☀ INSIGHT GUIDES

ISRAEL

DISCOVERY
CHANNEL

APA PUBLICATIONS L

Part of the Langenscheidt Publishing Group

INSIGHT GUIDE
ISRAEL

ABOUT THIS BOOK

Editorial
Edited by
Brian Bell
Updating Editor
Simon Griver
Picture Editor
Hilary Genin

Distribution
United States
Langenscheidt Publishers, Inc.
36–36 33rd Street 4th Floor
Long Island City, NY 11106
Fax: 1 (718) 784 0640

UK & Ireland
GeoCenter International Ltd
Meridian House, Churchill Way West
Basingstoke, Hampshire RG21 6YR
Fax: (44) 1256 817988

Australia
Universal Publishers
1 Waterloo Road
Macquarie Park, NSW 2113
Fax: (61) 2 9888 9074

New Zealand
Hema Maps New Zealand Ltd (HNZ)
Unit D, 24 Ra ORA Drive
East Tamaki, Auckland
Fax: (64) 9 273 6479

Worldwide
**Apa Publications GmbH & Co.
Verlag KG (Singapore branch)**
38 Joo Koon Road, Singapore 628990
Tel: (65) 6865 1600. Fax: (65) 6861 6438

Printing
Insight Print Services (Pte) Ltd
38 Joo Koon Road, Singapore 628990
Tel: (65) 6865 1600. Fax: (65) 6861 6438

©2008 Apa Publications GmbH & Co.
Verlag KG (Singapore branch)
All Rights Reserved
First Edition 1992
Fifth Edition 2006
Updated 2007, 2008

CONTACTING THE EDITORS
We would appreciate it if readers
would alert us to errors or out-
dated information by writing to:
**Insight Guides, P.O. Box 7910,
London SE1 1WE, England.
Fax: (44) 20 7403 0290.
insight@apaguide.co.uk**

www.insightguides.com
In North America:
www.insighttravelguides.com

The first Insight Guide pio-
neered the use of creative
full-colour photography in guide-
books in 1970. Since then, we
have expanded our range to
cater for our readers' need not
only for reliable information
about their chosen destination
but also for a real understanding
of that destination. Now, when
the internet can supply
inexhaustible (but not
always reliable) facts,
our books marry text
and pictures to provide
that much more elu-
sive quality: knowl-
edge. To achieve this,
they rely heavily on the authority
and experience of locally based
writers and photographers.

How to use this book

The book is carefully structured
both to convey an understanding
of the State of Israel and its culture, and to guide readers through
its diverse sights and activities:

◆ To understand modern
Israel you need to
know something of its
past. The **Features**
section explores the
history of the dynamic
young state, and the
complex cirumstances

standing religious and historical sites, and the beauty of the landscape, but also to convey an impression of the everyday lives of the Israeli people.

The contributors

This edition was edited by **Brian Bell**, Insight Guides' editorial director, and builds on earlier editions by **Pam Barrett** and **George Melrod**. The book has been comprehensively revised by **Simon Griver**, British-born but resident in Israel since 1978. His authoritative journalism is much in demand in the UK and the US. Even after so long in the country, he still values "the year-round sunshine, the exotic desert landscapes, and the informality of the people."

Israel's recent turbulent history meant that Griver needed to rewrite sections of the book, but significant portions of text remain from the specialist writers whose in-depth knowledge made past editions of the book so valuable to readers over the years. They include **Geoffrey Wigoder**, **Walter Jacob** and **William Recant** (who wrote the original history chapters), **Helen Davis**, **Barbara Gingold**, **Mordechai Beck**, **Asher Weill**, and **Nancy Miller** (who contributed to the Features section), and **Matthew Nevisky**, **Michal Yudelman**, **Daniel Gavron**, **Muriel Moulton**, **Leora Frucht**, **Bill Clark**, and **Amy Kaslow** (all contributors to the Places chapters).

Most of the stunning photography is by **Richard Nowitz** and **Gary-John Norman**, but there are also fine contributions by **Sammy Avnisan**, **Dinu Mendrea**, the **Israelimages** agency, and others.

that brought it about, after the years of exile.

◆ The main **Places** section provides details of the sights most worth seeing. The main places of interest are coordinated by number with full-color maps.

◆ The Travel Tips section provides a convenient point of reference for practical information on accommodations, restaurants, public holidays and religious festivals, travel, and specialist tour operators. Information may be located quickly by using the index printed on the back cover flap.

◆ The **photographs** are chosen not only to illustrate the out-

Map Legend

— ·· —	International Boundary
— —	Disputed Boundary
▬▬	Palestinian Autonomy
⊖	Border Crossing
—·—·—	National Park/Reserve
— — — —	Ferry Crossing
Ⓜ	Subway
✈ ✈	Airport: International/Regional
⛴	Bus Station
🅿	Parking
❶	Tourist Information
✉	Post Office
✝ ✝	Church/Ruins
✝	Monastery
☪	Mosque
✡	Synagogue
🏰	Castle/Ruins
∴	Archaeological Site
⋂	Cave
🛈	Statue/Monument
★	Place of Interest

The main places of interest in the Places section are coordinated by number with a full-colour map (e.g. ❶), and a symbol at the top of every right-hand page tells you where to find the map.

INSIGHT GUIDE

ISRAEL

CONTENTS

Left: the Ramon Crater, with the Mitspe Ramon Visitors Center.

Travel Tips

Places

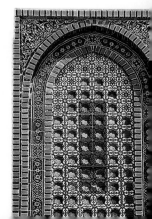

THE BEST OF ISRAEL

The unique sacred attractions of the Land of the Bible, absorbing museums, a dynamic culture, sun-soaked beaches, breathtaking landscapes... here, at a glance, are our recommendations, plus some tips that even Israelis won't always know

ABOVE: Jerusalem's distinctive Dome of the Rock.

ONLY IN ISRAEL

● **Sacred Sites.** For Jews, Christians and Muslims, these bear testimony to the lives of Abraham, King David, Jesus and Mohammed.

● **Dead Sea Scrolls.** On display in the Israel Museum is a real treasure: the oldest known version of the Old Testament and other scriptures. *Pages 290–1*

● **Sea of Galilee.** This is really a lake, while the Jordan is more like a stream. *Page 196*

● **Lowest Point On Earth.** 400 metres below sea level, the Dead Sea's excessive salt enables bathers to float. *Page 299*

● **Only Land Link Between Africa and Europe/Asia.** Israel's geographical location nourishes unique flora and fauna. *Page 114*

● **Red Sea.** Incredible marine life and the closest tropical waters to Europe. *Page 315*

● **Rebirth of a Nation.** Revival of biblical Hebrew, the Jewish ingathering and establishment of unique social units such as the kibbutz. *Pages 88, 95*

SACRED HOLY SITES

● **Western Wall.** Only remaining structure of the Second Temple is the most sacred site for Jews. *Pages 140, 205*

● **Dome of the Rock & El-Aqsa Mosque.** On the site of the Temple, Muslims believe Mohammed ascended to heaven from here. He also prayed in the mosque. *Pages 141, 143*

● **Via Dolorosa.** Christians believe that Christ took this path en route to his crucifixion at the present Church of the Holy Sepulchre. *Pages 145–7*

● **Garden Tomb.** Many Protestants believe this was the actual site of Christ's crucifixion. *Page 147*

● **Church of the Nativity.** Birthplace of Christ in Bethlehem. *Page 281*

● **Church of the Annunciation.** On the site of Mary's home in Nazareth. *Page 182*

● **Ein Tabgha.** Christ reputedly performed the miracle of the fishes and loaves here. *Page 197*

● **Mount of Olives.** Overlooking Jerusalem's Old City. Jews believe the Messiah will enter the city from this direction. *Page 155*

LEFT: Church of the Holy Sepulchre, Jerusalem.

FREE ISRAEL

● **Holy Sites.** The Western Wall and most of the major churches charge no entrance fee.
● **Yad Vashem Holocaust History Museum.** Entrance is free to this harrowing exhibition of man's inhumanity. *Page 174*
● **Jewish National & University Library.**

ABOVE: taking the Dead Sea mud treatment.

On the Hebrew University's Givat Ram campus the library exhibits the papers in which Einstein first scratched out his theory of relativity. *Page 174*
● **Baha'i Shrine and Gardens.** Costs nothing to tour the gold-domed shrine and the world's longest hillside gardens but you must book in advance. *Page 221*
● **Golden beaches.** Almost all the country's Mediterranean and Red Sea beaches are free. though some remote locations charge for parking.
● **Art Galleries.** Walking around the art galleries in Tel Aviv's Gordon Street in the late evening is part of the city's night life. *Page 348*

BEST BEACHES

● **Bograshov Beach (Tel Aviv).** It's in the heart of the city – but it gets crowded.
● **Sheraton Beach (Tel Aviv).** This is sexually segregated for religious bathers and for women who don't want to risk being pestered by men.
● **Hof Hacarmel (Carmel Beach).** Haifa's most popular beach can be found close to the city's southern entrance.

RIGHT: an antidote to the dry summer heat.

● **Caesarea.** Bathe amid the Roman and Crusader ruins.
● **Nitzanim.** Between Ashkelon and Ashdod. Its main attractions are palm trees and powdery white sand.
● **Coral Beach.** South of Eilat, snorkelers and divers seek out coral formations.

ABOVE: the fortress of Masada, facing the Dead Sea.

TOP VIEWS

● **Mount Scopus.** On this hill, armies encamped before attacking Jerusalem. *Page 164*
● **East Talpiyot Promenade.** See not only the golden glory of Jerusalem but in the winter the Jordan Valley. *Page 171*
● **Azrieli Tower.** From atop the tallest building in Tel Aviv, you can see much of Israel (on a clear day). *Page 257*
● **Mount Carmel.** Meander along the Yefe Nof promenade and enjoy the view of the bay. *Page 225*
● **Mount Meron.** Commanding view of

the Mediterranean and Sea of Galilee. *Page 184*
● **Masada.** The Herodian fortress provides a breathtaking view of the Dead Sea moonscape. A group of Jewish zealots killed themselves here in AD73 to avoid being captured by the Romans. *Page 293*
● **Mitspe Ramon Visitors Centre.** Not only explains the massive desert crater but offers a splendid view of it. *Page 307*
● **Mount Tzefahot.** Appreciate the changing colors of the desert mountains from

ISRAEL FOR FAMILIES

These attractions are popular with children, although not all will suit every age group.

● **Mini Israel.** Miniature model park with 350 scale models of the country's top buildings. *Page 268*

● **Sorek Cave.** Children will love the breathtaking beauty of the stalactites and stalagmites. *Page 267*

● **Jerusalem Biblical Zoo.** Attractive zoo, with relevant biblical quotations by each animal. *Page 172*

● **Israel Museum.** Has a children's wing where youngsters can be left while adults tour the exhibits. *Page 173*

● **Second Temple Model:** Scale model conveying the temple's vastness. Now relocated to the Israel Museum complex. *Page 172*

● **Bloomfield Science Museum.** This venue in Jerusalem is designed for curious young minds. *Page 173*

● **National Museum of Science.** Ditto, with the added delight of being housed in the original 80 year-old Technion in Haifa. *Page 219*

● **Ramat Gan Safari Park.** Make sure the kids keep the windows closed. *Page 258*

● **Rosh ha-Nikra.** Ride by cable car down to an enchanting grotto filled with water on the Mediterranean coast by the Lebanese border. *Page 232*

● **Underwater Observatory Marine Park.** The best place to survey the remarkable marine life of the Red Sea. *Page 320*

● **Dolphin Reef.** Swim with the dolphins in Eilat. *Page 320*

● **Ride a Camel.** Posted outside tourist sites in Jerusalem and by the Dead Sea, this is the essential Middle East experience.

● **Beaches.** Always fun for the family but watch out for the deceptively strong undercurrent in the Mediterranean.

ABOVE: feeding the dolphins at Eilat.

BEST MARKETS

● **Old City** *Souk.* Jerusalem's Old City market offers the essence of the Middle East. Enter from either Jaffa or Damascus Gates. *Page 137*

● **Makhane Yehuda.** Savor the fresh fruit, vegetables and spices of Jerusalem's leading food market. *Page 92*

● **Carmel Market**. Tel Aviv's leading market for food, clothes and vendors' witty banter. *Page 249*

● **Flea Market.** Located in Yafo, this is the country's most popular antiques market. *Page 253*

● **Bedouin Market**. Thursday morning in Beer Sheva is the time to buy a camel, goat or Bedouin bric-a-brac – or just to watch the spectacle. *Page 105*

● **Daliyal-El-Karmel**. Popular market in Druse village near Haifa. *Page 92*

LEFT: Carmel Market, popular in Tel Aviv.

BEST MUSEUMS

● **Israel Museum.** Showcase for the country's archaeology, art and Jewish ethnography and the Dead Sea Scrolls. *Page 173*

● **Yad Vashem.** This moving memorial tells the story of the Holocaust. *Page 174*

● **Tower of David Museum of the History of Jerusalem:** Just inside the Jaffa Gate exhibits the history of the holy city. *Page 137*

● **Eretz Israel Museum.** This Tel Aviv museum explains the complex history of Middle Eastern civilization. *Page 245*

● **Museum of the**

ABOVE: ancient stones in the Christian Quarter of Jerusalem's Old City.

Jewish Diaspora. Located on Tel Aviv University's campus, this recounts the story of Jewish culture in exile. *Page 244*

ABOVE: remembering the Holocaust at Vad Yashem.

BEST WALKS

● **Jerusalem's Old City.** Vehicles cannot negotiate the narrow alleyways anyway. Enter by the Jaffa Gate and turn right in the Arab *souk* into the Cardo, the ancient Roman thoroughfare. *Page 137*

● **Valley of the Cross.** Start from the Monastery of the Holy Cross, head for Jerusalem's Sacher Park, the Knesset, Israel Museum and Hebrew University. *Page 173*

● **Tel Aviv Promenade.** From old Yafo (Jaffa) in the south to Tel Aviv Port in the north, stroll the vibrant seafront. *Page 250*

● **Old Akko.** Take in the Crusader walls, fishing port and Arab market. *Page 207*

● **Mount of the Beatitudes to Ein Tabgha.** You don't have to be a practising Christian to enjoy this delightful stroll down hillside track to the Sea of Galilee. *Page 197*

● **Safed.** Take in the mystical atmospherics of the city's artists' quarter. *Page 184*

MONEY-SAVING TIPS

● **Israel Parks Authority:** From Masada to Caesarea and Rosh Ha-nikra, almost all rural sites are run by this authority, which is responsible for entrance fees. A nationwide family ticket can mean enormous savings. Tel: 02-5006245 (Jerusalem).

● **Egged Bus Company:** A range of passes at valuable discounts can be bought at Central Bus Stations.

● **Highway Six:** Except during the morning and evening rush hours, you won't get to your destination much faster by using this toll motorway. Find another route and save $5 per journey plus the additional $11 handling fee that car rental firms add.

● **Falafel stalls:** If you like salad, then for the small cost of a falafel in pita bread you can have as much of it as you want.

THE PROMISED LAND

*Israel defies indifference. Its long history draws visitors
but the real attraction is its great diversity of people*

Israel is intense. Few locations offer as much per square kilometer to sustain the spirit, feed the intellect and stimulate the senses. It is a place where three continents – Africa, Asia and Europe – meet, and the landscape and the people are a fusion of these three continents, a sometimes infuriating mixture of conflict and harmony. After all, this is the Promised Land to which, it is said, Moses led the Children of Israel. It is where Abraham forged his covenant with God, Christ preached his sermons, and Mohammed ascended to heaven.

You don't have to be a believer to savor all this. The miracles may be a matter of personal faith, but what can't be historically disputed is that this is the land of the Bible, the cradle of monotheism, a geography familiar from childhood religious instruction. The names resonate in visitors' minds and stimulate their curiosity: Jerusalem, the Galilee, Bethlehem, Nazareth, Yafo, Jericho, and the River Jordan.

At the site of the Temple you can pray at the one remaining wall the Romans left intact. You can walk along the Via Dolorosa to the Church of the Holy Sepulchre. You can visit the El-Aqsa Mosque on the Temple Mount where the Prophet Mohammed came to pray during his lifetime. Around the River Jordan you can drink in the atmosphere of a place where so much history has been made in the past two millennia – most recently, the emergence of modern Israel, "the Jewish State" and the focus of much recent conflict.

The enduring attraction

The empty stretches and open blue skies of the Arava and Negev deserts aside, this is one of the world's most densely packed pieces of real estate. Israel's population is more than 7 million, while over 3 million Palestinians live in the adjoining Gaza Strip and West Bank. For many visitors, the enduring attraction of Israel is its people – the inheritors of the rich tapestry of many invading cultures that have woven their history into the region.

Contrary to perceived stereotypes, most Israelis are neither right-wing religious zealots nor left-wing Peace Now activists. Most are middle of the road, more concerned about the performance of Tel Aviv's stock market, their favorite soccer team, or the Israel Philharmonic Orchestra. One attribute shared by all Israelis, whether they are religious or secular, of European or Afro/Asian origin, right-wing or left-wing, Jew or Arab, is a desire to talk to strangers. In chatting to tourists, Israelis may be simply wanting to practice their English, or vent their anger at Israel's perceived misrepresentation in the inter-

PRECEDING PAGES: praying at the Western (Wailing) Wall; modern Tel Aviv by night.
LEFT: an Orthodox Jew with a *shofar* (ram's horn) at the Western Wall.

national media, or more conventionally sell something, or have an enjoyable time with a good-looking visitor.

Whatever the motivation, Israelis are undeniably friendly. They can also be incredibly rude and abrasive, though this should be viewed within the context of their candid behaviour and tendency to treat even passing strangers like "family." Israelis are known as sabras after the indigenous prickly-pear cactus like fruit, which has a spiky, tough skin but is delicious, soft and juicy inside.

Israelis consider themselves to be part of Europe, although in fact the country via the Sinai peninsula forms the only continental land bridge between Asia and Africa. The European illusion is maintained in the spruce streets of Tel Aviv and Haifa, while because of Israel's geo-political isolation from the Arab world, the country is permitted to be an associate member of the European Union and a full member of most European institutions including the UEFA soccer federation and Eurovision. Palestinians get in on the act, too, frequently describing themselves to visitors as European Arabs.

However, from the narrow alleyways and markets of Jerusalem's Old City to the stunning desert landscapes of the Dead Sea – at 400 meters (1,300 ft) below sea level the lowest point on earth – the cultural and physical landscape is clearly not Europe.

The missing peace

Of course, the major blot on the landscape is the failure of Israelis and Palestinians to reach a lasting peace. Don't be deceived by off-the-cuff angry and chauvinistic comments by each group about the intransigence of the other side. Visitors who engage in more extended conversation with Jews and Arabs – and they are very eager to talk – will be surprised to discover how much enthusiasm, desire and goodwill there are towards reaching a historic compromise over the land, even if it is only because there is little stomach for the alternative.

The garrulousness and infectious energy of its people ensure that Israel is seldom boring. The hedonistic visitor seeking sunshine, golden beaches and pulsating nightlife, the nature lover in search of desert vistas and unique flora and fauna, and the historically curious seeking remains from biblical, Roman or Crusader times will not be disappointed. Most of all, religious visitors will usually come away with their beliefs reinforced, while non-believers have been known to return home with glimmerings of a faith they didn't have when they set out on their journey. ❑

RIGHT: a street in the Muslim Quarter of Jerusalem's Old City.

Decisive Dates

10,000BC–6000BC: Some of the world's first human settlements are established in the Jordan Valley, Judean Desert and Mediterranean coast.
3,000BC: Canaanite city kingdoms develop, based on trade between Mesopotamia and Egypt.

The Biblical Period

c.2000BC: Abraham settles in Be'er Sheva.
c.1280BC: Moses leads Israelites out of Egypt.
c.1225BC: Joshua captures Jericho.
c.1000BC: King David declares that Jerusalem

will become his capital.
c.950BC: King Solomon builds the First Temple.
722BC: Assyrians destroy the kingdom of Israel.
586BC: The First Temple is destroyed after the Babylonians conquer Jerusalem and send the Jews into exile.
546BC: The Jews return to Jerusalem after the Persians defeat the Babylonians.
520BC: The Second Temple is built.
444BC: Jerusalem's walls are rebuilt.
333BC: Alexander the Great conquers Jerusalem but allows the Jews freedom of worship.
164BC: Successful Jewish uprising led by Maccabees after Seleucid Greeks defile the Temple.
63BC: The Romans conquer Judea; it is subject

to Roman decree but it remains autonomous.
37BC: King Herod assumes the throne, founds Caesarea and rebuilds the Second Temple.

The Christian Era

c.AD30: The crucifixion of Christ.
66: The Jews revolt against Rome.
70: The Romans recapture Jerusalem after a long siege and destroy the Temple.
73: Jewish zealots in Masada commit mass suicide rather than be taken by the Romans.
132: Bar Kochba's revolt against the Romans fails, and most of the Jews go into exile.
325: Constantine, the Byzantine emperor, converts to Christianity. Palestine is recognized as the Holy Land, and Constantine's mother Helena arrives a year later to identify the sacred sites.

The Muslim Conquest

638: Fired by the new religion of Islam, Muslim armies conquer Jerusalem.
691: The Dome of the Rock is built on the Temple Mount.
705: The El-Aqsa Mosque is built.
750: Abassid caliphs succeed the Umayyads.
969: Fatimid rule begins.
1009: Fatimids destroy the Church of the Holy Sepulchre.

Crusaders, Mamelukes and Ottomans

1099: The Crusaders establish the kingdom of Jerusalem.
1149: The current Church of the Holy Sepulchre is consecrated.
1187: Saladin defeats the Crusaders.
1260: Mamelukes take control of the Holy Land.
1267: Nahmanides re-establishes Jerusalem's Jewish community.
1291: The last Crusader stronghold in Akko falls to the Mamelukes.
1492: Many Jews return to the Holy Land after expulsion from Spain.
1516: The Ottomans capture Palestine.
1541: Suleiman the Magnificent completes the construction of Jerusalem's walls.
1799: Napoleon occupies parts of the Holy Land.
1832: The Egyptian Mohammed Ali captures Palestine and holds it for eight years.

The Birth of Zionism

1878: First Zionist settlements established in Rosh Pina, Rishon Le-Tsiyon and Petakh Tikvah.
1881: Anti-Semitism in Russia, after the assas-

sination of Tsar Alexander II, forces millions of Jews to emigrate. Many go to the United States and Western Europe; some come to Palestine.
1897: Theodor Herzl convenes the first-ever Zionist Congress in Switzerland.
1901: The Jewish National Fund is established to acquire land in Palestine.
1917–18: The British capture Palestine and publish the Balfour Declaration favouring "the establishment in Palestine of a national home for the Jewish people."
1925: Large-scale Jewish immigration from Central and Eastern Europe.
1933: Adolf Hitler assumes power in Germany, increasing Jewish emigration.
1945: World War II ends, and the full horrors of the Holocaust become known. Survivors emigrate to Palestine but many are imprisoned by the British in Cyprus.
1947: The UN votes for the partition of Palestine into Jewish and Arab states, and the British prepare to withdraw.

The Establishment of Israel

1948: David Ben Gurion proclaims the State of Israel and becomes the first prime minister.
1949: An armistice agreement is concluded after the War of Independence.
1950: The Law of Return guarantees the free immigration of world Jewry. The Jordanians formally annex East Jerusalem and the West Bank, and Egypt takes the Gaza Strip.
1956: Israel captures and then returns the Sinai following the Suez campaign.
1964: The PLO is formed.
1967: Israel captures East Jerusalem, the West Bank, Gaza, the Sinai and the Golan Heights during the Six Day War. Golda Meir becomes PM.
1973: The Yom Kippur War.
1977: Likud's Menachem Begin becomes prime minister, ending 29 years of Labour government.
1978: Egyptian President Anwar Sadat visits Jerusalem. An Israel-Egypt peace treaty is signed the following year.
1982: Israel invades Lebanon, and the PLO is expelled to Tunisia.
1987: The first Intifada begins.
1991: Gulf War: Iraqi missiles fall on Israel.

1992: Yitzhak Rabin becomes prime minister.
1993: Israel and the PLO conclude a secret deal in Oslo. Rabin and PLO chief Yasser Arafat shake hands at the White House in Washington, DC.
1994: A peace agreement signed with Jordan.
1995: Yitzhak Rabin is assassinated, and Shimon Peres takes over as prime minister.
1996: Right-winger Binyamin Netanyahu is elected prime minister but lasts only three years.
2000: Palestinian leader Yasser Arafat rejects Prime Minister Ehud Barak's offer of most of the West Bank and Gaza and East Jerusalem. The second Intifada starts in September.
2001: Ariel Sharon is elected Prime Minister.

2004: Yasser Arafat falls ill and dies.
2005: Israel withdraws all Jewish settlements from the Gaza Strip.
2006: Ehud Olmert elected Prime Minister after Sharon is felled by a massive stroke. Olmert launches the Second Lebanon War after Hizbullah militants cross into Israel and kidnap two soldiers but the IDF fails to defeat the Shiite militia.
2007: The Palestinians are left divided after the Hamas Islamic fundamentalists elected in 2006 as the majority party in the Palestinian parliament stage a military coup in the Gaza Strip, while the West Bank is taken over by Arafat's elected successor, President Abu Mazen, the head of Fatah. ❑

PRECEDING PAGES: a 1584 map of Israel, with Jonah and the whale portrayed at the lower left corner. **LEFT:** a mosaic depicting an ancient Hanukkah Menorah. **RIGHT:** prime minister Ehud Olmert.

THE DAWN OF CIVILIZATION

The early history of Israel, familiar to many through biblical stories, laid the foundations of Jewish faith and sowed the seeds of future conflict

The dusty desert sign on the highway down from Jerusalem points northwards to "Jericho – The World's Oldest Known City". At the northern tip of the town is a rather unimpressive series of wooden fortifications. Remarkably, however, scientists estimate that these fortifications were built 9,000–10,000 years ago.

Evidence suggests that mankind first established farming communities, and the other trappings of civilisation as we know it, several thousand years before that. Caves in the Mount Carmel range near Haifa on the Mediterranean Coast have yielded jewelry and agricultural implements from 12,000 years ago.

But, as the remains at Jericho indicate, 7,000 BC was an important era in the evolution of Neolithic man. In the 1980s Israeli archaeologists discovered a treasure trove of artefacts dating from this period in a cave in the Judean Desert 48 km (30 miles) south of Jerusalem. The find, which includes woven fabrics, agricultural tools, decorated human skulls, carved figurines and painted masks, is on display in the Israel Museum. From these objects, anthropologists have concluded that late Stone Age man was far more advanced than had previously been believed.

According to Genesis

Such archaeological evidence is anathema to ultra-Orthodox Jewry, which has always insisted that the Creation took place nearly 6,000 years ago. By then, both ancient Egypt to the southwest and Mesopotamia to the northeast had been established as powerful and sophisticated civilisations. Canaanite tribes emerged about 5,000 years ago, founding city-kingdoms based on trade.

About 4,000 years ago, the book of Genesis relates, Abraham, the son of a wealthy Mesopotamian merchant family in the city of Ur (today in Iraq), became the first man to recognize a single deity. Rejecting the idolatry of his father, he traveled westwards and pitched his tent near Be'er Sheva.

Abraham is today revered as the father of monotheism. Although he believed in one God, he did not keep to just one woman, and the world might have become a less complicated

place had he done so. The Arab and Islamic heritage traces its roots to Abraham through his first son, Ishmael, born to his concubine Hagar, while the Judeo-Christian lineage can be traced back to Isaac, Abraham's second son, born to his wife, Sarah.

Sibling rivalry, Genesis tells us, compelled Abraham to cast out Hagar and Ishmael, whose descendants would forever bear enmity to the offspring of Sarah's son Isaac. Even a complete atheist would have to admit that the Bible got that right. The precise location of Abraham's tent is not known, which is probably just as well, for his burial site, the Tomb of the Patriarchs in Hebron, has seen far too many corpses.

LEFT: Moses receives the stone tablets from God.
RIGHT: early shekels show fruits of the earth.

Jews and Arabs have massacred each other in Hebron throughout history.

Sibling rivalry, beginning with Cain and Abel, is an ever-present theme in Genesis. Isaac's own twin sons quarreled when Jacob, egged on by his mother Rebecca, cheated Esau out of his birthright by tricking his blind father. And Jacob saw the pattern recur when his own sons sold Joseph, his favourite child, into slavery in Egypt.

The Children of Israel

Jacob was also known as Israel (Hebrew for "he struggles"). The name was given to him the wilderness. During the Children of Israel's 40 years wandering in the wilderness Moses was given the Torah, including the Ten Commandments, on Mount Sinai. His successor, Joshua, took the Children of Israel back to the Promised Land, scoring his first success in the Battle of Jericho in 1225 BC.

Though the Israelites defeated the indigenous Canaanites and settled on the inland hills, making Hebron their capital, they were unable to conquer the coastal plain where the Philistines in the south and the Phoenicians in the north reigned supreme. The historical importance of these peoples, especially the Phoenicians, who

after a dream in which he fought with an angel descending from a ladder leading up to heaven. All told Jacob had 12 sons and one daughter whose descendants are known to us as the Children of Israel.

Joseph prospered in Egypt, where he became a senior advisor to the Pharaoh. He was reunited with his family after a drought compelled them to look for food and shelter in the Land of the Nile. The Book of Exodus relates how successive generations of Pharaohs subsequently enslaved the Children of Israel.

In one of the most enduring of all biblical narratives, Moses, the Israelite, led his people out of bondage, across the Red Sea and through

LAYING THE FOUNDATIONS

It was during Joshua's era that many of the tenets of Judaism were first established. The festival of Passover (Pesach), held in the spring, recalls the Exodus from Egypt, and the miracles which preceded it, while Pentecost (Shavuot) marks the giving of the Torah to Moses on Mount Sinai.

Religious Jews today congregate at the Western (Wailing) Wall for dawn prayers at Pentecost, after spending the night studying the holy book. The Feast of Tabernacles (Succot), which is also known as the Festival of Rejoicing, recalls the 40 years spent in the wilderness and celebrates the joy of returning to the Promised Land.

had migrated from Greece, is often overlooked.

The Phoenicians, who settled in the cities of Akko and Tyre in Northern Israel and Southern Lebanon, are believed to have devised the first alphabet and invented glassmaking. And the Philistines in Ashdod and Ashkelon in the south were skilful metalworkers who were able to manufacture sophisticated weaponry.

The Israelites coexisted with their coastal neighbors, sometimes trading, sometimes fighting. Led at first by warrior-judges such as Gideon and Samuel, they felt the need for a king who would strengthen the people by uniting the tribes. Saul was selected, and he set the

though he did win access to the Mediterranean.

Most importantly, in historical retrospect, David conquered a Jebusite hilltop enclave. He decided that the fortress settlement, perched near commanding mountain peaks, with a plentiful supply of fresh underground spring water, would make an excellent new capital. So he moved his court and administration there from Hebron and called his new capital Jerusalem. The city also helped unite the 12 tribes because it was located on neutral territory.

David's son Solomon became renowned for his wisdom. He consolidated his father's achievements and extended the Israelite

scene for the golden age that his successor David was to bring about.

The establishment of Jerusalem

David ascended the throne a little over 3,000 years ago. A scholar, poet and notorious womaniser, he secured his place in history through military prowess and leadership, extending the Israelites' borders to the Red Sea in the south and Syria in the north. But despite his early victory over the mighty Goliath, with a slingshot, he was unable to vanquish the Philistines,

empire down to the Arabian peninsula and northeastwards to the Euphrates. He inherited his father's taste for beautiful women, and sealed strategic alliances by marrying princesses. His exact relationship with the Queen of Sheba remains unclear.

Most significantly, Solomon constructed the resplendent Temple to house the Ark of the Covenant, the focus of Jewish faith that was believed to contain the actual tablets of the Ten Commandments that were given to Moses on Mount Sinai. A stroll around the Temple Mount in Jerusalem today conveys what a vast building it must have been.

Despite his reputed wisdom, Solomon left no

LEFT: Joshua's men hang enemy kings.
ABOVE: a medieval view of Solomon and Sheba.

strong successor. Soon after his death tribal jealousies resulted in civil war and the secession of the 10 northern tribes who set up their own state, known as Israel in Samaria. The southern state of Judah, based on the tribes of Judah and Benjamin, remained faithful to Solomon's descendants. For two centuries an uneasy coexistence prevailed.

This was the age of the prophets. Isaiah attacked corruption, and Elijah denounced the idolatrous cult of Baal introduced by Israel's King Ahab and his wife

> **YEARNING FOR HOME**
>
> In Psalm 137, an exiled poet wrote the oft-quoted lines: "By the waters of Babylon we sat down and wept when we remembered Zion."

Jezebel. In 722 BC Israel fell to the Assyrians, and the people were dispersed. The fate of the "Ten Lost Tribes" is still unknown, and people in every corner of the globe occasionally claim descent from them.

The southern state of Judah survived by accepting Assyrian hegemony. This status quo endured for 150 years. Its end was foretold by the prophet Jeremiah, who preached gloom and doom and the destruction of Jerusalem.

By the waters of Babylon

Jeremiah's prophecies came true in 586 BC. The Babylonians, led by Nebuchadnezzar, superseded the Assyrians, sacked Jerusalem, destroyed the Temple, and transported the élite of Judah to Babylon.

In fact, this exile only lasted 40 years, until the Babylonians were defeated by the Persians, whose leader Cyrus the Great allowed all exiled peoples to return. The Temple was rebuilt, but the glorious age of Solomon was not recaptured. Judah remained an obscure Persian province for the following two centuries.

The balance of world power moved west to Europe, away from Egypt, Assyria and Persia. In 333 BC Alexander the Great conquered the region, and Greek rule began. For several centuries the Jews were allowed freedom of worship, but policies gradually became more obtrusive, culminating in the 2nd century BC with the sacrificing of a pig in the Temple and the prohibition of Jewish rituals such as circumcision and the observation of the Sabbath.

Armed resistance led by the Hasmonean family known as the Maccabees saw the Greeks defeated and Jewish control over Jerusalem restored. In 164 BC the Temple was rededicated, a victory celebrated to this day during the festival of Hanukkah.

The Roman Empire

The subsequent century of Jewish sovereignty saw prosperity, as past glories and lands were recaptured. But this taste of freedom was then lost for 2,000 years. In 63 BC the Romans conquered Judah, which, as Judea, was subject to the decree of the Roman governor of Syria but remained an autonomous province with its own kings. The best known was Herod the Great, who reigned from 37–4 BC, and was given extra territory, expanding his kingdom to include all of Israel and much of today's Jordan. He rebuilt the Temple and constructed grand new cities, such as Caesarea on the coast, which he dedicated to Rome. But Herod and his successors were ruthless despots who even killed their own children in their paranoia over potential conspiracies. Oppressed by Rome and its merciless vassal kings, the Judeans were ripe to be influenced by messianic preachers. ❏

LEFT: a romantic depiction of Noah's Ark.
RIGHT: Marc Chagall's depiction of David with his harp.

EMPIRES AND EXILE

*Successive empires conquered, flourished, then disappeared, while the Jews
were scattered across the globe without a land of their own*

The son of a Galilean carpenter, Christ had a limited impact in his own lifetime, at least in Jerusalem. Few historical accounts even mention him and the best-known contemporary historian, Josephus, devotes only a few sentences to an obscure Galilee preacher. The Romans felt threatened enough to execute him, although in those days of massacres and constant bloodshed that fate was no great distinction.

But a devoted band of Christ's followers were convinced that their leader was the messianic saviour the Jews craved. In the following decades the determination of these disciples was to change history. Christianity spread north and east to Armenia and Byzantium, and southwards, taking root in Africa, especially in Egypt and Ethiopia, and subsequently took hold in Rome and the rest of Europe.

The Jews themselves were unimpressed. For them Christ remains just one of a string of false messiahs, distinguished only by the fact that so many Gentiles accepted his teachings and interpreted them as good reason to persecute the Jews themselves, who were branded as Christ-killers. There is no historical evidence that the Jews conspired in the crucifixion of Christ, but when Rome subsequently embraced Christianity a convenient scapegoat was needed to draw attention away from its own culpability. The claim that the Jews were Christ-killers became the basis for anti-Semitism down the centuries.

Zealotry and defeat

Not that the Jewish establishment of the time would have shed a tear at Christ's execution. The aristocratic Sadducees, who controlled the priesthood, and the scholarly Pharisees, who interpreted the law, would have regarded Christ – those who were aware of his existence – as an undesirable subversive element.

The Essenes might have been more impressed. This ascetic cult was in all likelihood a major influence on Christ's philosophy. As a result,

LEFT: the Madonna and Child. **RIGHT:** an illuminated manuscript depicts Christ's death.

the Essenes' culture and writings in the Dead Sea Scrolls (which are displayed in the Israel Museum and include the oldest known version of the Old Testament) are of major interest to Western society.

The Zealots would have been too wrapped up in the nationalist struggle against Roman

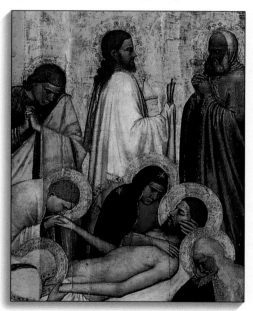

occupation to pay much attention to a Galilean preacher. Increased Roman oppression, most notably the decision by the Roman emperor Caligula to have his image installed in the Temple, strengthened the Zealots' popularity.

In AD 66 the Jews rebelled. The Romans imported major reinforcements, and the revolt was slowly crushed. By 69 only Jerusalem and several fortress outposts were holding out. After a year-long siege, Jerusalem was captured. The Romans sacked it, burning the Temple and carrying its sacred contents back to Rome. The city was renamed Aelia Capitolina, and all vestiges of Jewish culture were destroyed, except one wall of the Temple – the Western

Wall – which was left standing to remind the Jews of Roman sovereignty.

Masada was the most famous of the fortresses which held out, but resistance was futile; the soldiers of the Roman 10th Legion finally conquered the hilltop stronghold in AD 73. But they were denied the satisfaction of capturing its inhabitants: the Zealots – nearly 1,000 of them – committed mass suicide.

Another failed Jewish uprising against the Romans in 132, led by Simon Bar Kochba, saw most Jews executed, sold into slavery, or exiled, and this date is often considered as the start of two millennia of exile.

From Christianity to Islam

It is one of the great ironies that in the Holy Land, where Christ was born, preached and died, Christians have remained a small minority. By the 5th century they did form a majority, but the Roman Empire was already crumbling. The Persians temporarily conquered the region in the 7th century (before the Byzantines reasserted control), and in 640 the Arab followers of Mohammed swept through the region converting many to Islam. Mohammed's emphasis on the Oneness of God and the need to revive Jewish rituals such as circumcision and dietary laws struck a popular chord.

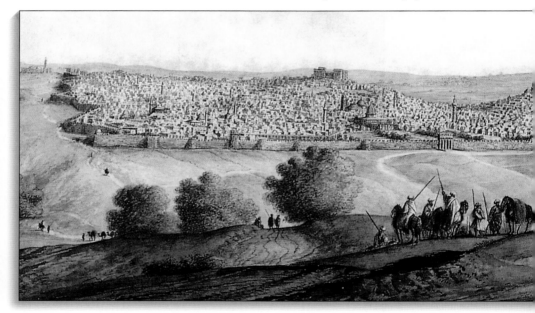

Jewish culture continued to flourish, especially in the Galilee. The Mishna, the Talmudic commentary on the Old Testament, was written by sages in Tiberias in the 2nd and 3rd centuries, while rabbinical scholars in the Mount Meron region near Safed penned the mystical texts that comprise the Kabbalah. But as Christianity took root in the region, after being embraced by the emperor Constantine the Great and the Eastern Roman Empire early in the 4th century, the Jewish presence in the Holy Land dwindled into insignificance. From that point until modern times, the glory of Jewish culture was to be accomplished in what became known as the Diaspora.

EMPRESS HELENA'S ROLE

After Emperor Constantine the Great embraced Christianity in the 4th century, his mother, Empress Helena, became an enthusiastic convert to the new religion, and played a key role in its dissemination. It is believed that she made a pilgrimage from Byzantium in the 4th century in order to identify the principal sites of Christendom, and to initiate the construction of shrines in these places. These holy sites include the Church of the Nativity in Bethlehem, the Church of the Holy Sepulchre in Jerusalem and the Church of the Annunciation in Nazareth, all sites which are revered by most branches of Christianity to this day.

Islam and the Arab world have coveted the Holy Land ever since. Abraham, the father of the Arab people, is buried in Hebron, while Mohammed is believed to have made a journey on horseback, after his death, to the Temple Mount in Jerusalem from where he ascended to heaven. In 691 Caliph Abd Al-Malik, horrified by the neglect of the Temple Mount, built the Dome of the Rock over the supposed site of Mohammed's ascension. Several decades later the El-Aqsa Mosque was built on the southern section of the Temple Mount. Jerusalem was now sacred to three major religions – Judaism, Christianity and Islam – attracting pilgrims

Templars, while the El-Aqsa Mosque was transformed into a church. The Kingdom of Jerusalem, ruled by King Baldwin I, who was installed in 1100, held sway over several subservient principalities.

The ostensible aim of the Crusades was to fight the infidel, but in reality the Crusaders slaughtered far more Christians than nonbelievers. En route, especially in the Balkans, they laid waste entire Orthodox Christian communities. In the Holy Land itself, Christian villagers turned out to greet their supposed liberators, only to be put to the sword. Although the Crusaders were sponsored by the Church,

from all three. But if individuals were content to visit, others wanted not only to come and see but also to conquer.

Crusaders and infidels

Islamic control of the Holy Land especially irked the Christians of Europe. As a result, during the 11th century the Pope inaugurated a series of crusades which saw Christianity in possession of virtually the entire Holy Land by the end of the century. The Dome of the Rock was commandeered as the headquarters of the

ABOVE: Jerusalem from the Mount of Olives, painted by Luigi Meyer in the late 18th century.

many of their number were motivated by imperialist ambitions.

The Crusaders built a network of hilltop fortresses, from Nimrod in the north to Jerusalem in the south, and ruled until 1187, when the Egyptian leader Saladin was victorious at the Horns of Hittim in the Galilee. Slowly the Europeans lost their foothold in the Holy Land. Even Richard the Lionheart, who led the Third Crusade in 1188, could not turn the tide. Four more Crusades delayed the inevitable, but in 1291 Europe lost St Jean d'Acre (Akko), its last stronghold in the region, to the Mamelukes, who in their turn had defeated Saladin.

Mamelukes and Ottomans

The Mamelukes are the least remembered of the Holy Land's conquerors. For nearly 250 years these slave warriors to the sultans of Egypt, who had been brought from Asia to be trained as elite soldiers, ruled over the region from Egypt to Syria. Despite their ornate architecture, this was an era of decline from which the Middle East has never fully recovered. As Europe flourished and America was discovered, the balance of world power slipped further away from the Eastern Mediterranean.

The rise of the Ottoman Turks stopped the rot, at least for a while. The Holy Land, too,

regained some luster after the Ottoman conquest in 1517. Suleiman the Magnificent, who ruled from 1520 to 1566, revived the economy of the region and built the impressive walls around the Old City of Jerusalem.

But from the 17th century the Ottoman Empire went into a decline that was to last for 300 years. The Holy Land gradually became a semi-desert, and Jerusalem degenerated into a crumbling village. The Ottomans, like the Mamelukes before them, ruled Palestine as a province of Syria, further belittling the status of the region in general and Jerusalem in particular. Voltaire, in his philosophical dictionary compiled in the mid-18th century, described the

city as a barren wilderness of rocks and dust.

Napoleon's brief conquest of parts of Palestine in 1799 spelled a revival of interest in the Holy Land by the European powers. As the Ottomans weakened, the British and the French vied for hegemony. Offended by the fact that the Christian sites in the Holy Land were dominated by Greeks, Armenians and Ethiopians, the Catholic, Protestant and Russian Orthodox churches were encouraged by their governments to build their own institutions.

In the event, it was the British who wrested control of Palestine from the Ottomans in 1917 during World War I. However, the League of Nations mandate stipulated that the British were to be temporary custodians. Even though significant numbers of Jews had begun returning to their ancestral homeland from the late 19th century onwards, nobody could have predicted that in just three more decades possession of much of Palestine would return to its ancient owners.

In exile

In nearly 2,000 years of exile the Jewish people never forgot Israel. They faced Jerusalem when they prayed and took to heart the sentence from Psalm 137: "If I forget thee, O Jerusalem, let my right hand forget her cunning." But while the Jews never forgot Jerusalem, for many years they showed no great inclination to return. Many individuals made pilgrimages to the Holy Land, but there was no significant mass movement to return to Zion.

Over time, the conventional Orthodox belief took root that the return would occur only with the coming of the Messiah. Eventually it was a combination of European enlightenment, nationalism and anti-Semitism that shook this conviction and promoted the belief that a return to Zion was necessary, both for the physical survival of Jews threatened by extermination and for the perpetuation of Jewish culture corroded by assimilation.

For the most part, the first millennium of exile was unremarkable. Most Jews lived in the Middle East and the Mediterranean basin, where they suffered what was to become a familiar mixture of intolerance and persecution while being patronized for their skills, crafts and merchant abilities. But if Islam and Orthodox Christianity, centred in Constantinople, had occasional outbursts of anti-Jewish sentiment, these paled into insignificance compared with the experiences the Jews were to have in Europe in their second millennium of exile.

Inquisitions and pogroms

By the 11th century large Jewish communities had established themselves in France and Germany. They arrived just in time for the Crusades, and a familiar pattern of massacres was begun which was to haunt the Jews all the way to Auschwitz. The Church institutionalized the belief that the Jews were satanic Christ-killers, who craved money above all else.

Nevertheless, in the 11th, 12th and 13th cen-

into Africa in the 14th and 15th centuries, it turned its attention to the non-Spanish, non-Christian infidels in its midst. For a century, under the Inquisition, Jews were either massacred or forced at sword point to convert. Finally, in the 1490s – just as Columbus was discovering America where the Jews would enjoy a new golden age – they were expelled from Spain. Many stayed, worshipping secretly; others returned to North Africa or settled in the newly emerging Ottoman Empire. Several thousand returned to the Holy Land, settling in Jerusalem and in Safed, which became a center of Jewish scholarship. Some found their way to Holland

turies the Jews entered a golden age, especially in Spain, where Jewish aristocrats formed a bridge between the Christian north and Moorish Arab Muslim south. Communal life and autonomous religious institutions flourished in both Spain and Germany, and the Jews even developed their own languages – Ladino and Yiddish – medieval Spanish and German respectively, mixed with Hebrew and written with Hebrew characters.

But as Spain drove the Moorish infidels back

LEFT: an idealized view of 18th-century Jerusalem.
ABOVE: delegates to the Sixth Zionist Conference in Basle, 1903.

PERNICIOUS PROPAGANDA

The image of Jews as Christ-killers was a pernicious one which was very hard to dispel. Along with it went a number of other superstitions, fomented or at least encouraged by the clerical authorities. One particularly unpleasant myth that persisted into the 20th century was that Jews killed Christian children so that they could use their blood for Passover rituals. The Jews were also blamed for the Black Death which swept Europe in 1348, and it was widely believed that they poisoned wells to spread the epidemic. Additionally, the fact that Jews were the only money-lenders, when the church forbade Christians to engage in usury, gave them a reputation for avarice.

and subsequently to England, when Oliver Cromwell legalized the community "expelled" in the 13th century.

Germany's Jews fared no better. Hounded by the Church, communities moved to Poland and Russia, establishing *shtetls*, small self-sufficient communities. The Pale of Settlement defined where they could live, excluding them from Russia itself, while pogroms kept them in constant fear. Ironically, the Pale of Settlement in Eastern Europe became a kind of homogenous Jewish state where Yiddish-speaking Jews evolved their distinct ethnic culture.

Emancipation and nationalism

The Industrial Revolution and the forces of the Enlightenment transforming Europe also affected Jews. Some turned to messianic cults such as Hassidism, but with nationalism sweeping across Europe many became secularized.

At the same time Europeans started investigating Jewish culture. The discovery that Hebrew was a Semitic language related to Arabic, outside Indo-European linguistic evolution, contributed to the rise of anti-Semitism. Previously the Jews had suffered religious persecution but were at least accepted into the Church, albeit often through forced conversions; now they were set apart racially.

Some Jews were assimilated into middle-class European society. In England, Benjamin Disraeli's father had the country's future prime minister baptised rather than bar mitzvahed when he was 13. But baptism did not make many Jews of mainland Europe seem European enough. Ultimately, they were still persecuted. The Enlightenment, with its anti-religious liberal emphasis, often worked against the Jews, who were viewed as religious fundamentalists.

Voltaire railed against them, and his anti-religious rationalist writings were developed in the 19th century by a young German Jew, Karl Marx, who rejected his heritage and spoke of a war against capitalists and clerics.

In this era of great change some Jews remembered Jerusalem. British philanthropists such as Moses Montefiore and the Rothschilds set up Jewish communities in Jerusalem and new agricultural villages like Rishon Le-Tsiyon, Zikhron Ya'akov and Rosh Pina.

Meanwhile, the assassination of Tsar Alexander II in Russia in 1881 was blamed on the Jews and unleashed awesome pogroms. Jews emigrated in their millions to Western Europe and especially to the United States, which from the outset had guaranteed religious freedom in its constitution. But some Jews, eager to return to Palestine, were persuaded by the philanthropists to settle in the Holy Land.

The birth of Zionism

But it was in France that modern political Zionism was conceived. In the 1890s a young Viennese-Jewish journalist, Theodor Herzl, was sent to Paris to cover the trial of Captain Alfred Dreyfus, the French Jewish officer who was

---

LOOKING FOR A PEACEFUL LIFE

The *shtetls* of Eastern Europe were small self-sufficient village communities in which Jewish people retained their own culture and way of life. They were portrayed romantically in the musical *Fiddler on the Roof*, based on the Yiddish stories by Sholom Aleichem about Tevya the Milkman, whose faith in God helps him to overcome all the trials and tribulations of life under the Tsars.

The rabbi's blessing in *Fiddler on the Roof* – "God bless the Tsar and keep him far away from us" – reflected the antagonism that the Russian rulers had developed towards the Jews, and the Jewish desire to be left undisturbed.

framed as a spy and blamed for his country's defeat in the Franco–Prussian war of 1870. As the trial unraveled, Herzl despaired of the fate of European Jewry. Though an assimilated Jew who knew virtually nothing of his cultural roots, Herzl wrote a book, *Altneuland* (*Old-new Land*), describing the re-establishment of a Jewish commonwealth in ancient Israel. He was written off as a dreamer, to which he responded, "If you will it, then it will be."

In 1897 Herzl convened the First Zionist Congress in Basle, establishing the World Zionist Organization, the forerunner of the Israeli government. He lobbied political leaders and

British support for a Jewish homeland. This lent the Zionist movement the international legitimacy it desperately needed.

If the likes of Herzl and Weizmann gave the Zionist movement diplomatic access, the foot soldiers in the field were the Jews of Eastern Europe. As Tsarist Russia hurtled towards the revolution, increasing numbers of ideologically motivated Zionist socialists found their way to Palestine. Between 1904 and 1917, some 100,000 came, though fewer than half stayed.

Among them was a young lawyer's son named David Ben Gurion who was to assume the leadership of the *yishuv*, the pre-state Jewish

courted European royalty, making his only trip to Palestine in 1898 to meet Kaiser Wilhelm II of Germany when the latter visited Jerusalem.

After Herzl's premature death in 1904, the unofficial leadership of the Zionist movement fell to Chaim Weizmann, a Russian-born professor of chemistry at Manchester University. Weizmann won the confidence of the British ruling elite, and after the conquest of Palestine in 1917 that meant everything. Most importantly, he persuaded the British Foreign Secretary, Arthur Balfour, to issue a declaration promising

entity. These men, products of pre-revolutionary Russia, were essentially Bolsheviks with a more liberal, humane streak. They set up trade unions, rejected the capitalist villages of the Rothschilds, and established their own agricultural collectives, called kibbutzim.

At first the indigenous Palestinians welcomed the Jewish settlers. Their numbers were small, they brought wealth and development, and, while most Palestinians lived on the inland hills, the newcomers were prepared to settle the humid, sparsely populated coastal plain. But the Balfour Declaration took the Arabs by surprise and indicated that they had greatly underestimated the Zionist potential. ❏

LEFT: Zionist visionary Theodor Herzl.
ABOVE: Turkish cavalry officers in Palestine, 1917.

PERFIDIOUS ALBION

The Balfour Declaration promised British support for a Jewish homeland,
but Israel soon became embroiled in international realpolitik

E ven today, the question is often asked in the Middle East: did the British favor the Arabs or the Jews during the Mandatory period? The answer is probably that they favored neither and that, as elsewhere, they pursued their own interests.

In the aftermath of World War I, Arthur Balfour and David Lloyd George were strong supporters of the Zionist cause because they perceived a Jewish homeland as a potentially friendly outpost of Empire. The notion also appealed to the religious sentiment of British Protestants. But Balfour had underestimated the strength of Arab nationalism that would emerge from the ashes of the Ottoman Empire, as well as the emerging economic and strategic importance of Middle East oil.

The British government's most hostile opponent of the Balfour Declaration was Edwin Montagu, Secretary of State for India, and the only Jew in the cabinet. Like a large section of secular world Jewry, he fiercely opposed Zionism because it called into question his national loyalties. He insisted that Judaism was a religion, not a nationality.

Arab riots

Britain's miscalculation in making the Balfour Declaration soon became apparent. In March 1920 a bloody riot in Jerusalem left more than 200 Jews dead. Widespread Arab violence soon made the British regret the Declaration, and in 1921 Winston Churchill, the Colonial Secretary and previously a fervent Zionist sympathiser, told Chaim Weizmann that 90 percent of the British government was opposed to establishing a Jewish homeland in Palestine.

But the Zionists were better organized than the Arabs and more determined than the British. The Histadrut trade union organization was founded in 1920, while the Haganah, an underground paramilitary body, effectively defended

LEFT: a Henschel portrait of a Palestinian Arab.
RIGHT: Zionist Dov Ber Borochov and friends in Plonsk, Poland, 1920.

Jewish settlements and became the forerunner of the Israel Defense Forces. Tel Aviv developed as the flourishing economic capital of the emerging Jewish entity, and kibbutz agricultural settlements made the local Jewish population self-sufficient in food.

Most vitally, large numbers of Jews began

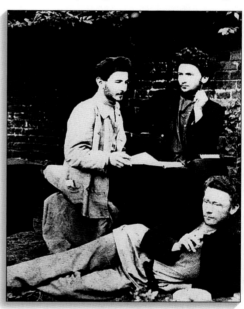

emigrating to Palestine. In the 1920s the Jewish population of Palestine doubled from 85,000 to 170,000. The Arab population numbered about 850,000. These Jewish newcomers included socialists disillusioned by the results of the Russian Revolution, as well as numerous middle-class merchants and professionals from Poland. While David Ben Gurion and his socialist followers became the establishment through the Jewish Agency, a kind of government in waiting, the right-wing nationalist revisionist movement of Vladimir Jabotinsky also enjoyed strong support.

In particular, Jabotinsky and his supporters vehemently opposed Churchill's unilateral decision in 1923 to cede all of Palestine east of the River Jordan, nearly two-thirds of the land mass of Palestine, to Britain's Arabian Hashemite ally Emir Abdullah.

The rise of Nazism

Adolf Hitler's 1933 assumption of power in Germany, together with the rapid economic development of Palestine, attracted even more Jewish immigrants. While most Jews saw Palestine as a safe haven from anti-Semitism, many were now being drawn there for other reasons. Palestine's coastal plain, where most Jewish towns were established, was no longer domi-

In an attempt to win Arab support for the impending war with Germany, the British passed a White Paper limiting Jewish immigration to 20,000 a year. So, as the Nazi stranglehold tightened around Europe, there was nowhere for Jewish refugees to flee. In effect, the British U-turn meant that, by refusing entry visas to Palestine for Jewish refugees trying to escape persecution, they were assisting Adolf Hitler in his Final Solution. Even after the full horror of the concentration camps was known, the British did not relent, keeping some 73,000 refugees, many of them concentration camp survivors, in detention camps in Cyprus.

nated by sand dunes and swamps. There were bourgeois boulevards lined with large houses, shops and banks, schools, universities and hospitals. An immigrant with means could live well here, while a poorer man could earn a reasonable working wage.

By 1939, on the eve of World War II, the Jewish population of Palestine had doubled again to 350,000. Bitter hostility to Zionism was led by Haj Amin Husseini, the Grand Mufti of Jerusalem, who consolidated his position as local Arab leader and formed an understanding with Hitler. The region might have been more peaceful had the more moderate King Abdullah of Jordan gained the upper hand.

POLITICAL MACHINATIONS

Shortly after World War II, Emanuel Shinwell, a Jewish member of Clement Attlee's Labour cabinet in Britain, was proud to identify with the Zionist cause and the establishment of the State of Israel. However, he pointed out that, as Secretary for Energy in His Majesty's Government, he was duty-bound to protect British interests, and that involved sympathizing with Arab states, whatever his personal feelings. Other British politicians were less candid about where their sympathies lay and also about the often unscrupulous choices involved in realpolitik. But, of course, the making and breaking of promises often seems to be an inevitable part of political life.

All the same, Ben Gurion and the Jewish Agency insisted that there was no alternative but for Jews to support the British war effort. The revisionists were not so certain. Irgun Zvi Leumi, led by Menachem Begin, agreed to a ceasefire with the British for the duration of the war, but an extremist fringe, Lehi, led by Yitzhak Shamir, continued to attack British targets throughout World War II. Many Jews, however, enlisted in the British Army, which even formed a Jewish brigade; this provided invaluable experience for subsequent battles.

The revelation of the Nazi atrocities made the Jews of Palestine all the more determined to achieve independence. The horrors of the Holocaust were no surprise to the Zionists, who had always feared something of the sort but had expected it to be Russian rather than German-inspired. The prevailing belief was that, had Israel existed at the time, 6 million Jews could have been saved.

Stalin to the rescue

Ben Gurion, grasping post-war realities, switched the focus of his lobbying from London to Washington. An intense diplomatic offensive was launched at the newly formed United Nations in New York, and quiet channels were opened to the Soviet Union. The support of Joseph Stalin in the establishment of Israel was to prove crucial. The United States, which voted against the UN-sponsored partition of Palestine in 1946, supported the same resolution a year later. Britain abstained both times. But Stalin, though undoubtedly anti-Semitic, saw a potentially socialist Israel as a Marxist bulwark against the puppet Arab administrations being set up by Britain and France. Consequently he threw his full weight, as well as that of his European satellites, behind the Zionists. He voted for the UN partition plan in November 1948 and even sent arms to help Israel during the War of Independence.

The right-wing Irgun and Lehi denounced Ben Gurion's diplomacy as futile. Their strategy was simple – to bomb the British out of Palestine. British soldiers were killed, Irgun and Lehi members were hanged, and more British soldiers were killed in retaliation. Following the bombing in 1947 of the British administra-

tive HQ at the King David Hotel, which killed 91 people, British public opinion clamored for a withdrawal. After much government deliberation, the pullout was fixed for 15 May 1948.

Although the socialists and revisionists had a violent mutual hatred, it was probably their joint efforts that brought about the establishment of Israel. Ben Gurion's diplomatic success at the United Nations and in gaining the support of both Stalin and the US president, Harry Truman, gave the Jewish state international legitimacy. The revisionists' all-out war against the British forced their withdrawal.

And so modern Israel arose from the ashes

of the Holocaust. Yet it is one of the myths of our time that this is why Israel came into existence, a romantic idea that appeals to a poetic sense of justice: the Jewish people suffered but were compensated with their own state.

This is not the way Israelis see it. They argue that Israel came into being despite the Holocaust, and that had just 1 million of the 6 million who perished reached Israel, the birth of the state would have been easier. They recall that, while Israel enjoyed much international sympathy after the Holocaust, little was done to help. Israel had to work hard to swing the UN vote, and when the British withdrew it was left completely alone to face the Arab world. ❑

LEFT: British soldiers in Jerusalem, 1917.
RIGHT: young David Ben Gurion in Turkish fez.

THE SECOND EXODUS

*The birth of the new state was a difficult one, and in subsequent years
political and economic vision were vital for survival*

As Israelis danced in the streets following the Declaration of Independence in May 1948, they knew that there would be little to celebrate in the ensuing months. Though vastly outnumbered by the surrounding Arab armies, better organization saw the Israel Defense Forces not only defend Jewish territory but also conquer large areas of the Negev and Western Galilee that had been allocated to Palestine under the UN partition plan.

However, if subsequent Israeli military victories were relatively swift, this first war ground on for nearly a year, costing the new country 6,000 lives, about 1 percent of the Jewish population. Jerusalem saw especially fierce fighting. Under the UN plan the city was meant to enjoy international status, but Jordanian Legionnaires overran the Old City, including the Jewish quarter, while the western, Jewish half of the city was besieged for months, relieved only when a new road was built through the hills. Eventually the city was divided into two, with the Israelis controlling the western half and the Jordanians annexing the eastern section, including the holy sites, as well as the entire West Bank. Egypt helped itself to the Gaza Strip, and Arab Palestine never came into existence.

The fate of the Palestinians

The Israelis have always officially claimed that the Palestinians ran away from their homes in 1948 to escape the fighting, expecting to return after an Arab victory. The Palestinians claim that they were forcibly expelled. Research shows that there is some truth in both versions. About a third of the 500,000 Palestinians living in the region that was to become Israel were coerced into leaving, becoming refugees in surrounding countries; about a third voluntarily fled, and the final third stayed put and eventually became citizens of Israel, which today has an Arab minority of some 20 percent.

LEFT: British troopships become a temporary home.
RIGHT: the first glimpse of the Promised Land.

Meanwhile, David Ben Gurion set about building his new nation. The architect of such institutions as the Histadrut trade-union movement and the Haganah, now renamed the Israel Defense Forces, Ben Gurion was easily able to outflank the world Jewish leader Chaim Weizmann, who also aspired to lead the new nation.

Ben Gurion offered Weizmann the post of president, the titular head of state.

At the same time, while allowing the revisionists led by Menachem Begin to participate in Knesset elections, Ben Gurion acted tough, outlawing their paramilitary organizations and blowing up a ship, the *Atalena*, bringing arms for Irgun in June 1948. Menachem Begin and his Herut Party, which won 14 out of 120 seats in the 1948 elections, were to remain in the political wilderness for nearly 20 years until, in the run-up to the Six Day War in 1967, Begin was invited by prime minister Levi Eshkol to join a national unity government. In elections a decade later, he won outright power.

Although harsh with his opponents, Ben Gurion knew how to delegate responsibility. After his socialist Mapai Party won 46 seats in the 1949 Knesset elections, he formed a coalition with the Stalinist Mapam Party to the left and religious and liberal groups to the right. Ben Gurion became prime minister and defense minister. Moshe Sharett, as foreign minister, became his heir apparent and eventually the second prime minister.

Within the army, Ben Gurion advanced the promotion of the daring one-eyed Moshe Dayan, a notorious womaniser who had sustained his injury while fighting for the British in Syria.

Another man who caught Ben Gurion's attention was the dashing young Yitzhak Rabin, commander of the Harel brigade, who was given a leading role in the armistice agreements negotiated after the War of Independence.

The Law of Return

The most significant new legislation introduced by the Knesset was the Law of Return of 1950, guaranteeing free immigration of world Jewry to Israel. The religious parties wanted to restrict immigration to candidates whose mothers were Jewish, but in the wake of the Holocaust and of the Nuremberg Laws, which had defined any-

THE ARMS INDUSTRY

Ben Gurion had a good eye for young talent, both inside and outside the army. In particular, he spotted the creative organizational abilities of a young Polish immigrant called Shimon Peres (who would become prime minister in 1984) and charged him with the task of developing a defense manufacturing infrastructure. Peres's accomplishments were remarkable, giving Israel a nuclear capability and enabling the country to produce its own tanks and fighter aircraft. Many Israeli weapons, such as the versatile Uzi sub-machine gun, became sought-after export items, and the existence of this successful industry no doubt boosted Israel's confidence during decades of war.

body with one Jewish grandparent as Jewish, this same yardstick was adopted.

In the years following the establishment of Israel, waves of immigrants flooded in. Nearly 700,000 arrived between 1948 and 1951, doubling the population. By 1964 another 500,000 had arrived and the population passed 2 million. But the European-born founding fathers were surprised to find that large numbers were arriving not only from Eastern Europe but also from Morocco, Egypt, Yemen, Iraq and other Arab countries, where entire Jewish communities were expelled in an anti-Zionist backlash.

By the 1960s Israel's Jewish population was split 50–50 between Ashkenazi European Jews and Sephardi Oriental Jews. This cultural divide, accentuated by socio-economic gaps, would generate major tensions in the 1970s.

International orientation

Ben Gurion had planned to pursue a neutral policy in the Cold War. During the War of Independence the USSR was the only country to send arms, though the USA had turned a blind eye to the military aid given to Israel by American Jewry. But, although a Stalinist party shared power in Israel's first government, the country was a parliamentary democracy with more in common with the West.

Moreover, Israel needed financial aid, and only the USA could supply that. So in 1949, when Israel took a loan of $100,000 from the USA, a pattern of economic dependence was begun. In parallel, Israel's relations with the Soviet Union were strained as Stalin refused to allow free emigration of Soviet Jewry.

However, Israel, in partnership with Britain and France, antagonized both the USA and the Soviet Union in 1956 when it launched the Suez campaign. Following the nationalization of the Suez Canal by Egypt's president, Gamal Abdel Nasser, British and French paratroopers seized the canal, and in less than a week Israeli troops had occupied all Sinai. But the Americans sided with the Egyptians, forcing the British and French to relinquish control of the canal and compelling the Israelis to withdraw from Sinai. Instead of being humiliated, Nasser became a hero.

Economic development

Despite Israel taking in so many impoverished immigrants and illiterate newcomers, plus the cost of remaining on a constant war footing, the economy developed steadily during the 1950s and 1960s. Major national projects were undertaken, including the draining of the Hula Swamp in the Upper Galilee and the building of the national carrier bringing water from the north to the Negev. The desert literally turned green. Forests were planted on the barren hillsides, and the arid land was transformed.

Even with its burgeoning population, the country was self-sufficient in food, and a major export industry, especially in citrus fruit, devel-

oped. Highways were built, and a health, education and energy infrastructure was put in place. In this formative stage, the Arab boycott and the unwillingness of overseas investors to put money into a country that might soon be driven into the sea turned out to be an asset, for Israel developed a home-owned industrial infrastructure. The economy was heavily centralized and socialist, but there was scope for entrepreneurs with the patience to unravel bureaucratic red tape.

In this stage of the country's development, donations from overseas Jewry, especially from North America, were a vital source of capital.

In addition, a reparations agreement was concluded with the West German government which compensated hundreds of thousands of survivors, or relatives of victims, for the loss of life, the suffering, and the property lost during the Holocaust. Menachem Begin bitterly opposed this agreement, insisting that no amount of money could atone for the devastation caused by the Nazis.

In 1963, when Levi Eshkol became the third prime minister, Israel was not a wealthy country, nor a full member of the industrialized world, but fortunately it did not suffer from the food shortages, disease and illiteracy which characterized most developing nations. ❑

LEFT: illegal immigrants gaze out from a British ship.
RIGHT: a waxwork model of Chaim Weizmann.

COMING OF AGE

*Through wars and internal strife Israel has struggled to maturity while
world opinion has fluctuated between praise and blame*

The Arabs have always maintained that Israel instigated the Six Day War in 1967 in order to seize more Palestinian territory. This interpretation of history overlooks the blockade of the Straits of Tiran by the Egyptian president, Gamal Abdel Nasser, which cut off the shipping route to Israel's Red Sea port of Eilat, as well as his boast that he would drive the Jews into the sea.

With hindsight, Nasser's threat was probably bluff, but Israel was not to know. As the Yom Kippur War revealed six years later, Israeli intelligence was poor at the time, and a first strike was crucial for such a tiny country with no strategic depth. So Israel took Nasser's threats at face value and attacked, and the Egyptian air force was destroyed on the ground minutes after the war started. The Golan Heights, from which Syria had been bombarding northern Israel, were captured. Israel also won the Sinai peninsula and Gaza Strip from Egypt, and the West Bank from Jordan. Jerusalem was reunited. Defense Minister Moshe Dayan and Chief of the Army Yitzhak Rabin were hailed as heroes.

Permanently on the map

Israel was never the same after the Six Day War. It wasn't only that the borders had changed and more than a million Palestinians had fallen under Israeli occupation. Perceived worldwide as the underdog in the Middle East conflict, Israel was now viewed as the oppressor. But the West, especially the United States, saw Israel as a potentially strong and reliable ally in the Cold War confrontation with the USSR. Military collaboration strengthened between Israel and the USA, while Britain and France maintained the arms embargo imposed at the start of the Six Day War.

Israel itself was intoxicated by its own success. Prime Minister Levi Eshkol died and was replaced by Golda Meir, who had grown up in the United States and was able to consolidate

LEFT: celebrating Independence Day in Jerusalem.
RIGHT: soldiers reach the Western Wall, 1967.

the US–Israeli romance. The country's new euphoria was not even tempered by a war of attrition between 1967 and 1970, in which Egypt shelled Israeli forces across the Suez Canal, nor by the emergence of the Palestine Liberation Organization (PLO), which carried out bloody terrorist attacks against Israeli tar-

gets, including the killing of 11 Israeli athletes during the Munich Olympic Games in 1972.

When Jordan and Egypt annexed the West Bank and Gaza Strip, the PLO had been suppressed and its leader, Yasser Arafat, imprisoned. But after 1967 the PLO was encouraged to spearhead the Arab nations' campaign to regain "the Zionist entity." By 1970 the PLO was so strong that Arafat tried, with Syrian backing, to take over Jordan. In a 10-day bloody war, King Hussein quelled the attempted Palestinian coup. Syrian troops who were massed on the border turned back when Israel said it would intervene to support the Hashemite Kingdom. Arafat and his fighters resettled in Lebanon.

War and peace

The PLO was popularly viewed as a terrorist organization that would eventually go away, and Israel considered itself invincible. In 1973 the Yom Kippur War stunned the nation. With a surprise assault, the Egyptians, under President Anwar Sadat, conquered much of Sinai while the Syrians nearly broke through to the Galilee. Israel recovered, counter-attacked, re-took the Golan Heights and even managed to cross the Suez Canal before the Americans, who for the first time became committed allies of Israel by airlifting emergency military supplies to the Middle East, forced a ceasefire.

Yom Kippur War. Moreover, Begin's populism appealed both to young Oriental Jews, alienated by the Ashkenazi socialist establishment, and to Orthodox Jewry, attached to the biblical sites in the West Bank, now called Judea and Samaria.

Yitzhak Rabin had first allowed right-wing Jews to settle Hebron and other West Bank towns in 1975, and in so doing opened a floodgate. Under Begin and his successor, Yitzhak Shamir, tens of thousands of Jews settled the West Bank and the Gaza Strip, and the Palestinians saw the little that was left of their homeland slipping away from them.

All the same, the right-wing Likud, though

But the war restored Egyptian pride and was portrayed by Sadat as a great victory. He signed a peace treaty with Israel in 1979 in exchange for the return of the Sinai peninsula. Remarkably, he did not shake hands with Golda Meir, or her successor Yitzhak Rabin, but with Menachem Begin, the implacably right-wing nationalist who won the 1977 election.

The birth of two-party politics

Menachem Begin's success changed the face of Israeli politics, which became a two-party affair, characterized by bitter divisions over the direction of Israeli society. After 29 years in power, Labor lost office because of its failures in the

SUPPORT FROM THE USA

By the late 1970s the United States had come to view Israel as a significant player in its Cold War global strategy, and also a vital support to NATO's vulnerable southeastern flank, which comprised the two bitter enemies, Greece and Turkey. This meant that large sums of money – about $1.5 billion a year – were plowed into Israel to pay for arms and to improve the country's military capabilities. Another $1.5 billion was given annually to help repay the loans taken out for previous acquisitions and, subsequently, for the expensive redeployment needed after the Sinai withdrawal in 1982. Such close ties with the USA naturally deepened the USSR's hostility towards Israel.

nationalist in character and reluctant to relinquish land, tended to make pragmatic concessions when pressured by the USA. Begin gave up Sinai after American arm-twisting, and received the Nobel Peace Prize for his pains.

Anti-Zionism

Israel's close identification with the USA made it a target for Soviet Union hostility. The communist bloc, Arab and Muslim nations and the developing world combined to isolate Israel as a pariah nation. The country was depicted as a racist state; Zionism was denounced by a UN resolution as an intrinsically fascist ideology.

The tactic was extremely effective, and even many of Israel's friends in the liberal West distanced themselves from Zionism. Remarkably, this was even before Likud came to power and when there was barely a settler in the West Bank. For Israelis, anti-Zionism was the flip side of anti-Semitism. Persecuted in Europe as Semites, they were now being denounced by the Semitic Arabs as European colonialists.

Ironically, while the Soviet Union was hounding Israel diplomatically and arming Syria, it eased restrictions on Jewish emigration. More than 180,000 Jews reached Israel from the USSR in the 1970s, and an even greater number emigrated to the United States.

Begin won a second election victory in 1981 and the following year turned his attentions on Lebanon. Israel's northern neighbor had been a model of democracy and affluence despite its divisions between Maronite Christians, Druze, Sunni and Shi'ite Muslims and Palestinian refugees. But the arrival of the PLO and its fighters in 1970 had disturbed the delicate balance, and the country plunged into civil war in 1975. The PLO used Lebanon as a base for attacks on Israel from sea and land.

Ariel Sharon, the Minister of Defense, convinced Begin that a military incursion into Southern Lebanon was required to clear out PLO bases. An invasion was launched in June 1982. Begin, like the rest of the nation, was surprised to learn a short while later that Israeli tanks were rolling through the streets of Beirut. The Americans intervened to prevent the Israel Defense Forces from finishing off Yasser Arafat, who was given safe passage to Tunisia.

LEFT: President Sadat is greeted by Begin in 1977.
RIGHT: checking Palestinian work permits.

In the aftermath of the war, Begin lost his previous vigor. The great orator fell silent and resigned the following year. He felt betrayed, not only by Sharon but also by his Finance Minister, Yoram Aridor, whose economic policies led to three-digit annual inflation.

The years of power sharing

The 1984 election result was inconclusive, and a rotation pact was agreed, with Labor's Shimon Peres serving as prime minister until 1986, followed by Likud's Yitzhak Shamir for the subsequent two years. Peres withdrew Israeli troops from Lebanon, with the exception of a security

belt closest to the Israeli border, and stabilized the economy, reducing the annual rate of inflation from 425 percent to 16 percent.

During the two decades that Israel had occupied the West Bank and Gaza, relations between the Israelis and Palestinians had deteriorated. Immediately after 1967 the Palestinians were infatuated with Israeli liberalism and the economic opportunities that occupation brought. A free press flourished, municipal elections were held, and employment in Israel, although mainly in menial jobs, led to improvements in the Palestinians' standard of living.

But things turned sour, especially after the Likud triumph in the 1970s, as it became clear that Israel was integrating the Palestinian territories into a Greater Israel. Right-wing settlers were becoming more powerful, and the Israeli government was talking of annexing the biblical Land of Israel.

Palestinian frustration exploded in 1987 with the outbreak of the Intifada, which was characterised by the throwing of rocks and Molotov cocktails at Israeli troops, and by strikes preventing Arab workers from coming to Israel. World opinion strongly sympathized with the Palestinians, and the demographic debate was renewed in Israeli politics, with Labor speaking of territorial concessions. The elections of

1988 saw Likud win the upper hand in a closely fought contest. Shamir continued to lead a national unity government, which broke down in 1990; he then formed a right-wing coalition.

The collapse of the Soviet Union

The unexpected disintegration of the USSR meant that, from 1990 onwards, Russian-speaking Jewry flooded into Israel. Over 800,000 immigrants had arrived by 1998. The demise of the Soviet Union saw Israel renew diplomatic relations with the states of Central and Eastern Europe and the former republics of the USSR. Another benefit was that the supply of Russian-made arms to Syria and the PLO dried up.

Before the post-Cold War situation could be digested, Iraq invaded Kuwait, and the Gulf War ensued in 1991. Scud missiles fell on Israel but, under American pressure, the right-wing government did not retaliate in order not to disrupt the allied coalition, which included Syria.

By November 1991 Israel was sitting round the table with the Palestinians and Syrians at the Madrid Peace Conference. In the wake of these preliminary peace talks, China, India and much of Asia established full diplomatic relations with Israel for the first time. African countries such as Nigeria renewed ties, and the UN resolution equating Zionism with racism was repealed. But Shamir stalled on progress in the talks, continuing to expand settlements in the West Bank. A confrontation with the United States was averted by Yitzhak Rabin's election victory in 1992.

Peace accords and assassination

Though Rabin had been elected on a dovish platform, Israelis and the wider world were surprised by the secret agreements concluded with the PLO in Oslo. In September 1993 Prime Minister Rabin and PLO Chairman Yasser Arafat shook hands on the White House lawn, and by 1994 Israel had withdrawn from most of the Gaza Strip and all the towns on the West Bank except Hebron. A peace agreement was signed with Jordan, and Morocco and Tunisia opened low-level diplomatic offices in Tel Aviv.

The peace process, combined with the end of the Arab economic boycott, ongoing immigration and a penchant for developing innovative high-tech products, saw the economy boom. Average annual growth of 6 percent in the early 1990s enabled the standard of living to rise rapidly to Western European levels.

But Rabin's right-wing religious and nationalist opponents were unimpressed by the economic benefits of peace. The opposition to territorial compromise strengthened following a terrorist bombing campaign by the extremist Palestinian Hamas movement. Vociferous anti-government demonstrations took place as the right's supporters took to the streets.

A young law student, Yigal Amir, took matters into his own hands. He stalked Rabin for several months, with a pistol in his pocket. His opportunity came following a peace rally in Tel Aviv in November 1995, when he took advantage of a lapse in security to pump three bullets into Rabin's back from point-blank range.

In the shocked aftermath of the assassination of a widely respected leader, the premiership was assumed by Foreign Minister Shimon Peres. As architect of the Oslo Accords, he had won the Nobel Peace Prize, along with Rabin and Arafat, and he now pushed ahead vigorously with the peace process. However, Syria's President Hafez El-Assad refused to meet him, even though Peres had agreed in principle to return the Golan Heights.

Persuaded by a large lead in the polls, Peres brought forward elections by six months to May 1996. But a lackluster campaign, combined with further terrorist attacks by Hamas and Hizbullah missiles raining down on the Galilee, saw Peres defeated by the narrowest of margins.

Netanyahu puts on the brakes

Binyamin Netanyahu became the first prime minister to be chosen directly by the electorate. He would have won more handsomely under the old system, by which the Knesset faction with the best chance of forming a government received a mandate from the president. He won because he made a late, pragmatic move to the center: in contravention of traditional Likud policy, he agreed to abide by the Oslo Agreements and to meet Yasser Arafat, and in 1997 he even withdrew from half of Hebron.

If Netanyahu lost allies to the right because of his diplomatic policies vis-à-vis the Palestinians, much of his center-ground support fell away as a result of his domestic incompetence. A polished speaker in both Hebrew and English (he had been raised and educated in the US by his Israeli parents) he began talking hesitantly after receiving the reins of power.

Most damagingly, he was implicated in a scandal over the appointment of a new Attorney-General (the State's chief prosecutor), who had been handed the appointment on condition he dropped charges of corruption against the Interior Minister, Arye Deri, of the ultra-orthodox Shas party. Netanyahu escaped prosecution due to lack of evidence and doggedly refused to resign. But the mud stuck and his majority in

---

LEFT: Yitzhak Rabin, assassinated in 1995.
ABOVE: Shimon Peres in pensive mood, with a portrait of the assassinated Yitzhak Rabin in the background.

> ### MINOR INCONVENIENCES
> The Intifada had one trivial but inconvenient aspect for some Israelis: no more popping over to dine in their favourite West Bank restaurant in Ramalla, or to buy cheap groceries in Gaza.

the Knesset was eroded, eventually compelling him to call elections in 1999.

Barak plays the dove

Netanyahu faced the Labor party's new star, Ehud Barak, a former chief of the army whom the late Yitzhak Rabin had groomed as his successor. Barak won on a landslide and a dovish platform, although he had no clear Knesset majority and needed support from the rightist ultra-orthodox Shas party. Relations with the Palestinians

improved, the economy boomed as Israel consolidated its position as a global high-tech leader, and the number of immigrants from the former Soviet Union surpassed the 1 million mark in less than a decade.

Barak gambled everything on a peace summit with the Palestinians at Camp David in the summer of 2000. President Bill Clinton acted as mediator as Barak stunned Israelis by agreeing to relinquish most of the West Bank and Gaza, including much of East Jerusalem and the Old City. To balance the 10 percent of the West Bank that Barak wanted to hang onto, he offered a strip of the Negev desert alongside Gaza as compensation. But Arafat was playing hard to get. He refused to yield any of the land captured by Israel in 1967 and demanded the right of return of all Palestinians to pre-1967 Israel, which would wipe out the country's Jewish majority. Shas withdrew from the government and Barak soldiered on for several months in the Knesset before calling elections.

Back to the Intifada

The conventional wisdom at the time among proponents of peace was that Arafat's hard line at Camp David was a bargaining posture to squeeze greater concessions from Israel. With hindsight, many Israelis – even on the left – feel

mind. In the first stage of hostilities, attacks took place mainly in the West Bank and Gaza against settlers and soldiers. Arafat and Barak carried on talking but the impetus for peace was buried in bloodshed.

Sharon enters the fray

In the 2001 elections Ariel Sharon, the hard-line general, convincingly defeated Barak. Demonized and despised for his role in the Lebanon war of 1982, Sharon was to surprise everybody, most of all his own supporters, by becoming a peacemaker.

But first Sharon had to handle intensified sui-

that the Palestinian leader was simply unable to bring himself to conclude a final agreement with the old enemy.

Certainly, after the Intifada broke out on 30 September 2000, Arafat appeared re-charged with a new energy. The nominal reason for the outbreak of hostilities was an insensitive visit by the opposition Likud leader, Ariel Sharon, to the Temple Mount. Rioting broke out across the West Bank – even among Israeli Arabs, 13 of whom were killed by police. The rioting may have been spontaneous, but Arafat's decision several days later to release all Hamas prisoners, who had been responsible for attacks on Israelis, suggested he had a more extended conflict in

cide bombings. After 9/11, Palestinian suicide bombings, inspired by what could be achieved by a small cadre of *shaheedin* (Muslim martyrs), escalated their attacks on crowded buses and public places. Sharon was initially restrained but eventually launched a massive attack on the West Bank against Palestinian fighters after a suicide attack at a Passover festive meal in 2002 killed 30 Israelis. "Targeted killings," in which Hamas and Jihad leaders were assassinated by aerial missiles and the construction of a security wall, cutting deep into Palestinian territory, sealing the West Bank from Israel, eventually quelled the suicide threat. Sharon, together with his Finance Minister Netanyahu, also won popularity by pulling Israel out of a deep recession, which at one time threatened to collapse the entire economy.

Disengagement from Gaza

Sharon was transformed into statesman seeking peace. The Labor party left the government coalition and Sharon called new elections in 2003, sweeping to victory and forming a right-wing government without Labor. To the horror of his own supporters, Sharon announced that Israel would withdraw unilaterally all Jewish settlements from Gaza. Labor re-joined the government coalition as Sharon's right-wing allies

though his deputy Ehud Olmert was elected prime minister in 2006 with a mandate for territorial compromise, the election victory by Hamas, who refuse to recognize Israel's existence, torpedoed any negotiated settlement.

Events in the north also worked against a rapprochement. Iran's nuclear program and the belligerence of their Lebanese Shiite Hizbullah proxies resulted in the Second Lebanon War in July 2006 when Israeli soldiers were attacked inside Israeli territory. Yet, despite massive air raids on Shiite targets in Lebanon and a full-scale invasion of Shiite strongholds near the Israeli border, the IDF failed to defeat Hizbullah, or halt

left. The far right bitterly opposed disengagement, but to no avail. Sharon achieved what even Rabin had never dared undertake, when Israel abandoned its settlements in Gaza in 2005.

Arafat's death the previous year, combined with the Gaza disengagement, created an opportunity for peace as Sharon and Arafat's elected successor Mahmoud Abbas (Abu Mazen) renewed the peace process. Sharon broke with the right-wing Likud and formed his own centrist Kadima party. But the opportunity was fleeting. Sharon was felled by a massive stroke and,

LEFT: Binyamin Netanyahu meets Yasser Arafat.
ABOVE: Ariel Sharon meets Abu Mazen.

missile attacks on northern Israel. Minister of Defense Amir Peretz and IDF Chief of Staff Dan Halutz resigned, but Olmert soldiered on.

The military failure in the north, Iran's nuclear aspirations and an emboldened Hizbullah are new anxieties for Israel, while the situation vis-à-vis the Palestinians offers little comfort. The Palestinians were left divided after the coup by Hamas in Gaza, while Abu Mazen's Fatah has control of the West Bank. The Israelis themselves remain divided between secular society, whose majority is prepared to relinquish virtually all of the West Bank, and the religious right and hawkish supporters who are determined to preserve a Greater Israel. ❏

ISRAEL TODAY

Despite divisions between left and right, religious and secular, Ashkenazi and Sephardi, Jews and Arabs, the country's democracy remains robust

Israel confounds expectations. It is a nation rooted in religion, yet the majority of the Jewish population are brazenly secular, turning to religion only for births, barmitzvahs, weddings and funerals. There are picturesque bastions of orthodoxy in Jerusalem, in Bnei Brak near Tel Aviv, and elsewhere a quaint mixture of medieval Poland and the Middle East, but for the most part long rabbinical beards are rare, many restaurants serve forbidden unkosher foods, the Sabbath is barely observed, and women dress anything but modestly.

It is the army generals rather than the rabbis who have forged the nation's values. Modern Israel is a nation whose military has a peerless reputation for executing the swift, the precise and the dramatically unexpected. Yet the ubiquitous Israeli soldier, rifle slung casually over his shoulder, appears slovenly and unregimented. This informality extends even to the Israel Defense Forces (IDF), but it was these long-haired paratroopers, unshaven officers and pot-bellied reservists who undertook the Entebbe rescue, bombed the Iraqi nuclear reactor and triumphed in the Six Day War.

Vigorous democracy

Israel's greatest achievements, however, have not been on the battlefield. A nation has been created out of immigrants from more than 80 countries, who shared a religious heritage and a desire to return to their ancestral homeland, but little else – not even a language. In the street you will hear an astonishing Babel of languages: Russian, English, Arabic, Amharic, Hungarian, French, Persian, Spanish, Yiddish. But Hebrew, the language of the Bible, has been resurrected and adapted to everyday life.

Even more surprisingly, parliamentary democracy has flourished – despite the fact that most Israelis originate in countries with no experience of such democracy; despite the frictions between

LEFT: Tel Aviv's Azrieli Towers bathed in pink light to publicize Breast Cancer Awareness Month.
RIGHT: anti-Aids campaigners challenge orthodoxy.

religious and secular, right and left, Arab and Jew; and despite the centrality and power of the army. Even when Prime Minister Yitzhak Rabin was gunned down in 1995, there was no danger of the Knesset's sovereignty being overthrown.

If a general seeks political power, he does not plan a coup d'état, as might happen else-

where in the Middle East, but resigns his commission and enters the political fray. And the chances of success are good: before becoming prime minister Yitzhak Rabin and Ehud Barak were both chiefs of staff in the Israel Defense Forces, while Ariel Sharon was a high-profile general. In the current cabinet, at least six ministers were former generals.

Another political safety-valve is the system of proportional representation, which allows all interest groups to be represented in parliament, enabling small parties to hold the balance of power between the major blocs, often granting them disproportionate powers. Civil rights, freedom of the press and an independent judiciary further reinforce democratic values in a country that takes an exuberant pride in flouting authority, and disobeying regulations.

Organized chaos

Consequently, the eye may initially see Levantine chaos and Mediterranean madness, but beneath the surface is a society that functions effectively. The wars have been won, the desert has bloomed, high-tech industries compete in – and sometimes lead – world markets. From a socialist base, a dynamic capitalist economy has been built with sustained economic growth, enabling Israel to enjoy high living standards.

The diverse landscape and climate complement the heterogeneous nature of the people. The heat of the summer leaves the country parched and brown except for the ripening grape vines, cotton fields and well-watered lawns. But, come November, the rains begin, driving forcefully down throughout the winter, and occasional snowfalls can cover inland hills. Flash floods in the desert uproot trees and shift boulders. By spring the countryside is ablaze with flowers and fields are as emerald as Ireland. But then the rains cease and gradually the land becomes thirsty and faded. The land, like its people, is in a state of constant flux and renewal.

In-gathering of the exiles

The essence of this ongoing change is *aliyah*, Hebrew for immigration. Since 1989 more than a million immigrants have reached Israel from the former Soviet Union alone. Over the same period, 40,000 immigrants have come from Ethiopia. This represents 15 percent of Israel's population, the equivalent of Britain taking in 9 million immigrants, or the USA 45 million.

The process has been tackled with relish, though inevitably there are problems. The Russian-speaking newcomers have assimilated easily into the country's economic life but often remain culturally apart. They are highly secular (about 300,000 of them are not recognized by the rabbinate as Jewish because only their fathers are Jewish, or their Judaism is in doubt) and they tend to have right-wing political views. Many are highly educated scientists, engineers, musicians and artists. Statistics show that the average immigrant who reached Israel from the former Soviet Union in the early 1990s already earns above the national average salary.

The exception to this rule are the Jews who came from the former southern Soviet republics of Uzbekistan and Azerbaijan and the Russian Caucasus. The economic profile of the Bukharian and Mountain Jews has more in common with Ethiopian Jews than their compatriots from

ica and Turkey fleeing military juntas; from Iran escaping the ayatollahs, and most recently from the Soviet Union and Ethiopia.

There has also always been a steady flow of immigrants from North America, Europe, South Africa and Australasia – immigrants prepared to forgo comfortable lives to rebuild Zion. Golda Meir, prime minister from 1969 to 1974, grew up in America, while the late President Chaim Herzog was born in Belfast. There are prejudices against newcomers, but immigrants can reach the top despite their heavily accented and awkward Hebrew.

Nurtured by government attempts towards

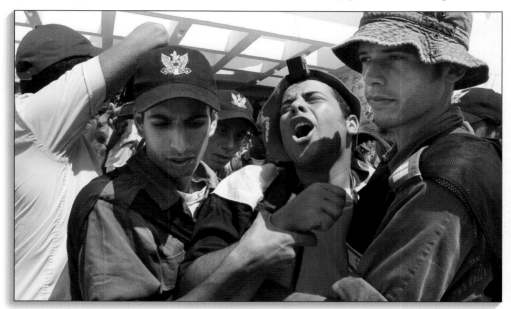

European Russia. Like Ethiopian Jews, the older generation struggles to adjust to Israel's high-tech society and seldom assimilates but their children, with much soul-searching pain, try hard to become Israeli and bridge the gap.

Israel is good at blending waves of newcomers into its society. Jews came from Russia before the revolution; from Germany and Austria fleeing the Nazis; from Poland, Hungary and Romania out of the ashes of the Holocaust; from Iraq, Syria, the Yemen and North Africa escaping Arab anti-Zionism; from Latin Amer-

social integration, the cultural mosaic becomes a melting pot. Contemporary Israeli music reflects a fusion between East and West. Strange food combinations include *felafel* and chips, goulash and couscous, chicken soup and *kubbe*.

A stable economy

David Ben Gurion built Israel's economy around the powerful Histadrut trade-union movement. Onto this socialist base – which encompassed agricultural production through the kibbutz collectives and moshav cooperatives, much of the health service, and many industrial conglomerates that included the country's largest bank – a dynamic capitalist system

LEFT: a Passover meal brings families together.
ABOVE: settlers being evicted from Gaza in 2005.

has been grafted. In the 1980s, three-digit inflation caused chaos, but since 1986 economic
order has been restored, with Western levels of
inflation and economic growth
averaging 6 percent annually
during most of the 1990s and 4
percent in recent years.

Meanwhile, the Histadrut is
in decline, and almost all its
business assets have been sold
off. Even so, union membership
today is remarkably universal, from the blue-
collar industrial workforce to senior management and members of the professions. The

agricultural produce failing to earn enough foreign currency to support a Western standard of
living. Contributions from world Jewry, German
compensation for the Holocaust,
a limited tourist industry and,
from the 1970s, US government
defense aid enabled the country
to balance its books. But, with
wars and mass immigration, it
was always a struggle.

The picture changed dramati-
cally in the 1990s. The emergence of high-tech
in the global economy was a godsend for Israel,
which was always strong on technological inno-

MIXES AND MUDDLES

In the 1980s, when three-digit
inflation raged, Israelis spoke of
their "muddled" economy as
opposed to the "mixed"
economies of Western Europe.

high-status composition of its membership has
seen the Histadrut retain much of its influence
when union movements elsewhere in the world
are diminished. But while the Histadrut is still
capable of calling a general strike – visitors may
be surprised to find all the banks on strike, or
doctors seeing only emergency cases – its power
has been diluted by a combination of Likud rule,
incompetent management of its pension funds
which required the government to take them
over, and the kind of competitive-edged capitalism needed to sell commodities overseas.

For the fact is that Israel must export to survive. In its formative years this was no easy task
with polished diamonds, Jaffa oranges and other

EXPORT EXPERTISE

In contrast to polished diamonds, of which Israel exports
$14 billion a year, and where the rough stones must be
imported, high-tech goods have high added-value. Israel
continues to export $1.5 billion worth of agricultural pro-
duce a year and a similar amount in agricultural inputs like
irrigation equipment. The country also exports nearly $3
billion a year of natural resources – minerals from the
Dead Sea and phosphates from the Negev Desert.

About 35 percent of goods are sold to Western Europe,
40 percent to North America and 20 percent to the Far
East. It has negotiated tariff-free trade with the European
Union and NAFTA (the US, Canada and Mexico).

vation. More than half of the US$47 billion of goods that Israel currently exports annually are advanced technology systems in telecom, mobile telephone and internet applications, software solutions, semiconductors, electro-optics, medical devices, pharmaceuticals, biotech and more. Military and security systems are a major export item.

Israel also enjoys an income approaching $3 billion a year from donations by the country's Jewish and Christian supporters. In addition, aid from the United States amounts to more than

A PEACEFUL MAJORITY

Opinon polls have shown that 70 percent of Israelis support the peace process and territorial compromise with the Palestinians.

The quest for peace

The main anxiety caused by dependence on the US concerns peace and territorial compromise. Many Israelis fear that US pressure to hand back more land to the Arabs will leave Israel vulnerable to future attack. The return of the Golan, for example, which the US has pressed for, is strongly opposed. Giving up Sinai for peace with Egypt was one thing; it is now a vast, demilitarized desert providing an effective trip-wire should Egypt ever want to attack but the Golan Heights and Mount Her-

$2 billion a year. This aid began in the 1970s when Israel was perceived as an important ally against the USSR, and was once a vital source of income for Israel. But today not only has the sum been gradually reduced but it has also become only a small proportion of Israel's national budget. However, although no longer economically dependent on Uncle Sam, Israel would find it difficult to thrive without US diplomatic support, and the country also needs advanced American weaponry.

LEFT: a post office employee shows one of the thousands of letters addressed to God and Jesus.
ABOVE: Ben Gurion International Airport.

mon tower menacingly over northern Israel.

But it is peace with the Palestinians that poses the greatest challenge. The two sides seem far apart. Despite the intransigent positions adopted by both Palestinians and Israelis, most people do not have the stomach for extensive bloodshed. But the sense of injustice is strong enough to enable Hamas in Gaza and Hezbollah in Lebanon to gain sufficient support to fan the flames of armed conflict, as they did in 2006. If the root causes of that injustice could be effectively tackled, the desire for peace and prosperity and an abhorrence of war, more than international pressure, may eventually bring a resolution to the so far elusive final accord. ❏

THE PEOPLE OF ISRAEL

This tiny country comprises an exotic mixture of people, many born
elsewhere but all regarding Israel as home

The only valid generalization to make about Israelis is that there is no such thing as a typical Israeli. The in-gathering of the exiles has brought Jews to Israel from 80 countries, and, beneath their sometimes surly surface, they can behave with Latin American panache, European civility or overwhelming Middle Eastern hospitality.

Israeli society itself has distinctly different sectors, including black-hatted ultra-Orthodox Jews and more modern Orthodox Jewry, as well as secular European (Ashkenazi) Jews and more traditional Oriental (Sephardi) Jews in addition to the indigenous Arab population.

Immigrants from the former Soviet Union now comprise 15 percent of Israeli society, while Ethiopian Jews add diversity to the social landscape. Slick Tel Aviv city businesspeople are increasingly prevalent, but the pioneering spirit lives on and rugged, bronzed kibbutz-nikim can still be found.

An urban emphasis

Kibbutz dwellers aside, Israelis are predominantly urban and suburban creatures. More than half the population lives in the country's three largest cities. Jerusalem has a population of 800,000, over 2½ million people live in the Greater Tel Aviv area, and an additional 500,000 in the Haifa Bay conurbation.

The Arabs are more rural. More than one-fifth of Israel's population of over 7 million belongs to the Arab minority, which is mainly Muslim but also includes Christians and Druze. Many Arabs are still loyal to their nomadic Bedouin tribes even though they have moved to permanent accommodation. Discussion of Israeli Arabs doesn't include the 3 million Palestinians of the West Bank and Gaza.

Israel's other minorities include several thousand Circassians, Turkic Muslims from the Southern Russian Caucasian mountains brought

PRECEDING PAGES: Orthodox Jews in Me'a She'arim.
LEFT: Tel Aviv's cosmopolitan youth culture.
RIGHT: the classic sabra (a native-born Israeli).

to the region in the 1800s to protect Ottoman interests. The Samaritans are an ancient Samarian sect, and the Baha'i religion has its world headquarters in Haifa. The Negev town of Dimona is home to several hundred Black Hebrews, and since the 1970s the country has taken in hundreds of Vietnamese boat people,

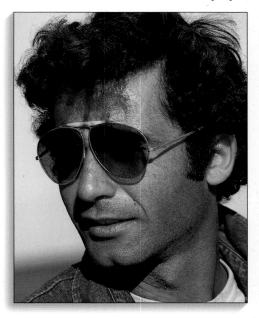

Bosnian Muslim refugees and former pro-Israel Southern Lebanese Christians. Israel also has an estimated 200,000 guest workers.

Educational institutions and the army have been powerful influences for social assimilation. The Hebrew language enhances social cohesion, although communities may jealously guard their distinct Jewish traditions.

Despite their diversity, native-born Israelis do have much in common and, perhaps because of their diversity, social niceties are rare. Native Israelis are brash, self-confident and always in a hurry. Yet they can also be considerate, and their openness and curiosity delight the gregarious as much as they intimidate the reticent.

Secular Jewry

For many non-Jews the term "secular Jewry" would seem contradictory. Many Jews, too, argue that Judaism is a religion and not a nationality and, therefore, Jews can be Orthodox or not Orthodox but never secular. Such semantic discussions overlook the realities of everyday Israeli life. The fact is that most Israeli Jews define themselves as both secular and Jewish.

It is difficult to ascertain who is a secular Jew. By and large, European Jews clearly identify themselves as secular, Orthodox or ultra-Orthodox and tend to be more extreme in their allegiances. It was secular Ashkenazi Jews from

Oriental Jews have made it out of the poor apartment buildings constructed for them when they arrived, and many have prospered. Take, for example, some of the most senior men in recent governments: President Moshe Katzav and Defense Minister Shaul Mofaz came from Iran, Minister of Infrastructure Benjamin Ben Eliezer hails from Iraq, and Transport Minister Meir Shetreet was born in Morocco.

Politics and religion

Israel's secular Jews share the liberal, universalist views of their North American and Western European counterparts. Democracy,

Europe who were the architects of the state in the early 1900s. Oriental Jews, who mostly came later, in the 1940s and 1950s, are more traditional. Many non-religious Oriental Jews have assimilated the European contempt for Orthodoxy, but most remain more respectful and even deferential and are more likely to be contemptuous of secularism.

The divide between Ashkenazi and Oriental Jewry remains today, although inter-marriage is common. But virtually all of the most impoverished Jewish Israelis are Oriental. This disadvantaged sector of society also tends to have strong religious leanings and is hostile to the secularism of Ashkenazi Jewry. However, most

McDonald's Bends the Rules

Where religious rules are concerned it's sometimes hard for outsiders to know where lines are drawn between the acceptable and the unacceptable. Take dietary laws, for example. McDonald's, the multinational hamburger chain, undertook detailed market research before moving into Israel. The result was that bacon McMuffins were non-starters, because pork of any kind is forbidden, but cheeseburgers were introduced successfully, even though kosher laws prohibit the mixing of meat and milk products. But bread is definitely not permissible during Passover, so McDonald's gets round this by serving cheeseburgers in buns made of potato flour instead of wheat.

freedom of expression and minority rights are the sacred values. Most would not mind if their daughter wanted to marry a non-Jew but might well be more bothered if she brought home a black-hatted ultra-Orthodox Jew. Though secular Jews firmly hold the reins of political power, there is an almost paranoid belief that they are slipping out of their hands.

Secular Jewry, especially in Jerusalem, feels it is a besieged community, threatened demographically by both the Arab minority and ultra-Orthodox Jewry, both of which have much higher birth rates.

Secular Jewry often complains about the exis-

ular Jewry commands only minority support. There is often plenty of backing on the right for secular causes. In recent times, for example, such senior politicians as Ariel Sharon, Ehud Olmert and Benjamin Netanyahu have been staunchly secular.

Political expediency has led to an alliance between the essentially anti-religious Likud and religious elements. Likud's reluctance to relinquish the West Bank and Gaza stems from security and nationalistic concerns, while the religious cherish the biblical concept of the Land of Israel. Moreover, Likud traditionally relied on support from the Oriental communi-

tence of Orthodox religious parties, but the fact is that it is impossible in Israel to separate politics from religion. The left-wing Meretz faction, which together with allies on the left of the Labour Party, probably commands the support of a third of Israelis, together with the centrist anti-clerical Shinui party, spearheads the political fight to break the Orthodox rabbinical monopoly on issues of personal status such as marriage, divorce, conversion and burial.

But it would be a mistake to assume, by reading the political map from left to right, that sec-

ties, who incline towards tradition. After the disengagement from Gaza, however, Likud's stock fell in the eyes of the right-wing religious community, and it was further devalued by Ariel Sharon's leaving to form a new party.

Family values

Although many people are surprised by the extent to which Israel's secular majority disregards religious practice, it would be misleading to think that Israelis have no regard at all for religion. On substantive issues such as marriage and burial, opinion polls consistently show that the majority of Israelis support the Orthodox monopoly of these rites. This has greatly

---

LEFT: backgammon game in Sheinkin Street, Tel Aviv.
ABOVE: Israel has some of the region's best beaches.

anguished the Reform and Conservative movements, imported to Israel from America, which attempt to adapt Judaism to the modern age, and in particular to integrate women into the synagogue service.

The fact is that secular Israelis have Zionism, which remains an ideology capable of attracting a high level of commitment to the building of the state and is closely linked to conservative family values. And even the most outwardly secular of Jews still tends to have an inner belief in the essential Jewish values – belief in God and a divine plan. This fills the spiritual vacuum. In the wake of Yitzhak Rabin's assassination,

young Israelis found these values helped them to cope with their grief over his death.

Like the post-Christian West, post-Jewish Israel suffers from rising crime, violence, drug addiction and inner-city poverty. But, despite a growing divorce rate, family ties remain strong; there is a deep respect for symbols of state, and, on the whole, young people are highly motivated to serve in the army.

Secular Israel is at once both radical and conservative. The long-haired teenager with an earring through his nose, for example, doesn't usually complain about having a short back and sides and submitting to army discipline at the age of 18. The divisions in Israeli society, though real, are misleading. The assassination of Yitzhak Rabin, a left-of-centre secular Ashkenazi, by Yigal Amir, a right-wing religious Jew from a Yemen-born family, seems to epitomize enmities. But this violent deed was an exceptional event. When the chips are down, Israelis have a surprising capacity for joining ranks.

Orthodox and Ultra-Orthodox

To a secular Jew the Orthodox and ultra-Orthodox groups have much in common. Both strictly observe the all-encompassing world of Halacha – Jewish Orthodox practice. This means that the men keep their heads covered and pray at least three times a day. Kosher dietary laws are strictly followed, and the Sabbath is a day for absolute abstention from work, including "lighting a spark" – thus prohibiting traveling, cooking, switching on a light and even smoking.

The diverse head coverings of the men often indicate degrees of Orthodoxy. Generally, the larger the *kippa* (skull cap) the more Orthodox the wearer. The *kippot* range from the small knitted variety, worn by the modern Orthodox, to the big black knitted ones of the mainstream Orthodox, and the large black skull caps worn beneath even larger black hats by the ultra-Orthodox.

A woman's clothes are a good indication of the Orthodox Jew's lifestyle. A man with a small knitted *kippa* is likely to be accompanied by a woman wearing immodest jeans or other contemporary Western clothing. Women in the large mainstream community will wear long dresses and keep their arms covered, but many no longer wear wigs or head scarves.

Women in the ultra-Orthodox communities are literally kept under wraps. Not a square inch of flesh is seen other than the face and hands.

The ultra-Orthodox woman cannot be in an enclosed room with men other than her immediate relatives. At weddings and parties women will sit in a separate area.

Ultra-Orthodox Jewish society comprises a collection of sects as much medieval Eastern European as biblical in their origins. This is why, on Saturdays (Sabbaths) and festivals, the men wear fur hats more suitable for a Russian winter than a Middle Eastern summer.

Anti-Zionism to ultra-Zionism

Historically all Jews were by definition Orthodox, and three or four centuries ago all of Eastern European Jewry would have followed a moral code similar to that of Me'a She'arim today. Growing secularism in 19th-century Christian Europe compelled Jews to find other outlets of cultural expression, and Zionism emerged as a secular movement. Therefore all Orthodox Jews were anti-Zionist to begin with, opposed to the use of Hebrew, the holy tongue, for everyday use and to the notion that a Jewish state could contemplate any degree of separation between synagogue and state.

However, in the 1920s a strong national religious movement emerged, combining the nationalistic values of Zionism with the tenets of Orthodoxy. With its own kibbutzim and workers' movements, it was bolstered by the mass immigration of Oriental Jewry, which had deeper ties with Jewish tradition.

Commanding the political support of about 10 percent of the population, the national religious movement, which historically contained strong elements of liberalism, veered sharply to the right after 1967 when the Gush Emunim settlers' movement sprang from it. Holding the Land of Israel to be sacred, the movement has come to be perceived as the fiercest opponent of territorial compromise. The national religious movement runs its own schools, distinct from their secular counterparts.

Ultra-Orthodox Jewry, known in Hebrew as *Haredim*, also has its own education system. These black-clad communities are at best critical of Zionism, at worst still opposed to the Jewish state. Each sect has its own rabbinical leaders, and most of them are based in New York rather than Jerusalem.

The largest *Haredi* sect is the Lubavitchers. Under the late Rabbi Schneerson, revered by his followers as a messianic figure, the Lubavitchers took a pro-Israel hawkish stand supporting continuation of Jewish control of the West Bank. The Satmar, on the other hand, which also has its headquarters in New York, refuses to recognize the government of Israel as the legitimate representative of the Jewish people.

An extreme Jerusalem-based sect called Netorei Karta even supported the PLO when its charter called for the destruction of the Jewish state. This sect holds that the Zionists are worse than the Nazis, for while the latter sought to

destroy the Jews physically, the former are destroying the Jewish people spiritually.

Prayer power

All these sects, even those with pro-Zionist leanings, tend to have contempt for the institutions of modern Israel – the flag, the army, the Supreme Court, etc. Few ultra-Orthodox Jews serve in the army, and those who do will often end up in the Rabbinical Corps, checking that kitchens are kosher. Even the right-wing Lubavitchers argue that praying for the strength of Israel is as important as fighting for it.

As a result, secular Jewry dislikes ultra-Orthodox Jewry's lack of patriotism, while the

---

LEFT: at Jerusalem's Western (Wailing) Wall.
RIGHT: an Orthodox Jew at prayer.

ultra-Orthodox condemn secular Jews' non-religious lifestyle. Orthodox Jewry is caught in the middle, justifying and condemning both sides.

Despite this lack of common ground, secular Israel exercises a certain degree of tolerance, mainly because the ultra-Orthodox parties hold the balance of power between left and right. Moreover, many Jews believe that to harass the ultra-Orthodox communities could leave them open to charges of anti-Semitism.

Oriental Jewry

Religious Jews from Asian and African countries have never fitted neatly into the European

the past decade for, though Orthodox Jewry has a higher birth rate, the overwhelming majority of Jewish immigrants from Russia are secular.

Russian-Speaking Jews

"Let My People Go" was the slogan used by campaign activists pushing for the right of Soviet Jewry to emigrate freely. Nobody believed it would actually happen even in the 1970s, the era of détente when nearly 400,000 Soviet Jews were allowed out, about half of them reaching Israel, the rest heading for the United States.

But as glasnost gained momentum in the late 1980s, the right to emigrate was suddenly

pattern of sects, though Israel's European religious establishment did succeed in imposing black hats and suits on many Jews from Yemen and North Africa. But ultimately Sephardi religious leaders like the charismatic former Chief Rabbi Ovadia Yosef, who retains his oriental robes, have prevailed. His Shas political party controls 10 percent of Knesset seats. Much of Shas's support comes from traditional rather than Orthodox Oriental Jews, indicating that the divide between observant and non-observant Sephardis is narrower than that between their European counterparts.

About 20 percent of Israeli Jews are Orthodox. This number has remained constant over

LANGUAGE OF CHANGE

As a result of the huge waves of Russian immigration since 1990, Israel's urban landscape has taken on a decidedly Slavic feel. Cyrillic shop signs abound, vying for space with Hebrew, English and Arabic lettering. Newsstands are bursting with Russian-language publications, and in some suburbs of Tel Aviv and Haifa, Russian is the lingua franca. Russian-speakers have their own state-run radio station, and cable TV brings them all the major television channels from Russia.

The newcomers are learning Hebrew as they become assimilated, but in the meantime it is interesting to see the impact of yet another language in this polyglot nation.

granted to Soviet Jewry. For Israel the event was as momentous as the breaching of the Berlin Wall. It was like a dam bursting. During 1990, more than 200,000 Jews reached Israel; in 1991, the figure was over 170,000. After the break-up of the Soviet Union the pace slackened, but still some 60,000 Jews arrived each year from the former Soviet republics throughout the 1990s.

Not every Russian-speaking Jew wanted to go to Israel. Several hundred thousand preferred North America, while after the start of the Intifada in 2000 more Jews moved each year to Germany than to Israel. More than a million Jews remain by choice in the former Soviet Union, keeping their options open.

Transforming Israel

During the 1990s, Russian-speaking Jews surpassed Moroccans as Israel's largest immigrant group. More than a million Russian-speaking immigrants have reached Israel since 1990, adding to the 180,000 who came in the 1970s.

Although secular, the Russian-speaking immigrants tend to be right-wing. Their best-known political leaders are the former refusenik Natan Sharansky and Avigdor Lieberman of the far-right Israel Is Our Home party. Both led the campaign against withdrawal from Gaza.

The latest wave of Russian immigrants has a high educational profile. Many are scientists and engineers, musicians and teachers. Even before this latest wave of immigration, Israel had the world's highest per capita proportion of doctors. With 15,000 more doctors among the newcomers, many could not at first qualify for medical licences or find work in their professions, but they have proved to be very flexible and willing to undergo re-training where necessary.

Understandably, it took a little while for some of the Russian-speaking newcomers to master Hebrew and become accustomed to the more assertive behavior of Western society, but most have adjusted well if not fully. After serving an immigrant's apprenticeship sweeping the streets, washing dishes or doing some other kind of menial work, most immigrants have managed to find a job in their profession.

These new immigrants have changed the

LEFT: Russian immigrants arrive at Lod Airport in the early 1960s.
RIGHT: Russian-language newspapers are now widely available in Israel.

demographic balance of Israel. Before their arrival, Israel had a small Oriental Jewish majority. Russian Jewry has tipped the scales back in favor of Ashkenazi Jewry, although 10 percent of these newcomers are Oriental Jews from the ancient communities in Georgia, Azerbaijan and the Russian Caucasus as well as Uzbekistan.

Kosher and un-kosher

In the main, Russian-speaking newcomers are Ashkenazi and secular, but about 30 percent of newcomers, are not Halachically Jewish. This means that they qualify for Jewish citizenship by virtue of having one Jewish grandparent (as

stipulated in the Law of Return of 1950) but do not meet the Orthodox Jewish requirement of having a Jewish mother.

Even those who are fully Jewish had little opportunity to learn about their Jewish heritage while growing up under the Soviet regime. Israel was already a highly secular society before the newcomers arrived, but interestingly these immigrants have failed to make the political impact that their numbers should warrant. At present more than 300,000 Russian-speaking newcomers cannot get married in Israel, which has no civil wedding ceremonies – they must travel abroad. But most of these immigrants still adhere to the traditional Soviet belief that taking to the streets to protest is contemptible behavior and, as a result, their voice is often not heard in Israel's robust and demonstrative political culture.

Most of these newcomers are not Zionists who in the Soviet regime ideologically yearned to immigrate to Israel. The immigrants of the 1970s risked imprisonment in order to leave for the Jewish State. The majority of those who came in 1990 and 1991 had a profound sense of Jewish identity; they put out their wings and migrated at the first opportunity. But recent arrivals have a less clear agenda, although many are seeking a more secure economic life amid the greater

employment opportunities Israel offers.

The latest wave of immigrants represents over 20 percent of the Jewish population. They and their children are already assimilating Zionist norms of allegiance to the state, service in the army, and fluency in Hebrew. In parallel, they are contributing some of their old culture to their new home, and the influence of their secularism is likely to move large sections of Israeli society even further away from traditional Judaism.

Ethiopians

The dramatic airlifts of Ethiopian Jews from the heart of Africa to the Promised Land in 1984 and 1991 captured the world's imagination. For

centuries Ethiopian Jews had cherished the dream that one day they would return to Jerusalem. The dream finally came true, but the reality has not always matched their expectations.

Before arriving in Israel, most Ethiopian Jews had been semi-literate subsistence farmers living in simple villages, usually without electricity or any modern conveniences. Being thrust into a fast-moving, high-tech society has been traumatic, especially for those people who were over 30 when they arrived. For the young, change is always easier.

Some of Israel's 100,000-strong Ethiopian Jewish community have done well, especially the children of community leaders, but most struggle to keep their feet on the lower rungs of the social ladder. According to Yitzhak Dessie, who became the first Ethiopian-born Israeli lawyer when he qualified in 1998, the essential obstacle confronting Israel's Ethiopian-born community is not discrimination but lack of employment opportunities and their own ability to grasp how Israeli culture functions.

The sense of alienation felt by many Ethiopians has been exacerbated by the reluctance of Israel's rabbinical authorities to recognize the unequivocal Jewishness of the Ethiopians. Thus they are required to undergo symbolic conversion to Judaism by being immersed in a ritual bath. In addition the *kessim* are not permitted to officiate at state-recognized marriages.

Positive discrimination

The younger generation (half the community is under 18) have been adept at assimilating Israeli values. The vigor with which they have protested their grievances through demonstrations, the media and political lobbying bodes well for the future. For its part, the Israeli establishment has allocated major resources for the education of the young generation, though still short of the required amount, and has introduced positive discrimination measures, such as more generous mortgages than those available to other new immigrants.

While racism against the Ethiopians is rare (the most anti-Ethiopian racist sector in Israeli society is probably found among the Russian-speaking new immigrants), the community sometimes suffers in rather odd ways. For example, the Health Ministry decided that Ethiopians were not suitable blood donors because of a higher incidence of Aids, tuberculosis and other diseases. Instead of the decision being announced publicly, a secret memo was sent to donation staff asking them to accept Ethiopian blood and then throw it away. The discovery of the policy provoked a storm of protest. An enquiry found that the policy was justified on health and safety grounds but that its underhand method of implementation was inappropriate.

Dramatic rescue

The Ethiopians began reaching Israel via Sudan in the early 1980s, and Operation Moses in 1984 saw 7,000 people airlifted to Israel. Most of them had trekked hundreds of miles across the

modern times most were located in two regions of Africa. Those who reached Israel in the early 1980s came primarily from Tigre, while the subsequent wave originated principally from Gondar. Although the two groups use the same Amharic alphabet, they speak different Ethiopic languages.

After initially refusing to bring to Israel the Falash Mura, Ethiopian Christians who had converted from Judaism in the 19th century, the government has airlifted some 20,000 to Israel over the past decade and several thousand more budding immigrants remain in Ethiopia awaiting visas to emigrate. ❏

desert to the Sudanese border, and many others had died en route. Even more dramatically, during a single 24-hour period in 1991 14,000 Ethiopians were flown to Israel as part of Operation Solomon. These people had been gathering in Addis Ababa over the course of a year but had been prevented from leaving by the Marxist regime. The Israeli Air Force succeeded in rescuing them just as the regime was toppled by rebels.

The history and geographical dispersion of Ethiopian Jewry is somewhat unclear, but in

LEFT: when high tech becomes high fashion.
ABOVE: Ethiopian women selling their crafts.

THE LOST TRIBES RETURN

The origins of the Ethiopian Jews are shrouded in mystery. Known in Ethiopia as *falashas* (invaders), they are believed by some scholars to be remnants of Dan, one of the Ten Lost Tribes. Some claim they are descendants of King Solomon and the Queen of Sheba. Cut off from world Jewry for two millennia, the community has sustained remarkably similar traditions.

There are distinctions, though. For example, the Ethiopians took with them into exile the Five Books of Moses and the stories of the Prophets, but have no knowledge of the Oral Law, which was codified only after the fall of the Second Temple in AD 70.

ISRAELI ARABS

Israel's Arabs occupy an anomalous position, yet most live harmoniously with their Jewish neighbors while retaining cultural ties to the Arab world

Not all the Arab inhabitants of Palestine heeded the call of the surrounding states (and "promptings" from the nascent Israeli army) to flee their homes when the State of Israel was established, despite the promise that they would be able to return within weeks once the Jewish state had been snuffed out by the

invading armies. About 150,000 remained, and numbers have since grown to their present 1.5 million. Half of Israel's Arab population is urbanized in the towns and villages of the Galilee. There are large Arab communities in Nazareth, Haifa, Ramla, Yafo and Jerusalem, while with their high birth rate villages like Umm El Fahm have grown into cities.

Of Israel's Arabs 82 percent are Muslim, 12 percent Christian and 6 percent Druze and Bedouin. All are faced with the paradox of being at once Arab, with linguistic, historic, cultural, religious and familial ties to the Arab world, and also citizens of a state which, since its inception, has been in conflict with that

world. And yet they have managed to walk the tightrope between their Palestinian nationality and Israeli citizenship, although in recent years they have become more assertive and less acquiescent, with a more militant Islamic and Palestinian national identity.

The only legal discrimination against the Arab population is that they are not liable to military conscription – although they may volunteer – because it is deemed unreasonable to ask them to fight against their co-religionists and kinsmen. Only the small Druze community is subject to the draft – and that is at its own request.

But exemption from military service has proved to be a double-edged sword. The army is the great equalizer, the shared national experience, the common thread that unites Israelis from wildly differing backgrounds. Exclusion from it inevitably involves social handicaps. In a more tangible form, it renders Israeli Arabs ineligible for certain jobs and state benefits and exacerbates the already disproportionate allocation of government land and economic resources.

The stain of discrimination

The plight of Israel's Arabs was acknowledged for the first time by the Israeli government in 2003 following a state commission of enquiry into the killing of 13 Arab demonstrators by police in 2000. The commission not only

A WOMAN'S PLACE

Israeli laws granting women equal rights have helped to liberalize attitudes towards women in Arab society. The changing aspirations of women (and of their husbands) are reflected in the birthrate – down from an average of 8.5 children per family in 1968 to 4.8 in the late 1990s and 4.2 today – although it is not expected to fall in the foreseeable future to the Jewish average of 3.2 children per family.

For all that, there is a strong trend towards the polarization of Jewish and Arab Israelis, despite the programs to foster understanding among youngsters, which are arranged by Israel's Education Ministry.

blamed the police for over-reacting but also spoke of an historical injustice to Israel's Arabs and "the stain of discrimination."

In spite of this and other disabilities, the Arabs of Israel have flourished, making great strides in health, education, and generally improved living standards. The impact of education and of involvement with Israel's vigorously open and democratic society have been profound. These days most young Arabs live with their own Western-style nuclear families and are economically independent of their elders. There is still, to be sure, strong attachment to traditional values and customs, but these are tinged with a clear

sent there are 13 Arab members of the Knesset out of a total of 120, representing a broad spectrum of opinion.

The Druze community

Although some of the first clashes between the Jewish pioneers in the 1880s and the local residents were with Druze villagers in Metula and other parts of the Galilee, Israel's Druze community has traditionally been loyal to the Israeli state. Young Druze are conscripted into the Israel Defense Forces (at the community's own request), and many serve in the regular army in the paratroops, armored corps and reconnai-

preference for the comforts of the affluent West.

A spiral of radicalism is not inevitable. A new breed of young Arab mayors and leaders – educated in Israel and at ease with the Israeli system – is emerging at a grass-roots level. They are demanding that facilities in their areas be brought up to the standard of those of their Jewish neighbors, and their style demonstrates a self-confidence that is at once proudly Arab and unequivocally Israeli.

The increasing Arab clout in the political arena is another significant development. At pre-

sance units, and border police. Traditionally a warlike people, always ready to defend their interests, they have proved to be first-class soldiers, and large numbers of Druze have been decorated for bravery.

In the Lebanon War of 1982–84, Israel's Druze found themselves in a delicate position when the IDF was aligned with Christian forces in Lebanon fighting the Lebanese Druze. It is a tribute to the strength of the friendship between the Jews and the Druze that their alliance survived this period.

The Druze have been a persecuted minority in the Middle East since they broke away from mainstream Islam in the 11th century, accepting

LEFT: a dignified Druze village elder.
ABOVE: waiting for customers by the Jaffa Gate.

the claims to divinity of the Egyptian Caliph El-Hakim Abu Ali el-Mansur. For this reason they have tended to inhabit inaccessible mountain ranges, where they could hold out against their enemies. Most Druze today live in the Mount Lebanon region of Lebanon and in Jebel Druze in Syria; some 80,000 of them are in the hills of the Galilee and on the Carmel Range in Israel, with a further 20,000 in the Golan Heights. There are records of Druze communities in the Galilee as early as the 13th century, but the first Mount Carmel settlement was established in 1590 when Syrian Druze fled their homes after an abortive revolt against the Turkish sultan.

Druze villages are not very different from Arab villages in the Galilee and the coastal plain, although the elders do not wear black headbands with their *keffiye* head-dresses. The older Druze tend to cultivate impressive moustaches. The women dress in modern clothes, the younger ones in jeans and short-sleeved blouses. The young men are indistinguishable from Israeli Jews, and indeed many of them affect Hebrew names, such as Rafi or Ilan.

There are conflicting tendencies to assimilate into the Jewish society, or to convert to Islam and assimilate into the local Arab community, but these are definitely minority movements, and most Druze are proud of their own identity

and culture and do not inter-marry with other communities. Some Israeli Druze live in mixed villages, notably Pekiin in Galilee, where they coexist with their Christian Arab neighbors and some Jewish families, who have lived there since Second Temple times.

The Druze were recognized as a separate religious community with their own courts in 1957. Their religion is said to be similar to that of the Ismai'li Muslims. The sheikhs, the religious leaders of the community, guard its secrets, and the ordinary Druze are simply required to observe the basic moral laws prohibiting murder, adultery, and theft.

They have their own interpretations of Jewish, Muslim and Christian prophets, believing that their missions were revealed to a select group, the first of whom was Jethro, father-in-law of Moses. One Druze religious festival is an annual pilgrimage to what is believed to be the grave of Jethro, near the Horns of Hittim in Galilee.

Serving alongside the Druze in the minorities unit of the IDF are the Circassians, about 3,000 of whom live in Israel. They are a Caucasian mountain people, originating in Russia; most of them are fair-haired, with blue or green eyes. Although many of the Russian Circassians are professing Christians, the Middle East branch of this people are Muslims. Almost all the Israeli Circassians live in the village of Kfar Kama, overlooking Lake Kinneret in Galilee, and in Rehaniya, just north of Safed.

The Bedouin

The Bedouin is the quintessential Arab, the nomad herdsman, dressed in flowing robes, riding his camel across the sands, pitching his tent

TRADITIONAL CRAFTS

Traditionally the Druze were successful hill farmers, but with the development of modern agriculture this activity has declined. However, their traditional weaving, carpet-making, basketwork and other crafts are still flourishing. There are a number of Druze villages with interesting markets selling handicrafts. Daliyat el-Karmel, south of Haifa, is an attractive village, a popular spot for tourists; and the Golan Heights villages of Majdal e-Shams and Mas'ada also specialize in local craftwork. But handicrafts don't keep an entire community employed, and most young Druze these days find work in either industry or the flourishing service sector.

under the palms before riding on to his next camping site. Like many romantic images, this one, fostered by old Hollywood films, is false – or at least somewhat out of date.

Some 20 percent of Israel's 140,000 Bedouin people live in the Galilee and the coastal plain, in settled villages which are virtually indistinguishable, to an outsider's eye, from other Arab villages. Traditions are stronger in the Negev, and you may still be invited for coffee, reclining on cushions and rugs of black goat's hair, but few Bedouin still live in the traditional manner. Some do still live in tents, and quite a few possess camels and herd sheep and goats, but increasing numbers are moving into permanent housing and finding work in construction, industry, the service sector and transportation.

Life on the land

The Bedouin farm the loess soil extensively, growing mostly barley and wheat but also cucumbers, tomatoes, peppers, watermelons, almonds, figs and vines. For irrigation they use dams, which they have built themselves, as well as former Nabatean structures, which they have carefully restored. They also utilize ancient water cisterns, which they have excavated.

Scores of Bedouin fled from the Negev from 1947 to 1949, around the time of Israel's War of Independence, but later returned. The situation was stabilized in 1953 when a census was conducted, with all those present at the time being accepted as citizens of Israel. About half the Negev Bedouin live in settlements not recognized by the government and therefore lack running water, electricity and other basic utilities. They are resisting government attempts to move them into permanent housing in small towns.

Formerly wandering freely between Transjordan, the Judean Desert, the Negev and Sinai, the Bedouin were forced to recognize the new international realities in the early 1950s. Israel's Bedouin are now confined to an area east of Be'er Sheva extending north as far as the former border with Jordan, and south as far as Dimona. This is only around 10 percent of the area over which they once wandered, but includes some

LEFT: a Bedouin stall in Be'er Sheva market.
RIGHT: tending the fire in a traditional tent.

excellent farming land. Today, there is no tribe that does not farm as well as herd its flocks.

The traditional life of the Bedouin shepherds which involved moving the herds from pasture to pasture, is a thing of the past, and their camps have long been permanent in the Negev. Their nomadic tradition, and their tendency to live with their dwellings spread out all over the desert, have made it difficult to plan modern villages for them.

Today most of the major tribal centres have

USING DESERT SKILLS

Bedouin are not conscripted into the Israel Defense Forces, but many of them serve in the army as scouts and trackers, utilizing their traditional skills, and several have reached senior rank.

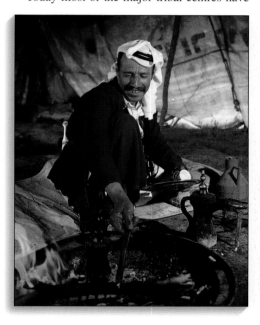

their own elementary schools, and there are now new high schools at Kuseifa near Arad. Bedouin take education seriously, and because of a lack of educational resources are often compelled to walk more than 16 km (10 miles) to school where necessary. It is a common sight, when driving from Be'er Sheva to Arad or Dimona, to see a Bedouin boy walking through the desert, his nose buried in the pages of a book, or sitting on a rock, writing in a notebook.

Bedouin arts and crafts still exist, with a flourishing home industry, based on weaving, sewing and embroidery. These wares are on sale in many places, notably in Thursday's Be'er Sheva market, a popular tourist attraction. ❏

THE PALESTINIANS

Nobody pretends that the Israelis and the Palestinians will ever be best friends,
but on both sides there is a genuine desire to end the conflict

Palestinian nationalism was a reaction to Zionism. As Jews began buying up Arab land in the early 20th century, so the indigenous Arab population was compelled to question its own identity. Historically that identity had revolved around the extended family, the village, the Arab people and Islam. But in

the modern world of emerging nations such an identity was either too parochial or too broad.

Just as many people – Jews and non-Jews – originally denied that the Jewish people constituted a nation, so Palestinians found their legitimacy under fire from both friends and foes. Many Arabs spoke of pan-Arabism and of one Arab nation encompassing North Africa and Asia Minor. Often such talk cloaked the expansionist ambitions of Syria, Jordan and Egypt.

Irreconcilable aims

For the Jews, of course, the Palestinian national movement, which denied the right of a Jewish state to exist, could never be reconciled with Zionist aspirations. Moderate Palestinian leaders, as well as the Hashemite kings (King Abdullah and his grandson, King Hussein, and his son, the reigning King Abdullah), were amenable to coexistence with the Jews. But they were unable to counter the militant rejectionism of Syria and Egypt and of local leaders such as Sheikh Haj Amin Husseini.

The tragedy of the Palestinian people was the inability of its leadership to accept the *fait accompli* of a Jewish state. Arab anger is understandable, because European anti-Semitism, which drove Jews back to the Middle East, resulted in the loss of Palestinian land. But attempts to drive the Jews into the sea in 1948 and 1967 and the expulsion of over a million Jews from Arab countries saw Israel strengthened territorially and demographically.

The founding of the PLO in 1964 was a crucial stage in the evolution of the Palestinian national entity. Even so, Yasser Arafat, its leader since 1965, was imprisoned in Damascus. Since the Muslim conquest, Palestine had been ruled from Damascus, and the Syrians saw Palestine – and, for that matter, Lebanon and Jordan – as an integral part of the modern Syrian nation.

The Six Day War of 1967, and the further expansion of Israel, saw the PLO come into its own. It was now in Syria's interest to encourage Arafat to regain Arab lands. Before 1967 the West Bank was in Jordanian hands, while Gaza was under Egyptian rule. But if the PLO and its many factions, each owing allegiance to a different Arab leader, were puppets designed to restore Arab sovereignty over as much of Israel as possible, Arafat – and most especially the Palestinians of the West Bank and Gaza – proved to be more independently minded than either Israel or the Arab world had anticipated.

Occupation and acrimony

Israel, after its occupation of the West Bank and Gaza in 1967, enjoyed good relations with its newly-conquered Palestinian subjects. Many of the Arabs of the West Bank and Gaza, for their part, were initially beguiled by Israeli liberalism and other Western ways. A free press was set up, universities were established, elections were held for the local municipalities, and the economy flourished. It must be said that one reason it flourished was through the menial work done cheaply by Palestinians in Israel.

Israel presumed that the Arabs of the West Bank and Gaza would prove as malleable as those who had stayed behind in 1948 and taken up Israeli citizenship. But Israeli Arabs were mainly village people, while those of Gaza and the West Bank had a large urban intelligentsia who identified strongly with the Palestinian

The effects of the Intifada

PLO tactics in the 1970s and 1980s were a mixture of terrorism and diplomacy. Terrorist attacks against civilians in Israel and around the world forced the Palestinian question onto the international agenda. Moreover, Arafat forged powerful alliances with the Soviet bloc and the Third World, which unswervingly supported the Palestinian cause. But, while the PLO succeeded in causing Israel untold political and economic damage and creating a climate of national insecurity, it was unable to achieve its goal of an independent Palestinian state.

nationalism espoused by Arafat and the PLO.

But while rejecting Israeli hegemony, the Palestinian notables in the West Bank and Gaza also felt alienated from the PLO leadership. Arafat, who built his own organizational hierarchy first in Jordan, then in Lebanon and finally in Tunis, was often viewed as a wealthy Diaspora leader who represented the millions of Palestinians living in Jordan, Syria, Lebanon, Egypt, the Gulf and elsewhere in the world, but was out of touch with the Palestinians on the front line of Israeli occupation.

LEFT: catching up with the latest news.
ABOVE: riding on the beach in Gaza.

A WANDERING GOVERNMENT

When given the right to assume Israeli citizenship, the 150,000 Arabs of East Jerusalem refused the offer to a man. It took the Israelis, even those on the left, many years to appreciate that Palestinian nationalism was not going to go away. The Palestinians' declared aim is to establish their own government in Jerusalem. After the return of the PLO to the West Bank and Gaza, Palestinian government meetings were held alternately in Gaza City and Ramallah near Jerusalem until the Hamas takeover in 2007. In 2000 Prime Minister Ehud Barak proposed giving much of East Jerusalem, including half of the Old City, to the Palestinians – so the dream is not entirely unrealistic.

The momentum for change came from within the West Bank and Gaza. The Intifada began in December 1987 in the Gaza Strip as a spontaneous uprising against Israeli occupation. Within days it had become an orchestrated campaign against Israeli troops, characterized by the throwing of rocks and occasional Molotov cocktails. The rebellion spread to the West Bank.

A new young Palestinian leadership began to emerge in the West Bank and Gaza. While it didn't discourage stoning the Zionist enemy, it was also prepared to enter into dialogue with Israel. Faisal Husseini, nephew of the arch anti-Zionist Sheikh Haj Amin Husseini, learned flu-

Arafat's stock fell even further after he threw his support behind Iraq's Saddam Hussein after the 1990 invasion of Kuwait. This isolated him from many of his Arab allies and caused the mass expulsion of the affluent Palestinian communities of the Gulf. The collapse of the Soviet Union, the PLO's superpower patron, saw Arafat down and, many assumed, out.

Gaza via Madrid and Oslo

But Yasser Arafat proved more resilient and compromising than many gave him credit for. He was allowed to attend the Madrid Peace Conference in 1991 as part of the Jordanian

ent Hebrew as a gesture of goodwill.

Arafat jumped on the Intifada bandwagon. But it was the local Palestinian leadership that was calling the tune, while Arafat and his entourage in Tunis looked increasingly remote from the Palestinians in the front line. Arafat put out diplomatic feelers, letting it be known that he was prepared to recognize Israel and discontinue terrorist tactics. But a brief flirtation with American diplomats in the late 1980s ended when Arafat was unable to prevent his own people from launching terrorist attacks against Israel. Nor was the right-wing government in Israel prepared even to contemplate an indirect dialogue with Arafat.

delegation. After the election of the Labor government in Israel in 1992, he seized the olive branch held out by Rabin's dovish advisors, and in less than a year he was shaking hands with the Israeli prime minister on the lawn of the White House in Washington. In 1994 he arrived in triumph in Gaza as Israel withdrew its troops from most of the Gaza Strip.

By 1995 the Palestinian Authority's jurisdiction comprised Gaza and the major West Bank cities, and Arafat's rule was confirmed through democratically held elections.

Until 2000, Arafat forbade terrorist attacks against Israelis – there had been a spate of suicide bombings in 1995 and 1996 and sporadic attacks afterwards – and he had imprisoned Hamas and Islamic Jihad leaders who did not obey his prohibition. But, after the failure of the Camp David peace talks in the summer of 2000, a visit by Ariel Sharon, then in opposition, to the Temple Mount sparked the second Intifada.

Unlike the first Intifada, which attracted international support as Palestinians threw rocks at Israeli soldiers, the second Intifada's use of guns and suicide bombers was looked on less sympathetically in the West, especially after the terrorist attacks on the US in 2001. Moreover, Arafat was perceived by the international community to have unilaterally pulled out of a viable impossible, and widespread expropriation of land as Israel built a separation wall.

Attempts by the US to erode Arafat's power through encouraging government reforms as part of their "Road Map" peace plan came to nothing. A French-style form of government was introduced with the new post of Prime Minister beneath Arafat's presidency. Mahmoud Abbas, popularly known as Abu Mazen, was the first to be appointed to the new post. But the veteran PLO leader refused to relinquish any real power. Isolated in the Palestinian government complex in Ramallah, surrounded by destruction, Arafat battled on against the

peace process. But, for the Palestinians, the second Intifada was a War of Independence. During 2002 constant suicide bombings even gave the fleeting illusion that the Zionists might be completely defeated and all of pre-1948 Palestine regained. But Israel hit back hard, and so widespread was the destruction that much of the West Bank resembled a war zone. Daily life became unbearable as a result of constant raids by IDF soldiers, aerial and artillery bombardment, targeted killings, a virtual siege on towns making movement around the West Bank

LEFT: group portrait in a café in Jerusalem's Old City.
ABOVE: a Palestinian policeman on duty.

THE PALESTINIAN AUTHORITY

If Palestinians had hoped that a more prosperous lifestyle and democratic regime with an independent judiciary and free press would be part of their emerging national entity, they were initially disappointed. Instead, a police state and corrupt administration were established, with Yasser Arafat's cronies diverting overseas aid and Israeli payments into their own overseas bank accounts. The Palestinian in the street felt resentful that life seemed no better in the Palestinian Authority than it was under Israeli occupation. Many turned to Islam and Hamas. But, when the second Intifada broke out in 2000, the corruption of the 1990s was largely forgotten in the passion of war.

Israelis. To Israelis and the world, his situation seemed hopeless, but the Palestinian people stood loyally behind him.

The sudden deterioration of Arafat's health and his death in France in 2004 acted as a catalyst for a ceasefire between the Palestinians and Israelis. The Intifada had anyway been running out of steam and more and more Palestinians had been questioning the point of continued hostilities against Israel. Abu Mazen, the natural successor to Arafat, met with Ariel Sharon in Sharm El Sheikh in Egypt and the two leaders agreed to end the bloodshed. Abu Mazen would prevent suicide bombings and other attacks, including the firing of mortar shells into Israel, while Israel would stop its targeted killings.

Fatah and Hamas

Abu Mazen was elected president in 2005 with a mandate to pursue peace, although he was never able to generate the strength and popularity of Arafat. Hamas pragmatically agreed to stop hostilities with Israel and instead nurtured its political base. Their success in this endeavor was reflected in their election victory in 2006 when they won 44 percent of parliamentary seats ahead of Fatah's 41 percent, compelling

THE COST OF THE INTIFADA

Whether Palestinians like it or not, their economic health depends on good relations with Israel. Before the second Intifada more than 70,000 had daily work permits to enter Israel and hundreds of thousands more worked and traded illegally. All that stopped in 2000. The World Bank reported a 23 percent drop in the Palestinian GDP over the four years of the Intifada, with unemployment rising from 14 to 37 percent. Nearly half the 3½ million Palestinians in the West Bank and Gaza lived below the poverty line, and the Palestinians' biggest source of income was an average $950 million a year in international donor aid. Most of this aid was cut off after Hamas was elected in 2006.

Abu Mazen of Fatah to preside uncomfortably over a Hamas-led parliament.

The international community cut off aid to the Palestinians as a protest against Hamas's militant refusal to recognize Israel. Tensions between Abu Mazen's Fatah and Hamas erupted in 2007 as Hamas seized control of the Gaza Strip, forcing Fatah officials to flee their homes, while Fatah took over the West Bank. The two-state solution had worked, joked one cynic: the Gaza Strip was run by Muslim fundamentalists and the West Bank by secular Fatah leaders. ❏

ABOVE: Yasser Arafat's "mobile grave" in Ramallah, designed to be moved one day to Jerusalem.

Guest workers

Israel attracts hundreds of thousands of tourists each year. But above and beyond the short-term visitors, whether they are pilgrims drawn by the holy sites or sun-worshippers attracted to the country's beaches, Israel also has a large number of longer-term guests.

These include youngsters from around the world wishing to experience Israel in a more profound way on a longer stay, either as a kibbutz volunteer or on an archaeological dig, or perhaps studying in a religious institution. Back-packers traveling around the world often stay longer than planned, attracted by the informality and vitality of Israel and the fact that casual work is easy to find and there is no shortage of cheap, youth-hostel-type accommodations.

In fact, the availability of unskilled employment in Israel has attracted workers from around the world. There are an estimated 200,000 foreign workers in the country, about half of whom are on legal contracts. This category includes Romanian construction workers, Thai agricultural laborers and Filipino domestic servants. (Somewhat ironically, there are more than 200,000 unemployed Israelis.) In addition there are around 100,000 illegal workers, mainly from Nigeria and Ghana, the majority of whom live in Tel Aviv where they work as house cleaners and factory hands.

These overseas workers took the place of the many Palestinians who worked in Israel until the outbreak of the first Intifada, which compelled Israeli employers to seek alternative sources of labor from overseas. The second Intifada from 2000 onwards consolidated the position of foreign workers, although the recession of 2002 resulted in sporadic expulsions.

The abundance of foreign workers in Israel contradicts the Zionist tenet of a Jewish state based on Jewish labor. Many Israelis decry the situation from an intellectual standpoint, but nonetheless are happy for someone else to do the menial work. Like most middle-class parents in the Western world, they would rather their own children became managers and professionals than blue-collar or manual workers.

While legal Romanian and Thai workers tend to be males on contract, sending money home to

their families, the West Africans are often in Israel en famille, creating a guest-worker-style environment similar to that in parts of Western Europe. There are so many West African workers in the area around the old bus station in Tel Aviv that it is sometimes known as "Little Lagos." These workers tend to maintain a low profile, fearing expulsion, but their children are a lot less passive. Some local authorities accept the children into schools, others don't.

Israel's newspapers regularly carry articles and comment on the subject, some urging mass expulsions of the guest workers, others promoting the granting of legal residency status to those who

apply. Some denounce the dilution of the State's Jewish character, others applaud an enriching cosmopolitan element. Despite these conflicting opinions, the fact remains that, while the foreign workers continue to constitute an important cog in the Israeli economic wheel, the status quo is likely to prevail.

Ultimately, politics as much as economics will dictate the outcome. If Arab terrorism is quelled, then the Israeli government will once again give preference to Palestinians seeking employment in Israel. In such an instance Israel's guest workers, whether legal or illegal, may suddenly find themselves out of a job and unwelcome in a land that many have come to look on as home. ❑

RIGHT: the thriving construction industry depends heavily upon guest workers.

THE ARMY

Toting sub-machine-guns, troops are everywhere: riding on buses, hitchhiking at roadside stations, sitting at pavement cafés, and strolling through shopping malls

The Israel Defense Forces (IDF) are considered to be one of the world's smartest armies. A quick glance at the ubiquitous, scruffy Israeli soldiers slouching around the streets makes it clear that this refers to high-tech innovation rather than military dress code. From satellite surveillance to fighter jets fitted with the latest computer electronics capabilities and the world's only anti-tactical ballistic missile (the Arrow), Israel's army is streets ahead of its Arab neighbors.

Dramatic victories such as 1967's Six Day War have been won, while daring operations such as the Entebbe raid on Uganda (when hostages were rescued from a hijacked plane) earned the IDF widespread admiration. There have also been failures such as the inability of army intelligence to anticipate the surprise attack by Egypt and Syria in the Yom Kippur War in 1973. Most recently the IDF's image was tarnished by its failure to defeat Hizbullah militants in Lebanon in 2006.

An independent attitude

Yet many overseas observers are left initially unimpressed when first encountering the Israeli military, for the Israeli army is like no other army in the world. During basic training, soldiers learn to salute their superiors, accept orders without question and stick to clearly defined dress codes. Thereafter, rules are made to be broken. Officers are never saluted, orders can be negotiated, and a pink T-shirt worn as a vest keeps the soldier warm in winter. Yet the IDF are highly effective, so a soldier's right to question an officer's orders may be a strength rather than a weakness. In the heat of battle orders are usually obeyed, and dramatic victories have been won. It is often said that, if the US and British armies do things "by the book," Israeli soldiers will often ignore the book and use their heads to adapt to the situation.

Male soldiers fall into several categories. There are young conscripts aged 18 to 21 doing their three years' national service, and a small number of professional soldiers, usually officers,

who carry on afterwards. Then there are the reservists. *Miluim*, Hebrew for reserve duty, involves men being plucked away from their families for a month or six weeks a year (more during times of military tension) to serve on the Lebanese border or the West Bank. There are, of course, rugged types who enjoy the lifestyle,

but most Israelis see *miluim* as a burden they would rather evade. The unpopularity of *miluim* does have a dovish effect, however, putting pressure on the government to solve the border problems, which make reserve duty necessary.

However, military service isn't as compulsory as many believe. About a third of Israeli Jewish men do not enrol for the army when they are 18. Ultra-Orthodox Jews can request a deferment to study, and youngsters deemed unsuitable because of delinquent behaviour are not called up. Also, any 18-year-old who insists that he does not want to serve will not be drafted. The number of teenage applicants for combat units is still higher than the places available, so regiments can pick and choose. National service is officially compulsory for Jews, but Muslims and Christians are exempt. Bedouins, who are renowned for their tracking abilities, serve as volunteers. Druze and Circassians are conscripted, at their own request.

Women at war

Women often fought as front-line soldiers in the struggle for independence, but the IDF confined them to non-combat roles after 1948, although conscripting women for two years. The Supreme Court ruled in 1995 that the army must accept women for pilots' courses; many

in Israeli culture, therefore, is the notion that a soldier has a right to refuse an immoral order.

Ironically, the IDF's greatest moment – the capture in just six days in 1967 of East Jerusalem, the West Bank, Gaza, the Golan Heights and Sinai (returned to Egypt in 1982) – has tarnished the army's image. Hundreds of Israeli soldiers have refused to serve in the West Bank and Gaza on the grounds that the occupation is illegal. The relatively lenient punishment is usually a short prison sentence.

If most of the "conscientious objecting" in the IDF has traditionally come from the left, that all changed in 2004 when the army began

have enrolled, and some have qualified. Although the numbers are still small, women are increasingly serving in combat units alongside men. Sexism aside, the army is not a bastion of conservatism in Israel. Homosexuals, for example, have always been accepted.

Another radical departure from global military practice is the IDF's long tradition of "purity of arms." This concept stemmed from the classic defence of the German soldier who took part in the Nazi extermination of Jews: "I was only following orders." Deeply enshrined

implementing withdrawal from Gaza and the northern West Bank. Dozens of religious Israeli soldiers heeded the call of their spiritual rabbinical leaders that an order to expel a Jew from his home in the Land of Israel was illegal and refused to fulfill the mission. Like their left-wing comrades before them, they received short prison sentences.

Overall, the IDF remains strong, not only as a military force but perhaps more significantly as the great melting-pot institution of Israeli society in which every new recruit, whether he (or increasingly she) is a new immigrant or veteran Israeli, fair-skinned or dark-skinned, has the opportunity to rise through the ranks. ❑

LEFT: a soldier on guard near the Lebanon border.
ABOVE: a female instructor teaches a new recruit.

RELIGIOUS VARIETY

Israel is the Holy Land to followers of three different religions,
who are joined by members of many alternative sects

The sheer intensity of the religious ardor in this small country is overwhelming: in Jerusalem's Old City, Jews at the Western Wall, Muslims at the El-Aqsa Mosque and Christians at the Church of the Holy Sepulchre may well be saying their prayers simultaneously, to say nothing of the myriad other synagogues, churches and mosques in the Old City alone.

Likewise, the diversity of religious experience here is in a category all its own. Hassidim wearing 18th-century *kapotas* and *shtreimels* (coats and hats) rub shoulders with robed monks and nuns from every Christian denomination, East and West, while Muslim *imams* in *galabiyah* mingle with secular Israelis and pilgrims to the Holy Land. Many of the holiest biblical sites have hosted synagogues, churches and mosques over the centuries, and even today visitors of one faith may well find themselves paying respects to a chapter of their own history in the house of worship of another.

The Jewish presence

Jewish spiritual life revolves around the home, house of study (*cheder* for youngsters, *yeshiva* for adolescents and adults) and synagogue – of which the latter is the most accessible to the visitor. Jerusalem's hundreds of synagogues range from the humblest *shtible* (several simple rooms) and Sephardi community synagogue to the gargantuan Belzer Center (which seats 3,500) and the Great Synagogue in King George Street. Other synagogues worth visiting include the Central, Yeshurun and the Italian.

The Orthodox pray three times a day, but it is on Sabbaths and festivals that the liturgy is at its most elaborate. The modest Hassidic premises are compensated for by the fervor of the prayers. Such groups exist in Safed, Bnei Brak, and throughout Jerusalem's northern neighborhoods, although the Me'a She'arim and Geula districts are the most picturesque. Among the warmest

and most approachable of the Hassidic groups is the Bratslav, whose Me'a She'arim premises contain the renovated chair of their first and only *rebbe*, Rabbi Nahman. He was famous for his stories and sayings. "The world is a narrow bridge; the main thing is not to be afraid at all" is one that Israelis have taken to heart.

At the other end of Me'a She'arim is Karlin, whose devotees screech their prayers – unlike their Geula neighbors, Ger, whose tightly-knit organization is reflected in their operatic music and self-discipline: "A true Ger Hasid," says one believer, "never looks at his wife." A similar outlook is espoused by Toledot Aharon, whose purity of purpose is matched by their animosity towards political Zionism, which they view as usurping the divine process of redemption. In this they follow the line of Netorei Karta (Guardians of the City), which has its own government-in-exile and campaigns for political autonomy. What unites all ultra-orthodox and orthodox groups is their opposition to the Conservative and Reform

LEFT: a Torah scroll and its keeper.
RIGHT: a rabbi officiates at a bar mitzvah at Jerusalem's Western Wall.

Movements, which have their own centres and desegregated houses of prayer in Jerusalem (on Agron and King David streets, respectively) as well as in other parts of the city.

The cycle of the Jewish year

The framework of Jewish piety is determined by the lunar cycle, beginning in September with Rosh Hashana (the New Year) and Yom Kippur, the Day of Atonement – a rigorous 25-hour fast. Synagogues are packed; services are long but moving. If you're Jewish and you hail from Minsk, Marrakesh or Manhattan, you're sure to find at least one service meeting your liturgical

is also Simchat Torah when the annual cycle of reading the Torah ends and begins again.

More lights burn during Chanukah, in December, when eight-branched candelabra shine in most homes in celebration of the Maccabean victory over the Greeks some 2,300 years ago. The fate of the cruel Persian leader Haman, thwarted in his attempts to kill the entire Jewish community by Queen Esther a couple of centuries earlier, is recorded in the Scroll of Esther and read on Purim (a cheerful, noisy festival held in March – a Jewish carnival when everybody goes about in fancy dress). In April, everyone spring-cleans for Pesach

needs. An unusual and controversial custom precedes Yom Kippur: Kaparot, which entails swinging a white chicken above the head of the penitent, after which the slaughtered fowl is sold or given to charity. This ceremony can be witnessed in most open market places.

During Succot (Tabernacles), which combines harvest gathering and prayers for winter rains, celebrants live in temporary tabernacles for seven days to remind the Jewish people of their 40 years in the desert. During the evenings, the pious let down their sidelocks to dance, somersault and juggle to intoxicating music. Some Hassidic sects cap off the ceremonies with a children's candlelit procession. The seventh day

ULTRA-ORTHODOX OUTREACH

The most familiar ultra-orthodox sect to worldwide Jewry is the Habad movement, which is famous around the planet for its successful outreach programs to secular Jewry. Habad's Israeli headquarters is at Kfar Habad, near Ben Gurion Airport. It was here that the late head of the sect, the revered Rabbi Menachem Mendel Schneerson (1902–94), the Lubavitcher Rebbe, had a redbrick home built identical to his New York mansion, which he planned making his residence when the Messiah arrived. In the event, Rabbi Schneerson never visited his Israeli home. Some followers expected him to return as the Messiah – a belief condemned by other Orthodox groups.

(Passover), the annual feast celebrating the Exodus from Egypt when bread is prohibited. Seven weeks later comes Shavuot (Pentecost), the Feast of Weeks, when thousands congregate at the Western Wall for dawn prayers, having spent the night studying the holy book, the Torah.

Between Passover and Shavuot, the Orthodox invest Independence Day and Jerusalem Unity Day with spiritual significance, creating new festivals. The cycle reaches full circle in summer, with the three-week period of mourning for the Temples, culminating in a day-long fast on Tisha B'Av.

New Messiahs

There is a growing Evangelical presence in Israel whose belief in the redemption has made them enthusiastic supporters of Zionism. These fundamentalist Christians celebrate Tabernacles by marching through Jerusalem in solidarity with Israel and many suggest that this time of the year was the real time of Christ's birth rather than Christmas, which has pagan origins relating to the re-birth of the sun and has become too commercialized for their taste.

Most of the traditional Arab Christian communities in Israel (roughly 130,000 people) are traditional rather than devout, while thousands of Catholic and Orthodox clergy devote themselves to lives of prayer and meditationand watch over traditional New Testament shrines. Israel and the Palestinian Authority hold practically all the Holy Land, and the devoted visitor can follow in the footsteps of Jesus from his birth in Bethlehem and his early life at Nazareth, to his Crucifixion at Golgotha, in Jerusalem.

Christian groups celebrate some 240 feasts and holy days a year, using two separate calendars, the Julian and the Gregorian. This provides three dates for Christmas: 25 December for Western Christians, 7 January for Greek and other Orthodox churches, Syrians and Copts, and 19 January for the Armenian, and two sets of Holy Weeks. The highlights of the year for Christian celebrants is at Bethlehem, where the main events take place at the Church of the Nativity, and during Easter Week, when there is a re-enactment of Jesus's last days: walks from the Mount of Olives and along the Via Dolorosa to the Church of the Holy Sepulchre. Here, two ceremonies take place: the Washing of the Feet on Maundy Thursday, and the Kindling of the Holy Fire – a ceremony in which people have been accidentally burned to death down the centuries – by the Orthodox and Eastern Churches on Holy Saturday. The carrying of the cross on Good Friday between the Praetorium and Calvary (Golgotha), along the Via Dolorosa, is repeated weekly by the oldest resident group of priests, the Franciscans. One of the most revered Christian sites is the place of Jesus's baptism on the River Jordan. Since the Six Day War this West Bank site has not always been open to pilgrims, depending on the political situation.

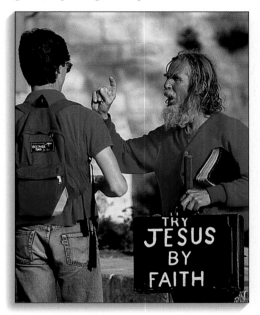

Uneasy coexistence

Judaism, Christianity and Islam live alongside each other in the Holy Land in suspicion rather than in harmony. For the most part, Jews and Christians have buried historical differences and fear Islamic militancy, although indigenous Christians are first and foremost Palestinians. The deepest hostilities are reserved for arguments over property and land rather than over tenets of belief and dogma.

Ironically, when they do meet for inter-faith dialogue, Orthodox Jews, Christians and Muslims often find they all seek to preserve the same conservative values, which are under fire in the Western World where secularism prevails. ❏

LEFT: Bethlehem's Milk Grotto.
RIGHT: a latter-day prophet emphasizes his message.

THE CHRISTIANS

A plethora of denominations flourishes among Israel's Christians,
the majority of whom are Arabs

Nowhere in the world is the observant traveler more aware of the rich and fascinating diversity of Christianity than in the Holy Land. On a morning's stroll through the Old City of Jerusalem you might encounter Greek Orthodox or Syrian Orthodox monks, Ethiopian and Coptic clergymen, Armenian

priests, Catholic priests and, without knowing it, clerics and scholars from virtually every Protestant church in Christendom.

There is no mystery to the extraordinary variety of Christian congregations in the Holy land. From the time of the Byzantines (324–636) through the era of the Crusader kingdoms (1099–1291) and 400 years of Ottoman rule (1517–1917) until today, churches sought to establish – then struggled to retain – a presence in the land where their faith was born.

The result is a plethora of denominations served by thousands of clergy from almost every nation on earth. The older churches, such as Greek Orthodox and Russian Orthodox, own many sites in Israel and have sometimes quarreled bitterly over them *(see box below).* The "younger" churches – such as the Anglicans, the Church of Scotland, Mormons, Lutherans, the Pentecostals, the Church of Christ, the Baptists, the Brethren and the Mennonites – also maintain institutions and congregations, as do the Seventh Day Adventists and the Jehovah's Witnesses. While the indigenous Arab Christians (mainly Orthodox and Catholic) take a strong pro-Palestinian line, thousands of evangelical Protestants who take a right-wing Zionist line have made their home in Israel in the past few decades.

Guaranteed freedoms

The founding of Israel provoked unease among Christians, who were deeply suspicious of Jewish intentions (the Vatican recognized Israel only in 1994). But Israel's Declaration of Independence pledged to "guarantee the freedom of religion, conscience, education and culture [and] safeguard the holy places of all religions." Moreover, Israel's reliance on support from the US and other western powers has also ensured that Israeli governments protect Christian interests.

The Six Day War of 1967, which left Israeli forces in control of the old city of Jerusalem, revived religious misgivings. Yet the Israeli government has been scrupulous in its attitude

---

THIS LAND IS MY LAND

The Greek Orthodox, Roman Catholics, Syrian Catholics, Russian Orthodox, Maronites, Chaldean Catholics, Armenian Catholics, Greek Catholics, Armenian Orthodox, Syrian Orthodox (Jacobites), Copts and Ethiopian Orthodox have all secured claims to holy sites, and own vast amounts of property in the Holy Land. Ownership is respected by the government of Israel but passions often reach crisis point over disputes between the churches themselves such as within the Church of the Holy Sepulchre in Jerusalem. Indeed, the Crimean War (1853–56) was caused by an argument between the Catholics and Greek Orthodox over ownership of part of the Church of Nativity in Bethlehem.

towards the churches' rights and prerogatives, adhering to the intricate balance created by the Ottoman rulers and British Mandatory authority in apportioning responsibility for the holy places. As a result, relations have been good between the Jewish state and the churches. Indeed, at times the Israeli government has found itself a reluctant referee of intra-Christian rivalries.

Evangelical claims

A recent phenomenon that is having an impact on the face of the Holy Land and Christian-Jewish relations is the world-wide growth of Christian evangelical Zionism, which regards the birth of the State of Israel as a fulfilment of biblical prophecy. Over the past decades, theological and ecumenical institutions have mushroomed to cater to this movement and enable young Christians to study in Israel, such as the International Christian Embassy in Jerusalem, the Mormon University on Mount Scopus, and groups such as Bridges for Peace. These evangelical Christians often live permanently in Israel and fully understand that attempts to convert Jews results in expulsion. Their views place them on the extreme right of Israel's political spectrum and most were opposed to Israel's withdrawal from Gaza in 2005.

Christian-Jewish reconciliation is not the sole preserve of the new churches. The Roman Catholic order of the Sisters of Zion, established in Jerusalem in 1855 by French Jewish converts, has been working towards such understanding for many years.

Every year, some 250,000 pilgrims visit the order's Ecce Homo Convent next to the Second Station of the Cross on the Via Dolorosa, and many stay to hear the sisters speak of Jesus the Jew and of Judaism as the wellspring of their faith. The sisters hold language classes for Jews and Arabs, and have set up a department of adult education at the Hebrew University. The German Mary Sisters also have a presence in Jerusalem and are in the forefront of the reconciliation movement.

Arabic language

The grassroots language of Christianity in Israel is Arabic. The great majority of Israel's 130,000 Christians (including the 15,000 Christians of

LEFT: a Russian Orthodox pilgrim.
RIGHT: a Greek Orthodox priest in Bethlehem.

East Jerusalem) are Arabs, and their clergy are either Arabs or Arabic-speaking.

The allegiances of Christian Arabs in Israel clearly favor the established Patriarchates: Greek Catholic, Greek Orthodox, and Roman Catholic. These divisions and ties are not very strong and Catholics will often convert to Orthodoxy and vice-versa for the sake of a marriage which has the blessings of both families. There are small communities of Anglicans and Lutherans (both churches are stronger on the West Bank than in Israel itself), and despite over 100 years of missionary work by more than 50 organizations, there are fewer than 1,000

local Arab adherents of Evangelical churches.

The Roman Catholic Church has established indigenous orders, including the Rosary Sisters and the Sisters of St Joseph, and at its seminary trains Arab priests from both Israel and Jordan.

Arab Christians, while growing in numbers and flourishing economically, have been hesitant about asserting themselves politically to press issues of specifically Christian concern. As a group, the Christian community displays many of the characteristics of a marginal minority: trying to maintain a balance between its Christian identity, Arab nationalism and delicate relations with Muslim neighbors within the context of a Jewish society. ❑

THE ECLIPSE OF THE KIBBUTZ

Israel's kibbutzim are no longer run as socialist settlements,

and the government is even prepared to see them privatized

The kibbutz, the Israeli version of a socialist collective commune, was considered one of the great socio-economic experimental successes of the 20th century. Even if Zionism was unpopular among the left from 1967 onwards, the Israeli farming communes inspired several generations of revolutionaries, who cited the communities as living proof that communism works.

But, like the Soviet Union, that other great communist experiment, the kibbutz looks set to become extinct. However, if the macro-socio-economic communism of the USSR disappeared because it simply failed to deliver even the most basic standard of living, the kibbutz in contrast is a victim of its own success and growing affluence.

Economic equality is one thing when dividing up food, clothes and other fundamentals. But when a kibbutz is rich, then the range of consumer choices, business decisions and diversity of lifestyles makes egalitarianism difficult to put into practise.

Change of style

Even so, the kibbutz is for the time being still alive. Some 110,000 Israelis live on 268 kibbutzim (the plural of kibbutz) representing 1.6 percent of the population. This is down from a peak in absolute numbers of 125,000 in 1990 (2.5 percent of the population).

The kibbutzim produce 40 percent of the country's agricultural output and export $1.5 billion of industrial goods a year. The vast amount of real estate owned by the kibbutzim has enabled them to open shopping malls, gas stations, fast-food outlets, hotels, wedding halls, country clubs and much more.

Kibbutz lifestyles have changed out of all recognition since 1909 when the first Russian-born pioneers established the original kibbutz at Dganya, where the River Jordan flows out of the Sea of Galilee. Within a decade there were 40 more kibbutzim. Moreover, these settlements enjoyed greater prosperity and social cohesion than the capitalist farms founded by the Rothschilds and other philanthropists in places like Rishon Le-Tsiyon, Petakh Tikva and Zikhron Ya'akov.

By the time the State of Israel was established in 1948 the kibbutz formed the backbone (and 6.5 percent) of Israeli society. Kibbutz members were looked up to as the social and

moral ideal of what a person should be, not least because the kibbutzim had transformed large tracts of arid land into fertile fields. But even more importantly the kibbutzim, which had been strategically located as pioneering outposts, were created in order to define the borders of the Jewish state.

Most of the Palmach, the elite fighting force of pre-state Israel, were kibbutz members, because by definition the kibbutzim attracted people who were eager to defend the country's borders from the battlefront. The combative traditions of the kibbutz have been maintained today, and most young members are still eager to volunteer for prestigious combat units.

From austerity to affluence

The kibbutz initially succeeded because members were motivated to work together, pool very limited resources and prevail against the odds in overcoming both a hostile environment and the Arab enemy.

It was in a climate of austerity that the kibbutzim laid the foundations for future prosperity. By the effective harnessing of agriculture and technology, the finest fruit and vegetables were grown, bringing premium prices on European markets. Varieties of cows were bred to produce the highest milk yields, and chickens that laid large numbers of eggs.

turing facilities in eight countries, 30 subsidiaries and a strong distribution presence in more than 100 countries.

In the 1960s and 1970s austerity was gradually replaced by a more middle-class lifestyle. But a kibbutz member's home remained a modest place, and money was channeled into communal projects such as dining halls, swimming pools, sports and educational facilities and cultural amenities.

Thousands of members left the kibbutzim, lured by the more individualistic lifestyle of the city. Many kibbutz children would choose not to return home after serving in the army. But

But perhaps the greatest kibbutz invention was drip irrigation, developed by members of Kibbutz Netafim in the 1960s. This system uses networks of pipes that drip water onto crops or trees, thus penetrating deeply into the soil and utilising minimal amounts of water. Drip irrigation works on a time clock and can be very simple, but in recent times sophisticated options have been added, such as computer control and fertilisers in the pipes.

Today Netafim has annual sales of more than $400 million, 1,700 employees, 12 manufac-

LEFT: life was tough for the pioneers.
ABOVE: a celebratory lunch, kibbutz-style.

THREE DIFFERENT PATHS

There are three kibbutz movements in Israel today: the national religious kibbutz movement combines a communal way of life with Jewish Orthodoxy, while the other two – Meuhad and Artzi – are secular in outlook. The latter two movements split from each other back in 1951, when Meuhad members denounced Stalin as an anti-Semitic dictator while adherents of Artzi remained faithful to the USSR and the party line. The Artzi movement realised that the Soviet experiment was going wrong long before the collapse of the Soviet Union in 1991, but it still leans more towards orthodox socialism than does the Meuhad.

there was always an equal number of veteran Israelis or new immigrants eager to take their place as the new pioneers.

Tarnished image

It is difficult to know when the kibbutz stopped being universally admired as a place for selfless pioneers. One important date was 1977, when the Labor Party lost the reins of power. The right-wing prime minister Menachem Begin poured scorn on the kibbutzim, not least because they had traditionally given their support to Labor governments.

Begin described kibbutz members as mil-

butzim got themselves into an economic mess. They borrowed large sums of money from Israeli banks in the early 1980s when annual inflation was triple-digit and the banks charged high interest rates. The economy stabilized in 1986, but the interest rates remained locked at exorbitantly high percentages.

Many kibbutzim staved off bankruptcy through loan repayment arrangements with bank and government help. However, this bailing out succeeded only in further tarnishing the kibbutz image, and, although as part of the deal the kibbutzim were forced to give the government some of their land, they held onto most of

lionaires who sit around their swimming pools all day. It was an unfair label, but it stuck. In particular Begin was politically exploiting the fact that kibbutzim were almost exclusively Ashkenazi, and even at its most austere their lifestyle was, nevertheless, considerably more desirable than the poverty suffered by the Oriental Jews in the nearby development towns of the Negev and the Galilee.

Somewhat unfairly, in view of their prominent role in both the Palmach and the contemporary army, the kibbutznikim were now portrayed as traitors rather than patriots, because they were left-leaning.

It was also during this period that the kib-

it. The disadvantaged and new immigrants resent the vast amount of land remaining in the hands of the kibbutzim.

Economic evolution

Today the nuclear family has replaced the Marxist belief in alternative social structures. Kibbutz children were once brought up in communal baby houses by educational professionals, seeing their parents only at certain times of the day, as it was believed that they should be part of the community first and foremost. But these days a child's place in the modern kibbutz is once more with his or her parents.

Family rather than communal living is being

reinforced by the gradual disappearance of the kibbutz dining room. Some 20 percent of kibbutzim have closed down their dining rooms and all members eat at home. And 80 percent of the remaining kibbutzim have transformed their dining rooms into "pay as you eat" restaurants, open to the public at large, but in which kibbutz members pay lower prices for meals. Some 82 percent of kibbutzim make members pay for all services and utilities, including their laundry and electricity, while most significantly 51 percent of kibbutzim have instituted pay differentials in which members receive salaries related to the work they are performing.

> ### KIBBUTZ CUISINE
>
> Kibbutz Dan's restaurant serves fresh trout from local tributaries of the Jordan. Kibbutz Mizra, near Nazareth, antagonizes Israel's religious community by rearing pigs and selling pork products.

An attractive lifestyle

From the point of view of socialist ideology, the kibbutz may not be what it used to be but it is still a very attractive place to live. It offers a rural life-style, guaranteed work in a number of different professions, and comfortable living standards, including a house and garden.

But it may be some time until the final nail is hammered into the kibbutz coffin. New legislation allows the kibbutzim to privatize themselves and sell their houses and gardens on the real estate market after buying their land from the government. However, the State and kibbutzim are very far from agreeing the value of the properties, so that only a few kibbutzim on the Lebanese border, where real estate is almost worthless, are fully privatized.

Meanwhile, the question of whether market forces will choke out traditional idealism is a matter of fierce debate.

The moshav movement

The privatization of a kibbutz would in fact turn it into a moshav (cooperative settlement). For the Jewish pioneers who wanted a less socialistic form of communal living when the earliest settlements were founded, the moshav offered a more individualistic alternative. Nahalal in the Galilee, the first moshav, was set up in 1921 by a breakaway group of settlers who were disillusioned by the socialist constraints of Dganya, the very first kibbutz. One member of this breakaway group was Shmuel Dayan, the father of Moshe Dayan, who was to become a high-profile defense minister and hero of the Six Day War in 1967.

In the moshav, each family runs its own household and farms its individual plot of land, but machinery is shared and marketing is done jointly. There are about 400 moshavim in Israel, but most members now work in regular jobs, renting out their land to private farmers. ❑

> ### FINDING OUT FOR YOURSELF
>
> Visitors wishing to sample life on a kibbutz or moshav can either stay at one of the many kibbutz and moshav guesthouses, or volunteer to work for a period of not less than a month. Guesthouses are often in isolated rural areas in the northern Galilee, but a few are within easy reach of Jerusalem and Tel Aviv. They usually offer all the facilities of a comfortable hotel. You can make a booking through the Kibbutz Hotels Chain (tel: 03-5608118; www.kibbutz.co.il). Prospective volunteer workers should contact Kibbutz Programme Center, 18 Frishman Street Tel Aviv (tel: 03-5278874; email: kpc@volunteer.co.il; www.kibbutz.org.il/eng/welcome.htm).

LEFT: the swimming pool at Ein Gedi kibbutz.
RIGHT: harvesting tomatoes.

WHERE TO FIND THE BEST BARGAINS

Shopping malls offer air-conditioned comfort, but it's the traditional markets which convey the true taste and aroma of the Middle East

Markets around Israel display a diverse range of goods, from the tempting fresh fruit and vegetables in Jerusalem's Makhane Yehuda and Tel Aviv's Carmel Market to the antique trinkets in Yafo's Flea Market.

The market that should on no account be missed is in the Muslim Quarter of Jerusalem's Old City. It is not so much that there is anything on sale which is particularly worth buying, but simply that the "souk" offers Western visitors the ultimate oriental experience.

This is a bazaar in the classic sense of the word. The narrow alleyways are bustling with raw energy, chaotic noise and the smells of exotic spices. Straight down from the Jaffa Gate along David Street are all the kitsch stalls selling T-shirts, religious icons and a variety of Holy Land paraphernalia. Store owners will invariably ask well above the value of an item, so visitors should be prepared to bargain. But the real heart of the "souk" is the spice market – turn left into Shuk Ha-Basamim just before the end of David Street. This dark, narrow labyrinth is no place for those who suffer from claustrophobia, but it is heaven for anyone who loves the pungent aromas of coffee and spices.

Gastronomes will also enjoy the huge array of pickles, spices, dried fruits and nuts on offer in Jerusalem's Makhane Yehuda, while the best bargains in the country in clothes as well as food are to be found in Tel Aviv's Carmel Market. Other markets of interest include the one in Akko's Old City and the Druze market in Daliyat el-Karmel, just south of Haifa.

◁ **NUTS ABOUT NUTS**
Israelis love dried fruit and nuts, but much of the produce is imported from as far afield as California.

△ **FIELD-FRESH FOOD**
As the seasons change, so does the fresh home-grown produce on the stalls of Makhane Yehuda market.

BE'ER SHEVA'S BEDOUIN MARKET

Thursday is the day to be in Be'er Sheva. Neither the recent removal of the Bedouin market to a location just south of the Central Bus Station, nor the increasing profusion of tourist trinkets, has entirely dulled the ethnic authenticity of the market, where Negev nomads come to trade their wares. Although it's open all day, it's best to get here shortly after dawn to enjoy the full essence of the market as the Bedouin trade camels, goats, and agricultural produce. Carpets, clothes, jewelry and other arts and crafts are also available. The highway to the south is strewn with traditional encampments but, with government land appropriations and financial inducements, most Bedouin are moving to fixed villages, a change increasingly reflected in the character of the market.

▽ **BUSINESS, OLD & NEW**
Contrasting lifestyles in Tel Aviv's Nakhalat Binyamin arts and crafts market, held every Tuesday and Friday.

▽ **ANTIQUE ATTRACTIONS**
Yafo's flea market offers bargain-hunters a selection of antique goods from Europe and the Middle East.

△ **OLD CITY VENDORS**
The shopkeepers in the Muslim Quarter of Jerusalem's Old City reflect the essence of the Orient.

◁ **BARGAIN TIME**
Towards the end of the day fresh market produce is often sold at throw-away prices.

▷ **THE TRENDY END OF THE MARKET**
A sax player in Florentin, a ramshackle but trendy neighborhood in south Tel Aviv.

LANGUAGE AND CULTURE

In just over a century a language has been reborn and a new culture
forged from the talents of Israel's diverse population

Had one to name the single most fundamental contribution made by Israel and the Jewish people to mankind, the immediate answer is the Old Testament which, together with the New Testament writings, forms the philosophical and moral web underlying most of Western civilization's values. And that book, for all its five millennia or so, remains the most important source and inspiration for much of Israel's cultural creativity.

It is, of course, only one of the strands, but it is the most pervasive. Other distinct strands are the great literary creations of post-Old Testament commentary – the Mishna, the Talmud, and the fashionable mysticism of the Kabbalah – the accumulated wisdom of 2,000 years of Jewish thought. No less important is the cumulative experience of modern statehood in a society whose population has multiplied nearly tenfold since independence, bolstered by immigration from diverse cultures.

Israel, like the United States before it, has often been described as a melting pot: as it has struggled with the integration of 2½ million immigrants from 80 nations, speaking dozens of languages. But a better image would be a *bouillabaisse*, the classic Mediterranean fish stew in which all the elements form a homogeneous whole, while each retains its own character, distinct identity, and flavor.

Hebrew: a language reborn

One of the most remarkable facets of the rebirth of the Hebrew nation was the revival of the Hebrew language. Through the 2,000 years of dispersion it had become almost solely a language of worship and expression of the yearnings for Zion. The *lingua franca* of the Jews in exile became either the language of the country in which they found refuge; or Yiddish, a combination of Hebrew and medieval German; Ladino, which was Hebrew mixed with Spanish; various forms of Judeo-Arabic such as

Mughrabi, a North African blend of Hebrew, Arabic and French; and Judeo-Persian dialects like Tat in the Caucasian mountain region. The first pioneers who arrived in 19th-century Palestine brought with them their own languages, usually Yiddish or Russian, but they insisted on using Hebrew in conversation in the early agri-

cultural communities, and its re-creation became a cornerstone of Zionist ideology.

The rebirth of Hebrew was virtually the work of one man, the Zionist thinker and leader Eliezer Ben Yehuda. Born in Lithuania in 1858, he immigrated to Palestine in 1881 and saw the revival of the language as an indispensable aspect of the political and cultural rebirth of the Jewish people. With single-minded, almost fanatical determination, he embarked on a lone campaign to restore the Hebrew tongue as a vibrant, living vehicle for everyday expression. When he and his new wife Dvora arrived in Yafo he informed her that they would converse only in Hebrew, and their son Itamar became the

---

LEFT: studying hard on the Hebrew University campus. **RIGHT:** a Torah scribe.

first modern child with Hebrew as his mother tongue. Ben Yehuda's efforts horrified the Orthodox population of Jerusalem who, when they realized he proposed using the holy tongue to further secular, nationalist and political causes, pronounced a *herem* (excommunication) against him. To this day, the Ashkenazi ultra-Orthodox Jewish community shun the secular use of Hebrew and the defilement of the holy language, and prefer Yiddish for everyday speech.

The introduction of Hebrew for everyday use was not greeted with universal acclamation even by the non-Orthodox, or the supporting Zionist bodies and organisations abroad. Bitter battles

were fought over the language of instruction at the Betsalel School of Art in Jerusalem (founded in 1906) and the Technion in Haifa (founded in 1913). German was the official language of the latter, and it took a strike by faculty and students to compel the supporting institution, the Hilfsverein, to give way. A few years later the language of instruction in all schools in the country (except for those of the ultra-Orthodox) was established as Hebrew.

Ben Yehuda compiled a dictionary of Hebrew, established an academy, and founded and edited several periodicals. Through these media he coined thousands of new words relating to every aspect of life and every discipline. Not all of

them took root; modern Hebrew, the all-purpose language of the country in every field, still borrows words from other languages which sound familiar to non-Hebrew speakers. Ben Yehuda's *sah rahok* ("long-distance speech"), for instance, never displaced "telephone", nor did *makushit* ("something that is tapped upon") take the place of "piano".

The question of slang

No one has yet successfully coined Hebrew words to replace the ubiquitous *automati*, *mekhani and democrati* etc, although the existence of such words in the language seriously disturbs Hebrew purists. Some slang neologisms would undoubtedly make Ben Yehuda turn in his grave: *Tremp* (clearly from "tramp") is the Hebrew for "hitchhiking", a sweat-shirt is a *svetcher*, over which you might pull a *sveder* if it gets cold. When your *breks* fail, the garage might find something wrong with your *beck-exel* or even, God forbid, with your *front beck-exel*.

Most of these words have Hebrew equivalents, but they have usually been pushed aside in common usage. Yet pure Hebrew words like *machshev* (computer), *tochna* (software) and *nayad* (mobile/cellular phone) have been happily integrated into everyday usage by Israelis.

There's no denying that Hebrew is once more a thriving, and still-evolving, vehicle of daily discourse employed in great works of literature and emails alike.

The written word

If the heartbeat of a nation's culture lies in the written word, then Israel has a problem because, despite the revival of Hebrew, there are no more

CROWNING ACHIEVEMENT

The crowning achievement of Ben Yehuda's life was his *Dictionary of Ancient and Modern Hebrew*, completed after his death by his son Ehud and his second wife, Hemda (Dvora's younger sister). This dictionary, and the Academy of the Hebrew Language, which he established in 1890, were the main vehicles through which a new, modern vocabulary was disseminated. Ben Yehuda wrote in the introduction to his dictionary: "In those days it was as if the heavens had suddenly opened, and a clear, incandescent light flashed before my eyes, and a mighty inner voice sounded in my ears: the renascence of Israel on its ancestral soil."

than 8 million people worldwide (including many Palestinians) who can speak and understand it, and certainly no more than 5 million who can comfortably read it. Hebrew can be considered an arcane, rather exotic language, one where those who choose to write in it must inevitably be faced with the frustrations of writing for a limited audience. But a lively, articulate and robust body of literature has evolved nevertheless. While the giants of modern Hebrew – Bialik, Tchernikhovsky, Brenner, Agnon (who won the Nobel Prize for Literature in 1966), and others – are still required reading in schools, they are supplemented by indigenous, increas-

drawn from the kibbutzim). Among them are Haim Guri, Moshe Shamir, S. Yizhar, Benjamin Tammuz and Hanoch Bar Tov.

An important phenomenon of the past 15 years or so has been the maturing of a group of writers of Sephardic origin for whom Arabic, rather than Yiddish, was a formative influence. Such writers include A.B. Yehoshua (who was short-listed for the first International Booker Prize), Samy Michael and Amnon Shamosh, whose *Esra Safra and Sons* became a popular television series.

Another literary phenomenon was Ephraim Kishon, Israel's best-known humorist who died

ingly Israeli-born writers whose work can stand comparison with the best of the world's contemporary authors.

One of Israel's best writers (and certainly the best-known abroad) is Amos Oz. A former member of Kibbutz Hulda who now lives in Arad, Oz is heavily influenced by the "return to the soil" labor-Zionist mores espoused by the founding fathers of the kibbutz movement. Many writers who maintain a prolific literary output belong to the "Palmach Generation" (the Palmach was the pre-state elite fighting force

in 2005, a prophet somewhat without honor in his own country, although his books have sold millions of copies overseas, especially in Scandinavia and Germany.

Literature has been deeply influenced by the deaths of millions of Jews in the Holocaust. It is that theme which is the all-pervasive *leitmotiv* in the writings of Aharon Appelfeld, whose books have been widely translated, and in those of Abba Kovner, "Ka-Tsetnik" (the pseudonym of Benzion Dinur) and many others, all of whom experienced that period themselves. A younger generation of writers is exploring more universal literary themes; they include David Grossman, Meir Shalev, Orly Castel-Blum and Irit

LEFT: the language in secular use.
RIGHT: Israeli novelist Amos Oz.

Linor. Shulamit Lapid and the late Batya Gur have adapted the detective story to the Israeli landscape.

The center ground in Israeli writing is held today by those who came to literary maturity after the Palmach days and whose vision was tempered through the fires of austerity, of absorption of immigrants, and four wars of survival. Such writers include Yitzhak Ben Ner, Shulamit Hareven, the late Ya'akov Shabtai, Yoram Kaniuk, and others.

Poetry holds a special place in Israel's literary life and the great poets of pre-Inquisition Spain such as Yehuda Halevy are still widely read.

According to a calculation based on books and the literary magazines, 10,000 new poems are published in the country every year. In addition to Bialik and Saul Tchernikovsky, the best-loved poets of past and present include Yehuda Amichai, Dan Pagis, Natan Zach, T. Carmi, Lea Goldeberg, Uri Zvi Greenberg and Rachel. Emerging contemporary poets like Asher Reich, Arieh Sivan, Ronny Somak and Moshe Dor make greater use of slang and colloquial Hebrew and less formal use of rhyme.

Music, from Classical to Jazz

The musical life of Israel is a good example of the country's bipolarity. There is a constant inflow of immigrant musicians, and an outflow of performers who have reached the highest international peaks. Yitzhak Perlman, Pinchas Zuckerman, Shlomo Mintz, Daniel Barenboim: all received their training in Israel and went on to glittering careers on the world's concert platforms. Israel's orchestras, including the Israel Philharmonic, the Jerusalem Symphony, the Beer Sheva Sinfonietta and many chamber groups, have provided homes for hundreds of players. Their rehearsals are a babel of Russian, German, Romanian, French and English – united by a lot of music and a little Hebrew. Reinforced by mass immigration from the former USSR, there are now also major orchestras in Rishon LeZion, Haifa, Netanya, Ramat Gan and Holon.

Israelis are a concert-going people: subscription series to the major orchestras are sold out, and a subscription to the IPO is jealously handed down from parents to children. Zubin Mehta, born in Bombay in 1936 and one of the world's foremost conductors, has led the IPO since 1991, and has done much to involve himself with Israel's struggle for survival. Music-loving tourists have many opportunity to hear well-loved pieces performed by some of the world's greatest talents. Placido Domingo, incidentally, got his first job at the Israel Opera (recently revived as the New Israel Opera), where he spent a year. The standard of choral singing is also very high, especially among the United Kibbutz Choir, the Rinat National Choir and the Camaran Singers.

Israel hosts a series of international musical events, including the Artur Rubinstein piano competition, the Pablo Casals cello competition, a triennial international harp contest, the Zim-

DANA ROCKS THE BOAT

Dana International reflects the clash of cultures which so often characterizes Israeli life. The glamorous pop singer won the 1998 Eurovision Song Contest but is as famous for her sex change operation (she was born Yaron Cohen) and for her numerous platinum-disc releases. The ultra-Orthodox community is not amused, particularly as Dana cannot easily be dismissed as a passing phenomenon, appealing only to teenage audiences. Having gaining followers in all sorts of unexpected quarters, she has become a symbol of secular resistance to ultra-Orthodox attempts to impose restrictions on Israel's cultural life and media output.

riya choirs festival, and annual music festivals in Jerusalem and Abu Ghosh (liturgical), Kibbutz Ein Hashofet, Kibbutz Ein Gev on the shores of the Sea of Galilee, Kibbutz Kfar Blum in the Upper Galilee (chamber music) and the Red Sea Jazz Festival. The Klezmer Festival in Safed each summer has revived the Hasidic Jewish musical tradition.

Classical music is often too Ashkenazi for the taste of many Oriental Jews and Arabs. They have their own musical traditions, and the Israel Andalusian Orchestra reflects the culture of North Africa. But in pop music east and west are integrated. The best known songwriters, such as Naomi Shemer, Ehud Manor and Uzi Hitman (who all died in 2004 and 2005), were Ashkenazi but deeply loved by all Israeli Jews. The late Ofra Haza, who died of Aids, and living artists such as Rita and Gali Atari and bands like Typex are Oriental but popular among all Israelis.

Dance greats

Israel owes its place in the world of dance to four women. The first was a Russian-trained ballerina, Rina Nikova, who came to Palestine in the 1920s determined to create a local art form incorporating themes from the Bible, Middle East tradition, folk dance and Russian classical ballet. The second, Sarah Levi-Tanai, harnessed the Yemenite dance tradition, one of the richest and most exotic of the Middle East, into a modern framework, creating the Inbal Dance Theatre, the forerunner of several other successful ethnic groups.

The third, Baroness Bethsabee de Rothschild, founded the Batsheva and Bat Dor dance companies, which remain leading exponents of modern dance in Israel. In recent years the two companies have been joined by the Kibbutz Dance Company and the Israel Ballet, the country's only classical ballet company. The fourth woman was Martha Graham, who was undoubtedly the formative influence on modern dance in Israel. The Israel Ballet was set up by Berta Yampolsky and Hillel Markman.

A company rare in concept and achievement is Kol Demama ("Voice of Silence"), a group composed of deaf and hearing-impaired dancers, whose performances are electrifying. The training method developed by director Moshe Efrati

is based on vibrations through the floor transmitted by the dancer's feet. Vertigo, founded in 1992, combines ballet and contemporary dance.

Folk-dance groups abound, and there is no kibbutz or town that doesn't have its own troupe. Outstanding among them is Hora Yerushalayim, a Jerusalem-based group, whose four companies perform at home and overseas. Israelis love to dance, and many festive occasions end up with exuberant *horas, krakoviaks, debkas,* Hassidic dances and other European and Arab dances, are now part of the heritage. Each summer the Karmiel Dance Festival brings folk troupes to Israel from around the world.

Theatrical roots

Israeli theater owes its origins to the melodramatic tradition exemplified in the first Hebrew theater in the world, Ha-Bimah, founded in Moscow in 1917 (and moved to Palestine in 1931). Since then theater has come a long way in style, presentation, method, and especially content. Of all the arts in Israel, theater is perhaps the most socially involved, with a new generation of playwrights breaking taboos, tackling controversial topics, and attempting to act as the mirror and conscience of society.

Concerns of the past, the Jewish experience in pre-war Europe, the Holocaust, all these still manifest themselves on the Israeli stage, but,

LEFT: Zubin Mehta takes a bow.
RIGHT: ballet flourishes in Israel.

increasingly, dramatists are addressing themselves to contemporary issues, problems of daily life in Israel, the Arab-Jewish conflict, alienation between ethnic, religious and other social groups. A new play by Hanoch Levin, Yehoshua Sobol or Hillel Mittelpunkt is a major event which will be dissected, analysed and discussed as energetically as political events. Hanoch Levin, especially, is a defiant, iconoclastic writer whose works inevitably cause controversy and attract attempted censorship. But his irreverent, nihilistic, often obscene satire makes him Israel's most interesting and original theatrical talent.

Most major repertory theaters – such as the Ha-Bimah, Cameri, Beit Lessin Haifa Municipal Theater, Be'er Sheva Municipal Theater and Jerusalem Khan – enjoy substantial official support and are very well attended. The language barrier prevents visitors from sharing in the rich offerings, but simultaneous translations are often available. The Arab Theater and Beit Hagefen are Arabic-language companies while Gesher (meaning bridge) produces Russian and Hebrew drama.

The Israel Festival each spring in Jerusalem brings drama companies to Israel from around the world, while the Akko Fringe Festival in October is Israel's equivalent of the Edinburgh Festival. Haifa holds a Children's Theater Festival each year.

Cinema blossoms

The best actress award won by Hanna Laszlo at the 2005 Cannes Film Festival for her role in Amos Gitai's movie *Free Zone* demonstrates that Israeli films can compete in the global marketplace. *Free Zone* is the story of three women: an Israeli, American and Palestinian traveling in Jordan. But it is the exception rather than the rule. For the most part, limitations of budget, the need for subtitles and a tendency to focus on parochial rather than universal themes have stymied Israeli cinema. The pick of the Hebrew movies down the decades is *Beyond the Walls*, *A Siren's Song*, *Life According to Agfa* and *Tel Aviv Stories*.

Most cinema productions are strictly for local consumption and are based on sitcoms, sex-coms, and in-joke situations such as teenage affairs, marital conflicts and army life. TV soap operas such as *Ramat Aviv Gimmel* and *Love Around the Corner* combine poor acting with predictable scripts.

Israelis have made it on the international stage including actors Haim Topol (best known in *Fiddler on the Roof*) and movie moguls Menahem Golan and Yoram Globus.

The Jerusalem International Film Festival and Haifa International Film Festival each summer are the showcases of the Israeli film industry and non-Hollywood international movies.

Painters and sculptors

Israeli art owes its fundamental quality to a combination of two factors: a classical European tradition brought here by the country's early painters and art teachers, and the influ-

MOVIES WITH A MESSAGE

Serious film-making in Israel began in the early 1920s and 1930s. Most of the output consisted of documentaries, whose main purpose was as a fundraising device aimed at demonstrating the Zionist effort to audiences abroad. These early films, with their images of muscle-rippling pioneers making the desert bloom, against a background of stirring music and an exhortatory soundtrack, became known as "Keren Kayemet" films after the Hebrew name of the Jewish National Fund which sponsored them. Today they seem amateurish, but, like the propaganda films made in post-revolutionary Russia, they are interesting social documents.

ences of the special quality of the light and the natural attributes of the country.

Israeli visual art, possessing its own individual character, has been created in a comparatively short space of time, since the establishment of the Betsalel School of Art in Jerusalem in 1906. Israeli artists have experimented with all the movements and trends of the contemporary art world from expressionism to cubism, from Russian social realism to environment and performance art, but few have managed to make the quantum leap from local to universal recognition. Among contemporary artists who have are Ya'akov Agam (his kinetic room at the

At the end of the 1970s, following in the steps of the USA and Europe, Israeli art entered the post-modernist era. The work is energetic and forceful, often containing violent images, which are, perhaps, part of the war reality in Israeli life. Currently, Tel Aviv artist David Reeb is among the few whose works have an overtly socio-political theme.

Museums and galleries all over the country cater to the art lover. The main ones are concentrated in two areas: Gordon Street, in central Tel Aviv, and Old Yafo. There are others in Jerusalem, Haifa, Ein Hod (an artist's village to the south of Haifa which staged the Sculpture

Pompidou Centre in Paris is a seminal work), Menashe Kadishman, Avigdor Arikha, Mordechai Ardon and Joseph Zaritsky.

Dany Karavan and Ygael Tumarkin are two sculptors well known abroad whose work can be seen all over Israel. Marcel Janco (1895–1984), founder of the Dadaist Movement, Reuven Rubin (1893–1974), painter of lyrical large-scale canvases, and Anna Ticho (1894–1980), with her exquisite line drawings of the Jerusalem hills, have also gained a following.

LEFT: street theater in Jerusalem.
ABOVE: Mordechai Ardon's stained-glass windows at Givat Ram.

Biennale in 1990), and Safed, a Galilean town full of artists.

Tel Aviv Museum has a large and representative collection of Israeli modern art on permanent display, along with many temporary exhibitions. The Israel Museum, which has impressive collections of classic, impressionist and foreign modern art (as well as its vast collection of archaeology, Judaica and Jewish art and ethnography), rather tended to neglect Israeli art before the opening in 1985 of the Ayala Zacks-Abramov Pavilion of Modern Art. This has now become the nation's main repository of contemporary Israeli painting and sculpture. ❑

CUISINE

Eastern Mediterranean fare such as falafel, hummous and mezze salad
complement such global staples as pizza and hamburgers

Jewish and Muslim (kosher and halal) dietary laws are very similar, with both religions prohibiting pork and insisting that animals are prepared for consumption in the same very specific way. There is considerable variety, though, since every Jewish community – whether Ashkenazi, Sephardic, Yemenite or Russian – has interpreted the culinary requirements of Judaism in its own way.

Most hotels in Israel serve only kosher food and they display a sign to this effect. But most restaurants (except in Jerusalem) are not kosher, though often this is because they are open on the sabbath and therefore not entitled to certification.

Another fundamental tenet of kosher laws is that milk and meat cannot be mixed. So you shouldn't expect to have coffee and a dairy dessert in the same kosher dining room where you can eat a meat dish. Surprisingly, McDonald's in downtown Jerusalem and most of its branches throughout the country are not kosher; in other words, you can wash down your cheeseburger with a milk shake. For the unadventurous, many other fast-food joints have outlets throughout Israel.

The Arab influence

What people traditionally associate with "Jewish food" is actually Eastern European – *matzo* ball soup, *gefilte* fish, *latkes* and *cholent*. But most Jewish restaurants in Israel are owned by Jews who came from Arab countries, and thus the main food that both Jews and Arabs cook and eat in the country is the kind of fare eaten across the whole of North Africa and the Middle East.

In the Mediterranean tradition this involves a great deal of culinary ingenuity. The best example of this is the chick pea, a humble legume and on the face of it an unexciting Middle East staple. But, either fried into small balls and eaten as falafel, together with salad and spices in a pitta bread, or mashed into houmous and mopped up with pitta bread together with olive oil and beans, these make delicious, cheap, filling and highly nutritional meals. Another pop-

ular fast-food dish is *schwarma*. Usually made from turkey, this is carved off the spit and put into pitta bread or *laffa* (a type of bread originating in Iraq), again with a choice of salads and spices. *Borekas*, a Balkan-style pastry filled with cheese, potato or mushrooms, is another filling fast-food solution.

If you are sitting down to a meal then it is customary to start with *mezze*, a selection of salads eaten with pitta bread. Try houmous, *tahina* (sesame-seed paste) and *tabule* (cracked wheat salad). Some restaurants in Tel Aviv's Kerem Hatamanim, West Jerusalem's Agripas Street and East Jerusalem's Bab e-Zarha will go overboard with the *mezze*, serving up as many as 20 different salads, including pickled cucumbers and olives. It is best to specify which salads you actually want.

The meat, typically beef – *shashlik* kebabs or a steak – can be a bit of a disappointment and relatively expensive. The fish, such as the St Peter's fish and Nile perch, can also be an anti-climax. It is generally well seasoned but lacking in body. Often the best option is to fill up on the nutritional salads and forgo the main course altogether. However, the quality of both meat and fish has improved over the past decade.

Kosher laws prohibit the consumption of shellfish and stipulate that fish for cooking must have both fins and tails that can be detached from the skin. Removing bones is also prohibited, hence the popularity of the supposedly boneless *gefilte* fish. Authorities can differ: some deem swordfish acceptable, for example, while others don't.

Other dishes worth trying are stuffed dumplings *(kube)*, stuffed peppers and stuffed vine

exotic pastries such as *katayeef*, flavored with vanilla and honey, and *baklawa*, a very rich delicacy with delicious, coarsely chopped pistachio nuts, walnuts or almonds.

Fruit

The range of local fruit and vegetables is best appreciated at Makhane Yehuda market in Jerusalem or Carmel Market in Tel Aviv. On a hot summer's day nothing quenches the thirst better than the rich, red water-melons on sale at these colorful markets. Also on offer are all manner of spices and pickles. But the meat and fish being sold here are nothing special. ❑

leaves. The steak restaurants in Agripas in Jerusalem also offer a "Jerusalem mixed grill" stuffed in pitta bread, though this is not for the anatomically squeamish. Indeed, the Jerusalem mixed grill is offered throughout the country.

Jews and Arabs have a sweet tooth, and here visitors can go European or Middle Eastern. Ben Yehuda Street, and elsewhere in West Jerusalem, and the cafés of Tel Aviv and Haifa's Hadar and Central Carmel have many Central European-style cafés serving delicious apple strudel. Arab restaurants offer a range of more

LEFT: Jerusalem's climate encourages outdoor dining.
ABOVE: fresh fish is the basis for much local cuisine.

ISRAELI WINE

In 1875 Benjamin Disraeli, Britain's prime minister, likened a bottle of kosher red wine from Palestine to cough medicine. Happily, Israeli wines have improved enormously in recent years, though many restaurants will still tell you that they serve two types of wine – white and red. Beer is best avoided altogether (one visiting Irish soccer fan recently told Israel TV he wouldn't wash his car with it) and the local spirit, arak, is a variation on the Greek ouzo. Though Arab restaurants will serve alcohol, for obvious reasons heavy drinking is not encouraged. Israelis, too, though they have no prohibitions about alcohol, are intolerant and suspicious of drunkenness.

JUDAICA

Jewish arts and crafts experienced a revival with the birth of Zionism,
inspiring contemporary artists to give a new twist to old traditions

As in ancient times, Jerusalem is the center of Israel's arts and crafts industry, and workers are to be found in their own centrally located quarters. One feature of the arts scene is the accessibility of its artists, enabling collectors to buy directly from the studio shops.

Jewish ritual art, the bulk of Judaica, is

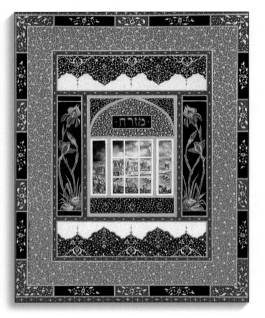

divided into two categories: holy vessels, directly associated with the Torah, and ritual utensils, used for tasks in the home and synagogue. While not intrinsically holy, the latter acquire sanctity in the performance of religious duties (*mitzvot*). If a ritual object adds an aesthetic dimension, users have the benefit of fulfilling an additional commandment, *hiddur mitzvah* – glorification of the commandment.

The rules of creation

Halacha, Jewish law, offers only a few rules for creating specific ritual objects. The Chanukah lamp is perhaps the most clearly defined. It must have eight separate lights of the same height, and a distinguishable ninth light for kindling the others. They must burn, in a publicly visible spot, for at least 30 minutes past sundown. The rest is left to the artist.

In most cases, form and decoration followed the fashions of the time and place in which they were produced. Chanukah lamps, from the 12th century onwards, have French Gothic windows, Moorish arches, or Italian garlands; wine cups and candlesticks are reminiscent of the Renaissance and baroque periods, a single Hebrew letter the only sign that they were used by Jews.

Symbols of the artists' surrounding cultures were given new significance when combined with classic Jewish symbols. Long-standing favorites include (Torah) crowns and double columns invoking the Temple; biblical scenes and signs of the Zodiac; lions of Judah, grape vines and pomegranates, griffins and fish; and, of course, the seven-branched Menorah. Representations of the human figure and face were generally avoided in deference to the Second Commandment ("Thou shall have no graven images") but they appear from time to time.

Contemporary artists

Israel's contemporary Judaica artists, like their ancestors, favor semi-precious and precious metals, but items can be found in almost every other material, from rare woods and in particular olive wood, to Lucite. Two distinct schools have recently emerged. One is highly traditional, basing its shapes and decorations on patterns from the baroque period or earlier. Many of these works are imitations or adaptations of well-known museum pieces; others are brought up to date by incorporating the lines of modern Jerusalem or devices such as whimsical moving parts. The second school is strictly, sometimes aggressively, contemporary. Form prevails over function; the artist strives to create art works, which may be used in ritual.

An informal arts and crafts tour could begin at one of the two non-profit galleries which offer an instant overview of Israel's craft scene. Neither gallery sells anything but refers visitors directly to its selected artists. At the House of Quality this means going upstairs to the studios where several silversmiths, including veterans Arie Ofir and Menachem Berman, work full-time. At the Alix de Rothschild Crafts Center the director may be on hand for tea and a chat about his latest discoveries.

Nearby, the Courtyard Gallery is the place for fibre-art fans seeking chic handmade baskets, fabrics and wall hangings. Those who prefer a strictly ethnic look can go across town to Kuzari, now with its sales outlet in Yoel Salomon Street in the center of town. It is in the Bukharim Quarter, where local women embroider every-

among the world's top designers of contemporary Judaica, and Michael Ende is a chief purveyor of the "nouveau antique" school.

Fans of the latter should also visit Yossi's Masters' Workshop (King David Street) and The Brothers Reichman (in Geula). Both offer extraordinary workmanship and classic designs in fine metal. Similar style characterizes the ceremonial pieces by Catriel, a carver of rare woods, in Yohanan MiGush Halava.

Close to Catriel are silversmiths Davidson and Amiel, calligraphic artist Korman, and jeweler Sarah Einstein, who transforms antique Middle Eastern beads into high-fashion jewelry. ❑

thing, from tea cosies to Torah covers, in traditional patterns for the Kuzari store.

Khutsot ha-Yoster (Art & Crafts Lane) near Jaffa Gate has top craftspeople like Uri Ramot (ancient glass and beads in modern settings); the Alsbergs (antique coins in custom-made jewelry); and Georges Goldstein (hand-woven tapestries and *tallitot* – prayer shawls). But the lane's greatest distinction is its concentration of outstanding silversmiths. Yaakov Greenvurcel, Zelig Segal and Emil Shenfeld are ranked

LEFT: a *mizrach* (wall hanging) depicts Jerusalem.
ABOVE: a silversmith crafts Menorahs and other ceremonial objects.

OTHER ARTS AND CRAFTS

From the artists' quarter in old Safed to the seaside boutiques in Eilat, on every major city avenue and in the oriental markets, there's an almost endless array of local handicrafts. In addition to Judaica, Israel is rich from the arts and crafts of other communities. Bedouin weaving and handicrafts include special embroidered bags, pillows and table cloths and weaving for carpet. These items can be found at the Bedouin market in Be'er Sheva on Thursday mornings. Similar Druze handicrafts are on sale in the Carmel village of Daliyat el-Karmel. Distinctive Armenian pottery is available on the Via Dolorosa of the Christian Quarter in the Old City which makes a delightful gift.

APPLETONS' JOURNAL

of LITERATURE ❖ SCIENCE ❖ AND ART

ENTERED, according to Act of Congress, in the year 1871, by D. APPLETON & Co., in the Office of the Librarian of Congress at Washington.

No. 99.—Vol. V.]　　　　SATURDAY, FEBRUARY 18, 1871.　　　　{ PRICE TEN CENTS.
　　　　　　　　　　　　　　　　　　　　　　　　　　　　　　{ WITH SUPPLEMENT.

THE RECOVERY OF JERUSALEM.*

THIS is the somewhat pretentious title of the narrative of recent English explorations of Jerusalem, by means of excavations conducted by Captain Wilson, of the Royal Engineers, under the auspices and at the expense of the Committee of the Palestine Exploration Fund. Without, perhaps, fulfilling the meaning of the old crusading war-cry,

exact knowledge of the scenes and localities in which their reli[gion] first appeared on earth. The explorations have solved many diff[icult] problems, and settled many fierce and protracted controversies. Sh[afts] have been sunk and tunnels made in the most secluded and myster[ious] parts of the sacred city, and structures brought to light that have [not]

WILSON'S ARCH, DISCOVERED AT JERUSALEM IN 1867.

the "Recovery of Jerusalem," it is undoubtedly a record of researches and discoveries of the highest value, and of the greatest interest to scholars, antiquarians, and, above all, to Christians who desire an

been seen by mortal eyes since the days of Titus, or perhaps of S[olo]mon.

The beginning of this great work was the Ordnance Survey [of] Jerusalem, made by Captain Wilson, of the English Royal Engine[ers,] in 1864–'65. Early in the year 1864 the sanitary state of Jerusa[lem] attracted considerable attention; that city, which the Psalmist described as "beautiful for situation, the joy of the whole earth,"

---

* The Recovery of Jerusalem. A Narrative of Exploration and Discovery in the City and the Holy Land. By Captain Wilson, R. E., and Captain Warren, R. E. With an Introduction by Arthur Penrhyn Stanley, D. D., Dean of Westminster. D. Appleton & Co.

DIGGING UP THE PAST

Archaeology is Israel's national hobby, fascinating all age groups, and tourists and natives alike are encouraged to unearth a rich past

With 20,000 recognized archaeological sites in an area of around 21,000 sq. km (8,100 sq. miles), and finds dating back to 150,000 BC, Israel has several dozen archaeological museums in addition to numerous private collections. Yet only a few potential sites have been thoroughly explored; time, money and manpower have all placed limits on the scope of such exploration.

A gentlemanly hobby

Adherents past and present to what one scholar called the "study of durable rubbish" have been drawn to biblical archaeology for a range of reasons: greed, adventure, religion and scholarship. During the Victorian period it was something of a gentlemanly hobby.

The first known "archaeologist" to work in Israel was inspired by religious belief. In AD 325 Empress Helena, the mother of Constantine the Great, the emperor who declared Christianity the official religion of his empire, ordered the removal of a Hadrianic temple to Venus built on a site, which she had determined was the hill of Golgotha. Constantine erected the Church of the Holy Sepulchre to commemorate the alleged site of the crucifixion and entombment of Jesus.

During the next 16 centuries the territory changed hands numerous times. Explorers of all religions crossed its borders, armed with little more than compasses, picks, shovels, and curiosity. Stories of bribery, untimely deaths and mystical reunions with long dead sages and prophets pepper their accounts. Medieval adventurers report that those who dared to enter the burial cavern of the patriarchs and their wives at Hebron were struck blind or senseless or worse. Such tales did not deter others.

Interest in the Holy Land intensified after Napoleon conquered Egypt in 1798 and the Rosetta Stone was subsequently discovered. Scholars, amateurs and snake-oil salesmen

LEFT: an 1871 journal recounts the discovery in Jerusalem of Wilson's Arch.
RIGHT: the underground city at Amatzia.

descended on Palestine, then a sparsely populated backwater. Some of these adventurers became the victims of archaeological fever. For example, when the British Museum rejected as fake certain "ancient" parchments that Moses Wilhelm Shapira had bought from a Bedouin, the amateur archaeologist simply disappeared.

In 1911, Captain Montague Parker and his crew of treasure hunters barely escaped with their lives when they were caught excavating under the Mosque of Omar on the Temple Mount. The British mission had been following the hunch of a Swedish clairvoyant who insisted that this was where they would find a cache of objects from King Solomon's temple. Offended Jerusalemites rioted in the streets.

Method in the madness

The foundations of modern archaeology as we know it were not laid until the late 19th century, and were marked by the establishment of major academic institutions sponsoring field trips and publication societies. The Palestine Exploration Fund, founded in London in 1865, is the grandfather of these groups, which include such venerable institutions as the American Schools of Oriental Research and the Ecole Biblique et Archaeologique Française. The work which Edward Robinson, Claude R. Conder, Sir Flinders Petrie and other giants carried out during this period continues to cast a long shadow on modern archaeology.

It was Petrie who first recognized the importance of stratigraphy – that is, the examination layer by layer of a tel, the artificial mound formed by successive settlements. He was also

Today an eclectic approach to tel excavating prevails. Technological advances enable surveyors to provide archaeologists with considerable information before a single shovelful of earth has been removed. Carbon-14 dating has further improved the possibility of fixing an artefact in time. Archaeologists can now dig underwater, cross-reference finds on computers and learn more quickly what their colleagues have discovered. They can call on a host of specialists, including paleo-botanists, osteologists, ethnologists, philologists and biblical exegetes to interpret their finds.

Most importantly, archaeologists now

among the first to recognise the importance of using pottery to date each layer. He realised that, in different periods, particular types of pottery would be associated with particular strata.

After World War I, Mortimer Wheeler and Kathleen Kenyon refined the debris analysis method of pottery dating. At about the same time a separate methodology arose, emphasising the importance of uncovering large areas to expose the architecture of a settlement.

Devotees of the so-called architectural method accused those of the debris analysis school of overlooking the big picture. The latter in turn accused their colleagues of ignoring the importance of stratigraphy.

emphasize that once a locus – a three-dimensional area designated for excavation – is dug and artifacts are removed, the site will have been ineluctably altered. By the very nature of their work, they destroy irreplaceable evidence in their search for remnants of the past.

A passion for proof

Archaeology is a field whose study bolsters or threatens religious and political beliefs – as well as pet scholarly theories. Since the late 1970s, when a small but vocal ultra-Orthodox minority tried to stop a dig at the City of David, claiming it was desecrating ancient graves, archaeologists have faced fierce opposition throughout the country from these devout Jews determined to protect perceived burial grounds.

Jordan has filed formal complaints with UNESCO – largely for political reasons – against Israeli digs in East Jerusalem, although the Israeli government has done much to preserve important archaeological sites there.

Among secular, apolitical scholars the real value of the Bible in their archaeological work is hotly debated. Many doubt its utility as a historical document and a source of verifiable reference. Others cling firmly to the Bible's documentary importance and infallibility.

The careers of Israel's greatest archaeologists

Sea Scrolls, Yadin writes "He found something symbolic in the thought that this was happening at the very moment when Jewish sovereignty in Palestine was about to be restored after almost 2,000 years – the very age of the parchment he had seen." That parchment is now part of the collection at the Shrine of the Book, in the Israel Museum.

An impressive amount of history has been uncovered from the Roman and Byzantine cities of Caesarea, Bet Shean, Banias and Tzipori in the north to the Nabatean settlements of Avdat and Mashit in the south, as well as Masada, the mighty fortress overlooking the Dead Sea. ❑

were hewn from this complex web of scholarly debate and political instability. Benjamin Mazar, who directed the 1960s excavations next to the Western Wall in Jerusalem, remembers his 1936 dig at Beit She'arim in northern Israel. "Everyone had a keen interest in the excavation, because finding Jewish antiquities reinforced the meaning of Zionism and strengthened the reason for creating a Jewish state. We were… building a homeland, and Jewish antiquities were part of its foundation."

Of Sukenik's discovery in 1947 of the Dead

LEFT: visiting a site at Mount Gerizim, Samaria.
ABOVE: archaeologists debate a vital point.

POPULARIZING THE PAST

The late Yigael Yadin, the son of Eliezer Sukenik, followed in his father's footsteps, and conducted many digs of his own. His books on Masada, Khatsor ha-Glilit and the Dead Sea Scrolls have dramatized the history of the "people of the book". In addition, much of his work has been popularized by others. Khatsor, a site in northern Israel with an underground water system, is the subject of James Michener's novel *The Source*. And Yadin's dig at Masada – where he discovered a ritual bath and synagogue – became the focus of a TV mini-series from which millions learned about the heroic but futile stand of a handful of Jews against the Roman forces in AD 73.

CONSERVING FOR THE FUTURE

Since the State of Israel was created, forests have been planted and the land regenerated, but creeping urbanization remains a threat

Intrinsic in Zionist ideology was love of the Land of Israel and the re-birth of its entire eco-system. Many admirable things have been achieved over the past century, and while it was true that the land had been previously neglected, all too often the European settlers tried to create an environment that was too

green, especially in the southern half of the country, and in many instances deserts have been transformed into unnecessary forests.

However, the main environmental failure has been caused by the transplanting of too large a population into too small an area. As affluence increases, more and more Israelis are forsaking their small apartment in an urban high rise for a more spacious house and garden. Shopping malls, high-tech parks and highways swallow up the countryside. Industrialization has taken its toll and it is said that more than 1,000 Israelis die each year from the consequences of polluted air – more annual deaths than from road accidents and terrorism combined.

That said, Israel's environment is unique. The Sinai peninsula, together with Israel and Jordan, form the only land link between Africa and Europe/Asia, and the flora and fauna represent a unique mix of the three continents. Each spring it is estimated that more than a billion birds migrate northwards from their breeding grounds in Africa, flying along the Great Syrian-African rift valley. At Israel's more verdant northern border the birds, which include 200 species and 34 different types of birds of prey, can sense journey's end.

But Israel has been good to the birds. In the 1980s the US government pressed to build a $2 billion Voice of America antenna in the Arava desert, which would have impeded the birds' flight path. Under pressure from environmentalists the Israeli government said no; the installation was eventually built in Kuwait.

Preparing for salvation

The Jewish concept of redemption sees not only people but all God's creations including animals, trees and flowers being redeemed when the Messiah comes. In the meantime it is Man's duty to tend the environment so that there is something to redeem when salvation arrives. The early Zionists may not have been "greens" in the modern sense but they were horrified by the swamp-ridden arid land that they found. The region was a desolate backwater of the crumbling Ottoman Empire and nature had been ravished. The hand of havoc, it seemed, had reached into the Garden of Eden.

Lions had disappeared in Crusader times and crocodiles did not survive the 19th century. Few may regret the demise of these predators but the more widespread introduction of modern firearms was a tragedy for less threatening wildlife. Within a few decades, large numbers of the gazelles and ibex, which had lived here since the days of the prophets, had been ruthlessly killed. A monstrous hunting binge shot several species such as the wild bear into extinction but the leopard just survived in the south, though probably no more than a dozen exist.

The local race of ostrich, which so perplexed Job, was blasted to nothingness. Israel's native race of Asiatic wild ass, a creature some scholars identify as the animal Jesus rode on Palm Sunday, was annihilated. The spectacular white oryx antelope, the *re'em* of the Hebrew Bible, translated in the King James Version as unicorn, suffered a similar fate. Fortunately, a few specimens were captured for breeding before the last of the wild population was exterminated.

Flora was also destroyed. For centuries Christian pilgrims had scoured the countryside for biblical wildflowers. These were picked, pressed and sent back to Europe to serve as

were burned as fuel. By the time T. E. Lawrence (Lawrence of Arabia) was attacking the Ottoman trains, Israel had less than 3 percent tree cover. With the loss of vegetation, the soil turned to dust and was swept out to the desert by the wind. The scant winter rains had no absorbent material to hold them, and water ran quickly to the sea while the wells dried out.

Early Jewish settlers determined to recreate the biblical Land of Israel were confronted by severe problems. The land was exhausted, and could not support either a human population or its own natural processes. The ecological integrity of the land had to be restored.

bookmarks in family Bibles. Generations of Europeans could "consider the lilies" of the Holy Land – but these lilies were lifeless, dried, and incapable of reproduction. Today, Israel's native Madonna lily is a very rare plant.

Loss of vegetation

The big disaster came when the Ottoman Turks built a railway into the Arabian Desert, and the region's forests were leveled. The heavy timbers were used to bridge ravines, middle-sized logs became rail ties, and the smaller pieces

HOLDING BACK THE DESERT

Much of the regeneration of the land has been achieved by the Jewish National Fund (JNF), Israel's afforestation agency, which was also responsible for planting the northern hemisphere's most southerly non-equatorial forest, the Yatir Forest, in the northern Negev desert.

The agency is particularly concerned with combating desert encroachment. But, despite its achievements, the JNF comes in for criticism. Some environmental organizations in Israel accuse it of overkill, claiming that it is trying to create European-style forests in places where a semi-arid desert environment should naturally exist. Others accuse it of over-reliance on the Aleppo pine.

LEFT: the Pillars of Solomon at Timna National Park.
ABOVE: wildflowers bloom in the Judean Desert.

The 15th day of the Jewish month of Shevat, Tu B'Shvat, is an Israeli Arbor Day, celebrated by planting trees in any of the scores of special planting zones in the nation's forests. Israelis plant trees on other days, too – to mark birthdays and weddings, for example. In one forest about 20 km (12 miles) west of Jerusalem 6 million trees have been planted as a memorial to Holocaust victims.

Since Israel was founded in 1948, planted forests have grown to cover 2,000 sq. km (770 sq. miles) – 10 percent of the country's land area. With the return of the trees, winter rains were captured and channeled to the aquifers.

mushrooms in the Jerusalem forest after the first winter rains, or the growth of colorful mosaics of lichen upon fallen logs. Others are so dramatic that they are impossible to miss. The majestic golden eagles have returned to the skies, and one pair even builds its nest each year in the branches of a planted pine forest just south of Jerusalem.

Nature reserves

There are 280 established nature reserves in Israel, covering more than 4,000 sq. km (1,540 sq. miles) – more than than one-fifth of the country's land area. By international standards,

Wells again became productive. With the return of the trees, particularly the fast-growing Jerusalem pine (*Pinus halepensis*), soil was regenerated. In many places the pines were cut once the soil was adequate and replaced with apricot, almond and other fruit and nut trees.

With the return of trees, soil and water, agriculture prospered. Israel is one of the very few arid lands which grows enough food to feed itself – and has enough surplus for exports.

With the return of the trees, nature also flourished, and the land began to recover. Life processes dependent upon a good vegetative cover were regenerated. Some are hardly noticed – for example, the sprouting of orenit

UNWELCOME IMPROVEMENT

The Hula Nature Reserve in the Upper Galilee is perhaps an example of over-zealous attempts by Israel to "improve" on the existing environment. In the 1950s the Hula Swamp was drained to make way for agriculture. Of the 4,000 hectares (10,000 acres) drained, 80 hectares (200 acres) were left as a nature reserve, the habitat of water buffalo and diverse wildlife. But the farmland beneath the swamp, rich in peat, is becoming less and less fertile, and recently 400 hectares (1,000 acres) were reswamped.

This well-intentioned project has been acknowledged as a noble failure, and there are plans to restore the Hula Swamp in the long term.

the reserves are strictly run. They are maintained in as pristine a state as possible, and visitors are forbidden to pick flowers, camp or picnic. Administered by the Nature Reserves Authority, they serve a variety of functions. Generally, they reflect the need for humanity and nature to coexist. An example can be seen at Banias, a beautiful nature reserve at the foot of Mount Hermon, on Israel's northern border. The name Banias is a corruption of the Greek "Paneas," and here there are the remains of an ancient Greek temple dedicated to the god of the forests. Other archaeological treasures in the area include the remains of the ancient Nim-

They flow from taps in Tel Aviv and Haifa, help irrigate the fields of the Galilee, and fill the fish ponds of the Beit She'an Valley.

Many nature reserves are established solely for the preservation of particular natural features: a seasonal pond, a secluded valley where rare flowers blossom, a sunny cliff with good nesting ledges. Some of these reserves are off-limits to human visitors because of their importance to nature and the ecological equilibrium of the region.

One of the most interesting projects is the Khai-Bar programme. Khai-Bar is a Hebrew term which simply means "wildlife" but to

rod Fortress and the Crusader town of Belinas.

The reserve's colorful wild oleander and thick groves of myrtle, plane and willow trees appeal to the naturalist's eye. It is a haven for a great variety of birds and mammals. The rare stone marten and wild cat live here, and otters splash with carefree abandon in the waters which flow from the slopes of Mount Hermon.

These waters give a human dimension to this nature reserve, for they are the headwaters of the Jordan River, and much of them eventually enters Israel's national water-carrier system.

ABOVE: spring flowers bloom among the cacti at Yitzrael Valley in the Galilee.

Israeli conservationists it also identifies an international effort to "return the animals of the Bible to the land of the Bible." Conservationists have searched the world to find remnants of the species which once inhabited these lands. Some of the discoveries were prosaic: addax antelope were found in a Chicago zoo, and a few Asiatic wild ass came from the Copenhagen Zoo.

Deer with false documents

A few of the discoveries have involved some spectacular rescue work. Mesopotamian fallow deer, for example, were spirited out of revolutionary Iran during a howling storm, on false export papers. White oryx – the unicorns of the King James Bible – reached their ancestral home in the Negev after a globe-trotting journey of tens of thousands of kilometers. Their source was a few hundred kilometers southeast of the Negev – in the personal zoo of the late Saudi King Faisal. And a flock of ostrich chicks was airlifted out of Ethiopia's Danakil desert when the Israeli Air Force was sent on a special mission to fetch some new immigrants to Israel.

All the animals, regardless of their origin, are first brought to special reserves set up to rehabilitate them to life in Israel's wild areas.

Geological diversity

Topography in Israel is a matter of spectacular contrasts. Mount Hermon, on the northern border, towers to a snowcapped 2,814 meters (9,223 ft); the Dead Sea, at 400 meters (1,300 ft) below sea level, is the lowest point on the face of the earth. Broad plains stretch across parts of the Galilee, and fringe the northern Negev with expanses of steppe grasslands.

Makhtesh Ramon, a natural crater 40 km (25 miles) across, is carved from the central Negev highlands. The north–south range of the Judean Mountains forms a continuous ridge, nearly 1,000 meters (3,280 ft) high, an

One Khai-Bar reserve is deep in the Negev, about 40 km (25 miles) north of Eilat; it specializes in desert animals. Another is on top of Mount Carmel, on the Mediterranean coast near Haifa; its speciality is wildlife of the Mediterranean oak-forest region.

The restoration process is comprehensive and involves years of painstaking work. Indeed, 14 years passed between the acquisition of the Asiatic wild ass from the Copenhagen Zoo, and the day when their offspring were judged tough and experienced enough to live freely in the wild. Today they are repopulating remote areas of the Negev and giving birth to wild foals.

hour's drive east of the Mediterranean coast.

The great geographical and topographical diversity is responsible for tremendous biological diversity. There are sub-alpine meadows on the slopes of Mount Hermon, and just 25km (16 miles) south, at the Hula Nature Reserve, there is a lush tropical jungle: the world's northernmost papyrus swamp. Israel is a land of Eurasian oaks and African acacias, Eurasian foxes and wolves and African Dorcas gazelles and rock hyrax. It is a land of blending continents, flora, fauna and geology.   ❏

ABOVE: a pair of scimitar-horned oryx grazing at a Khai-Bar reserve.

Protecting the Coast

Israel's Mediterranean coast is 200 km (120 miles) long but fast dwindling. The golden beaches stretch from the sand dunes dividing Israel from the Palestinian Gaza strip in the south to Rosh Hanikra, a delightful network of underground caves on the coast by the Lebanese border reached by cable car from cliffs down to the sea. About half of the coastline falls under the jurisdiction of Israeli municipalities, which for the most part have lined the seafront with expensive housing developments and hotels.

Even the beaches are not always accessible to the public for free as local authorities often charge a fee. Elsewhere, marinas have been built in Ashkelon and Ashdod, Tel Aviv and Herzliya and the deep seaports of Ashdod and Haifa are being greatly expanded, while power stations, military installations and private developments deny the public access to several kilometers more of the coastline.

The Coastline Protection Law, which was enacted by the Knesset in 2004, is designed to stop this erosion of one of Israel's most important environmental assets. The Law dictates that, in those areas where the coast does not belong to a city's municipality, there can be no major construction within 300 meters (980 ft) of the beach.

Unique ecosystem

For many "greens" the Law is too little too late. The 300-meter limit fails to protect the huge sand dunes that remain just inland from the coast, brought up from the North African deserts by winds and currents over millennia.

Many of the Jewish settlements in the Gush Katif region of the Gaza strip are scheduled to be re-built in the Nitzanim region north of Ashkelon, the country's last major unspoiled area of these sand dunes and their unique ecosystem. High-rise coastal developments also spoil the view of the sea and block the breezes which cool the inland regions.

Nor does the Law touch on the dire state of Israel's rivers. Although best known for the north–south River Jordan, Israel has several dozen smaller east–west rivers, which flow into the Mediterranean Sea. And while the River Jordan provides much of the country's drinking water, a mouthful of the hopelessly polluted River Yarkon in Tel Aviv or the River Kishon in Haifa will almost certainly result in a fatal lung infection. The River Poleg near Netanya is frequently contaminated with sewage, although elsewhere progress has been made in cleaning rivers. Sea turtles have returned to the mouths of the Alexander and Hadera rivers north of Netanya.

One continuing difficulty is that, despite the good intentions of a large proportion of the population, "green" issues are rarely on the political agenda. This isn't because Israelis are indifferent to them, but because issues of war and peace tend to shoulder other concerns to one side.

Despite the problems, Israel's Mediterranean coastline is still dominated by golden, sun-soaked beaches while the sea itself, with its dangerously deceptive strong undercurrents, is cleaner than it once was when particles of oil would annoyingly stick to bathers' bodies.

The best beaches are at Nitzanim in the south (when it's not being used for pop concerts in the summer), Caesarea in the center of the country, where you can bathe amid the Roman ruins, and at Achziv north of Nahariya.

Other delightful seaside spots, romantically enhanced by civilization's concrete onslaught, are the ancient ports and fishing villages at Yafo, near Tel Aviv, and Akko, north of Haifa. ❑

RIGHT: the old fishing village of Akko.

A HIGH-TECH ECONOMY

From internet and mobile phone applications to medical devices and biotech,
Israel's industry has invested heavily in new technology

With more than 300 million downloads worldwide, ICQ (standing for I seek you) is the most disseminated item to have come out of the Holy Land since the Bible. ICQ and the messaging clones, which have since imitated it such as Microsoft's Messenger, have revolutionized the lifestyle of young

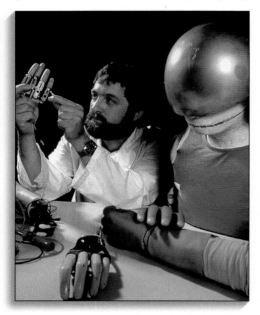

people and the way they communicate. The story behind ICQ also reflects Israel's success in establishing itself as a leading player in the global high-tech economy.

Back in the mid-1990s four Israelis in their early twenties had an idea. Arik Vardi, Sefi Vigiser, Amnon Amir and Yair Goldfinger loved the internet but felt frustrated that computers could only find other computers on-line but could not bring together specific individuals. For two years they set about rectifying the matter through a company they set up called Mirabilis, which created peer-to-peer architecture with a central server that provides users with other users' internet addresses. Arik's father

Yossi, one of Israel's leading businesspeople who had set up Israel Chemicals in 1967, provided capital and entrepreneurial know-how, and in 1998 Mirabilis (and ICQ) were sold to America On Line for $407 million.

In Israel itself the Mirabilis effect was felt far beyond the computer screen. It inspired thousands of young high-tech entrepreneurs in the country to dare to transform their dreams into viable business products thorough their own start-up companies rather than existing corporations. And it persuaded the business world that there were huge returns to be reaped from carefully selected investments in high-tech start-ups. For an investment of several million dollars, Mirabilis had hit the jackpot. And it emphasized to the international business community that Israel had unique systems and solutions to offer.

Despite the downturn in high-tech in 2002–03, Israel's advanced technology industries have gone from strength to strength. In the past decade Israel's commercial landscape has been transformed from a sluggish economy, which often seemed to draw on the worst aspects of capitalism and socialism, to a dynamic marketplace attracting billions of dollars in overseas investments. The gleaming glass high-rise towers sprouting up throughout Tel Aviv testify to the country's new-found affluence. Elsewhere there are impressive high-tech industrial parks in Haifa and Beer Sheva, Herzliya and Petakh Tikvah, Rekhovot and Jerusalem.

A new business model

Small operations like Mirabilis, which then sells the technology it has developed to a global corporation, have become an industrial sector of their own and created a new business model in Israel. Cisco Systems alone has acquired eight Israeli communications start-ups for $950 million, while Kodak has spent $1.5 billion purchasing six Israeli digital imaging firms. Intel bought just one Israeli firm, which makes chips for mobile phones for $1.6 billion and Marvell Technologies acquired a firm which develops advanced communications on silicon for $2.7

million. The biggest acquisition of an Israeli start-up was the $4.8 billion that Lucent Technologies paid for Chromatis Networks and its optical communications systems.

In addition, Israeli start-ups have raised billions of dollars on overseas stock markets. More than 100 Israeli firms are traded on international markets, mainly in New York and London. The country's 70 venture capital firms have generated over $15 billion in investment funds over the past decade and mobilized more than $40 billion in transactions related to the Israeli high-tech sector. Companies investing in Israeli venture capital firms include Boeing, BT, Deutsche

puter software and laser technology have enabled Israeli cutters to improve their competitiveness.

But it was military necessity more than anything else that enabled the country to develop leading-edge industries. Israel is one of only eight countries worldwide with an independent space launch capability and is a global leader in Unmanned Aerial Vehicles, missile technology, electro-optics, lasers, radar and intelligence systems, and homeland defense solutions.

Israel's only natural resources – the bromine, potash and magnesium in the Dead Sea and phosphates in the Negev – were of little use until the 1980s and '90s when scientists devel-

Telekom, France Telecom, Alcatel, Siemens, Samsung and the like.

High-tech oranges

Israel has always been strong on technology. Even the Jaffa orange and Israel's other agricultural exports have been based on developing new species of fruit and vegetables, irrigation techniques, greenhouse technology, pesticides and fertilizers. The country is the world's largest producer of cut and polished diamonds, selling $7 billion worth of stones a year, and here too com-

LEFT: cybernetics at the Haifa bio-med faculty.
ABOVE: the Diamond Exchange, Ramat Gan.

PROTECTING MURDOCH

In the late 1980s Professor Adi Shamir (no relation to the other Shamirs) of the Weizmann Institute in Rekhovot persuaded Rupert Murdoch to acquire his encryption system to protect his new Sky TV satellite service. Murdoch's News Data Corp. also set up NDS, headquartered in London but with its development and manufacturing plant in Jerusalem. In a business revolving around code breaking – counterfeit cards giving access to satellite channels are a potential money-spinner for crooks – many of NDS's senior executives are former Mossad agents. NDS Israel, a global leader in its field, has annual sales of nearly $500 million.

oped more efficient ways of extraction and uses for them. More than $3.5 billion of these minerals are now sold each year.

Typically an Israeli high-tech executive is a graduate of one of the country's leading universities and an elite combat army unit. Indeed, many global firms will invest in or acquire an Israeli firm, not only for its systems and solutions, but also to have access to a high-tech team capable of fast-tracking a complex project.

Intel's investment

For many years, though it happens less frequently these days, Israel would lose its best

FROM RUSSIA WITH LOVE

The million new immigrants from the former Soviet Union who arrived in the 1990s brought new technological ideas, which could be developed with local entrepreneurs. One Russian immigrant, for example, approached Israel Chemicals with some interesting information. Back in the Soviet Union, he had worked for a Russian mining firm that had developed a highly efficient way of extracting magnesium from the sea. Israel Chemicals purchased the technology from the Russian company and set up Dead Sea Magnesium, a joint venture with Volkswagen, which extracts hundreds of millions of dollars worth of magnesium alloy each year for use as a lightweight metal in vehicles.

minds to the US. One such man was Dr Dov Frohman, who was part of the Intel team which developed the first computer chip in the 1970s. But he set a trend of returning home and set up Intel Israel in the 1980s, encompassing both an R&D center and semiconductor producing plant which today has annual exports of nearly a billion dollars. Motorola, Hewlett Packard, Philips, IBM and Microsoft and just some of the major multinational corporations which have established significant manufacturing and development facilities in Israel.

Not all Israeli technology has been sold off to the highest international bidder. Many local firms have hung onto their products and generated annual sales of hundreds of millions of dollars, including Amdocs (telephone billing), Comverse (telecom systems and software), ECI Telecom (advanced telecom solutions), Check-Point Technologies (internet security) and Alvarion (wireless broadband systems).

But by far the largest Israeli company is Teva Pharmaceuticals, the world's biggest manufacturer of generic drugs (pharmaceuticals whose patents have expired), with annual sales of over $9 billion. Teva is also tapping into Israel's fast growing biotech sector to develop its own original pharmaceuticals and one such drug – Copaxone, for the treatment of multiple sclerosis – has annual sales alone of $1.7 billion.

The poor get poorer

However, Israel's high-tech revolution has not benefited everybody. Alongside greater prosperity, governments have dismantled many aspects of the socialist state which existed prior to 2000. Although there is high-quality medical care for all citizens, government welfare payments to the unemployed, single parents, large families and the elderly, which were already low by western standards, were cut even further by Finance Minister Binyamin Netanyahu in 2003. Consequently the gap between rich and poor in Israel is wider than in any other developed country except for the US.

According to Israel's National Insurance Institute, 20 percent of Israeli families and 28 percent of children live below the poverty line. For them, faster internet, 3G mobile phones and satellite technology offer little comfort. ❏

LEFT: Israelis were early adopters of cellphones.

Sport

Historically, sport and Judaism did not mix. In biblical times the Greek love of physical prowess conflicted with the Jewish moral code and Ancient Greece's attempts to impose its culture throughout the region was resented by the Israelites. Even today ultra-orthodox Jews reject sport as "Hellenistic."

Down the centuries Jews maintained this aversion to sport. Emphasizing the spiritual and intellectual, Judaism rejected the physical world of sport. Secular Zionists determined to create the new Jew who was a soldier and farmer, saw sport as the ideal means to these ends. Sports movements were established in the early 20th century, tied to political movements – Hapoel (Labor), Betar (Likud) and Maccabi (the defunct Liberal party). Even the orthodox Jewish community got into sport, founding Elitzur. These sports clubs exist today and often the political connections have survived – Betar Jerusalem is a bastion of the right and Hapoel Tel Aviv is associated with the left.

Headline events

These clubs encompass amateurs and professionals. Professionally, Israeli sport was slow to take off. The national soccer team reached the World Cup finals for the one and only time in Mexico in 1970. Tragically, the only sporting headline Israel ever made was when Palestinians at the Munich Olympics in 1972 gunned down 11 members of the country's Olympic squad. It was not until the 1992 Olympics in Barcelona that Israel won its first Olympic medals, and the country celebrated its first gold medal in Athens in 2004 when Gal Fridman won the windsurfing competition.

In professional sport Israel benefited from its expulsion from Asian sporting federations in 1968. Consequently the country was accepted into the European sporting federations such as UEFA in soccer and is entitled to compete in such prestigious competitions as the UEFA Champions League. Maccabi Haifa and Maccabi Tel Aviv have both reached the lucrative Group stage with Haifa even enjoying a 3–0 victory over the mighty Manchester United. Individual players have had successful careers in Europe's top leagues, including

RIGHT: fans of the Maccabi Tel Aviv soccer club cheer on their team.

Haim Revivo in Spain's La Primera Liga and Eyal Berkovic, Tal Ben Haim and Yossi Benayoun in England's Premiership.

At club level Israel has best excelled in basketball, with Maccabi Tel Aviv winning back-to-back European titles in 2004 and 2005. In tennis Israel has had top 20 players in the 1980s (Shlomo Glickstein), 1990s (Amos Mansdorf) and more recently the appropriately named Anna Smashnova and Shahar Peer. Like Alex Averbukh, the European pole vaulting champion, Smashnova is an immigrant from the former Soviet Union.

However, with the exception of the occasional World Cup qualifier or Champions League match,

there is little to interest the visitor in terms of professional sport or major tournaments. The biggest sporting festival in Israel is the Maccabiah, recognized by the IOC as the Jewish Olympics, when Diaspora Jewish communities compete for medals. The event is held every four years, and the 18th Maccabiah will take place in July 2009.

Visitors to Israel will most enjoy the country's participatory water sports, with surfing and windsurfing, water skiing and swimming in the Mediterranean, the Sea of Galilee and the Red Sea. The country has the highest number of licensed divers proportionally in the world and diving is the best way to make the acquaintance of the Red Sea's remarkable marine life. ❏

PLACES

A detailed guide to the whole of Israel, with principal sites
clearly cross-referenced by number to the maps

Arriving at Ben Gurion Airport, visitors are likely to choose one of two directions: eastwards up through the Judean Hills to Jerusalem, with its history and religion, or westwards past the fragrant citrus groves to Tel Aviv, Israel's bustling, economic capital, a brash place with golden beaches and a pulsating nightlife, a city looking to its future rather than its past.

From east to west, Israel (including the Palestinian autonomous zones) is less than 100 km (60 miles) at its broadest points. Tel Aviv is at the heart of the coastal plain, a densely populated, narrow piece of land stretching from the Gaza Strip in the south to Lebanon in the north, with mild, wet, sunny winters and hot, humid summers.

The inland hills to the east offer cooler, drier climes. Jerusalem is perched on a peak 830 meters (2,700 ft) high, and other ancient cities such as the West Bank towns of Bethlehem, Hebron and Nablus are also built on hills. Here the hot, dry summers are tempered by delicious late afternoon breezes and in the winter there can even be a dusting of snow. In the spring, the best time to visit, the hillsides are ablaze with flowers. The terraced hillsides of olive groves and grapevines have a biblical charm, but otherwise the landscape has a Mediterranean familiarity.

The terrain east of Jerusalem has an alien, exotic charm, for, in addition to its social divisions, the Holy City is a continental divide. The western slopes lead down through forest and field to the Mediterranean, but to the east the land dips down dramatically through rugged desert to the Dead Sea basin, the lowest point on earth, and the northern stretch of the great Africa-Syria rift valley.

The craggy canyons and billowing beige hills of this desolate rock desert have historically attracted religious hermits, and contain concealed monasteries. The Dead Sea itself is really a lake with becalmed waters, that nestles amid a landscape of shimmering mountains and has a high salt content which enables bathers to float – a highlight of any trip to Israel.

The 500 km (300 miles) from north to south take the traveler from the majestic snow-covered peaks of Mount Hermon and the rolling hills of the Galilee to the tropical waters of the Red Sea resort of Eilat. En route are the Sea of Galilee, the Jordan Valley and Dead Sea, and the Arava Valley and Negev Desert. It is possible in the winter to ski on the slopes of Mount Hermon in the morning and go scuba diving in the Red Sea in the afternoon, where remarkable coral formations and exotically colored fish of all shapes and sizes are a feast for the eye. Use the itineraries in the following pages to discover the best that Israel has to offer. ❑

PRECEDING PAGES: agriculture in Samaria; anemones bloom in the Jezreel Valley, with Mount Tabor in the background; Bethlehem, surrounded by the Judean Hills.
LEFT: Rosh Hashana evening devotions on the beach at Tel Aviv.

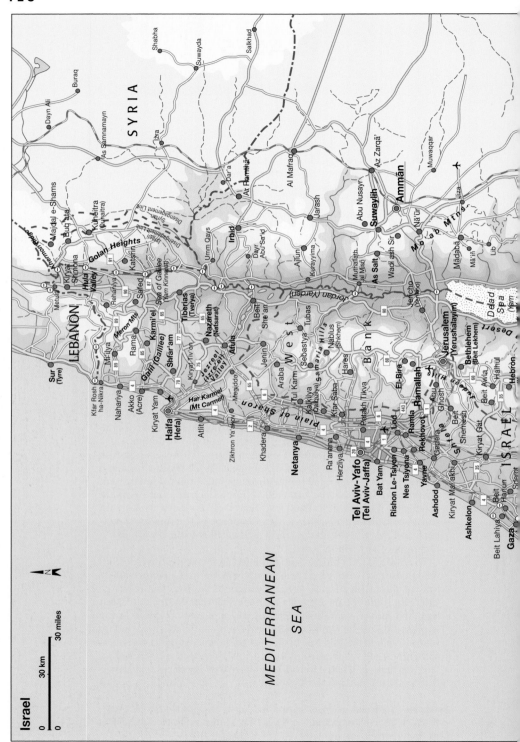

Israel

0
0

30 km

30 miles

SYRIA

LEBANON

ISRAEL

West Bank

MEDITERRANEAN
SEA

Dead
Sea
(Yam)

Desert

Moab Mtns

Jordan (Yarden)

Plain of Sharon

Samaria Hills

Judea Hills

Shabha
Suwayda
Salkhad
Buraq
Dayn Ali
As Samnamayn
Izra
Muwaqqar
Dar'a
Az Zarqā'
Liza
Ammān
Nā'ūr
At Ramtha
Al Mafraq
Irbid
Abu Nusayr
Suwaylih
Jarash
Mādaba
Umm Qays
Dayr Abu Sa'id
Ajlun
Kurayyima
Ma'in
Lib
Muthallith
al Misri
As Salt
Wadi ash Sir
Jericho
(Yeriho)
Jerusalem
(Yerushalayim)
Bethlehem
(Beit Lekhem)
Hebron
Beit Awla
Halhul
Ramallah
El-Bira
Abu
Ghosh
Beit
Shemesh
Kiryat Gat
Hares
Nāblus
(Shkhem)
Tubas
Sebastya
Jenin
Tul Karm
Araba
Kalkilya
(Qalqilya)
Kfar-Saba
Petakh Tikva
Lod
Ramla
Rehovot
Gedera
Yavne
Nes Tsiyona
Rishon Le-Tsiyon
Bat Yam
Tel Aviv-Yafo
(Tel Aviv-Jaffa)
Herzliya
Ra'anana
Netanya
Khadera
Zikhron Ya'akov
Atlit
Haifa
(Hefa)
Har Karmel
(Mt Carmel)
Kiryat Yam
Akko
(Acre)
Nahariya
Kfar Rosh
ha-Nikra
Sur
(Tyre)
Metula
Kiryat
Shmona
Buq'ata
Majdal e-Shams
Kuneitra
(Quhaitra)
Golan Heights
Katsrin
Hula
Valley
Safed
Rehaniya
Mi'ilya
Rama
Meron Mtns
Karmi'el
Shfar'am
Kiryat Tiv'on
Megiddo
Afula
Nazareth
(Natsarat)
Tiberias
(Tverya)
Sea of Galilee
(Yam Kinneret)
Bet
She'an
Ibtin
Galil (Galilee)
Jezreel
(Izrael)
Valley
Ashdod
Kiryat Malakhi
Ashkelon
Beit Lahiya
Beit Hanun
Sderot
Gaza

Thermon Line
Israeli Disengagement Line
Syrian Disengagement Line

1
91
90
87
65
77
70
85
89
75
4
2
6
4
4
5
1
28
4
40
431
443
4
3
5
80
60
90
1
1
1
35
35
1
1
4

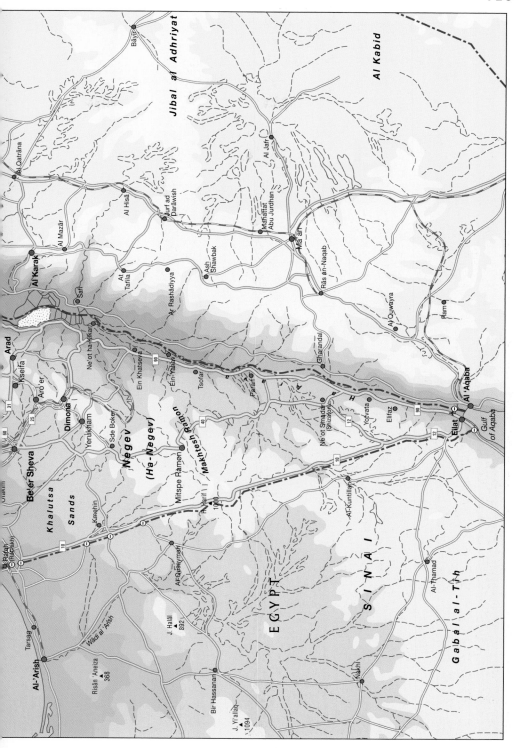

JERUSALEM YESTERDAY AND TODAY

Map on pages 160–1

The followers of three major world religions demand a say in the future of the Golden City. To appreciate why, you need to understand its turbulent past

Jerusalem has been called many things: the Golden City, the Holy City, the City of David, the City of Peace. Sadly, it is also a city of strife. To Jews, it is their national and spiritual epicenter: the incarnation of ancient Israel; the place where Abraham went to sacrifice Isaac; the site of David's glory and Solomon's Temple; the eternal capital of the Jewish people. To Christians, it is the city where Jesus spent his last days on earth: the site of the Last Supper, the Crucifixion and Resurrection. To Muslims, it is Al Quds ("The Holy"), the place where Mohammed is said to have ascended to Heaven on his steed; indeed, it is Islam's third holiest city after Mecca and Medina.

From its enduring power as a spiritual symbol, to the quality of the light, Jerusalem is unique. And today, more than 3,000 years after David made the city his capital, Jerusalem still has the ability to stir emotions and fire the imagination like no other city on earth.

LEFT: sunset from the Mount of Olives.
BELOW: opposition to a road scheme.

Visiting Jerusalem

Still the centerpiece of many a journey to Israel, as it has been throughout the centuries, Jerusalem continues to reward the traveler with its riches. The market-places, shrines, ruins, hotels, temples, churches and mosques are all readily accessible, and the city's tourist board (www. jerusalem.muni.il) is more than willing to provide directions. Yet the soul of the city is more elusive. The rhythm of daily life here is governed by prayer, usually channeled through tightly-knit religious communities, and the visitor who merely barters for trinkets in the Old City between hops to famous churches or museums is missing the source and substance of the place.

Also, as the seat of government for the state and a major academic and high-tech center, Jerusalem has an important secular profile.

Physically, Jerusalem is actually many cities in one, totalling nearly 800,000 residents. The modern part of the city, spreading out to the west, north and south, has been a Jewish enclave since its inception in the late 1800s, and from 1948 the capital of the State of Israel. Vast new Jewish neighborhoods have been built in open areas captured in 1967. In many suburbs secular, traditional and orthodox Jews live alongside each other. Meanwhile, ultra-orthodox Jews with a prolific birth rate have overflowed from Me'a She'arim in the center to Sanhedria and large new neighborhoods in the north of the city.

Most of Jerusalem east of the old "green line" that

divided it from 1948 to 1967 (during which time it was Jordanian) remains Arab, although many neighborhoods have again been cut off from Jewish Jerusalem by the new Security Wall *(see page 277)*. In the center of it all is the Old City, wrapped in its ancient golden walls, containing much of historic Jerusalem and its shrines. It, too, was in Jordanian hands up to 1967.

The Israeli victory in 1967 not only rolled away the wall but also fulfilled the 2,000-year Jewish dream of returning to the Western Wall and the Old City. Israel officially annexed the Old City and East Jerusalem in 1967, although the world still looks upon these areas as occupied territory. Ehud Barak, Israel's former prime minister, proposed keeping the Jewish and Armenian Quarters and giving the Christian and Muslim Quarters to the Palestinians.

David's capital

In ancient times it was said that the world had 10 measures of beauty, of which nine belonged to Jerusalem. The city's acclaim (or immodesty) only served to make it attractive to conquerors, and it has been the object of repeated siege and conquest. In part, this was due to its strategic situation on a vital trade route, at the crossroads between East and West. Ironically, however, it was later the very holiness of the city that inspired its would-be champions' relentless ferocity.

Jerusalem first crops up in biblical narrative during Abraham's migrations from Ur to Canaan. Here he was greeted warmly by Melchizedek, King of Salem, "Priest of the most high God". The Israelites were already well-ensconced in the hills of Judea when David captured the city from the Jebusites around 1000 BC. Building an altar for the Ark of the Covenant on the crown of Mount Moriah, he made the city his capital, renaming it Jerusalem "the Dwelling of Peace."

The Menorah at Heikhal Shlomo.

BELOW: the classic panorama of the walled city.

The 35 years under David's rule, and the subsequent 40 under Solomon, brought splendor to the once modest fortress town. The site of David's altar saw the rise of Solomon's magnificent Temple, incorporating the much-sought-after cedar wood from Lebanon, copper from the mines at Timna, and a wide variety of rich metals and carved figures. The city was embellished with the wealth of an expansive empire, its walls reaching in an oblong shape to include David's city on the slopes of Ha-Ofel and down to the pool of Silwan below.

Around 926 BC King Solomon died, and in the absence of his authority the kingdom was split in two by his successors. Jerusalem remained the capital of the southern Kingdom of Judah, as the following centuries saw the city and its kingdom succumb to the expanding control of the Assyrians. In 586 BC Nebuchadnezzar of Babylonia plundered the city, sending its inhabitants into exile. They returned in 539 BC under the policy of the new king, Cyrus the Great of Persia, and set at once to the task of building a Second Temple.

Greeks and Romans

Alexander the Great's conquest of Jerusalem in 332 BC initiated a brief Hellenisation of Jewish culture in the city and then in 198 BC the Seleucids took control. Deprived of religious rights, the Maccabees spearheaded a Jewish uprising, leading to the re-consecration of the destroyed Temple in 165 BC.

Hasmonean rule gave way in 63 BC to Rome, with the conquering armies of the Roman general Pompey. In 40 BC the Roman Senate conferred the rule on Herod the Great and sent him to Judea; during his reign his psychopathic behavior was matched only by his extensive architectural endeavors, most notably the Second Temple which, according to the historian Josephus, was built by 10,000

Map on pages 160–1

Alexander the Great exhibited great tolerance for Judaism and personally encouraged Jews to continue practising their religion.

**Map
on pages
160–1**

TIP

The Model of the
Second Temple in Bayit
Vegan near the
Holyland Hotel gives an
idea of how Jerusalem
looked 2000 years ago
(tel: 02-6437777; open
daily 8am–10pm, fee).

BELOW: wall plaque
in the Garden
of Gethsemane.
RIGHT:
at the Church of
the Holy Sepulchre.

workmen and 1,000 priests. It took eight years to complete the courtyard and another couple of years to finish the Temple itself.

When it was completed, it was widely regarded as one of the wonders of the world. Jerusalem was still a Jewish city under Roman rule when Jesus's crucifixion was ordered by the procurator Pontius Pilate around AD 30.

The increasingly insensitive Roman administration was challenged by the Jewish Revolt of 66, crushed four years later by Titus, who razed Jerusalem and plundered the Second Temple. A second rebellion was instigated by Emperor Hadrian's decree to lay the city out anew on a Roman plan and call it Aelia Capitolina; but the Bar-Kochba revolt of 132 was stamped out, and in 135 Hadrian initiated the reconstruction of the city, banning any Jew from entering its boundaries.

Christianity takes over

The great Christianization of Jerusalem was inaugurated in the 4th century by the Byzantine Emperor Constantine; in the 7th century the city fell to Muslim rule, and in 1099 to the bloody grip of the Crusaders for some 80 years. It once more came into its own under the Ottoman Emperor Suleiman, who rebuilt its walls from 1537 to 1541. After his death, until modern times, it fell into decline.

To this day, Suleiman's walls remain the most impressive monument to the city's multi-layered history. From stone stairways at various points in its span you can mount the restored Ramparts Walk, which follows every circuit but that by the Temple Mount. A "green belt" of lawns surrounds much of the circumference, adding to the view. The seven gates of the city are a source of fascination in themselves *(see page 158)*. Just inside the Jaffa Gate, which serves as the main entrance to the Old City from West Jerusalem, is the famous Citadel, or Tower of David. In reality the structure doesn't have much to do with David; it was built by Herod, who named its three towers after his wife Mariamne, his brother Phaesal and his friend Hippicus, and was so impressive that Titus let it stand after burning the city. The Mamelukes and later Suleiman reinforced it, adding its minaret.

Exploring the city with this guide

For practical purposes, we have divided the rest of the city into three chapters. "The Old City" *(page 137)* describes the sites within the city walls. "Outside the City Walls" *(page 151)* covers the many places of interest just outside the ancient boundaries; and both East and West Jerusalem are discussed in the chapter on "The New Jerusalem" *(page 163)*.

Visitors should follow their instincts in exploring this city and take detours to the less obvious sites. For any guidebook to attempt to describe Jerusalem in a few chapters is rather like asking a rabbi to describe the entire Talmud while standing on one foot, for no amount of explanation can hope to capture the spirit of this complex place: the patina of gold on the Dome of the Rock, the view from the Mount of Olives at sunset, the shifting moods of its houses and hills, the thoughtfulness and pride in the eyes of its citizens and the bizarre but beautiful echo of interwoven prayers – of all religions – that envelop the city walls, blowing in the wind, night and day. ❏

JERUSALEM: THE OLD CITY

Map on page 138

*A tour of the many sacred shrines, historic houses
and atmospheric markets contained within the
ancient walls of the Old City*

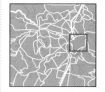

I t's a museum, a bazaar, a collection of sacred shrines. It also happens to be home for ten of thousands of residents crammed within the 4-km (2½-mile) circumference of its old battlements. Its gates never close, night or day, for the hundreds of thousands of overseas visitors who are drawn to the Old City of Jerusalem each year. The Jewish (www.myrova.com), Christian, Armenian and Muslim quarters of the Old City each have their own special significance, and this book will look at these as it suggests the most interesting walks.

Around the Jaffa Gate

The main portal between the Old City and West Jerusalem is the **Jaffa Gate ❶** The site offers a number of contemporary attractions which include the **Tower of David Museum of the History of Jerusalem ❷** (Sun–Thurs 10pm–4pm in summer until 5pm and 10pm on Sun, Tues & Thurs, closed Fri. Sat 10am–2pm; tel: 02-6265310; www.towerofdavid.org.il, fee) inside the body of the Citadel, which contains displays describing the tumultuous history of the city, figurines of Jerusalem characters, a 19th-century model of the Old City, and the multi-layered ruins of the structure itself. A multi-media show with a separate entrance describes the various moods of Jerusalem via numerous slide projectors. The walls themselves are the palette for the sound and light show presented here in a host of different languages (Apr–Oct: Sun–Thur 9am–5pm and 10pm on Sun, Tues and Thur, Fri, Sat and holidays 9am–1pm; Nov–Mar: Sun–Thur and 10am–4pm Fri, Sat and holidays 10am–1pm; tel: 02-6265333; www.towerofdavid.org.il; fee).

LEFT: visitors to the Dome of the Rock.
BELOW: the Jaffa Gate: the entrance to the Old City.

The Municipal Tourist Information Office is just inside the Jaffa Gate (Sun–Thur 8.30am–5pm; tel: 02-6271422). Also opposite the entrance to the museum is the **Christian Information Office** (Mon–Sat 8.30am–1pm; tel: 02-6272692; www.cicts.org). About 150 meters (165 yards) in from the Jaffa Gate is the narrow entrance to the labyrinthine **Bazaar** (El Bazar) **❸**. Go straight down into the Arab souk. Aggressively friendly shopkeepers will assault you with all manner of trinkets at "special prices" but take time to distinguish the quality from the trash, because both forms are plentiful. Prices in the stores nearest the Jaffa Gate are generally more expensive, and some shopkeepers even have the *chutzpah* to refuse to haggle. The further into the market, the better the bargains.

It's a wonderful place for bargain hunters. Palestinian pottery and Armenian tiles are attractive, but cheaper varieties have little glazing and will fade. Brass items such as coffee servers and tables should be judged by their weight: too light and it's probably plated tin. Too shiny is also suspect; a little tarnish suggests authenticity. Sheepskin jackets, gloves and

slippers are popular, but in time these may smell too much like sheep, especially if they get wet. At the end of the alleyway El Bazar, just before a T-junction, a black sign overhead points right to Ha-Kardo. Turn right here and almost immediately you leave the Muslim Quarter and enter the Jewish Quarter.

The Jewish Quarter

Inhabited by Jews as far back as the First Temple Period 3,000 years ago, the Jewish Quarter today is a modern neighborhood housing over 1,000 families, with numerous synagogues and *yeshivas* (academies for Jewish studies). This thriving little community was rebuilt out of the rubble following the reunification of Jerusalem in the 1967 Six Day War. Families who had lived in the quarter prior to their expulsion by the Jordanians in 1948 were the first to move back in. Religious Jews revived many of the old study houses and congregations. Artists, attracted by the picturesque lanes, soon took up residence. Today the Jewish Quarter is one of the city's most desirable (and expensive) areas.

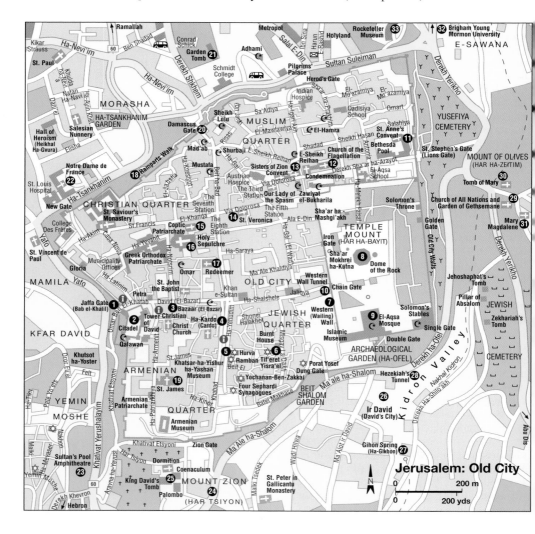

Jerusalem: Old City

Nowhere is the old-new character of the quarter more evident than in the **Ha-Kardo** (Cardo) ❹. With its modern lamps and smart shopfronts, this submerged pedestrian byway at first looks like a trendy shopping mall incongruously set next to the old bazaar. Ha-Kardo was the north-south axis of the garrison town that the Romans built after they destroyed Jerusalem in AD 70. Called Aelia Capitolina, the town was laid out geometrically like an army camp, with Ha-Kardo (from Latin: cardinal, or principal) as its main thoroughfare. In the Byzantine period this colonnaded avenue ran for 180 meters (600 ft) to a looming church called the Nea, built by Emperor Justinian in 543 and destroyed in an earthquake in the 8th century. Later the Crusaders used Ha-Kardo as a main market street. After they were expelled by the Muslims, Jerusalem reverted to a backwater and Ha-Kardo was eventually buried beneath 4 meters (13 ft) of rubble, to be excavated and brought to life again only in the 1980s.

Signs and diagrams posted along either side of the "new" Ha-Kardo pinpoint the remains of the various civilizations that conducted their daily commerce here. A large excavation reveals the outer wall of the city of the Judean King Hezekiah. At another point, Byzantine Corinthian-style columns have been restored, along with some roofing beams, to illustrate how shops once lined this thoroughfare.

The southern end of Ha-Kardo is open to the sky. Here the big paving stones lie bright in the sunlight, the columns exposed in all their classic beauty. It's also from this point outdoors that visitors can best appreciate the reconciliation of demands for a museum and a neighborhood. City planners wanted to build apartments along the route, while archaeologists insisted that the historical heart of the city be exposed. The compromise: apartments standing on stilts above the ancient avenue.

Museums and memorials

Running parallel eastwards to Ha-Kardo is **Ha-Yehudim** (Jewish Quarter Road), the site of the **The Last Ditch Battle Museum** (Sun–Thurs 9am–5pm Fri 9am–1pm; tel: 02-6288141), which offers a 15-minute multi-media presentation on the history of the area from the Israelite period to the present. The emphasis is on how the Jewish Quarter was lost to the Arab Legion in Israel's War of Independence in 1948; how it was subsequently regained in the Six Day War of 1967; and how it has since been reconstructed. The museum also has an unusual collection of pictures taken by *Life* magazine photographer John Phillips, both during the battle in 1948, and in 1975 when he returned to find and photograph the survivors.

A few steps away from the museum is a memorial to the fighters who fell defending the quarter. An electronic map recreates the battle, house by house.

Between the museum and the memorial is the Ashkenazi Court, a synagogue and residential complex established in 1400 by European Jews. The great **Hurva Synagogue** ❺ was burned by angry creditors in 1720 (hence its name, which means ruin). In 1856 it was rebuilt, but in May of 1948 it was blown up by the Arabs; today only the dynamic span of its front archway rises over the site.

Beneath the Hurva is the Ramban Synagogue, built shortly after the noted Bible commentator Rabbi

Map on page 138

When the Siebenberg family dug beneath their homes in the Jewish quarter, they found rare artifacts plus water systems and burial vaults from the First and Second Temple periods. For a personally guided tour, call the Siebenbergs at 02-6282341.

BELOW: buyers and sellers in an Old City market.

TIP

The most popular
places to eat are the
cafés on David Street;
the funky sweet shops
along Souk Khan
ez-Zeit; and
Abu-Shukri's on
El-Wad Street, which
sells wonderful
houmous.

BELOW: late after-
noon light bathes
the Jewish Quarter.

Moses Ben Nahman emigrated from Spain in 1267, and possibly the oldest of the
many houses of worship in the Jewish Quarter. Now it is used every day.

The most enchanting of the venerable houses of worship are on Ha-Kehuna in
the complex known as the **Four Sephardi Synagogues**. These synagogues have
been lovingly restored to serve both as houses of worship and as a museum documenting their destruction and rebirth. Of interest are the Italian hand-carved
Arks of the Law in the Stambouli and Prophet Elijah Synagogues, and the early
17th-century Yochanan Ben-Zakkai Synagogue with its cheery folk characters.

A short walk up Or Ha-Khayim, the **Old Yishuv Court Museum** (Mon–Thurs
10am–3pm, Fri 10am–1pm; tel: 02-6284636; fee) illustrates the lifestyles of the
Jewish community of the Old City in bygone days when immigrants from a particular village in, say, Poland or Hungary would cluster around one court, sharing many facilities. The grounds incorporate two courts and two synagogues.

At the end of Tif'eret Yisra'el is the most remarkable archaeological site in the
Jewish Quarter: the **Burnt House** ❻ (Sun–Thur 9am–5pm, Fri 9am–1pm; tel:
02-6287211; fee). This, apparently, was the residence of the priestly Bar-Kathros
clan at the time of the Jewish revolt against Rome. Among other clues, ashes from
a great conflagration indicate that the house was destroyed when Titus razed the
city. The numerous finds displayed within the house include a measuring weight
bearing the name Kathros, and the skeletal arm of a woman in the kitchen who
was apparently struggling to escape the fire.

The Western Wall

The wide stone steps at the end of Tif'eret Yisra'el lead down to the most important site – not only within the quarter, but in all of Jewish civilization. This, of

course, is the Kotel ha-Ma'aravi, or the **Western Wall** (always open; free) ❼. Clambering up and down these steps at all hours of the day and night – like so many angels ascending and descending Jacob's ladder – is a stream of worshippers, pilgrims and tourists. Below and to the left is the Western Wall plaza and the Wall itself.

Map on page 138

Above the Wall

The **Temple Mount** (Sat–Thurs 7.30–10.30am and 12.30–1.30pm, Sat–Thur 7.30am–1030am (during Ramadan); closed to non-Muslims Fri and Muslim holidays; free) is the biblical Mount Moriah where Abraham nearly sacrificed Isaac, where the First and Second Temples once loomed, and where the golden Dome of the Rock and the silvery **El-Aqsa Mosque** (same hours as Temple Mount; combined fee for Mosque, Dome and the Islamic Museum) now stand. To the right of the Temple Mount is a vast maze of archaeological excavations, which lead to the Old City Wall and the Dung Gate.

The Jewish Quarter area was known in Temple times as the Upper City. The plaza below occupies the lower end of what was called the Tyropoeon Valley, the rift that cuts through the entire length of the Old City. Because this was the lowest point in the Old City, rubble and trash have been dumped here over the centuries, filling in much of the space between the upper level and the Temple Mount (and giving the Dung Gate its inglorious name).

Rising to a height of 15 meters (50 ft), the Western Wall consists chiefly of massive carved stone blocks from the Herodian era, topped by masonry from the Mameluke and Turkish periods. Contrary to popular belief, it was not a part of the Temple itself, but merely the retaining wall for the western side of the Tem-

Gender segregation is strictly enforced at the Western Wall with men praying to the left and women to the right.

BELOW: praying at the Western Wall.

ple Mount. But because it was the only remnant of the Temple complex to survive the Romans' sack of the city, it has inspired the reverence of Jewish people for 2,000 years. Because Jews also gathered here to bemoan the loss of the Temple, the place earned the evocative sobriquet "Wailing Wall."

The tunnel-like enclosure at the northern end of the Wall is the site of continuing excavations. The main arch, named after the 19th-century British explorer Captain Charles Wilson, may have supported a huge pedestrian bridge between the Temple Mount and the Upper City. Below the arch is the deep shaft dug by Wilson's contemporary, Sir Charles Warren. Archaeologists have determined that the Wall extends another 15 meters (50 ft) below ground level.

The Temple Mount

Turkish coffee, a legacy of the Ottoman Empire.

Mosques and shrines dot the various quarters of the Old City, and most of the gates exhibit Islamic calligraphy, but the glories of Islamic Jerusalem are on the Temple Mount, which Muslims call **Haram esh-Sharif**, the Venerable Sanctuary, so this may be a good moment for a brief history of the Muslim impact on Jerusalem. It came essentially in three stages: the first was shortly after the death of Mohammed, when his successors spread the faith out of Arabia and wrested Jerusalem from the crumbling Byzantine Empire in 638. In this period Caliph Omar built a mosque on the Temple Mount, which was later expanded to the Dome of the Rock, and in the 8th century the El-Aqsa Mosque was constructed nearby.

BELOW:

celebrating a bar mitzvah at the Wall.

The second Muslim phase followed the brief Crusader occupation of the Holy Land. The Europeans were defeated by Saladin, and with the recovery of Jerusalem in 1187 the Muslims began a major reconstruction of the city and especially of the mosques. By 1249 the dominant Muslims were the Mamelukes, former slaves from Asia Minor who were highly accomplished architects and artisans. Much of the beauty of Islamic Jerusalem today is attributable to the work of the Mamelukes.

But corruption and dissolution marked their regime, and by 1516 the Mamelukes were easy prey for the invading Ottoman Turks. For the next 400 years Jerusalem was ruled from Constantinople. Early in this period (1520–66) Suleiman I built the city ramparts that we see today, the Damascus Gate and the greatest water system in the city from the time of Herod to the present. After Suleiman, however, the city simply stagnated until the collapse of the Ottoman Empire in World War I.

Today the Mount is the most disputed portion of this contentious city. The Arab nations are determined that an Islamic flag must fly over the site. In deference to the local Muslim authorities, Israel leaves the administration of Haram esh-Sharif entirely to Muslim officials. Israeli Border Police provide security in the area, but in cooperation with Arab policemen.

Israel's Chief Rabbinate, meanwhile, has banned Jews from visiting the Temple Mount, because somewhere on the hill is the site of the ancient Temple's Holy of Holies, the inner sanctuary which only the High Priest was allowed to enter, and even then only on one day of the year, Yom Kippur. Nevertheless, certain ultra-nationalist Israelis calling themselves the

"Temple Faithful" periodically attempt to hold prayer services on the mount, an act that invariably incenses both the Arab community and other Jews.

Dome of the Rock

The most eye-catching structure on Haram esh-Sharif is the **Dome of the Rock** ❽. The outside of the edifice, which is a shrine and not a mosque, is a fantasia of marble, mosaics and stained glass, painted tiles and quotations from the Koran, all capped by the gold-plated aluminium dome. Notable, too, are the curved pillars at the top of the steps, from which, according to tradition, scales will be hung on Judgement Day to weigh the souls of mankind.

The inside of the Dome of the Rock focuses on the huge boulder called the **Kubbet es-Sakhra**. This is the sacred rock on which Abraham was said to have prepared the sacrifice of Isaac. It is also the spot on which, during his mystical journey to Jerusalem, Mohammed is said to have mounted his steed and ascended to heaven. Appropriately enough, the heavenly interior of the famous golden dome shines down from above, a truly joyous achievement in gold leaf, mosaic and stained glass. Beneath the rock, meanwhile, is a crypt where the spirits of the dead are said to gather.

The silver-capped mosque at the southern end of the mount is **El-Aqsa** ❾, a vast complex that can accommodate as many as 5,000 worshippers. Serving essentially as a prayer hall, El-Aqsa is more functional in design than the Dome of the Rock. Probably built on the remains of a Byzantine basilica, it also straddles vast underground chambers known as **Solomon's Stables**, where a new mosque has been built recently which some fear has undermined the foundations of the El-Aqsa mosque.

Map on page 138

TIP

Shoes must be taken off before entering the Dome of the Rock and El-Aqsa Mosque. Islam looks upon shoes with disdain and to sit in anyway that shows a Muslim the sole of your shoe is considered the height of rudeness.

BELOW:
the monumental Dome of the Rock.

El-Aqsa features prominently in the modern history of the region. It was on the doorstep of this mosque in 1951 that a Muslim fanatic murdered Jordan's King Abdullah in sight of his little grandson, who became King Hussein, father of the present King Abdullah. In 1969 a deranged Australian set fire to the building, causing extensive damage (reconstruction is still in progress) and sparking off inflammatory calls throughout the Muslim nations for a *jihad*, or holy war, against Israel.

The **Islamic Museum** adjoining El-Aqsa has interesting exhibits covering centuries of Muslim life in Jerusalem, including lamps, weapons and ancient Korans. Also noteworthy are the mount's elaborately carved fountains, intricate wrought-iron gates, the miniature Dome of the Chain and the marble-and-stone *minbar,* or preaching pulpit, outside El-Aqsa.

Although this area can ignite so much political passion throughout the Middle East, it is a tranquil place, marked by sunny plazas and quiet gardens where the wind sighs through the trees.

Troublesome tunnel

In front of the Western Wall is the entrance to the controversial **Western Wall Tunnel ⑩**. Here archaeologists have dug out a 2,000-year-old street leading along the rim of the Temple Mount several hundred meters northwards to the Via Dolorosa as it passes through the Muslim Quarter. The Arabs have always feared that the tunneling was a Zionist plot to get under the Temple Mount and blow up the mosques, even though excavations are not actually under Haram esh-Sharif.

The **Jerusalem Archaeological Park** is to the right of the Western Wall

TIP

Tours through the Western Wall Tunnel must be booked in advance. For details, tel: 02-6271333.

BELOW: a doorway on the Via Dolorosa.
RIGHT: a Via Dolorosa street scene.

(Sun–Thurs 9am–4pm, Fri 9am–2pm; fee). It contains a broad stairway where prophets harangued the crowds on their way to the Temple, the abutment called **Robinson's Arch** (after its 19th-century American discoverer, Dr Edward Robinson), and the remains of palatial buildings and purification baths from Temple times. Seen from the walkway above the excavations, the site is a jigsaw puzzle of incomprehensible stone, but a licensed guide with Bible in hand brings the area to life. New excavations enable the public to see the actual shop-lined street that bordered the surroundings of the Second Temple before it was destroyed in AD 70.

The road to Calvary

Rome likes to think of itself as the center of the Christian world, and St Peter's Basilica is certainly grander than anything Jerusalem has to offer. Yet within the worn walls of Jerusalem are two places that stir the most casual Christian: the Via Dolorosa and Calvary. These names reside in the consciousness and reverberate in the vocabulary of all Western civilization.

Archaeologists, as they are wont to do, maintain that neither the Via Dolorosa nor any of the other major sites that we identify today with the Crucifixion corresponds to historical reality. But if the Via Dolorosa that we traverse was not walked upon 2,000 years ago, some ancient road is buried underneath the present ground level. Pilgrims should not be unduly distressed that today's Via Dolorosa is a commercial street, complete with a Jesus Prison Souvenir shop and a Ninth Station Boutique. Bear in mind that the lane was a bustling city street at the time of Jesus.

The **Via Dolorosa** begins near St Stephen's Gate (also called the Lions' Gate) which, despite, the surrounding churches, is actually in the Muslim Quarter. In the 1990s the municipality undertook an elaborate and delicate project of repairing the Via Dolorosa that included the restoration of collapsing buildings and overhead arches along the route, the replacement of the 400-year-old sewage system, and proper demarcation of the Stations of the Cross. When the plaza was cleared of rubble, huge paving stones dating from the Roman period were exposed. These stones, which have been revealed at a few points elsewhere along the route, may very well have been walked on by Jesus and his followers.

Stations of the Cross

Guided tours are recommended, especially as some of the Stations of the Cross are difficult to locate in the maze of the Old City.

Begin at the **Convent of St Anne** just inside from St Stephen's Gate (open Mon–Sat; fee) **⓫**, considered to be the best-preserved Crusader church in the entire Holy Land. In addition to a crypt designated as Mary's Birthplace, the church compound contains the Bethesda Pool where Jesus performed a miraculous cure.

The **First Station of the Cross**, where Jesus was sentenced, is tucked away on the left inside the courtyard of the Umariyah school, a Muslim boys' institution. The **Second Station**, where Jesus received the Cross, is opposite, on the street outside the **Chapel of Condemnation** and the **Church of the Flagellation** **⓬**. It

A street whose name is recognized around the world.

BELOW: a Roman road found beneath the Via Dolorosa.

Map on page 138

was here that Jesus was scourged and had the crown of thorns placed on his head. The latter church also has a graceful courtyard and quiet garden.

The events associated with the first two stations are believed to have taken place in Herod's **Antonia Fortress**, remains of which are found beneath the churches along the Via Dolorosa. In the nearby **Convent of the Sisters of Zion** , for example, is a huge underground chamber called the Lithostrotos (Mon–Sat; tel: 02-6277292; fee), often said to be the place where Pilate judged Jesus; on the paving stones outside are signs of board games played by Roman soldiers.

Outside is the **Ecce Homo Arch**, which some maintain was constructed by Emperor Hadrian in the 2nd century and which takes its name from Pilate's jeer "Behold the man." At the end of 1985 the Sisters of Zion dedicated a Roman arch inside the church which they contend is the Ecce Homo.

Almost all of the subsequent stations on the Via Dolorosa are marked by plaques bearing the appropriate quotations from the Bible, and many are accompanied by a fan-like design in cobblestones on the street.

The **Third Station**, where Jesus fell with the Cross, is commemorated by a column in a wall on Ha-Gai (El Wad), which the Via Dolorosa traverses. Just beyond is the **Fourth Station**, where Jesus encountered Mary. On this site is the **Armenian Catholic Church of Our Lady of the Spasm**, which has a notable Byzantine mosaic in its crypt.

The Via Dolorosa at this point becomes a fairly steep and crowded commercial lane ascending to the right from Ha-Gai. The **Fifth Station**, just at the juncture of Ha-Gai and the Via Dolorosa, is where Simon the Cyrenian helped Jesus carry the Cross. A bit farther on is the **Sixth Station**, at the **House of St Veronica** , where Veronica cleansed the face of Jesus with her veil.

Detail from carving at the Fourth Station of the Cross.

BELOW: Easter procession along the Via Dolorosa.

At the point where the Via Dolorosa bisects the souk's Khan ez-Zeit bazaar is the **Seventh Station**, where Jesus fell again. This is also believed to be the site of the Gate of Judgement from which Jesus was led out of the city to the place of crucifixion, and where his death sentence was publicly posted.

The Via Dolorosa at this point disappears; buildings cover the rest of the route to the Church of the Holy Sepulchre. But both the church and the last Stations of the Cross are close by. The **Eighth Station** is outside the **Greek Orthodox Chapel of St Charalampos**, constructed on the site where Jesus addressed the women with the words "Weep not for me, but weep for Jerusalem." At the **Coptic Patriarchate** compound ⓯ off the Khan ez-Zeit bazaar, a pillar marks the **Ninth Station**, where Jesus stumbled for the third time. This is one of the more unusual churches in the city. The monastery is a replica of an African mud-hut village, and the nearby Coptic chapel is located on the roof of the Church of the Holy Sepulchre, within which are located the final Stations of the Cross.

The Holy Sepulchre

Experienced travelers are probably aware that, the more venerated a shrine in the mind of the pilgrim, the more disconcerting the reality can be. In the case of the **Church of the Holy Sepulchre** ⓰ (daily, dawn to dusk) both its size and its complexity are rather bewildering. Here, at the highest point in the Old City, the Romans had a temple dedicated to Venus. Emperor Constantine the Great erected a church here in the 4th century, after his mother Helena identified the tomb of Jesus. Constantine's church was later destroyed, and the present church was built by the Crusaders in the 12th century. Much more has been added since the Crusaders left.

Map on page 138

Protestants doubt that the Church of the Holy Sepulchre is the true site of the crucifixion and resurrection. In the 19th century General Gordon identified the Garden Tomb as the possible site of Jesus's tomb and the garden today belongs to the Anglicans (see *page 151**).*

BELOW: a priest lights candles in the Holy Sepulchre.

TIP

Sahlab, a sweet,
spiced warm drink
peddled by vendors
outside the Damascus
Gate, is a combination
of cornstarch, water,
milk, vanilla and
sugar. It tastes espe-
cially good in winter
and is said to relieve
stomach problems.

BELOW AND RIGHT:
the venerated
Church of the Holy
Sepulchre.

Several Christian communities currently share the church, each maintaining its own chapels and altars and conducting services according to its own schedule. Each is responsible for the sanctity and maintenance of a scrupulously specified area. Church fathers have battled in the past over such issues as who cleans which steps. With its gloomy interior, its bustle of construction work, its competing chants and multiple aromas of incense, the Church of the Holy Sepulchre can seem intimidating. Freelance guides cluster about the doorway, offering to show visitors around for an unspecified fee. While some are competent and sincere, many have a routine in English limited "Here chapel, very holy. There picture, famous, famous."

Despite all this, the church maintains its magnificence. The focal points, of course, are the section built over the hillock where the Crucifixion took place (called Golgotha, from the Hebrew, or Calvary, from the Latin), and the tomb where Jesus was laid. These sites encompass the continuation of the Via Dolorosa and the final Stations of the Cross.

Stairs to the right just inside the door to the church lead up to **Calvary**. The **Tenth Station**, where Jesus was stripped of his garments, is marked by a floor mosaic. The next three stations are located at Latin and Greek altars on this same level and within a few paces of each other. They mark the nailing of Jesus to the Cross, the placing of the Cross, and the removal of Christ's body. The **Fourteenth Station** is below the Holy Sepulchre: the tomb is downstairs under the church's main rotunda. Within the Holy Sepulchre are the Angel's Chapel, the rock that was miraculously rolled away from the tomb entrance, the chapel containing the burial site, and the adjacent tomb of Joseph of Arimathea.

Other notable sites within the church complex include the Catholikon, the

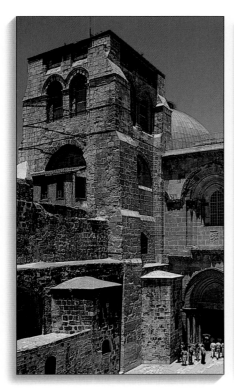

Greek cathedral close to the main rotunda, with its stone chalice on the floor marking the center of the world; chapels dedicated to St Helena, to Adam, and to the Raising of the Cross; and tombs of the Crusader Kings of Jerusalem. It is these side chapels and cavern-like tombs that offer contemplative visitors respite from the troops of tour groups that pour through the church. In a chapel beneath the main floor of the church one can sit in relative silence, listening to an Eastern Orthodox mass being chanted in a distant nave, or perhaps watching a solitary monk polishing a candlestick.

An Armenian choirboy.

Outside the Holy Sepulchre are churches of most denominations. To the right on the corner of Muristan outside the plaza's left exit (when leaving the Church of the Holy Sepulchre) is the graceful **Lutheran Church of the Redeemer ⑰**. Its tower, the highest point in the Old City (open Mon–Sat; fee), offers a magnificent view of the Old City.

The main access to the Christian Quarter is the **New Gate** – so named because it was punched through the Old City walls relatively recently, in 1887. Winding into the city from the gate are Ha-Patriarkhiya Ha-Yevanit, Ha-Notsrim and Ha-Latinim (Greek Orthdox, Catholic and Latin Patriarchate roads), all leading to their respective compounds, with churches that often contain interesting libraries and museums.

From the Church of the Holy Sepulchre the main thoroughfare northwards leads to the Damascus Gate. From here – as from most of the city gates – there is access to the **Ramparts Walk ⑱** (daily 9am–4pm; fee), a walk around the top of the city walls which provides marvelous views. To visit the Old City's remaining quarter – the Armenian Quarter – return via Muristan and David Street to the exit of the bazaar near the Jaffa Gate and then head southwards past the Christian Information Center.

BELOW: olive wood images of Mary and Jesus for sale.

The Armenian Quarter

Ha-Patriarkhiya Ha-Armenit is the street leading around the Citadel up from the David Street bazaar. Between the Christian Information Center and the post office stand Christ Church and the Anglican Hospice, the 19th-century base for many of the British diplomats and clergymen who encouraged the exploration and modernisation of Ottoman Jerusalem.

The road passes through a brief tunnel and into the **Armenian Quarter ⑲**, entered on the left through a gate – this is a walled enclave within a walled city. Entrance to the Armenian Quarter is permitted only on Mon–Fri 6.30am–7.30am and 3–3.40pm; Sat and Sun 6.30am–9.30am). A modest doorway leads to the 12th-century **St James's Cathedral**, one of the most impressive churches in the Old City.

A little further on is the **Armenian Museum**, a graceful cloister housing a fascinating collection of manuscripts and artefacts. Jerusalem's 2,000 or so Armenians live in a tight community behind the cathedral-museum complex. As one of the smallest ethnic groups, they have a reputation for keeping to themselves. But in fact they are quite outgoing, proud of being descendants of the first nation to adopt Christianity, usually fluent in English, and most hospitable to visitors. ❏

Map on page 138

OUTSIDE THE CITY WALLS

Just outside Jerusalem's ramparts are some of the most revered sites in Christendom and some extraordinary examples of excavation

Map on page 138

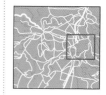

The sites surrounding the Old City walls are also redolent with religious significance. In addition, the streets just outside the Damascus Gate form the city center of Arab Jerusalem. The **Damascus Gate** ⓴, from where you may have begun the Ramparts Walk (*see page 149*), is the grandest entryway to the Old City. Landscaped in the 1990s, its plaza offers one of Jerusalem's best forums for people-watching. The **Roman Square Museum** (Sat–Thur 9am–5pm Fri 9am–1pm; fee) beneath the gate examines the Roman era of the city from the lower-level portal of that period. Also under the Old City walls close by are **Solomon's Quarries** (Sat–Thur 9am–5pm Fri 9am–1pm; fee), an ancient mine which tunnels deep below the alleys to Mount Moriah.

The **East Jerusalem Bus Station**, just opposite, operates buses to points in the West Bank, using independent Arab lines. From alongside the Old City, East Jerusalem's two main avenues, Derekh Shkem (**Nablus Road**) and **Salah E-Din**, lead into a cobweb of traffic.

Several hundred meters to the north of the Damascus Gate, along Derekh Shkem, you will come to the **Garden Tomb** ⓴ (Mon–Sat at 9am–noon, 2–5.30pm; free). Within a landscape reminiscent of a sumptuous English garden, this is a dual-chambered cave that Anglicans and other Protestants claim could have been the tomb of Jesus. The Garden Tomb is situated on a hill which, if viewed from the East Jerusalem Bus Station, suggests to many the shape of a skull, which is the meaning of the Hebrew word Golgotha.

A vast necropolis

The whole of East Jerusalem is in fact something of a vast necropolis, and is rife with caves and burial crypts. These include **Jeremiah's Grotto**, where the prophet supposedly wrote his Lamentations over Jerusalem, and the **Tomb of Simon the Just**, a Jewish high priest alive in the 3rd century BC. The most awesome chamber is **Tomb of the Kings** – although it is misnamed, being in fact the tomb of Queen Helena of Mesopotamia, who converted to Judaism in 54 BC.

The hill to the west of the Damascus Gate is dominated by the splendid 19th-century **Hospice of Notre Dame de France** ⓴ which is opposite the New Gate. The grandiose, ornate French architecture suggests that pilgrims were not expected to suffer deprivation – and indeed the building now houses a luxury hotel with a *cordon bleu* French restaurant. The building has a fascinating history, too. Badly damaged in the 1948 war, Notre Dame remained abandoned on the dividing line between Arab and Jewish Jerusalem. When it suffered further damage in the Six Day War, the French Assumptionists decided to cut their losses and sold the building to the Hebrew University in 1972. The Vatican

LEFT: an Arab shopkeeper.
BELOW: the Garden Tomb.

was livid that such a prime piece of Catholic real estate in the Holy Land had been relinquished. Rome decided to challenge the sale in Israel's civil courts, claiming that under canon law a Catholic property cannot be sold without Vatican consent. To avoid an awkward trial the Israeli government (which owns the Hebrew University) agreed to sell Notre Dame to the Vatican.

Turning left into Yafo and following the Old City walls, you can see that the new Mamila Project to the right is nearly completed. This 19th-century district of workshops and small traders has been transformed into a complex of luxury hotels and apartments with some of the quarter's original buildings, such as the St Vincent orphanage, retained. Beyond the Jaffa Gate is **Khutsot ha-Yoster** (Arts & Crafts Lane), which houses the studios and shops of artists and artisans.

Adjoining Khutsot ha-Yoster to the south, down Derekh Khevron, is **Sultan's Pool ㉓**. This former reservoir has been converted into an amphitheater and, located beneath the walls of the Old City, has to be one of the world's most inspiring venues for outdoor concerts.

On the far side of the Derekh Khevron bridge is the **Valley of Hinnom**. It is hard to realise that these pleasant parklands are believed, in Jewish tradition, to be the scene of child sacrifices in pagan Canaanite times, and therefore synonymous with hell, which is what *Gehenom,* the Hebrew word for Hinnom, means.

Mount Zion

Mount Zion (Har Tsiyon) ㉔, overlooking Hinnom, was used as a synonym for Jerusalem and came to symbolize the Jewish yearning to return to the homeland. Indeed, at the end of the 19th century Zionism was adopted as the official name of the national movement of the Jewish people. In 1948 the Old City fell

TIP

Check the *Judaica* chapter (*page 104*) for details of recommended places to see and buy arts and crafts.

BELOW: graceful arches span the Coenaculum.

to Jordan, but Israel retained Mount Zion, and from 1948 to 1967 the historic ridge was an important lookout point for the young country, as well as its closest approach to the shrines of the Old City and Western Wall. These days Mount Zion is less controversial, if no less beloved. Churches and *yeshivas* huddle side by side amid the gardens and wind-bent pipes. Mount Zion can be reached by walking along the delightful gardens southwards from the Jaffa Gate, or alternatively for drivers from the car park outside the Zion Gate.

Within the **Diaspora Yeshiva** (www.diaspora.org.il) complex is the site of **King David's Tomb** ㉕ (Sun–Thur 8am–5pm, Fri 8am–1pm; fee). Archaeologists maintain that this is another example of a site not corresponding to historical truth, but that hasn't prevented the tomb from being venerated.

Primary among the Christian sites here is the **Coenaculum** (daily 8am–5pm; free), believed to be the Room of the Last Supper (although the Syrian Orthodox St Mark's House on Ararat Street in the Armenian Quarter makes the same claim). Today the Coenaculum is basically an elegant but bare room, empty but for the flow of daylight, and it requires considerable imagination to fill it as Leonardo did in his classic fresco. The Coenaculum is located on the second floor of the large, rambling complex that contains David's Tomb.

Turn right outside David's Tomb/Coenaculum and then head left to the **Church of the Dormition** (daily 8am–5pm; tel: 02-6719927; free), a handsome Benedictine edifice commemorating the place where Mary fell into eternal sleep. The church has a noteworthy mosaic floor and crypt, and its basilica is the site for concerts of liturgical and classical music. On the eastern slope of Mount Zion on Malki Tsedek Road is **the Church of Peter in Gallicantu** (daily 8am–5pm; free) where Jesus was supposedly imprisoned by the high priest Caiaphas.

Map on page 138

TIP

For a magnificent view of the Kidron Valley and Mount of Olives, walk down from the Zion Gate to the Dung Gate and then along the newly built promenade.

BELOW: the Church of the Dormition, on Mount Zion.

Further down the slope on Mount Zion is the **Old Protestant Cemetery**, the resting place of the British subjects who figured in the religious, cultural, archaeological and diplomatic life of 19th- and early 20th-century Jerusalem.

Above the Kidron Valley

The **City of David** ❷⓺ (Sun–Thur 8am–5pm or 8pm in summer, Fri 8pm–1pm; tel: 02-6262341; www.cityofdavid.org.il; fee) excavations are on the steep hillside outside the **Dung Gate**. This hill is called **Ha-Ofel**, and the archaeological dig here has been the scene of violent protests by religious zealots claiming that ancient Jewish graves have been violated. The diggers dispute this, but say that the site is too important to leave buried, because the Ophel is where the earliest incarnation of Jerusalem stood: the Jebusite city of more than 3,000 years ago.

Around 1,000 BC, King David captured the city and made it his capital. Although his son Solomon was to build the Temple on the high ground above it, the main residential portion of the city itself remained clinging to this slope above the Kidron Valley. It did so because at the foot of the slope is the **Gihon Spring** ❷⓻, at the time Jerusalem's only water supply.

Since the spring was located in a cave on the floor of the valley, Jerusalemites were in danger of being cut off from their water when the city was attacked. But the stunning engineering project known as **Hezekiah's Tunnel** ❷⓼ carried out by King Hezekiah about 300 years after King David's time, managed to connect the Gihon Spring to the Silwan Pool inside the city some 530 meters (580 yards) farther down the valley. The intrepid 19th-century archaeologist Charles Warren not only explored the tunnel but also discovered a shaft reaching up through the Ophel to an underground passage from where city residents could come to draw

The gardens of Mount Zion are a peaceful spot to sit and reflect on Jerusalem's past – or simply to rest weary sightseers' feet.

BELOW: the City of David excavations.

water in buckets. In 1867 Warren had to crawl on his belly through the stream bed to explore the water system. Today visitors can study the schematics in comfort in the **City of David Archaeological Gardens**, and then stroll through the illuminated passageway to the top of Warren's shaft to peer at the water rushing below. In the Kidron Valley itself, visitors with candles can tramp along the knee-deep stream in Hezekiah's Tunnel from the Gihon Spring and through the Ophel until they emerge at the Silwan Pool.

The upper end of the Kidron Valley, also known as the Vale of Jehoshaphat, contains several Jerusalem landmarks. The slope off to the northeast is the Mount of Olives, and in the valley itself are the **Tomb of Absalom** and the **Tomb of Zekhariah**. Despite their traditional names, these stately tombs, with their graceful pillars and elaborately carved friezes, are not thought to be the resting places of David's rebellious son or of the prophet. Rather, archaeologists believe that they were part of the vast 1st-century necropolis that encircled Jerusalem, and probably served wealthy citizens or notables of the Herodian court.

The Mount of Olives

Wherever the historical Golgotha was located, it's agreed that Jesus made his triumphal entry into Jerusalem from the **Mount of Olives**. This hill, with its breathtaking view of the Old City, is mainly a Jewish cemetery dating back to the biblical period and still in use today. Round about the cemetery the Mount of Olives has numerous sites of significance for, in a meeting of faiths, many Jews and Christians believe that the Messiah will lead the resurrected from here into Jerusalem via the Old City's Golden Gate, which faces the mount.

Tradition has it that it was through a gate on this site that Jesus rode into

Map
on page
138

TIP

The walk through Hezekiah's Tunnel is not recommended for those with claustrophobic tendencies. Even the courageous should take a torch with them.

LEFT: the Tomb of Zekhariah.
BELOW: Jewish cemetery, the Mount of Olives.

Entrance to the Church of All Nations at the foot of the Mount of Olives.

BELOW: the Dome of the Ascension.

Jerusalem, just as an earlier Jewish tradition says that this is how the Messiah will enter the city at the End of Days. The gate, however, is tightly sealed. It is said that a Muslim ruler decided to have it bricked up to prevent any Messiah from arriving in Jerusalem and wresting the city from Muslim hands. The reverence for this most sacred of mountains is generally reflected in a spirit of mutual tolerance and understanding. As to why the Mount of Olives is so bare and rocky: tradition has it that the Romans cut down all the olive trees to build the siege machines used in the destruction of Jerusalem in AD 70 – but that with the Resurrection, the trees will flourish again.

The Garden of Gethsemane

At the foot of the mount is the handsome **Church of All Nations** (open daily; free), noted for its fine Byzantine-style mosaic facade. Also known as the Basilica of the Agony, it was designed by a Franciscan architect, Antonio Barluzzi. Its 12 cupolas represent the 12 nations, which contributed towards its construction. Adjoining it is the **Garden of Gethsemane** ㉙ where Jesus was betrayed, or at least, the largest of several gardens identified as Gethsemane. The olive grove here has been verified as being 2,000 years old – although this is not particularly remarkable for olive trees. It has been suggested that it was from one of these trees that Judas hanged himself.

Next to the garden is **Mary's Tomb** ㉚ (open Mon–Sat; free), deep within the earth and illuminated by candles placed by members of the Orthodox Churches. Midway down the stairs to the 5th-century chapel are niches that are said to hold the remains of Mary's parents, Joachim and Anne, and her husband Joseph.

Among the most notable churches on the way up the mount along the narrow side road to the left of the Garden of Gethsemane upon the right is the Russian Orthodox **Church of Mary Magdalene** ㉛ (Tues and Thur am only; free) built by Tsar Alexander III in 1886 and easily identifiable by its golden onion-domes.

Further up is the small but entrancing Franciscan **Basilica of Dominus Flevit** which marks the site where, according to Luke's Gospel, Jesus paused to weep over Jerusalem. Built over Canaanite burial caves and a ruined Crusader church, the lovely, tear-shaped chapel was designed by Antonio Barluzzi in 1953. Carrying on up and also on the right is the Church of **Pater Noster** (open Mon–Sat; free) a Carmelite Convent, with the Lord's Prayer in numerous languages on its interior walls. Here, too, are the ruins of the **Church of the Eleona**, on the site where Jesus revealed the mysteries to his followers.

You have now reached the ridge of the mountain. On the far side of the mount, with a view of the **Judean Desert** and the red hills of Edom across the Jordan, is the **Bethpage Chapel**, from where the Palm Sunday processions to Jerusalem begin. At the crest of the hill is the **Russian Orthodox Church of the Ascension** (open Tues and Thur am only; free) with its landmark bell tower. Nearby, the small octagonal **Dome of the Ascension** (open daily; free) marks the traditional site of Jesus's ascent to heaven. Converted to a mosque when the Muslims conquered

Map on page 138

the city in 1187, the structure is said to have been the architectural model for the Dome of the Rock.

Along the road to the south, which is a cul-de-sac, is the **Seven Arches Hotel** and the classic picture-postcard view of Jerusalem's Old City. This is also the best place for a brief ride on one of the camels, which are always lying in wait with their minders for adventurous tourists.

A Mormon presence

If you backtrack through the Arab village of E-Tur, which straddles the ridge of the Mount of Olives, you will find to the right of the steep hill (Derekh E-Tur) that leads back down to the Old City one of Jerusalem's most aesthetically pleasing new buildings: the **Jerusalem Center for Near Eastern Studies, Brigham Young University** ❷. The construction of this attractive campus and college complex, built into the hillside on eight levels, was fiercely opposed by Orthodox Jews in the 1980s. But in the interests of pluralism, the Mormons from Salt Lake City, Utah, were allowed to go ahead with their project after promising that no missionary activity will take place in Israel. Students who come to Israel for semester-long courses are warned that they will be sent home if they proselytize. The campus has splendid gardens and an inspiring view of the Old City.

Going back towards the Old City, on the corner of Sultan Suleiman opposite the walls between St. Stephen's Gate and Herod's Gate, you will find the **Rockefeller Museum** ❸ (Sun–Thur 10am–3pm, Sat 10am–1pm; tel: 02-6282251; fee). It has a stately octagonal tower, a gracious courtyard and an extensive collection of archaeological finds. Still battle-scarred from 1967, it is now part of the Israel Museum. ❏

TIP

From the Dome of the Ascension several paths lead down to the city. Walks here, especially at dawn or sunset, are some of the loveliest experiences that Jerusalem has to offer.

LEFT: the Pater Noster Church.
BELOW: camels wait for customers on the Mount of Olives.

SEVEN GATES AROUND FOUR QUARTERS

The Old City of Jerusalem can only be entered by seven gates while an eighth, the Golden Gate, is sealed pending the coming of the Messiah

Jerusalem's gates all have their own story to tell. The Jaffa Gate, as the name implies, was traditionally the main thoroughfare westwards to Jaffa (Yafo). It is known in Arabic as the Hebron Gate. The walls beside it were breached in 1898 so that Kaiser Wilhelm II of Germany could enter on horseback.

The Zion Gate, predictably, leads out to Mount Zion which was inexplicably left outside the city walls. The unfortunately named Dung Gate was the point from which the city's refuse was taken out. It offers best access to the Temple Mount and Western Wall.

St Stephen's Gate is also known as the Lions' Gate. It stands opposite the Mount of Olives, near the start of the Via Dolorosa. The Israeli army launched a surprise attack here when capturing the Old City from Jordan in 1967.

Herod's Gate, sometimes called Flowers Gate, is the least known of the gateways, and offers access to the Muslim Quarter.

The Damascus Gate is located opposite the highway which leads north to Nablus (it is called the Nablus Gate in Hebrew). It's the busiest gate linking Arab East Jerusalem and the Muslim Quarter market. The New Gate, as you would expect, is the most recent. The walls were breached in the late 19th century so that pilgrims staying in the Notre Dame Hospice opposite would have direct access to the Christian Quarter.

But the Golden Gate is special: set midway along the eastern wall of the Old City, it is blocked up. Through this gate, it is said, the Messiah will enter ancient Jerusalem after crossing a paper bridge from the Mount of Olives.

▷ **VENDORS AT THE GATE**
The main plaza outside the Damascus Gate is always busy, filled with Arab vendors peddling all kinds of food and drink.

△ **AESTHETIC ARCHITECTURE**
Ornate patterns by the Zion Gate characterize the painstaking aesthetic efforts of Suleiman's architects.

◁ **HELP FROM FRIENDS**
World Jewry contributed large sums of money to the renovation of the Old City walls in the late 1960s, as this plaque by the Jaffa Gate testifies.

▽ **NO ENTRY**
The Golden Gate remains sealed, awaiting the day of redemption when the Messiah will enter the city, bringing heaven to earth.

SULEIMAN'S GIFT TO JERUSALEM

The Old City's walls were constructed by the Ottoman sultan Suleiman the Magnificent between 1537 and 1541. The walls are 4 km (2½ miles) long, an average of 12 metres (40 ft) high and nearly 3 metres (9 ft) thick. Along the top of the wall was a patrol path for guards, now open to the public and known as Ramparts Walk.

By 16th-century standards the wall was not especially solid, and its main purpose was not so much to withstand a concerted attack as to protect Jerusalem's citizens from bandits and predatory creatures. The citadel (above), the city's main garrison, was incorporated within the walls by the Jaffa Gate, while Mount Zion was inexplicably left outside. Legend has it that Suleiman executed his chief engineer for the omission.

Suleiman supposedly embarked upon the project in the first place because of a recurring nightmare about being chased by a lion. His advisors interpreted the lion as being Jerusalem (the lion of Judah) which had been left naked (without walls) after being conquered by Suleiman's father.

◁ **GATEWAY TO PRAYER**
The Dung Gate is the most popular with Orthodox Jews due to its proximity to the Western Wall.

▽ **GUARDED BY LIONS**
St Stephen's Gate is also known as Lions' Gate because of the lions affixed to the wall outside.

▽ **GATE TO THE MUSLIM QUARTER**
Herod's Gate, to the north-east of the Old City, leads into the Muslim Quarter.

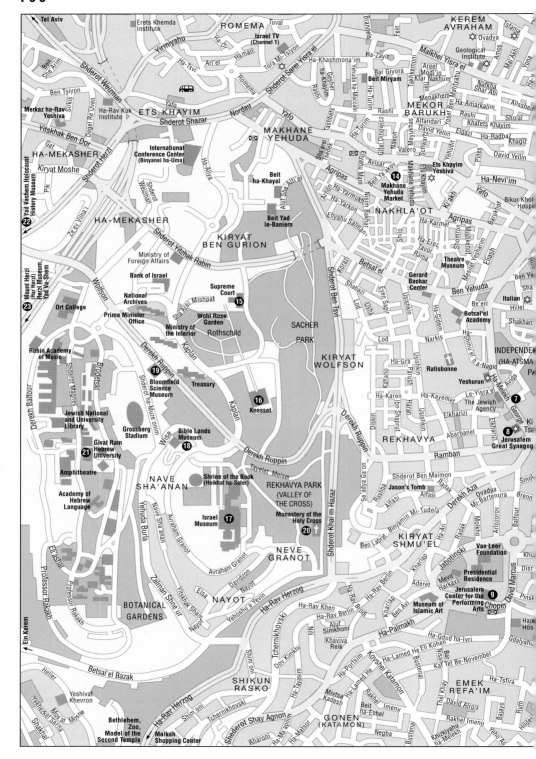

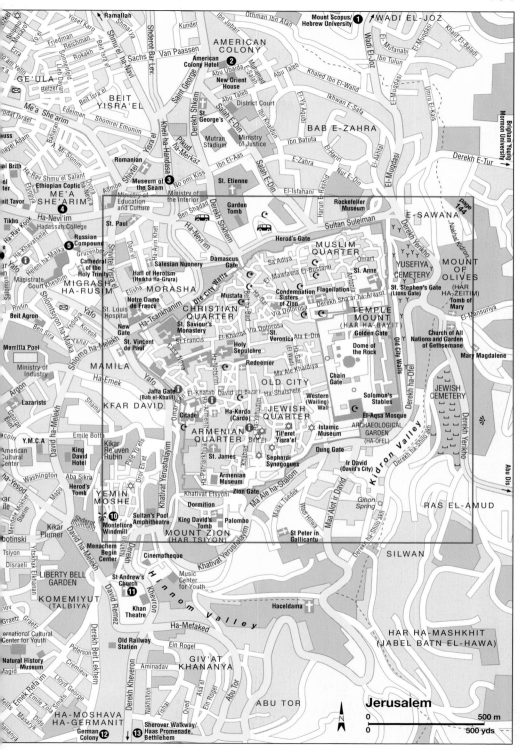

Jerusalem

THE NEW JERUSALEM

From Mount Scopus in the east to the somber Yad Vashem in
the west, this chapter explores the New Jerusalem,
its past history and its present development

Map
on pages
160–1

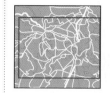

Throughout the ages Jews have wept, sung and prayed for Jerusalem. Above all, they prayed that one day they might return to their holy city. Yet the Jerusalem that confronted the first waves of Jews who came to start new lives here in the mid-19th century was a dismal contrast to the ideal spiritual capital they had dreamt of for so long. A backwater of the Turkish Ottoman Empire for 400 years, by 1917 the city had been left behind. It was filthy, decrepit and insanitary, cramped within the confines of its great protective wall.

Even the founder of Zionism, Theodor Herzl, during his 10-day sojourn in Palestine in 1898, noted his disgust with its squalid conditions, writing, "When I remember thee in days to come, O Jerusalem, it will not be with delight. The musty deposits of 2,000 years of inhumanity, intolerance and foulness lie in your reeking alleys. If Jerusalem is ever ours, I would begin by cleaning it up. I would tear down the filthy rat-holes, burn all the non-sacred ruins, and put the bazaars elsewhere. Then, retaining as much of the old architectural style as possible, I would build an airy, comfortable, properly sewered, brand new city around the holy places."

LEFT: Malkha
Shopping Mall.
BELOW: a native
of Jerusalem.

Modern metropolis

Herzl's words proved to be prophetic. The new Jerusalem is much more than airy, comfortable and properly sewered – it is the fitting capital to the Jewish State that he envisioned. Bold geometric architecture erupts from every hillside; sleek thoroughfares lead into tree-lined boulevards; high-rises tower over church steeples and elegant city parks. There are bars, theaters and luxury hotels.

Yet the city that has inspired so much Jewish yearning and Christian and Muslim passion over the centuries is no less reverent for its modernity; the Christian visitor today will be struck by the vast array of churches and hospices of every denomination spread across the streets and hilltops of the city, while for the Muslim pilgrim the resplendent Dome of the Rock and El-Aqsa Mosque are at the heart of their faith. But it is the tremendous blossoming of Jewish spirituality here that has characterized the past century. *Yeshivas*, synagogues and cultural institutions abound, each place of worship reflecting the specific religious or ethnic coloring of its congregation.

Shabbat is observed scrupulously; from dusk on Friday to Saturday evening most stores and buses cease their service, the streets empty, and a tranquil hush descends on the city, although towards midnight there is a surprisingly boisterous night life near Zion Square.

As the capital of the State of Israel, Jerusalem – Yerushalayim in Hebrew – holds a special meaning

TIP

A new tunnel recently opened through Mount Scopus provides the fastest route down to the Dead Sea.

even for its secular residents, who gripe that the city is far less cosmopolitan and lively than Tel Aviv. The new city is still not exceptionally wealthy or grand, but many of its structures exude a symbolic significance that outstrips their otherwise modest aesthetic merits. The domineering presence of a few undistinguished high-rises over the skyline, in particular, is jarring – if nonetheless useful for navigating one's way around. But from other perspectives the new city can be magical: old and new merge seamlessly, and Jerusalem seems as unearthly and splendid as any image its name evokes.

Perhaps the most lasting legacy of the British Mandate era is the 1918 declaration forbidding new construction to employ any material but the city's famous sandy-gold, sometimes pink, Jerusalem stone. While this has hampered architects' creativity, the result has been a rare sense of visual harmony, enhancing the city's unity, while moderating the damage of its less successful architecture.

No event has had more influence on the shape of the city in recent years than its unification in the 1967 war. Not only did this clear away the barbed wire and concrete that separated East and West, it also, for a time, took Jerusalem off the front line of the Arab-Israeli conflict. Since the late 1960s there has been an explosion of development, much of it is attributable to Teddy Kollek, Mayor of Jerusalem from 1965 to 1993. He attracted new institutions into the city, conserved Old City landmarks, and presided over the colorful sweeps of new public art as well as the hideous behemoths of rapidly erected housing.

Some 800,000 people live in Jerusalem, and the city continues to grow, balancing, with mixed grace, the calls of the past and future. However, since the start of the second Intifada in 2000, the divisions have re-appeared with large parts of Arab Jerusalem cut off from the city by the new Separation Wall *(see page 277).*

BELOW: a contemporary synagogue on the university campus.

Potent peak

There is no better place to start a tour of the new Jerusalem than **Mount Scopus** ❶. Isolated and aloof atop a ridge north of the city, it holds a special place in Jerusalem's history. Its prime importance is as the site of the **Hebrew University**, inaugurated here under the vision of Chaim Weizmann in 1925. It was cut off from the rest of Jewish Jerusalem during the 1948 War of Independence, after a Hadassah Hospital convoy of scientists and staff was massacred in April of that year. Reabsorbed into the city since 1967, the university has enjoyed a spectacular modernization of its campus. Among the most impressive sites here is the classical amphitheater, which hosts concerts and lectures and, when empty, offers an awesome view of the rolling Judean Hills. A new Hadassah Hospital has been built, and other notable monuments include a British cemetery dating from World War I.

Travel from the University down Churchill Boulevard and left into Aharon Katzir Stree. This leads to the the wealthy Arab quarter of **Sheikh Jarah**, which includes on its southern fringes along Nablus Road **New Orient House**. This was a Palestinian quasi-government building, but became less important after Faisal Husseini, the Palestinian Minister of Jerusalem Affairs, died in 2001.

On the adjacent street is the **American Colony Hotel** (www.americancolony.com) ❷, Jerusalem's oldest hotel and a favorite haunt of foreign journalists because of its neutral location on the border between East and West Jerusalem.

Along St George St and then Kheil ha-Handasa, at the old border, is the **Museum of the Seam** ❸, a former border post known as the Tourjeman Post (Sun–Thur 9am–5pm, Fri 9am–2pm; tel 02-6281278; www.coexistence.art.museum .org; fee). It displays contemporary art that deals with socio-political conflicts between different groups.

Map on pages 160–1

The American Colony Hotel, where writers Mark Twain and Herman Melville once stayed.

BELOW: sunset over the city.

Religious enclave

A few hundred meters down Shivtei Yisrael on the right is **Me'a She'arim**  ❹, where the mood is intense and unworldly. Nearly a third of all Jerusalem citizens are *Haredi*, or ultra-Orthodox, and these neighborhoods reflect the rigorous religious lifestyles of their inhabitants. Me'a She'arim, meaning literally "a hundred gates," is the most famous Orthodox community. Built as early as 1875 as a refuge for Hassidic families, the neighborhood has retained much of the intimacy and flavor of a European *shtetl*. The Orthodox Jews who live here speak Yiddish and wear the traditional styles: *peot* (side-curls), heavy, black garments for the men and shawls for the women. Signs warn that secular fashions, especially "immodest" female dress, are offensive and not tolerated. These admonitions should be taken seriously: immodestly dressed women are often spat at or even stoned.

Ha-Nevi'im (The Street of the Prophets) runs roughly parallel to the south of Me'a She'arim from behind the Russian Compound to near the Damascus Gate and is one of the main thoroughfares in Jerusalem. This street is famed for its historic architecture and beautiful buildings, whose wonders make a stroll down it an adventure. Where the road meets Shivtei Yisra'el, the Italian Hospital was once home to the Zionist leader Menachem Ussiskin and the author S.Y. Agnon. Today this beautiful 16th-century building houses the offices of the Ministry of Education.

The **Rothschild Hospital** at the corner of Ha-Rav Kook, was built in 1887 and is now occupied by students of Hadassah Hospital for paramedical training.

On the corner of Ethiopians' Street is **Beit Tavor**, built in 1889. Since 1951 it has been home to the Swedish Theological Seminary, and the beautiful courtyard is open to visitors daily. Off the Street of the Prophets lie several religious institutions, including the Ethiopian Coptic Church.

If I forget thee, O Jerusalem,
Let my right hand forget her cunning,
Let my tongue cleave to the roof of my mouth, if I remember not thee;
If I set not Jerusalem above my chiefest joy.
— Psalm 137

BELOW: aerial view of Me'a She'arim.

Russians and Prussians

Ha-Nevi'im's western end meets **Jaffa (Yafo) Road** at its mid-point between the city entrance and Jaffa Gate. The new city's main thoroughfare was paved in 1898 for the visiting German Kaiser, the Prussian Wilhelm II – for whose procession the wall between the Jaffa Gate and the Citadel was rent open. Today Jaffa Road remains the main axis for New City traffic, meandering from the gate to the northern bounds of the city, passing Makhane Yehuda, the Jewish food market, which is a colorful attraction in its own right (*see page 92*), before reaching the central bus station. But the entire road is to be pedestrianized and will become part of Jerusalem's first tram route.

Leaving the Old City behind, Jaffa Road passes the new **City Hall** municipal complex and plaza. In the basement of City Hall is a model of central Jerusalem used by architects planning new buildings. The model can be viewed by the public. City Hall also has a **Visitors Center** at 3 Safra Square, (Sun–Thur 9am–4.30pm, Fri 9am–1pm; tel: 02-6258844).

An alleyway to the north of City Hall leads to the **Russian Compound ❺**, covering several blocks to the right of Jaffa Road. These were purchased by Tsar Alexander II in the wake of the Crimean War as a refuge for thousands of Russian pilgrims who flocked to the city every year, often dirt-poor and under considerable duress from their trip. Started in 1860, this complex marked the first notable presence outside the Old City; most of the buildings, including the handsome green-domed **Cathedral of the Holy Trinity** and the Russian Consulate, were completed by 1864. The compound has been largely bought by the Israeli government, and the buildings now house law courts, a police station and part of Hadassah Medical School, as well as a plethora of bars, cafés and restaurants.

Map on pages 160–1

The Bukharim Quarter, to the northwest of Me'a She'arim, is a neighborhood inhabited today largely by the ultra-orthodox. It was built in the 1890s by Jews from Uzbekistan in Central Asia.

BELOW: the *Haredim* of Me'a She'arim.

The **Hall of Heroism** (Sun–Thur 9am–5pm, Fri 9am–1pm; tel: 02-6254000; fee) is a small museum at the back of the complex, within what was once a British prison; it is dedicated to the Jewish underground resistance of the Mandate period.

Downtown

On the other side of Jaffa Road are the winding lanes of **Nakhalat Shiva,** Jerusalem's second oldest residential suburb, now delightfully renovated. Founded by Joseph Rivlin in the early 1860s, the enclave had grown to hold some 50 families by the end of that decade. Now Rivlin and Salomon streets, which have been pedestrianized, cross the old neighborhood and, despite their decidedly narrow girths, they house quite a few of the city's favorite restaurants as well as much of its nightlife and upscale Judaica stores. At the end of Nakhalat Shiva, next to the car park, artisans sell their wares during the summer months.

At the hub of it all is **Kikar Tsiyon (Zion Square)** ❻ always crowded, always crazy. It was called after the Zion Cinema, now long gone, a rallying spot for young Zionists in the 1930s, but Zion Square is still a popular venue for both young Israelis to meet up and for occasional political demonstrations. A bulky glass tower stands on the site now.

A block up Ha-Rav Kook, on the north side of Jaffa Road and down an alleyway to the left, is an unexpected little nooks, **Beit Ticho**. In the early 20th century it was the home and office of the Jerusalem landscape artist Anna Ticho *(see panel, left)* and her husband Avraham, an eminent ophthalmologist. The childless couple bequeathed their home to the Israel Museum and the house contains its original furnishings, paintings by Anna, and Avraham's books and Hannukah menorahs. The lobby and the large garden contain a popular restaurant.

Anna Ticho (1894–1981), who moved to Jerusalem in 1912 from the Czech city of Brno, became one of Israel's most popular artists. "Her eyes can see real landscapes," said Dr Haim Gamzu, a former director of the Tel Aviv Museum, "but they can also penetrate into the soul of the landscape."

BELOW: the Russian Compound.

The Jerusalem café scene really gets into its stride at **Ben Yehuda**, the five-block long pedestrian avenue that begins at Zion Square. This is the place where everyone comes to see (and be seen), to drink (though drunkenness is rare), sip cappuccino, sample pastries, and simply mingle with friends and strangers. Musicians, young couples and would-be prophets are always out in force, and several local characters have established their reputations here.

Marking the city's main north-south axis, **Ha-Melekh George** (**King George V Street**) ❼, which cuts across Ben Yehuda at the top of the streeet, also has its share of hubbub. The contrast between old and new is most vivid at the plaza in front of the City Tower, where the preserved doorway facade of an earlier building stands oblivious to its new surroundings. Hillel, leading back down towards the Old City (parallel to Ben Yehuda on the south), is the site of the lovely, ornate **Italian Synagogue and Museum** (Sun, Tue, Wed 9am–5pm, Mon 9am–2pm, Thur, Fri 9am–1pm; tel: 02-6241610 www.jija.org; fee). It was transported here from Conegliano Veneto, near Venice, in 1952 and dates originally from 1719.

The YMCA building.

The **Beit Agron**, or press building, is further on, opposite the park and an ancient reservoir, **Mamila Pool**. In the basement of Beit Agron is the Time Elevator, a simulated ride through the city's history in a converted cinema.

The Jerusalem Artist's House on the western side of King George (corner of Betsalel and Shmuel Ha'Nagid) was originally the home of Jerusalem's premier arts and design college, founded in 1906 and moved in the 1990s to Mount Scopus. The delightful building houses art exhibits and is a popular eatery and bar.

Religion dominates Ha-Melekh George further to the south. The **Yeshurun Synagogue** across from the park is followed, further down the block, by the **Jerusalem Great Synagogue** ❽. The 18th-century ark covering the Torah scrolls was brought here from Padua, in Italy. Next door is the seat of the chief Rabbinate of Israel, **Heikhal Shlomo**.

BELOW: an earnest street musician.

Mamilla and King David Street

Between Ha-Melekh George and Mamila, Gershon Agron rims the final edge of Independence Park, a pleasant expanse of green in the center of the city. This avenue leads across to the **Mamilla Center**, a 19th-century lane of artisans' workshops converted into a pedestrian shopping mall with up-market stores and delightful cafés overlooking the Old City walls. The mall links the New City to the Jaffa Gate.

Nearby, David ha-Melekh (**King David Street**) hosts two of Jerusalem's most celebrated edifices. The **YMCA**, built in 1928–33, was the work of Shreve, Lamb & Harmon, who were simultaneously designing the Empire State Building. Its 36-meter (120-ft) tower offers an outstanding view of Jerusalem and its environs, and its symmetrical rotundas reflect an elegant harmony with modern Middle Eastern form.

The **King David Hotel** (tel: 02-6208888), opposite, was built with old-world grandeur by Egyptian Jews in 1930. It was a British base of command in the Mandate period, and the entire right wing of the building was destroyed in a raid by the Jewish underground in 1946. It is customary for visiting heads of state to stay at the King David or the nearby David's Citadel Hotel.

Map on pages 160–1

A good time to visit the Jerusalem Center for the Performing Arts is in May during the Israel Festival when there are visiting artists from overseas and outdoor performances in the plaza in front of the theatre complex.

BELOW: Montefiore Windmill.

Below the King David, an airy park holds the cavern of **Herod's Family Tomb**, where the stormy monarch buried his wife Mariamne and two sons after murdering them in a paranoid rage.

The **Jerusalem Center for the Performing Arts** ❾ can be reached by going up Jabotinski and turning left into Marcus. This attractive neighborhood, known as Talbiyah, contains the city's most expensive houses. The arts complex contains four theatres and auditoriums (www.jerusalem-theatre.co.il); it is also a delightful place just to sit around, and to have a meal or a cup of coffee.

Along Chopin, at the junction of Ha-Palmakh, is the **Museum of Islamic Art** (Sun–Thur 10am–3pm Tues until 8pm Fri & Sat 10am–2pm; tel:02-5661291 www.islamicart.co.il; fee). The **Presidential Residence**, home of the titular head of state, can be found to the right at the start of Jabotinski.

The Montefiore Windmill

Opposite the bottom end of Jabotinski is Shderot Blumfield which leads to the **Montefiore Windmill** ❿, a conspicuous landmark built by the British philanthropist Sir Moses Montefiore in the 1860s. It now houses a modest museum (Sun–Thur 9am–4pm, Fri 9am–1pm; free). There is another windmill behind the Jerusalem Great Synagogue, but the Montefiore Windmill, which stands above the oldest Jewish neighborhood outside the Old City, is the better known.

Until the 19th century the Old City walls served as the city limits for Jerusalem's Jews; outside, Muslims and Bedouin raiders posed a threat. Opposite the Old City, between the Jaffa Gate and Mount Zion, the first Jewish suburb to penetrate this barrier remains in situ. Wishfully called **Mishkenot Sh'Ananim** (Dwellings of Tranquillity), the long, block-like structure (on the steps just beneath the windmill) was built in 1860 by Sir Moses Montefiore with the bequest of Judah Touro, a New Orleans Jew.

In the next four years Montefiore bought an adjoining plot of land and expanded the quarter, calling it **Yemin Moshe**. In the wake of the 1967 war Yemin Moshe was revitalised as an artists' colony, and today its serene walkways and stone houses command some of the highest rents of any neighborhood in the city. Montefiore built the windmill at the edge of the quarter to provide flour for the settlement, and in 1948 it served as an important Israeli observation post.

As you head south, with the **Liberty Bell Garden** (Hapa'amon) on the right, the modern city opens onto the old. Embedded on the side of the **Valley of Hinnom** like a rugged gem, the **Cinematheque** on Derekh Khevron is a popular landmark. Its theaters show foreign and alternative movies, including first screenings at July's annual Jerusalem International Film Festival.

Opposite the Cinematheque is the **Menachem Begin Heritage Center** (Sun–Thur 9am–4pm, Fri 9am–noon; tel: 5652020; free, but tours must be booked in advance). This includes a museum dedicated to the life of the former Prime Minister and Nobel prize winner.

Above the heritage center, the Scottish **St Andrew's Church** ⓫ has a well-regarded hospice, and a memorial to the Scottish king Robert Bruce who, on his death in 1329, requested that his heart be taken to Jerusalem (unfortunately it was waylaid en route, in Spain, and

Map on pages 160–1

never made it). Around the corner, the **Khan Theatre's** atmospheric archways are the venue for drama, folk music and jazz performers.

The railway station a block further on dates from 1892. However, the daily service was discontinued several years ago with trains now running to Tel Aviv from the new station near the Malkha shopping mall.

The German Colony

Stretching due east from Hinnom is an area of tree-lined boulevards and peaceful homes. The area immediately east, called the **German Colony** ⑫, was founded in 1873 by German Templars and still has a subtly European air. The central street of the German Colony is Emek Refa'im, a fashionable boulevard of stores, restaurants and cafés which leads down to the large Arab-style houses of Baq'a and the Talpiyot industrial zone in the south, a less salubrious mix of discount stores, wedding halls and night clubs.

To the east is one of the city's most delightful spots. Turn left from Emek Refa'im into Pierre Koenig and left again into Yehuda and continue straight into Daniel Yanovsky to reach the **Sherover Walkway** and **Haas Promenade** (East Talpiyot) ⑬. Linking up the Arab village of Abu Tor with the Jewish neighborhood of East Talpiyot, these parklands offers a splendid view of the Old City and, when the summer heat haze dissipates, a breathtaking view of the Judean Desert. The promenade ends at Government House, now the HQ of the United Nations' regional operations. This is also known as the **Hill of the Evil Counsel**, where Judas Iscariot is said to have received his 30 pieces of silver.

Not far away, the kibbutz Ramat Rakhel also offers an inspiring view of the desert, and nearby to the south is the monastery of Mar Elias *(see page 285)*.

Given its 3,000 years of history, Jerusalem has acquired dozens of names over the millennia. In the Bible, it is variously referred to as Moriah (Gen.22:2), Jebus (Judges 19:10), Zion (II Samuel 5:8), Ariel, Lion of God (Isaiah 29:1) and Neveh Tzedek (Jeremiah 31:22)

BELOW:
Haas Promenade.

TIP

The train to Tel Aviv from the new Malkha station takes 75 minutes compared to 45 minutes by bus, but the hillside views make the railway a more worthwhile experience. There is also a station at the Biblical Zoo.

To the west is the sprawling suburb of Gilo, which overlooks Malkha. Adjacent to **Teddy Soccer Stadium**, home to Beitar Jerusalem, one of Israel's leading teams, is the **Malkha Shopping Mall** (Kanyon) and the new railway station. With air-conditioning in the summer and heating in the winter, the shopping mall can be a pleasant place to find gifts, entertain the children and eat a meal.

The road running east of the shopping mall (Kolitz) leads to the **Biblical Zoo**, also known as the Tisch Family Zoological Gardens (Sun– Thur 9am–7pm, Fri 9am–4.30pm, Sat 10am–6pm; www.jerusalemzoo.org.il; fee). The zoo is attractively landscaped into the hillside and contains animals mentioned in the Bible.

The government area

The various institutions of government can be found near the western entrance to the city. But to feel the political pulse of the country, journalists often wander through the colorful **Makhane Yehuda Market** ⓮ which straddles Yafo (Jaffa) and Agripas streets to the east of the Central Bus Station and the west of Zion Square. The vendors who offer a tempting array of fresh fruit and vegetables and other foodstuffs tend to lean to the right in their readily available opinions.

High on the hill above **Sacher Park**, the largest in the city, which is opposite the end of Agrippas and Bezalel Streets, is the **Supreme Court** ⓯ (tours in English Sun–Thur at noon; tel: 02-6759612; fee). Completed in 1992, this impressive edifice uses light, shade and glass to great effect. The Supreme Court justices comprise the highest court in the land and have the power to interpret Knesset (parliamentary) legislation.

Just to the south, past the Bank of Israel and the Prime Minister's Office, is the nation's Parliament Building, the **Knesset** ⓰ (open Mon–Wed during debates,

BELOW: the Shrine of the Book.
RIGHT: Model of the Second Temple.

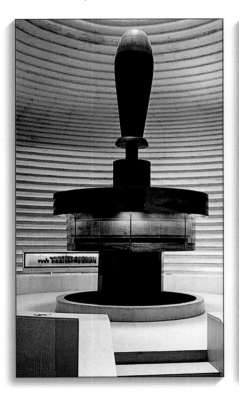

Sun and Thur 8.30am–2.30pm for guided tours, which must be booked in advance; tel: 02-6753420; www.knesset.gov.il; fee). This is the symbol of Israel's democratic system. Be sure you take the tour of the interior, which includes a tapestry designed by Marc Chagall (you must present your passport). The **Wohl Rose Garden** above is sweetest in the spring and late autumn.

The **Israel Museum** ⓱, (Mon, Wed, Sat, Sun 10am–4pm, Tues 4–9pm, Thur 10am–9pm, closed Sun; tel: 02-6708811; www.imj.org.il; fee) is reached from the Knesset along Kaplan to Derekh Ruppin, and is Israel's national museum and a leading showcase for the country's art, archaeology and Judaica. Its most famous exhibit is the **Shrine of the Book** which displays the Dead Sea Scrolls. These scraps of tattered parchment represent the oldest known copy of the Old Testament.

There is a **Model of the Second Temple** in the Israel Museum compound. This impressive 1:50 scale model of Jerusalem in AD 66 conveys just vast the Second Temple complex must have been. Price of admission to the museum includes a free shuttle and entry to the Rockefeller Museum *(see page 157)*.

Opposite are two more museums. The **Bible Lands Museum** ⓲ (Sun–Thur 9.30am–5.30pm, Wed 9.30am–9.30pm, Fri 9.30am–2pm; tel: 02-5611066; www.blmj.org; fee) in Avraham Granot displays artefacts dating from biblical times. Along Ruppin north-east is the hands-on **Bloomfield Science Museum** ⓳ (Mon–Thur 10am–6pm, Fri 10am–2pm, Sat 10am–3pm; tel: 02-6544888 www.mada.org.il; fee) is imaginative and is popular with children.

Beneath the Israel Museum is the Valley of the Holy Cross, a biblical landscape of olive trees dominated by the **Monastery of the Holy Cross** ⓴ (Mon–Sat 9.30am–5pm, Fri 9.30am–1.30pm, closed Sun; fee). Here, it is believed, grew the tree (planted by Abraham's nephew Lot after he was saved from Sodom's

Map on pages 160–1

Bust of Hadrian in the Israel Museum.

BELOW: hands-on at the Bloomfield Science Museum.

destruction) from which the wood was taken for the cross on which Christ was crucified. The Crusader-style monastery was built in the 7th century and belonged to the Georgian Orthodox Church until the 19th century when (for lack of funds) it was handed to the Greek Orthodox Church.

To the west of the Valley of the Cross is the **Botanical Gardens**, a small but pleasing garden of international flora, set by a lake. It is part of the **Hebrew University's Givat Ram Campus** ㉑, established after 1948 when Mount Scopus was cut off. The campus includes the science faculties of the university as well as the **Jewish National and University Library** (Sun–Thur 9am–7pm, Fri 9am–1pm; www.jnul.huji.ac.il; free), one of the largest libraries in the world. It counts among its treasures the actual papers on which Albert Einstein worked out his theory of relativity.

Blooms in the Botanical Gardens.

Yad Vashem and Mount Herzl

Remembrance is a key theme of modern Judaism, and Jerusalem has no shortage of memorials. The two most potent of these lie side by side on the western ridge of the city, and provide powerful testimony to the two events which altered the course of Jewish history in the 20th century: the Holocaust and the creation of the State of Israel. You can reach them by returning along Ruppin and Wolfson ands turning left into Shderot Herzl.

The new **Yad Vashem Holocaust History Museum** ㉒ (Sun–Thur 9am–5pm, Fri 9am–2pm; tel: 02 6443400; www.yadvashem.org.il; free) is a striking memorial to the 6 million Jews massacred by the Nazis. Daring in its design, the museum is housed in a linear, triangular structure (which some compare to a Toblerone container) stretching for 160 meters (525 ft) beneath a hillside *(see panel, right).*

BELOW: remembering at Yad Vashem.

The complex also includes a central chamber, **Ohel Yizkor**, or the **Hall of Remembrance**, which sits on a base of rounded boulders; inside, an eternal flame flickers amid blocks of black basalt rock engraved with the names of 21 death camps. Most visitors spend between one and three hours in the complex.

Mount Herzl honors the Viennese journalist Theodor Herzl, who founded the Zionist movement between 1897 and 1904. His remains were transported to Jerusalem in 1949, and his simple black granite tomb marks the summit of the mount. Also buried in the cemetery here are Vladimir Jabotinksy and other Zionist visionaries, joined most recently by the late Prime Minister Yitzhak Rabin, assassinated in 1995. On the northern slope of the ridge lie the graves of Israeli soldiers who died defending the state. The **Herzl Museum** (Sun–Thur 9am–5pm, Fri 9am–1pm; fee) stands guard at the entrance to the mount.

Biblical retreat

Ein Kerem, the small biblical town nestling in a valley to the west of the city proper, beneath Yad Vashem, is as timeless as the hills and well worth a whole afternoon to itself. It is rich in religious history. The most renowned sites include the **Franciscan Church of the Visitation**, designed in 1956 by the architect Antonio Barluzzi, on the spot where the Virgin Mary visited Elizabeth, John the, Baptist's mother, and the central **Spring of the Vineyard** (also known as Mary's Fountain), which gave the town its name. At the **Church of St John**, mosaics and a grotto mark the traditional birthplace of the Baptist.

The **Hadassah Hospital** complex, just above the town, is internationally known for Marc Chagall's stained-glass windows, depicting the 12 tribes of Israel. The town also has a number of galleries and restaurants. ❑

Map on pages 160–1

TIP

Since the opening of its new museum, Yad Vashem is so busy that the car park is usually full. An alternative is to take the shuttle bus from the Mount Herzl car park.

BELOW: Ein Kerem.

YAD VASHEM

The idea of establishing a Holocaust memorial in Palestine was first proposed in 1942 and the Holocaust Martyrs' and Heroes' Remembrance Authority, which runs it, was finally established in 1963. Today its archive holds 62 million pages of documents and 260,000 photographs, its library has more than 90,000 titles, and the International School for Holocaust Studies has more than 100 educators on its staff. The old Jewish tradition of *Vehigadeta Lebincha* ("And you will tell your children") is much in evidence.

A major expansion and refurbishment of the complex culminated in 2005 with the dedication of a new Holocaust History Museum, three times the size of the old one. The new Yad Vashem uses the latest multimedia means to recount the horrifying story of Jewish massacres from 1933 to 1945, and includes the world's largest collection of Holocaust art, comprising 10,000 works, many of them on carefully preserved thin scraps of paper.

Only the apex of the museum is above ground, forming a skylight. The gray concrete walls intensify the harshness of the structure, which gashes brutally through the Jerusalem hillside. The effect is powerful and, as the museum puts it: " Every visitor leaves Yad Vashem with a personal impression of an event that has universal dimensions."

THE GALILEE AND THE GOLAN

This tour takes in the Christian landmarks of Nazareth, mystic Safed of the Kabbalah, the Roman baths of Tiberias and the forbidding heights of the Golan

Map on pages 180–1

A white-robed Druze puffing away on his pipe in a mountain top-village; a bikini-clad bather soaking in sulphuric springs at a Roman bathhouse: these are the stark contrasts typical of Israel's dynamically diverse north – the Galilee and the Golan.

Extending from the lush Jezreel Valley to the borders of Lebanon and Syria, this relatively compact region, at one moment a desolate expanse of bare rock, can suddenly explode into a blaze of blood-red buttercups and purple irises. Here Christians can retrace the steps of Jesus, while Jews can reflect on the place that produced their greatest mystics.

Lying on the main artery that linked the ancient empires, the Galilee has been a battleground for Egyptian pharaohs, biblical kings, Romans and Jews, Christians and Muslims, Britain and Turkey.

Jewish pioneers established the country's first kibbutzim here. In subsequent decades the kibbutzim have mushroomed to cover much of this region where tribes of Bedouin still live and Arab and Druze villages lie nestled in the hills. A circular tour of the entire Galilee and Golan is less than 400 km (250 miles) – a day's leisurely drive – but even in a month's tour the visitor would get only a passing appreciation of this region's history's incredible history, sacred sites, diverse inhabitants and breathtaking landscapes.

PRECEDING PAGES: the foot of Mt Tabor. **LEFT:** the road to Afula in the Jezreel Valley. **BELOW:** the water system at Megiddo.

The valley

Highway 65 from the center of the country suddenly dips into the **Jezreel Valley**, which, stretching from the Samarian foothills in the south to the slopes of the Galilee in the north, is Israel's largest valley. Because of its strategic location on the ancient Via Maris route, the list of great battles that have scoured this seemingly tranquil stretch is long and colorful. But the greatest battle of all has yet to be fought here. It is the one that the Book of Revelation says will pit the forces of good against the forces of evil for the final battle of mankind at Armageddon.

The site referred to is **Tel Megiddo** (Mount Megiddo) ❶, a 4,000-year-old city in the center of the valley. Turn left at Megiddo Junction into Highway 66 and the Mount is 2 km (1¼ miles) to the north (daily 8am–4pm until 5pm Apr–Sept; tel: 04-6522167; fee).

Even the first written mention of Megiddo – in Egyptian hieroglyphics – describes how war was waged on the city by a mighty pharaoh some 3,500 years ago. Since then many a great figure has met his downfall on this ancient battleground. It is said of the Israelite King Josiah, who was defeated at the hands of the Egyptians around 600 BC: "And his servants carried him in a chariot dead from Megiddo" (I Kings 10, 26). In World War I the British fought a critical battle

against the Turks at Megiddo Pass, with the victorious British general walking away with the title Lord Allenby of Megiddo.

In the heap of ruins that make up the *tel* (mound) of Megiddo, archaeologists have uncovered 20 cities. At the visitors' center a miniature model of the site gives definition to what the untrained eye could see as just a pile of stones. It is actually a 4,000-year-old Canaanite temple, King Solomon's stables (built for 500 horses), and an underground water system built by King Ahab 2,800 years ago to protect the city's water in times of siege. Steps and lighting enable easier exploration of the 120-meter (390-ft) tunnel, and of the almost 60-meter (200-ft) high shaft, which was once the system's well.

Beit She'arim

Head north along highway 66 through the pleasant but unremarkable countryside of the Jezreel Valley and turn right at Hatishbi Junction into Route 722 and right again several kilometers later into 75. You will soon reach **Beit She'arim** ❷ (daily 8am–4pm, until 5pm Apr–Sept; tel: 04-9831643; fee). This is Israel's version of a necropolis and was the most important burial place in the Jewish world during the Talmudic period. The limestone hills have been hollowed out to form a series of catacombs. Inside the labyrinths, vaulted chambers are lined with hundreds of sarcophagi of marble or stone (depending on the social rank of the deceased). Each of the coffins – often elaborately engraved – weighs nearly 5 tonnes. When the Romans forbade the Jews to settle in Jerusalem, the center of Jewish national and spiritual life moved to Beit She'arim and this 2nd-century burial ground became a chosen spot not only for local residents but also for Jews everywhere.

It's worth climbing the hill for a good view the Jezre'el Valley and the Carmel Mountain Range. On the hilltop is a bronze statue of Alexander Zeid, who discovered the necropolis in the 1920s.

Back along 75, right along 77 and right again along 79 is **Tsipori** ❸ (daily 8am–4pm, until 5pm Apr–Sept; tel: 04-6568272;

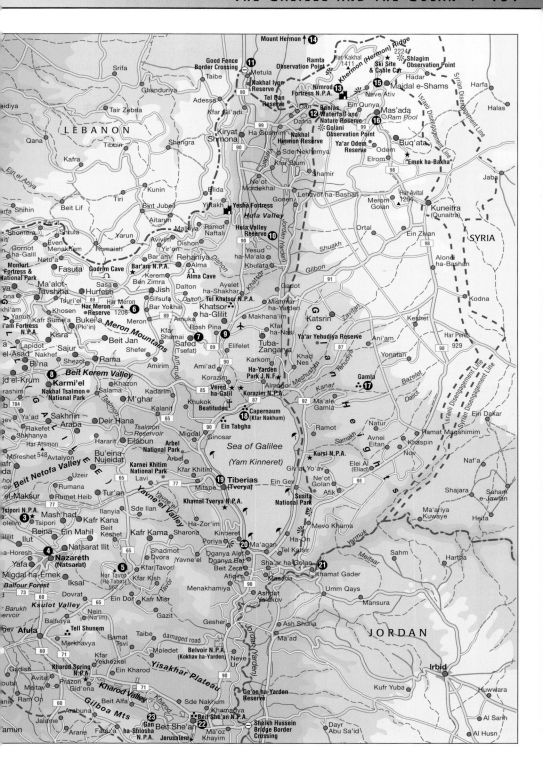

fee), known to the Greeks as Sepphoris. Reflecting this settlement's long history are a 4,500-seat Roman ampitheater, a beautifully preserved 2nd-century mosaic of a woman dubbed "the Mona Lisa of the Galilee" and a Crusader fortress.

Cradle of Christianity

Further along highway 79 is **Nazareth ❹** (www.nazareth.muni.il), a strange blend of the timeless and the topical, the sacred town where Jesus Christ spent much of his life and which is today a bustling city of more than 70,000, Israel's largest Israeli Arab city. "Can anything good come out of Nazareth?" (John 1, 46). This rhetorical question might seem puzzling today, particularly to millions of Christians for whom Nazareth is equated with Christianity itself. But when it was posed two millennia ago, the only feature that most distinguished this village in the lower Galilee was its obscurity.

A Franciscan waters his garden.

Since then, the quaint town where Jesus grew up has become renowned. Today, of almost two dozen churches commemorating Nazareth's most esteemed resident, the grandest of all is the monumental **Basilica of the Annunciation** (daily 8am–6pm; free). The largest church in the Middle East, it was completed only in 1969, but it encompasses the remains of previous Byzantine churches. It marks the spot where the Angel Gabriel is said to have informed the Virgin Mary that God had chosen her to bear His son. The event has been given an international flavor, and is depicted inside in a series of elaborate murals, each from a different country. In one, Mary appears kimono-clad and with slanted eyes; in another, she's wearing a turban and bright African garb. Not to be outdone, the Americans have produced a highly modernistic Cubist version of the Virgin.

BELOW: the Basilica of the Annunciation.

In the basement of the **Church of St Joseph** (next to the Basilica) is a cavern

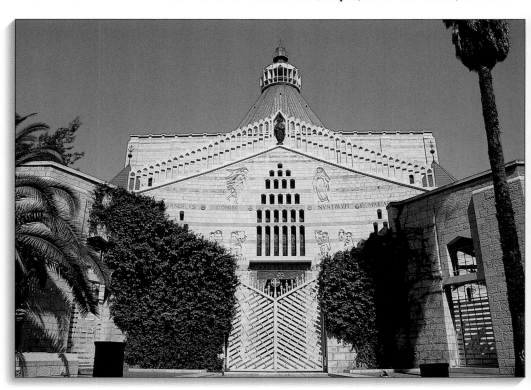

reputed to have been the carpentry workshop of Joseph, Jesus's earthly father.

Some of the simpler churches, however, capture an air of intimacy and sanctity that the colossal Basilica lacks. This is especially so in the **Greek Orthodox Church of St Gabriel**, nearly a kilometer further north at the end of Maria Road. Upon entering the small dark shrine you hear nothing but the faint rush of water. Lapping up against the sides of the old well inside the church is the same underground spring that provided Nazareth with its water 2,000 years ago. Another very atmospheric church is the tiny Catholic one which was previously a synagogue. At one time believed to be the actual one attended by Jesus, it is now thought to have been built on the same site, probably in the 2nd century AD.

Eight km (5 miles) north of Nazareth on Highway 754, nestled among pomegranate and olive groves, is the Arab village of **Kafr Kana**. Shortly after being baptised, Jesus attended the wedding of a poor family in this town. Here, says St John's Gospel, he used his miraculous powers for the first time, making the meagre pitchers of water overflow with wine. Two small churches in the village commemorate the feat.

Ha Tabor ❺ rises to the east of Nazareth and south of Kafr Kana, but it is necessary to travel around almost four sides of a square – best east along 77 then south on 65 – to reach this huge hump of a hill. Mount Tabor offers an overview of the whole Jezreel Valley – a patchwork of gold and green farmland. This strangely symmetrical hill dominates much of the valley. It was here that the biblical prophetess Deborah was said to have led an army of 10,000 Israelites to defeat their idol-worshiping enemies. Two churches commemorate the transfiguration of Christ, which is also said to have taken place here.

When his sermons began to provoke the Jews, Jesus took three of his disciples

Map on pages 180–1

Tensions between Nazareth's Muslim majority and Christian minority are never far beneath the surface and resentment runs deepest over a contested piece of property by the Basilica of the Annunciation on which a mosque has been built.

BELOW: Nazareth, the country's biggest Israeli Arab city.

Traditional themes get a contemporary look from an artist in Safed.

and ascended Mount Tabor. There, the Gospels say, "He was transfigured before them – his face shone like the sun and his garments became white as light." The Franciscan **Basilica of the Transfiguration** commemorates the event, which Christians believe was a foreshadowing of his resurrection.

Atmospheric Safed

About 30 km (18 miles) due north of Mount Tabor are the highest peaks in the Galilee. Many people believe that they exude an inexplicable air of something eternal that makes them seem even higher than they are. Travel north along 65, west along 85 and northeast on 866 to the Meron Mountains. To reach the highest peak, **Har Meron** ❻ – at 1,208 meters (3,955 ft), the highest summit in pre-1967 Israel – you have to continue on Highway 89 for 11 km (7 miles) and turn south onto the mountain road. When not marred by the summer heat haze, the sweeping view from the Mediterranean to Mount Hermon is exceptional. These mountains are filled with the magic of the tombs of the rabbis who composed the Kabbalah, the highly fashionable great Jewish mystical texts which have enchanted the likes of pop-singer Madonna.

At the base of the mountain, back on Highway 89, in **Meron** village, is the tomb of Shimon Bar-Yochai, the revered rabbi who drew Jews to the region in the first place. On the feast of Lag Ba'Omer in May you can still see tens of thousands of his devout followers gather outside nearby Safed's synagogues and make their way in a joyous procession to his grave at the foot of Mount Meron.

BELOW: old Safed has the atmosphere of past centuries.

Immediately east of Meron is **Safed** ❼ (www.safed.co.il). This attractive hilltop town can be reached by heading southeast along 89. Sheltered by the highest peaks in the Galilee, Safed seems also to be sheltered from time itself. Its

narrow, cobble-stoned streets wind their way through stone archways and overlook the domed rooftops of 16th-century houses. Devout men, clad in black, congregate in medieval synagogues, the echo of their chants filling the streets. A modern area of Safed, with some 27,000 residents, has sprung up around the original city core.

When the Spanish Inquisition sent thousands of Jews fleeing, many ended up in Safed, bringing with them the skills and scholarship of the golden age they had left behind in Spain. The rabbinical scholars of Safed were so prolific that in 1563 the city was prompted to set up the first printing press in the Middle East (or, in fact, in all of Asia).

The Shulchan Aroch, the basic set of daily rituals for Jews, was compiled here. But the real focus of Safed's sages was not the mundane but the mystical. Many had been drawn to the city in the first place because of its proximity to the tomb of Rabbi Shimon Bar-Yochai, the 2nd-century sage who is believed to have written the core of the Kabbalah, Judaism's foremost mystical text.

The efforts of Safed's wise men to narrow the gap between heaven and earth left not only great scholarly work and poignant poetry but also a legacy of legends about their mysterious powers. At one synagogue (Abohav) an earthquake destroyed the entire building but left unscathed the one wall facing Jerusalem.

Every synagogue here is wrapped in its own comparable set of legends, which the *shamash* (deacon) is usually delighted to share. Not all the synagogues are medieval, many of the original ones having been destroyed and replaced by more modern structures, but the spirit of the old still lingers in these few lanes off Kikar Meginim.

The special atmosphere that permeates Safed has captured the imagination of dozens of artists who have made it their home. Like the rest of the old city, the artists' quarter of Safed remains untouched. "Nothing has been added for the benefit of the tourist" is the claim. Nothing has to be. Winding your way through the labyrinth of lanes, you'll find more than 50 studios and galleries as well as a general art gallery and a museum of printing. Another highlight in Safed is the Klezmer Hasidic Musical Festival each August.

Towering above the center of Safed, littered with Crusader ruins, is **Citadel Hill**, an excellent lookout point, taking in a panorama that extends from the slopes of Lebanon to the Sea of Galilee.

Havens in the hills

The wide open spaces of the Western Galilee (west of Safed) act as a haven, attracting various idealists seeking to carve their own small utopias on its slopes. So, in addition to the more common settlements like kibbutzim, Bedouin encampments and Arab, Druze and Circassian villages, you'll find a community of transcendental meditationists at **Hararit** who have found their nirvana on these secluded slopes. There is also a colony of vegetarians at **Amirim** who have set up an organic farm as well as a guesthouse where visitors can indulge in gourmet vegetarian meals. The villagers of **Harduf** also eat only organically grown foods,

Map
on pages
180–1

Safed's **Israel Bible Museum** exhibits 300 visual scenes of the Bible by the artist Phillip Ratner. The **Kabbalah Museum** explains kabbalah teachings. Mila Rozenfeld's **Doll Museum** (Eshtam Building) has a collection of costumed dolls. **Beit Hameiri** is a historical museum documenting Safed's Jewish community.

BELOW: Safed, a town of the artistic and the Orthodox.

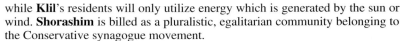

BELOW: a statue at Karmi'el celebrates life.

while **Klil**'s residents will only utilize energy which is generated by the sun or wind. **Shorashim** is billed as a pluralistic, egalitarian community belonging to the Conservative synagogue movement.

To be sure, even the mainstream Jewish inhabitants of this region tend to lead a lifestyle governed by environmental if not religious concerns. Many have left the crowded center of the country to seek a higher quality of life and fresher air. There are many high-tech opportunities in the region and the commute to Haifa is only 30 minutes.

Karmi'el ❽ has burgeoned into the largest town in the Western Galilee. It was established in 1964, and its population of 60,000 includes native-born Israelis as well as Jewish immigrants from 34 countries (including many Americans and, recently, Ethiopians and Russians). Clean, pretty and prosperous, Karmi'el is considered a model development town. Near its center, against a backdrop of desolate mountains, is a series of larger-than-life sculptures depicting the history of Israel's Jewish people. Each July, Karmiel hosts an International Folk Dance Festival.

Karmi'el is set in the **Beit Kerem Valley**, the dividing line between what is considered the Upper Galilee (to the north), with peaks jutting up to almost 1,200 meters (4,000 ft), and the Lower Galilee (to the south), a much gentler expanse of rolling hills, none of which exceeds 600 meters (2,000 ft). This area west of Safed has not been included in the formal route of this tour but the landscape is spectacular and many of the aforementioned "off-beat" villages offer accommodations.

The Galilee Panhandle

Descending eastwards from Safed on Highway 89 is the land extending north of the Sea of Galilee which gradually narrows into what is known as the finger of the Galilee in Hebrew or the Galilee panhandle in English, with Metula at its tip. This is particularly pretty countryside. The east opens up into the sprawling Hula Valley, beyond which hover the Golan Heights. Towering over the valley to the west are the **Naphtali Mountains**, beyond which loom the even higher mountains of Lebanon. These picturesque peaks were in the past a source of frequent Katyusha rocket attacks on the Israeli towns below.

Apart from the beauty it offers, the road to Metula is an odyssey through the making of modern Israel. The first stop on this trek is **Rosh Pina ❾**. On the rock-strewn barren terrain they found here a century ago, pioneers fleeing from pogroms in Eastern Europe set up the first Jewish settlement to be founded in the Galilee since Roman times. They called it Rosh Pina, meaning the "cornerstone" a name which came from the passage in Psalm 118 "The stone which the builders rejected has become the cornerstone." The original 30 families who settled here were part of the first wave of Jewish immigration that began in the 1880s.

Rosh Pina, a quaint town of about 1,000, has maintained something of its original rural character. Cobble-stoned streets line the old section of the town, and 19th-century houses, though badly neglected, still stand.

Continuing northwards towards Metula on Highway 90, the next stop after several kilometers takes you off the road of modern history, exposing instead the far more ancient foundations of the country. **Khatsor ha-Glilit (Tel Hazor)** (daily 8am–4pm, until 5pm Apr–Sept; tel: 04-6937290; fee) is one of the oldest archaeological sites in Israel – and by far the largest. With its 23 layers of civilization spanning 3,000 years, it was the inspiration for *The Source*, James Michener's 1965 novel.

Map on pages 180–1

The Hula Valley

This is the region of the **Hula Valley**, a stretch of lush land dotted with farming villages and little fish ponds that would seem like a mirage to someone who had stood on the same spot 40 years ago. Then you would have seen 4,000 hectares (10,000 acres) of malaria-infested swamp land – home to snakes, water buffalo and wild boar.

The draining of the valley was one of the most monumental tasks undertaken by the State of Israel in its early days. It took six years. By 1957 the lake had been emptied, leaving a verdant valley in its place but now part of the region has been re-swamped, as excessive peat in the ground is impeding agriculture. You can get an idea of what the area was like before the drainage by visiting the 80 hectares (200 acres) of swamp land that have been set aside as the **Hula Valley Reserve** ❿ (daily 8am–4pm, until 5pm Apr–Sept; tel: 04-6937069; fee). Three kilometers (2 miles) after Yesod Hama'ale junction, turn right into the reserve. There is also a museum devoted to the natural history of the region at **Kibbutz Khulata** just to the south known as the Dubrovin Farm; it recreates living conditions in the late 19th century. There is a guesthouse in the northern part of the valley at **Kfar Blum**, a kibbutz with a distinctly Anglo-Saxon tone.

The nearby town of **Kiryat Shmona** commemorates the heroes of Tel Hai

Hula Valley Reserve.

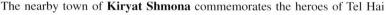

BELOW:
the war memorial
at Kiryat Shmona.

and is, in fact, built on the site from where the Arabs used to launch their attacks. It is one of scores of development towns founded shortly after Israel became a state, in order to integrate some of the 700,000 Jews who had poured into the new country. Kiryat Shmona, like many other "development towns," was hardly a town at all; it began life as a series of corrugated iron huts known as *ma'abarot* (essentially refugee camps). Situated close to the border, it has been for years the target of rocket attacks and terrorist infiltrations from the Lebanese mountains that overlook it, and the town was devastated by hundreds of missiles during the Second Lebanon War in the summer of 2006. The town is today quiet, with a population of 20,000, but it has little of interest to tourists.

Neat rows of crops near Kiryat Shmona.

The road to Metula

When the end of World War I left Palestine's status unclear, Arab gangs attacked the Jews in this most northern region, forcing them out of their settlements. The settlers at **Tel Khai** and **Kfar Gil'adi**, north of Kiryat Shmonah, though outnumbered, held out under siege for months until their leader, Joseph Trumpeldor, was shot and killed. The incident prompted the Jews to improve their self-defense and triggered the formation of the Haganah, predecessor of the Israel Defense Forces.

The building from which the settlers defended themselves is now a museum devoted to the Haganah. Nearby is a memorial to Trumpeldor and seven fellow fighters, including two women, who died in the attack. Thousands of Israeli youths converge on the Tel Hai site on the anniversary of Trumpeldor's death. There is also a youth hostel here and a guesthouse at neighboring Kfar Gil'adi, today a flourishing kibbutz.

BELOW AND RIGHT: the Galilee, as viewed from Khatsor ha-Glilit.

Just before Metula, in the **Nakhal Iyon Reserve** (daily 8am–4pm, until 5pm

Apr–Sept; tel: 04-6951519; fee), is a picturesque waterfall that flows impressively in the winter months (Oct–May) but is completely dry the rest of the year. This is due to a longstanding arrangement by which Israel permits Lebanese farmers to divert the water for agricultural use.

Until the Golan was captured from Syria in 1967, **Metula** ⓫ (www.metulla.muni.il), Israel's most northern point, surrounded on three sides by Lebanese land, was the target of frequent rocket attacks. Founded in 1896 by Baron Edmund de Rothschild who purchased land from local Druze for the same wave of Russian immigrants that had settled in Rosh Pina, it was for two decades the only settlement in the area. Even today, the nearest major shopping center is 10 km (6 miles) away in Kiryat Shmona. But one attraction is the **Canada Center**, the country's only Olympic-size ice rink.

Apart from the fresh mountain air, abundant apple orchards (much of the country's supply comes from here) and charming *pensions*, what draws tourists to this secluded town of 600 inhabitants is its now famous border with Lebanon. Since Israel withdrew from Lebanon in 2000, there is no daily stream of Lebanese workers coming to Israel each day, but the "Good Fence" border offers Israelis an opportunity to stare into the troubled territory of their northern neighbor.

The source of the River Jordan

Return to Kiryat Shmona and travel east on Highway 99. Some 10 km (6 miles) east of Kiryat Shmona, on the edge of the Golan Heights (and what used to be the Syrian border), is the archaeological site of **Tel Dan** (daily 8am–4pm, until 5pm Apr–Sept; tel: 04-6951579; fee). Situated at the northern tip of Israel, it was founded in biblical times by members of the tribe of Dan, after quarrels with the

Map
on pages
180–1

TIP

The fee to Tel Hazor includes free entrance to the museum at **Kibbutz Ayelet ha-Shakhar** and visitors are encouraged to stop off at the museum first in order to better understand the excavations. The kibbutz also runs a popular guesthouse.

Philistines forced them to leave the southern coast. It is also notorious as one of two cities where Jeroboam permitted worship of the idolatrous golden calf.

Today the site includes various Israelite ruins, a Roman fountain and a triple-arched Canaanite gateway. In the summer, volunteers help to excavate this active and scenic *tel* where the source waters for the Jordan River emerge in attractive bubbling brooks. The museum at **Kibbutz Dan** nearby has descriptions of the geology of the region and the reclamation of the Hula Valley below. The kibbutz also runs a very popular restaurant, the **Dag on the Dan**, specializing in fresh trout from the nearby streams.

The **Dan River** provides the greatest single source of the Jordan River – in fact, "Jordan" is a contraction of the Hebrew *Yored Dan* (descending from Dan), and that's precisely what this biblical river does. For its 264-km (165-mile) length, the Jordan flows from the snowy peak of **Mount Hermon** to the catchment basin of the Dead Sea, 400 meters (1,300 ft) below sea level, and the lowest point on the face of the earth.

The Golan

Several kilometers further east the **Banias Waterfall** is among the most popular natural attractions in the country – and has been for thousands of years. "Banias" is a corruption of the Greek *Panaeas*, and in a cave near the spring are the remains of an ancient temple built in honor of Pan, the Greek god of the forests.

Roman and old Crusader ruins may also be visited at **Banias**, which is in the **Mount Hermon Nature Reserve** (daily 8am–4pm, until 5pm Apr–Sept; tel: 04-6902577; fee), but the real attractions are the waterfalls, including the country's largest, and inviting pools.

Kibbutzim aren't what they used to be. In 2005 Kibbutz Shamir, just west of Kiryat Shmona, raised $48 million on the US NASDAQ market for its optical industries firm which makes quality lenses.

BELOW:
Banias Waterfall.

Before 1967, Banias was located in Syrian territory. Thus you are now officially on the fiercely contested Golan Heights. **The Golan** (www.golan.org.il) is a sombre massif doomed by history and bloodied by almost ceaseless war. It is a great block of dark grey rock lifted high above the Upper Jordan Valley, and those who have it have the power to rain misery upon their neighbors.

The Golan is a mighty fortress created by the hand of nature. During the Tertiary Age, geological folding lifted its hard basalt stone from the crust of the earth. Today it is a sloped plateau, rising in the north to heights greater than a full kilometer above sea level. It stretches 67 km (42 miles) from north to south and 25 km (15 miles) from east to west.

Israel considers the Golan Heights to be part of its territory (in 1981 Israeli military occupation of this former Syrian territory was replaced with civil law and administration), although few other countries accept this *fait accompli*. Israeli justification for absorbing the Golan focused on Syria's belligerence, and the fact that it was used as a base for artillery shelling of Israeli settlements below.

Since the beginning of the peace process there has been much talk of territorial compromise over the Golan, but many people in Israel vehemently oppose such a move, in particular the 15,000 Jewish settlers in the Golan.

Historic redoubt

The Golan has been disputed throughout history. In antiquity it was the greatest natural barrier traversed by the Via Maris, the "Sea Highway" that led from Egypt and the coastal plain across the Galilee and the Golan to the kingdom of Mesopotamia. The Golan was allocated to the tribe of Manasseh during the biblical era, but was frequently lost and recaptured over the centuries. Under

Map on pages 180–1

A camel decked out for tourist rides.

BELOW: most of Israel's apples come from the Metula region.

Roman rule, Jewish settlement in the Golan increased, and a few generations later, during the Jewish Revolt against Rome (AD 66), many of the descendants of those settlers met cruel deaths during the epic battle for the fortress of Gamla (*see page 195*).

The mountain range changed hands frequently during the following centuries, though archaeological evidence indicates a substantial Jewish population until the time of the Crusades; for the next eight centuries, the area was practically desolate.

At the end of the 19th century the Ottoman Turks tried to repopulate the Golan with non-Jewish settlers, to serve as a buffer against invasion from the south. Among those who put down roots here were some Druze, Circassians fleeing the Russian invasion of the Caucasus Mountains in 1878, and Turkomans who migrated from Central Asia. A village of Nusseiris (North Syrian Alawites) was also established here.

After World War I, when British troops under General Edmund Allenby drove the Ottomans off the Golan, the region was included in the British Mandate of Palestine, but in the San Remo conference of 1923 it was traded off to the French sphere of influence. From 1948 to 1967 the Syrians used the Golan Heights as a forward base of operations against Israel. Jewish villages in the Hula Valley were shelled by Syrian artillery mounted here. Syria continued to install fortifications in the Golan throughout the 1960s, converting the region into a military zone.

War finally broke out on 6 June 1967 with Syrian army attacks on Kibbutz Dan, Ashmura and She'ar Yashuv. The attack was blunted the following day, and on 9 June Israeli troops counter-attacked. Within 48 hours all Syrian units on the Golan had either retreated or surrendered.

Many of the ancient buildings in northern Israel are built from the black volcanic basalt rock taken from the Golan Heights.

BELOW: a church in the Golan Heights.

From war to peace

Only six inhabited villages, with a total population of 6,400 people, remained on the Golan at the time of the Israeli victory, these including five Druze communities and one Shiite village at Ghajar. Today these villages house more than 20,000 inhabitants, who live peacefully within Israel but have refused to take Israeli citizenship and "pragmatically" speak publicly in support of Syria for fear that they may one day find themselves looking to Damascus as their capital.

Within weeks of the 1967 conquest, members of Israeli kibbutzim began establishing communities in the unpopulated hills, the first being Merom Golan. During the following years the region was transformed as orchards were planted, including apples, pears, peaches, almonds, plums and cherries, as well as vineyards.

Syria attacked again on 6 October 1973, the Jewish Day of Atonement, when most Israeli troops were on leave with their families. The next day Syrian troops occupied nearly half the Golan. Israel responded on 8 October in what was to become the greatest tank battle in history. Within a week Syria had lost some 1,200 of an estimated 1,500 Soviet-built tanks. By 24 October, Israeli units were within sight of Damascus when the United Nations called for peace, and Israel complied. A dangerous legacy of minefields remains.

Now for more than three decades peace has pre-

Map on pages 180-1

vailed. Indeed, this has been Israel's quietest border, with first President Hafez el Assad and in recent years his son Bashir scrupulously adhering to the armistice agreement signed with Israel in 1975. As a result, domestic tourism to this region, which remains delightfully cool in the summer months, has flourished, although it remains rarely visited by overseas tourists. Ample but unexceptional bed-and-breakfast accommodation has sprung up on most of the region's settlements

Most Israelis see the Golan as a vital buffer zone between them and Syria, an enormous bunker filling its ancient role of blocking invasion. But visitors who do come usually tour the old Syrian fortifications that dot the area. The **Nimrod Fortress** ⓭ (daily 8am–4pm, until 5pm Apr–Sept; tel: 04-7762186; fee) on the northern Golan – turn left onto Highway 989 from 99 – is one of these. From this 13th-century Syrian fortress built to defend the waters of Banias below, one gains a spectacular view of the Northern Galilee and the Naphtali Hills beyond, and it is easy to understand the strategic reasons for its construction.

Mount Hermon

Towering above the north end of the Golan is **Mount Hermon** ⓮ (2,814 meters/9,230 ft) with several ranges radiating from it. It occupies an area roughly 40 by 20 km (25 by 12 miles) and is divided between Lebanon, Syria, Israel and several demilitarized zones under UN jurisdiction. About 20 percent of this area is under Israeli control, including the southeast ridge **Ketef ha-Hermon** (the Hermon Shoulder), whose highest point rises to 2,224 meters (7,296 ft).

The higher areas of Mount Hermon are snow-covered through most of the year, and each winter brings snow to all elevations over 1,200 meters (3,900 ft). Israeli ski enthusiasts have opened a modest ski resort on these slopes, with a

The Golan Druze still have strong ties with Syria. Many young people study at universities in Syria and marriages are often arranged usually between young Syrian Druze women and Golan men. The economic opportunities are greater on the Golan.

BELOW: the remains of Nimrod Fortress.

chair-lift and an equipment rental shop for skis, boots, poles and toboggans. The slopes are often compared to those found in New England – not particularly lofty, but nevertheless a challenge and a pleasure to ski. The ski resort (open 8am–4pm generally Jan–Apr, depending on snowfall; tel: 04-6981337) can be reached by continuing along highway 989 and turning north onto 98 in the outskirts of Majdel e-Shams.

Nature on Mount Hermon is of particular interest to Israelis because it's the only sub-alpine habitat in the country. Several birds, such as the rock nuthatch and the redstart, are at the southernmost extremity of their range here, while others, such as the Hermon horned lark, are found nowhere else.

Many dolinas are scattered around Mount Hermon. These are cavities in the surface of the rock formed by karstic action on the mountain's limestone. In the winter the dolinas fill with snow, and they are the last areas to melt in the spring, thus supporting lush green vegetation long after the rest of the slope has dried out under the intense sun.

Druze villages

At the foot of Mount Hermon is **Majdal e-Shams** ⓯, the largest of the Druze villages on the Golan, which is located as the junction of Highways 989 and 98. The town has good restaurants and souvenir shops, and is popular with tourists.

The Druze village of **Mas'ada,** 8 km (5 miles) to the south along 98 overlooks the **Ram Pool** ⓰, a fascinating geological phenomenon. This is one of only two extinct volcanos in the world, which over time has evolved into a small lake (the other is in Kenya) .

A popular tourist pastime in the spring and summer on the Golan is visiting

In the winter the adventurous sort will sometimes ski on the Hermon in the morning and drive down to Eilat to go scuba diving on the same day.

BELOW: skiing on Mount Hermon.

farms that allow you to pick (weigh and pay for) your own fruit such as cherries, blackberries and raspberries, which are expensive delicacies in Israel. Among other places this can be done at Elrom, 7 km (4 miles) south of Mas'ada.

Katsrin, 20 km (13 miles) to the southwest along Highway 91, is the modern "capital"of the Golan and the region's only municipal center. Established in 1977, it is designed in the shape of a butterfly and is home to the **Golan Archaeological Museum** (Sun–Thur 9am–4pm, Fri 9am–1pm, Sat 10am–1pm; tel: 04-6969634; fee) which exhibits artifacts from the ancient settlement of Katsrin.

With a population of 5,000, **Katsrin** is the home of Golan Wineries, one of the country's largest winemakers who in the 1980s revolutionized the country's wine industry, previously known for cheap sweet red wine used for religious purposes. For Israelis, Golan is synonymous with good wine and, assisted by Californian experts, it sells $30 million worth of quality wines a year, including $5 million in exports. Dozens of other smaller Israeli wineries have taken their inspiration from the Golan venture.

You can visit the Golan winery in Katsrin (Sun–Thur 8.30am–5pm, Fri 8.30am–1.30pm; tel: 04-6968435; www.golanwines.co.il; free entry and free samples). Teetotallers will prefer the tour of the nearby Mei Eden mineral water factory, also free with free samples (open Sun–Thur 9am–4pm but book the tour in advance; tel: 04-6961050).

Gamla

Another often-visited site on the Golan is **Gamla** ⑰. Travel south from Katsrin on 9088, left and right onto 808. Gamla (daily 8am–4pm, until 5pm Apr–Sept; tel: 04-6822282; fee) was the "Masada of the north," a fortified town of the south-central Golan which, in AD 66, was the focus of one of the early battles in the Jewish revolt against Rome. Initially, the rebels put Vespasian and three full Roman legions to shame. The over-confident Roman leader threw his troops against the Jewish bastion only to have them humbled by a much smaller and less professional Jewish force. Recovering, the embarrassed Romans besieged the Jewish town in one of the most bitter battles of the war. Vespasian vowed that no mercy would be shown.

The Romans gradually pushed the Jews to the precipice above which this mountain-top city was built, and, when Roman victory appeared imminent, many defenders committed suicide rather than surrender. Four thousand Jews were killed in battle; another 5,000 either committed suicide or were slaughtered by the Romans after Gamla had fallen to them.

"The sole survivors were two women," historian Josephus Flavius wrote, "They survived because when the town fell they eluded the fury of the Romans, who spared not even babes in arms, but seized all they found and flung them from the citadel."

The site was reduced to rubble by the Romans and then lost to history for precisely 1,902 years. In 1968, Gamla was rediscovered during a systematic Israeli survey of the region. Today it is possible for visitors to stroll through the ancient streets of this community and inspect the remains of many ancient houses, and

Map on pages 180–1

In English the Eagle is often considered the king of the birds, but in Hebrew it is the vulture which is given this title, outranking the eagle. See the vultures at Gamla and you'll understand why.

BELOW: a Druze shopkeeper.

even a synagogue, all of which were constructed out of the Golan's somber black basalt stone.

The ruins are clustered on a steep ridge, and, if you tour the area between late winter and early summer, there is a very good chance of seeing magnificent griffon vultures with a 2-meter (7-ft) wingspan soaring to their nests beneath you. The site also commands a fabulous view of the Sea of Galilee.

Among the fields to the east of Gamla it is possible to find several prehistoric dolmens. These are Stone-Age structures which look like crude tables, with a large, flat stone bridging several supporting stones. They are generally considered to be burial monuments, and most are dated to about 4,000 BC. Dolmens are found at several other sites around the Golan and the Galilee.

Jewel of the Galilee

Glowing like an emerald, its tranquil surface framed in a purplish-brown halo of mountains, the **Sea of Galilee** is probably the most breathtaking lake in the country. At 21 km (13 miles) long and 11 km (7 miles) wide and a depth of no more than 45 meters (150 ft), it may not be enormous by global standards, but it has, through some romantically inspired hyperbole, come to be known as a "sea" (the Sea of Galilee, the Sea of Tiberias, the Sea of Ginossar are its most popular names. In Hebrew it is called Yam Kinneret because it's shaped like a *kinnor* or harp.

Not surprisingly, these bountiful shores have been inhabited for millennia, with the earliest evidence of habitation dating back 5,000 years to a cult of moon-worshippers that sprouted in the south. Some 3,000 years later the same lake witnessed the birth and spread of Christianity on its shores, while high up on the cliffs above, Jewish rebels sought refuge from Roman soldiers. The dramas of the

Fish in the Sea of Galilee are so plentiful that catches of 270 kg (600 lb) don't make headlines. It is recorded that, in 1896, more than 4,000 kg (9,200 lb) of fish were caught in one massive net.

BELOW: an ancient dolmen near Ma'ale Gamla.

past, however, have since faded into the idyllic landscape. Today it is new water sports, not new religions, that are hatched on these azure shores.

Map on pages 180-1

Around the lake

Descend highway 869 to the lake and travel anti-clockwise along 92 and then 87 to Capernaum. It was in the numerous fishing villages around the Sea of Galilee that Jesus found his first followers. The village of **Capernaum** ⑱ on the northern tip of the lake, became his second home. Here he is said to have preached more sermons and performed more miracles than anywhere else.

It was a metropolis of sorts in its heyday, and at least five of the disciples came from here. (It is after one of them, a simple fisherman named Peter, that the Galilee's most renowned fish gets its name.) Today the site houses the elaborate remains of a 2nd-century synagogue – said to be built over the original one where Jesus used to preach. There is also a recently completed church shaped like a ship on what was believed to be the house of St Peter, and there is also a Franciscan Monastery here.

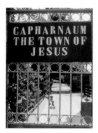

In the neighboring town of **Ein Tabgha**, Jesus is said to have multiplied five loaves and two fishes into enough food to feed the 5,000 hungry people who had come to hear him speak. The modern **Church of the Multiplication** (open daily 8.30am–5pm) was built over the colorful mosaic floor of a Byzantine shrine in 1982. Next to it is the Church of Peter's Primacy.

A claim to fame.

It was standing on a hilltop overlooking the Sea of Galilee that Jesus proclaimed to the masses that had gathered below: "Blessed are the meek, for they shall inherit the earth." This line from the Sermon on the Mount is immortalized by the majestic **Church and Monastery of the Beatitudes** (daily 8am–5pm;

BELOW: the Church of the Beatitudes.

free). This octagonal church, set in well-maintained gardens, belongs to the Franciscan order and was built in the 1930s. **Vered Hagalil**, (www.veredhagalil.co.il) adjacent to the Church of the Beatitudes, is a bit of an anomaly in these parts with its Wild West-style restaurant, chalet accommodation and horseback tours.

Moving back south along Highway 90, you will first come to the towering cliffs of **Arbel**. Today a rock climbers' haven, during Roman times they served as a hideout for Bar Kochba and his Jewish rebels.

Nearby is **Ginosar**, an especially beautiful kibbutz with a luxurious guesthouse. Ask some of the residents about the perfectly intact 2,000-year-old boat recently uncovered on the shores of the kibbutz.

Tiberias, a lakeside resort

The capital of the lake, **Tiberias** ⓳, has become known for its "fun in the sun" spirit. A sprawling city of 60,000, halfway down the west coast, it is one of the country's most popular resorts. On its new boardwalk, lined with seafood restaurants, you can dig into delicious St Peter's fish while enjoying a stunning view of the lake. On the marina you can have your pick of water-skiing or windsurfing, or go for a dip at one of the beaches along the outskirts of the city. During summer you'll need to dunk yourself in the water one way or another.

With all the distractions available in this popular playground, it's easy to forget that Tiberias is considered one of the four holy Jewish cities. To remind you, there are the tombs of several famous Jewish sages buried here, including the 12th-century philosopher Moses Maimonides and the self-taught scholar, Rabbi Akiva, who was killed by the Romans after the Bar-Kochba uprising.

When it was founded by Herod Antipas around AD 20, Tiberias failed to attract

Vered Hagalil Guest Farm was created by Yehuda Avni, who emigrated from Chicago to Israel in the late 1940s, and his Jerusalem-born wife, Yonah. They transformed barren land into a leisure complex.

BELOW: the Jordan Valley at the south end of the Sea of Galilee.

devout Jews because it was thought to be built over an ancient Jewish cemetery and so considered impure. But eventually economic incentives, as well as a symbolic "purification" of the city by a well-respected rabbi, cleared the way for settlement. During the 2nd and 3rd centuries it reached its zenith. With a population of 40,000, it became the focus of Jewish academic life. It was at Tiberias that scholars codified the sounds of the Hebrew script and wrote the Mishnah, the great commentary on the Bible.

By the eve of the Arab conquest of 636, Tiberias was the most important Christian center outside Jerusalem. A 12th-century battle between Muslims and Crusaders destroyed the city, and, after being resettled, it was again reduced to rubble in 1837, this time by an earthquake. The repeated destruction of the city has, unfortunately, left only meager souvenirs of its vibrant past. A few remains of Crusader towers dot the shoreline, and an 18th-century mosque is crammed in between ice cream stands in the main square.

For historians and hedonists alike, Tiberias's main drawing-card is the **hot springs** situated at the southern outskirts of the city. There are many hypotheses about the cause of this natural wonder. In fact, the same cataclysmic convulsions that millions of years ago carved the Jordan Rift also created these 17 springs that gush from a depth of 2,000 meters (6,500 ft) to spew up hot streams of mineral-rich water. The therapeutic properties of the springs have been exploited for centuries.

Spa treatments

For some contemporary healing, go to **Hamei Tiberias**. This hotel-spa offers a range of treatments, from whirlpools to electrohydrotherapy, that are reputed to

St Peter's fish for sale.

cure everything from skin ailments to respiratory problems and, some claim, sterility. In the winter, a soak in these mineral-rich jacuzzis can be a soothing respite from the damp Galilee air.

You can see the original baths the Romans used in the **National Archaeological Park** across the street in a fascinating little **museum** (Sun–Thur 10am–noon, 3–5pm; fee). Also within this national monument, which is the site of the ancient city of Khamat, archaeologists have uncovered a 2nd-century mosaic synagogue floor – undoubtedly the most exquisite ruins you'll find in Tiberias. Maimonides tomb on Ben Zakai St. just south of the hotel district is a popular site for Jewish pilgrims.

Just outside the city, 4 km (2½ miles) to the west along 77, are the **Horns of Hittim** (Karnei Khitim) where in 1187 the Muslim forces of Saladin defeated the Crusaders in the decisive battle that brought an end to the Crusader Kingdom.

Baptism in the Jordan

Shortly after Jesus left Nazareth at the age of 30, he met John the Baptist preaching near the waters of the Jordan. In the river that the Bible so often describes as a boundary – and, more figuratively, as a point of transition – Jesus was baptized. Once thus cleansed, he set out on his mission. One tradition holds that the baptism took place at the point where the Sea of Galilee merges with the Jordan River near what is today Kibbutz Kinneret, 12 km (7 miles) south of Tiberias on Highway 90.

BELOW: the open-air museum at Khamat Tverya.

The **Yardenit Baptismal Site** (Sat–Thur 8am–5pm, Fri 8am–4pm; tel: 04-6759111; www.yardenit.co.il; fee) has been established just outside the kibbutz in order to accommodate the many pilgrims who still converge on the spot. After

the Six Day War, the site was closed except for special occasions, but it is now open for more general access. There is also a rival "Site of the Baptism" further south, near Jericho.

Around the point where the lake merges with the Jordan River in the south are three kibbutzim: **Dganya Alef**, **Dganya Bet** and **Kinneret** ❷. Not having guesthouses, they attract fewer tourists than other kibbutzim around the lake, but they are the ones that are most worth noting because they were the first in the country. From the ranks of their members sprang many of Israel's legendary leaders, including Moshe Dayan. At the entrance to Dganya Aleph is a Syrian tank, stopped in its tracks in the 1948 War of Independence. Kinneret's cemetery, on the lakeside by Kinneret junction, is the burial place for leading Israeli artists and is a marvelous place for tranquil contemplation. The beaches around the lake are expensive and often crowded and dirty.

Several settlements have guesthouses and camping facilities, including **Moshav Ramot**; **Kibbutz Ein Gev**, site of a gala music festival every spring; **Kibbutz Ha'On**, which had an ostrich farm before they became popular in other parts of the world; and **Kibbutz Ma'agan**. Also on the east coast is the Golan Beach and its water wonderland, the Luna Gal. At **Beit Zera**, on the southern tip of the lake, are the ruins of an ancient moon-worshipping cult.

Ancient baths dating from the Roman period are found on the southern Golan at **Hamat Gader** ❷ (daily 9am–5pm; tel: 04-6659980; www.hamat-gader.com; fee), near the Yarmuk River and reached traveling eastwards on Highway 98. Set in a secluded mountain nature reserve and with Israel's only naturally flowing hot mineral springs, Hamat Gader is by far the country's most popular commercial tourist attraction. The site's renovated Roman baths and a range of other attrac-

Map on pages 180–1

TIP

Many kibbutzim such as Sedot Nehemia rent out inner tire tubes, on which you can float down the River Jordan – an extremely relaxing experience.

BELOW: by the lake at Tiberias.

A tempting bunch of ripe dates.

tions including treatments and massages, a water park, a crocodile farm and other animal exhibits, and restaurants draws 750,000 visitors a year. Hamat Gader was established in the 2nd century AD by the Roman Empire's 10th Legion. The spa soon became recognized as the second most beautiful baths in the empire, after Baia in Italy, and was known internationally as the Three Graces – symbolizing charm, youth and beauty. The baths were badly damaged by an earthquake in the 7th century and eventually abandoned in the 9th. The site also has an exclusive hotel and spa.

Beit She'an

Back along 98 and south for 30 km (19 miles) is the ancient *tel* of **Beit She'an** ㉒, reflecting 6,000 years of civilization and billing itself as Israel's Pompeii. Near it sits Israel's best preserved Roman theatre which once seated 8,000, and there is an archaeological museum featuring a Byzantine mosaic floor. Beit She'an was once a member of the Roman Decapolis, meaning that it was one of the 10 most important cities in the Eastern Mediterranean. Other structures here include a colonnaded street, on the east side of which is a ruined temple which collapsed in an earthquake in the 8th century. Excavations here have revealed 18 superimposed cities, so those in search of archaeological intrigue should not miss Beit She'an.

The modern town, however, is a rather dull little place, with little to offer. If you're thinking of going to Jordan, there is a Japanese-funded crossing here called the **Jordan River Crossing**, opened in 1999 sometimes known as the **Sheikh Hussein Bridge**. It is 90 meters (nearly 300 ft) long.

Easily accessible from the highway north of Beit She'an are the impressive ruins of the 12th-century Crusader fortress of **Belvoir** (daily 8am–4pm, until 5pm Apr–Sept; tel: 04-6581766; fee). Perched on the highest hill in the region, it offers an extensive view of the valleys below and of neighboring Jordan.

The Jordan Rift

South of Beit She'an and east of the Gilboa mountain range is one of the lowest points in Israel: the **Jordan Rift**. Encompassing the Jordan Valley and the Beit She'an Valley, it is part of the same 6,500-km (4,000-mile) rift that stretches from Syria to Africa and is responsible for the lowest point on earth – the Dead Sea. Even here at 120 meters (390 ft) below sea level (it gets to 390 meters/1,280 ft further south), it's like a kiln baking under an unrelenting sun during the summer. By way of comparison, Death Valley, California, the lowest point in the United States, is only 87 meters (285 ft) below sea level. But nourished by the Jordan River, the Yarmuk River and a network of underground springs (including the Spring of Kharod), this remains a lush region, bursting with bananas, dates and other fruit. It is home to some of Israel's most prosperous kibbutzim.

A water system not quite as historic as Megiddo's but impressive in its own way can be found at **Gan ha-Shlosha** (The Garden of Three) ㉓, west along 6667 from Bet She'an (daily 8am–4pm, until 5pm

BELOW: an ostrich at Kibbutz Ha'On.

Apr–Sept; tel: 04-6586219; fee). Modern developers have managed to recre-ate a tiny piece of Eden in this stunning park. It is also known as Sachne, meaning "warm" in Arabic, because of the warm waters of **Ein Kharod** (The Spring of Kharod) that bubble up from under the earth to fill a huge natural swimming pool.

The Spring of Kharod actually starts at the foot of the Gilboa Mountains, just east of Afula, and flows all the way to the Jordan, but for most of the way the warm waters are underground and diverted for use in local settlements. The only other spot where they surface is at Gid'ona where the Israelite warrior Gideon supposedly assembled his forces 3,000 years ago, and which in more recent times served as the training spot for the forces of the Palmach, the elite fighting unit of the Jews before the State of Israel was created.

There is also a memorial here to Yehoshuah Henkin, a Zionist leader, who purchased hundreds of thousands of acres of land – including this piece – for Jew-ish settlement.

About a mile west of Gan ha-Shlosha is **Kibbutz Beit Alfa** (daily 8am–4pm, until 5pm Apr–Sept; tel: 04-6532004; fee), where you'll find the country's best-preserved ancient synagogue floor. Discovered when kibbutz members were digging an irrigation channel, the 6th-century floor consists of a striking zodiac mosaic and a representation of the sacrifice of Isaac.

Overlooking the length of the Jezreel Valley are the **Gilboa Mountains**. Here King Saul met his untimely end at the hands of the Philistines, causing David to curse the spot forever, "Ye mountains of Gilboa, let there be no dew, nor rain upon you, neither fields of choice fruit." (II Samuel 20, 21–23). Return to Afula and eastwards on 65 to Megiddo. ❏

Map on pages 180–1

TIP

Israelis flock to the Gilboa Mountains in March to see the fleetingly rare and distinctive Gilboa Iris, symbol of the Society for Protection of Nature in Israel.

BELOW: the theater at Beit She'an.

THE CRADLE OF THREE RELIGIONS

For some pilgrims the Holy Land bears witness to the truth of the Bible, while the more cynical see tourism turning it into a religious Disneyland

From the historical point of view there can be no dispute. This is where Abraham first spoke of monotheism, to which Moses led the Children of Israel, and where Solomon built his Temple. During the Roman period Christ preached in the Galilee and was crucified in Jerusalem. Five centuries later Mohammed prayed in Jerusalem, and Muslims believe that after his death he came to Jerusalem on horseback before ascending to heaven.

For believers of all three religions the sites associated with all these events are sacred. For non-believers there is still a historical and archaeological fascination with the shrines.

Jews consider Hebron, Jerusalem, Tiberias and Safed to be holy cities. In Hebron the Tomb of the Patriarchs – Abraham and family – is located at the Cave of Machpelah. In Jerusalem the Western Wall, the one remaining structure from the Temple complex, is considered the holiest shrine. Tiberias was where the oral law section of the Talmud was compiled in the second century, the period in which the Kabbalah, Jewish mystical texts, was written in the hills around Safed.

The principal Christian sites are the Church of the Nativity in Bethlehem, where Christ was born, the Church of the Annunciation in Nazareth, where his family lived, and the Church of the Holy Sepulchre in Jerusalem, where he was crucified and rose again.

Muslims revere the Tomb of the Patriarchs in Hebron, as Abraham was also the father of the Arab people, as well as the Temple Mount where the El-Aqsa Mosque and the Dome of the Rock are holy sites, both associated with Mohammed.

▽ **THE MOSQUE ON THE MOUNT**
The El-Aqsa Mosque on the Temple Mount was built in 705 and restored by Saladin after the Templars used it as their headquarters.

▷ **CHRIST'S HERITAGE**
The Church of the Nativity in Bethlehem is shared acrimoniously by the Catholic, Armenian and Greek Orthodox churches.

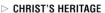

▽ **AWAITING THE MESSIAH**
Jews believe those buried on the Mount of Olives will be the first to return to life when the Messiah arrives.

◁ **CALLING THE UNFAITHFUL**
An ultra-Orthodox Jew urges his secular brethren to attend morning prayer.

THE VIA DOLOROSA

Unlike the other Christian shrines in the Holy Land, which date back to Byzantine times, the traditional route of the Via Dolorosa was only established in the late Middle Ages. Since then Christians have re-enacted Christ's last journey, bearing a cross through the narrow, winding streets of Jerusalem's Old City. Every Friday Franciscan friars lead a procession along the Via Dolorosa from the Church of the Flagellation. These processions are especially colorful and intense on Good Friday.

There are 14 Stations of the Cross, the last five inside the Church of the Holy Sepulchre where it is believed Christ was crucified, buried and resurrected. The Catholic and Orthodox Churches do not doubt the authenticity of the Via Dolorosa and the Holy Sepulchre, but some Protestants suggest that Calvary was at the Garden Tomb site, near the Damascus Gate.

△ **FERVENT PRAYER**
The large stone blocks of the Western Wall, the last remaining vestige of the Temple complex destroyed by the Romans, absorb Jewish religious fervor.

◁ **BARMITZVAH BOY**
A young Jewish boy reads from the Torah as he celebrates his barmitzvah by the Western Wall.

▷ **THE GOLDEN DOME**
The Dome of the Rock is a highly revered shrine, marking the spot from which Muslims believe that Mohammed ascended to heaven on a steed.

◁ **BAPTISM IN THE JORDAN**
The Yardenit Baptismal Site, located where the River Jordan flows out of the Sea of Galilee, receives streams of Christian pilgrims seeking baptism.

THE NORTH COAST

Wander into the past in ancient Akko, then return to the present along the delightful north coast with such pleasures as water sports, as well as grottoes and stunning views

Maps:
Area 180
City 208

Akko (www.akko.org.il) ㉔ is probably the most atmospheric place in Israel. Battered over the centuries by successive invaders, it holds its own against the flow of time and tourism. The old sea wall, built by the Crusaders, overlooks the expanse of the Mediterranean, on the northern tip of Haifa Bay, while Gothic archways and minarets mingle within the city. The ancient stone piers still give port to fishermen; the markets and cafés still overflow with friendly service and mysterious faces.

Chosen as the key port of the Crusader Kingdom by Baldwin I in 1104, and successfully defended against Simon Maccabeus and Napoleon Bonaparte, Akko has left behind the glorious fury of its past. Yet if it is a backwater, it is a dramatic one, as richly eloquent as any in the Holy Land.

Crusader capital

Akko is among the world's oldest known seaports. It was already a major population center when the Phoenicians dominated the northern coast. Its ancient industries include glassware (Roman historian Pliny credits Akko with discovering the art of glassmaking) and purple dyes – extracted from the *Purpura*, a seasnail which gave the color its name. Around 333 BC, Alexander the Great passed through the then-flourishing Greek colony; Julius Caesar came 300 years later, in the process laying the stones of the first paved road in Roman Judea – from Akko to Antioch.

The Arabs held the city from AD 636 to1104, fortifying and rebuilding much of it; yet Akko only hit its zenith during the Crusader era. The First Crusade was launched with the capture of Jerusalem in 1099. Five years later Akko fell, and the Crusaders immediately realised its value as a Mediterranean lifeline. Developed into a major trading center by Genovese merchants, and renamed St Jean d'Acre, it became the principal port on the eastern Mediterranean rim.

Many of the most powerful and colorful Crusader orders – the Knights Templar, the Teutonic Order, the Order of St Lazarus, and the Hospitaller Order of St John – established centers here. In 1187 Saladin defeated the Europeans at the Horns of Hittim, and many Crusader cities fell into Saracen hands. Led by Philip Augustus of Spain and Richard the Lionheart of England, the knights of the Third Crusade recaptured Akko, and made it the capital of their kingdom in 1192. The remains left from the ensuing century of Crusader rule testify that this was its finest hour, before it fell once more into obscurity.

In the mid-1700s the port was revived by the Bedouin Sheikh Dahar el-Omar, followed by Akko's

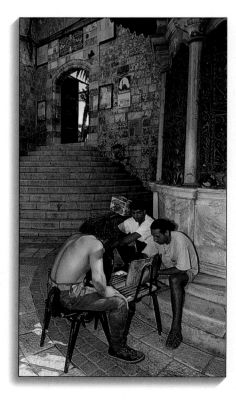

LEFT: the El-Jazzar Mosque from the air.
BELOW: board games in Akko.

If you are in Akko
during the Succot/
Tabernacles festival,
don't miss the Fringe
Theater Festival,
Israel's equivalent of
Scotland's Edinburgh
Festival. A major
emphasis in the
drama is the Jewish–
Arab coexistence that
the city exemplifies.

BELOW: the mosque
and the harbor.

most notorious prime builder, the Ottoman Pasha Ahmad, known as "el-Jaz-zar"(the butcher) on account of his penchant for cruelty. His architectural lega-cies include Akko's best-known landmarks. In 1799, aided by British warships, el-Jazzar accomplished what much of Europe could not: he defeated Napoleon in a two-month siege. Turkish rule and the advent of the steamship ended Akko's importance as a port, and the town regained prominence only in the last years of the British Mandate, when its prison held hundreds of Jewish freedom fighters, including the Zionist leader Ze'ev Jabotinsky, and was the scene of a remarkable jailbreak in 1947. Since independence the city has retained its maritime charac-ter while developing its industry, and today it holds close to 50,000 residents, both Jews and Arabs. In 2001 UNESCO declared Old Akko a World Heritage Site.

Entering Old Akko

To enter the old city from the new, follow the coastal strip or the parallel Weizmann Street, where the **Visitors Center** (daily 8.30am–5pm, and 6pm in summer; tel: 04-9813651) stands in the Enchanted Park on your left before entering the Old City. It's a good idea to stop off here because considerable savings can be made by pur-chasing multiple-entrance tickets for the Old City's major sights. The Center also shows movies about Akko and exhibits archaeological finds from the city.

Go into Old Akko through the dry moat and city walls, built by the Crusaders and later refortified. You can climb the wall here, and visit the northeastern com-mand post, the Burj el-Kommandar, with a strategic view and a restored prom-enade, which continues on to Land Gate, at the bay.

As you enter the city, the first prominent structure is the elegant **El-Jazzar Mosque Ⓐ** (open dawn to dusk; fee), built in 1781–82 by "the butcher" and

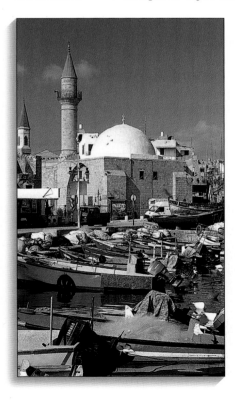

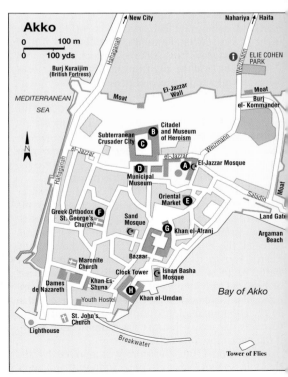

now the site of his tomb and that of his adopted son, Suleiman. Ringed with domed arcades and swaying palms, the mosque is considered the finest in Israel, and serves as a spiritual center for Israel's Muslim community. Except for a shrine containing a single hair from the beard of the prophet, the interior is as stark as it is magnificent.

On the right-hand side of Weizmann Street, dominating the old city skyline, is the towering **Citadel and Museum of Heroism** Ⓑ (Sat–Thur 9.30am–5pm, Fri 9.30am–noon; fee). Built by el-Jazzar on Crusader ruins, the fortress has been used variously as an arsenal and a barracks and, since Turkish times, as a prison. This was the center for the incarceration and execution of Jewish underground fighters during the British Mandate, and exhibits in the museum document this unsettling period.

Abutting the Citadel is the most interesting site of all, the dank and dramatic **Subterranean Crusader City** Ⓒ (Sat–Thur 9am–4.30pm, Fri 9am–12.30pm; fee). While not excavated in their entirety, the halls of the sprawling complex contain such unusual historical testimony as carved fleur-de-lys insignia. Now reclaimed, the halls are the venue for the October **Akko Fringe Theater Festival**, which brings together the best of Israel's experimental and alternative drama companies.

As you emerge from the subterranean city, turn off a small lane into a restored Turkish bathhouse, which is now the **Municipal Museum** Ⓓ (same hours as Crusader City; tickets valid for both). The museum contains exhibits on archaeology, Islamic culture, folklore and weaponry.

Wandering deeper into the maze-like streets of Akko, you may stumble across the Sand Mosque, off the **Souk**, the fascinating **Oriental Market** Ⓔ. Further in

Map on page 208

Oriental spices for sale in Akko.

BELOW: calling the faithful to prayer.

TIP

For information, maps and tours when traveling to inaccessible spots such as Monfort Fortress, contact the Society for the Protection of Nature, tel: (02) 6232936 (Jerusalem); (03) 6375063 (Tel Aviv); or (04) 8664136 (Haifa).

BELOW: view of the Rainbow Arch.

is the **Greek Orthodox St George's Church** , dedicated to two British officers who fell at Akko in 1799 and 1840. Of special interest are the *khans* (inns) that grace the port-side area. These include the imposing **Khan el-Afranj** (Inn of the Franks) , near the **Bazaar**, and the unequalled **Khan el-Umdan** (Inn of the Pillars) . The lower storeys of the latter were used as stables and its upper ones as lodgings. Its geometric courtyard is memorable, and the clock-tower (minus its clock) offers a glimmering view of the port.

Beneath the tower, wander by the fishing port, and up along the sea wall, which houses one or two lovely cafés among its layered arches. The youth hostel is here, and, further on, the lighthouse, and from this corner you can take in the sunset view of the sea wall heading north to the new city, the old stone houses huddled in its tired embrace.

North to the border

Arching north from Akko along the coast on Highway 4 lies the final architectural gift from el-Jazzar, the austere spine of the **Turkish Aqueduct**, which once ran 15 km (9 miles) to the spring at **Kabri**, now a picnic and camping site.

Just north of Akko the **Baha'i Tomb and Gardens** mark the burial site and villa of Mirza Hussein Ali, an early leader of the Baha'i faith, known also as Baha Ulla (Glory to God). Surrounding the tomb is a lovely formal Persian garden.

Further north, beyond the gardens, is **Nahariya** ㉕. A clean and modest resort community founded in 1934 by German Jews, it offers many amenities for water sports, and a fine coastline on which to enjoy them. Its most noticeable landmark is the quiet stream, the Ga'aton, which flows down the center of the main street.

From here continue northwards along Highway 4. **Ahziv National Park** ㉖,

5 km (3 miles) north of Nahariya along Highway 4 (daily 8am–5pm, until 7pm Mar–Sept; tel: 04-9823263; fee) is a rocky embayed coast and beach with lagoons, deep natural seawater pools and manmade seawater pools, shallow enough for children to splash in. Also here are the remnants of an ancient settlement and large, grassy lawns.

Several kilometers further north turn inland along route 899 where, at the Shlomi junction, lies an intriguing piece of nature. The **Rainbow Arch** was formed when a section of the cliff edge dissolved, leaving a large, almost perfect arch. Today, abseilers rappel down this beautiful natural arch to the lush valley below. From the roadside the marked footpath is a gentle uphill stroll to the arch and a panoramic view.

Some 15 km (9 miles) east of the coast along Highway 899, atop a steep ridge, and accessible only by footpaths, lies **Monfort Fortress** ㉗ (daily 8am–4pm, fee), the most important of a string of Crusader forts, now set in a national park.

On the way back to the coast, along the final few kilometers to the Lebanese frontier, there towers the rocky border point of **Rosh ha-Nikra** ㉘, Israel's northernmost coastal limit. The view from the chalk-white cliffs set off against the crashing azure waves is entrancing, but it is Rosh ha-Nikra's **grottoes**, formed by millennia of erosion, that are the prime attraction. A cable car (daily 8.30am–4pm, until Apr–mid Jul and mid-Aug–Sept, until midnight mid-Jul–mid-Aug; tel: 04-9857108; www.rosh-hanikra.com; fee) takes you down over the pounding tide, and a footpath is also there for the determined. Atop the cliff, the southernmost edge of the range known as the **Ladder of Tyre**, is a cafeteria, and a view over the now walled-up railway tunnel that once led to Lebanon. On a clear day, looking south, one can just make out the port of **Haifa** ㉙ (*see page 213*). ❏

Map on pages 180–1

Cable cars take you to the grottoes.

LEFT AND BELOW:
Rosh ha-Nikra: the grottoes and the snowy-white cliffs.

HAIFA

Haifa is a busy working port where Jews and Arabs live in relative harmony. The domed Baha'i shrine and resplendent gardens are the most prominent landmarks

Maps:
Area 180
City 216

I n 1750 the Bedouin Sheikh Dahar el-Omar destroyed a squalid coastal village because its inhabitants neglected to pay homage. The town lay in ruins for eight years, until, having made his point, the sheikh rebuilt it and improved its natural harbor. **Haifa ㉙** grew from that unpropitious beginning, and has since evolved into a bustling port city and maritime center.

Today Haifa (www.haifa.muni.il) is Israel's third-largest city, one of the centers of the nation's renowned high-technology industries. From its original cradle on the narrow coastal strip between the Mediterranean and the Carmel Range, Haifa has marched up Mount Carmel, settling itself lazily among the gentle slopes. The city is built on three levels, rising from its original location along the waterfront. The second level, in the Carmel foothills, is Hadar Ha-Karmel, the central business district and the oldest residential area. The newest neighborhoods have climbed all the way to the crests of the peak, and cling to its sides, connected by a network of excellent roads. At the very apex is the **Carmel Center**, where some of the city's most attractive homes and exclusive hotels and shops are located. Seeing the glorious views of the bay and azure Mediterranean, it is no surprise that the affluent have built their lives at the mountain's summit. In addition, however, an ugly urban sprawl of industrial chimneys and apartment blocks spreads northwards to Akko. Haifa itself has a population of more than 300,000, while half a million people live in the metropolitan area.

LEFT: the Baha'i Temple.
BELOW: the cable car to the Carmel Heights.

Historic port

Haifa had been known since the 2nd century as a safe haven for passing ships, situated as it was along one of the Mediterranean's oldest sea lanes, but at the time of its premature destruction in the mid-18th century it was little more than an assemblage of huts, with fewer than 250 inhabitants. Reborn, it thrived, and by 1890 some 8,000 people lived within its limits. Yet it took a combination of railroads, war and the need for deeper water ports to catapult the city into significance in the 20th century.

The causes were interlinked: under the impending pressures of war, the Ottoman Turks built the Hejaz Railroad connecting Haifa to Damascus in the north, while the British started the Sinai Military Railroad, which was later to link Haifa to Qantara on the Suez Canal. At the end of the war, when the British controlled Palestine under a League of Nations mandate, they gradually modernised Haifa's port, rejecting Akko's waters as too shallow for the bigger ships of the age.

With a steady increase in maritime traffic, and a continuing stream of immigrants, the population reached 25,000 by 1918. By 1923 it had more than doubled, and by 1931 doubled again to exceed 100,000. After

Israel's independence in 1948 further development of the port became essential. Israel's land borders were sealed, and Haifa's port became the Jewish state's only opening to the world.

From blue collar to high-tech

Today the port, monitored by a centralized computer system, bristles with massive electronically-operated cargo-handling equipment, berths the world's sea-going mammoths, and was Israel's premier maritime center, although it has now been overtaken by Ashdod. But Haifa has also become a versatile industrial center. Known affectionately as the "Red City" because of its long-standing identification with the nation's labor movement, it was for many years essentially a blue-collar city, though with the advent of high-tech fewer and fewer people perform manual work.

At the northern edge of the city, an industrial zone accommodates a very extensive petrochemical industry, oil refineries and many small manufacturing units. Israel's high-technology companies are centered in a new science-based industrial district at the southern entrance to the city.

Despite its industrial base, Haifa is a highly cultured city with a large number of museums, a theater company and two universities – Haifa University and the Technion, Israel Institute of Technology. The latter is the country's oldest university, opening its doors in 1924, a year before the Hebrew University in Jerusalem. The Technion has also become one of the world's leading science and technology universities. Many of Israel's foremost high-tech entrepreneurs are Technion graduates and two of the universities professors were awarded the Nobel Prize for Chemistry in 2004 for describing the way cells destroy unwanted proteins.

Proud of their industrious image, Haifa residents like to say that while Tel Aviv plays and Jerusalem prays, Haifa works.

BELOW: tasting the latest vintage in a Haifa wine cellar.

Arab communities

A Saturday bus service is unusual in Israel. The fact that it happens in Haifa reflects the formative influence of its Arab citizens on the city's social patterns. There has always been a significant Arab presence in Haifa, and Jews and Arabs here have a long history of mutual give-and-take. Israeli Arabs constitute about 10 percent of Haifa's population, and the city attracts thousands more every day from the surrounding villages. Although there are some mixed areas, most Arabs have remained in their own neighborhoods, in many cases in the same places where their families have lived for generations.

There are two distinctive Arab communities in Haifa; **Wadi Nisnas** is one of the area's oldest neighborhoods, adjacent to Hadar, near Bet Ha-geffen, Haifa's Arab-Jewish community center. With its buildings of massive sandstone blocks, window grilles and arched doorways, its prevalence of Arabic and Middle Eastern music, and the range of exotic food and clothing for sale, Wadi Nisnas is a graphic reminder that Haifa stands with one foot firmly planted in the Levant.

In sharp contrast to Wadi Nisnas, **Kababir**, perched high on a ridge overlooking the Mediterranean, is an Arab neighborhood of sumptuous dwellings and lush gardens. Established as an independent village in 1830, the community opted for annexation to Haifa when the State of Israel was established in 1948, anticipating the benefits of schools, health services, water and sewage systems. The majority of residents are Ahmdya Muslims, a small Islamic sect distinct from the larger Shi'ite and Sunni groups in Wadi Nisnas. Although fully integrated into the Haifa municipality, Kababir is administered locally by a committee of six elders elected annually by the men of the community. A new mosque, completed in 1984, is the only one of its kind in the Middle East.

Maps:
Area 180
City 216

TIP

Haifa is well served by Israel Railways. The main line from Tel Aviv stops at Hof Hacarmel at the southern entrance to the city, then at Bat Galim, the city center, and carries on through the northern suburbs to Akko and Nahariya.

BELOW:
sharing opinions.

A cheerful young resident.

The Carmel slope

The **Carmel Center** (Ha-Karmel) **Ⓐ** is where most of Haifa's hotels are located. Here, atop towering Mount Carmel, panoramic scenes of the city, sea and mountains burst into view at every turn. Shops line Shderot ha-Nasi along with sidewalk cafés and restaurants specializing in kosher, Chinese, Italian and Middle Eastern foods.

Atop the crest of Mount Carmel, reached by traveling south along Shderot ha-Nasi, looms the contemporary features of the **University of Haifa**, its distinctive tower thrusting resolutely against the sky. Founded in 1972, the university serves the entire northern district, and has branches in some of the more remote areas. The 25-storey **Eshkol Tower**, designed by the Brazilian architect Oscar Niemeyer, offers an unparalleled view of northern Israel, which makes the 5-km (3-mile) journey here from the Carmel Center worthwhile.

Tucked within the mountainous folds of upper Haifa are a number of hidden treasures. On the slope near the Promenade of the Carmel Center is the **Mane-Katz Museum Ⓑ** (Sun, Mon, Wed, Thur 10 am–4pm, Tues 2pm–6pm, Fri 10am–1pm, Sat 10am–2pm; tel: 04-8383482; free) is housed in the building where the Jewish-French expressionist lived and worked in his later years. Besides his paintings and sculptures, the display also includes his personal collection of Judaica and antique furniture. A short distance away is the Edenic Mothers' Garden, the biggest of Haifa's parks – and there are nearly 400 of them. Among curving paths, flowers and picnicking families is the **Museum of Prehistory and Haifa Zoo Ⓒ** (Sun–Thur 8am–3pm, Fri 8am–1pm, Sat 10am–2pm; tel:04-8371833; fee), displaying finds of the Carmel area, which way back then was home to Neanderthal Man. The zoo is pleasant and well maintained.

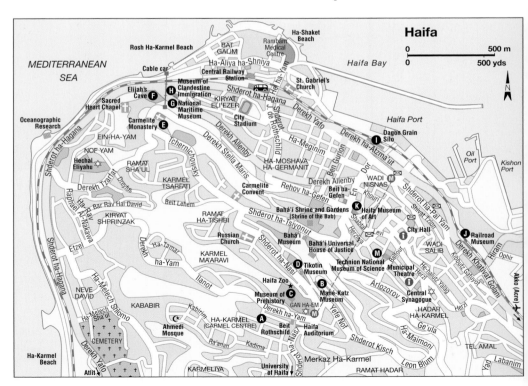

Israel's only museum of Japanese art, the **Tikotin Museum D** (Sun, Mon, Wed, Thur 10am–5pm, Tues 4–8pm, Fri 10am–1pm, Sat 10am–4pm; tel. 04-8383554; fee), is back in the heart of the Carmel Center, at 89 Shderot ha-Nasi.

Going down the slope for several kilometers, along Shderot ha-Nasi and then turning left down Techernikovsky, you reach that part of the city known as **French Carmel**, an expensive but cosy residential district. At the end of this area, Mount Carmel levels off into a promontory, and this is the site of the **Carmelite Monastery E** (daily 6am–1.30pm, 3–6pm; tel: 04-8337758), the world center of the Carmelite Order. Situated at the end of the mountain, along Stella Maris Road, the church commands one of the most spectacular views of the city. The site was selected in the 12th century by a small band of Crusaders who settled there to devote themselves to asceticism, solitude and prayer. The order which grew from that beginning was officially founded by St Brocard in the 13th century. The church was built in the 18th century, over a grotto associated in the Jewish and Christian traditions with the prophet Elijah and his disciple Elisha. The interior dome depicts events in their lives, and a small museum displays local archaeological discoveries.

Elijah's Cave F (Sun–Thur 8am–5pm) can be reached by a footpath from the monastery. The prophet is said to have rested and meditated here in the 9th century BC, before his momentous encounter with the Baalists on one of the peaks of the Carmel Range. After leaving the cave, he is said to have climbed to the top of Mount Carmel, where an altar had been erected by the worshippers of Baal and other Phoenician deities. Elijah challenged their priests to light a flame under a sacrifice by means of their religious powers.

According to tradition, the pagan priests failed; Elijah called upon the Lord and

Map on page 216

A main thorough-fares leading up Mount Carmel was once named UN Avenue. But on the day in 1975 that the UN passed a resolution equating Zionism with racism, the city renamed the road Zionism Avenue. When the resolution was repealed, the name was not changed back.

BELOW: Elijah's Cave, below the Carmelite Monastery.

the flames were instantly ignited. Ahab, the Jewish king who had angered the Lord by worshipping Baal, was witness to the event. Rejecting paganism, he ordered the massacre at the Kishon River of all the Baalists. The event is recorded in detail in I Kings 18, 17–46. Some Christians believe the cave to have sheltered the Holy Family on the way back from Egypt, and know it also as the **Grotto of the Madonna**.

Along the seafront

Opposite the monastery itself, a sinuous platform marks the upper terminal of Haifa's cable car system (daily 9am–11pm, closed on Fri in winter; tel: 04-8335970). Delayed for more than a year due to controversy surrounding its intended operation on the Sabbath, the system ferries passengers from the Carmel heights down to the seaside Bat Galim Promenade.

It is an easy walk to the **National Maritime Museum** ⑥ (Sun–Thur 10am–4pm, Sat 10am–1pm; tel: 04-8536622; fee) and the **Museum of Clandestine Immigration** ⑪ (Sun–Thur 9am–4pm, Fri 9am–1pm; tel: 04-8536249; fee). The immigration museum includes the tiny ship in which Jewish immigrants sought to evade the British Mandatory government's blockade in the years before the State of Israel was declared.

Adjacent to the port area, a 3-km (2-mile) bus or taxi ride northwards along the coast, is the **Dagon Grain Silo** ❶, probably one of the only architecturally pleasing silos in the world. Besides its commercial use for receiving and storing grain from ships anchored in the port, the silo houses a **museum** (guided tours Sun–Fri 10.30am; tel: 04-8664221; free) devoted to the history of bread- and beer-making. An assortment of old implements is displayed

BELOW:
Elijah's Cave,
Mount Carmel.

Map
on page
216

with explanatory photographs, murals and mosaics, and there is a working model of the silo's own mechanised system.

Hugging the waterfront, the **Railroad Museum** ❶ (open Sun–Tues and Thur 9am–noon; tel: 04-8564293; fee), opposite 40 Hativat Golani Street, is several kilometers further south. Housed in an attractive old Ottoman building, it pays tribute to the importance of the railway in Haifa's history. Steam engines that hauled freight from the hinterlands to the port are preserved, along with luxury passenger cars, ornate sleeping cars, and wood-paneled dining cars. Visitors are encouraged to climb aboard and try out the accommodation.

Hadar

The new **Haifa Museum of Art** ❻ (Sun–Thur, Sat 10am–1pm, Tues, Thur, Sat 5–8pm; tel: 04-8523255; fee) at the southern edge of Hadar, on Shabtai Levy Street, is crammed with displays. Comfortable viewing from good vantage points isn't always possible, but the variety and quality of the collections make a visit worth the effort. Special exhibitions are occasionally held. Work by contemporary Israeli artists is exhibited at the **Chagall Artists' House**, established in 1964 at 24 Hazionut Blvd (Sun–Thur 9am–1pm, 4–7pm, Sat 10am–1pm; admission free). Marc Chagall (1887–1985) visited Israel eight times, and his work can be found in the Knesset and in the Hadassah Medical School in Jerusalem.

The Germany Colony

One of the most attractive parts of Haifa is the **Germany Colony**, which can be reached along Derekh Allenby from the National Maritime Museum, or by descending Shederot Ha-Tsiyonut from Shderot ha-Nasi. Built in 1868 by the

The city's central bus station at Bat Galim was recently replaced by two smaller bus stations at the southern and northern entrances to the city called Hof Hacarmel (south) and Checkpost (north).

BELOW: the Dagon Grain Silo.

OTHER HAIFA MUSEUMS

In Hadar, the level above the waterfront (use the Carmelit subway), the original edifice of the country's preeminent Institute of Technology, the **Technion**, has been preserved as an architectural landmark and is now the home of the exciting hands-on **National Museum of Science** ⓜ (Mon, Wed & Thur 9am–5pm, Tues 9am–7pm, Fri 9am–1pm, Sat 10am–2pm; tel: 04-8628111; fee). The magnificent old building, constructed in 1924, was designed by Alexander Baerwald, combining European lines with an eastern dome, crenellated roofs and intricate mosaics. The Technion recently expanded into a large new campus in the Neve Shannon neighbourhood; free tours are offered daily.

Beit Dagon (Palmer Square, tel: 04-8664221; guided tours Sun–Fri 10.30am) shows how grains of wheat have been cared for from ancient times.

The **Israel Oil Industry Museum** (2 Tuvia St, tel 04-8654237; Sun–Thur 8.30am–3.30pm) is not concerned with the Middle East's "black gold" but instead illustrates the production processes of edible oils, yesterday and today.

The **Israel Electric Corporation Visitors Center** (Salman Road, Shemen Beach. tel: 04-8646176; Sun–Thur 8am–3pm; free but book in advance) is for those who have always wanted to visit a power station.

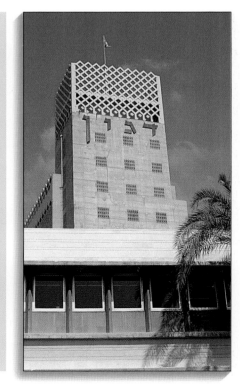

Map on page 216

There's plenty of decorated pottery for sale in Haifa.

German Templar, this area has become gentrified in recent years with delightful old houses and gardens. The beauty of the German Colony has been further accentuated by the recently completed Baha'i Garden, rising majestically up the hill with the gold-domed Baha'i Shrine at its peak *(see opposite page)*.

Food and fun

Pavement cafés are everywhere in Haifa, ranging from a couple of tiny tables on a sidestreet, where excellent Viennese coffee can be bought, to the umbrella-shaded elegance near the Cinemathèque at the Rothschild Center on Hanassi Street. Haifa also has a wide variety of restaurants, ranging from dinner-and-dancing in the Rondo Grill of the Dan Carmel Hotel to a Middle Eastern evening of folk-dancing at Al-Pasha on Hamman-al-Pasha Street. More local flavor can be sampled at The Pleasant Brothers, an unassuming place on the corner of Moriah and Pica streets in the Ahuza neighborhood. This is a long-time local favorite, popular for its *shish kebab*, *shishlik* and salads. After dinner, have a cup of coffee in one of the many coffee houses around the corner on Pica Street.

Israel's only subway

One block up the hill from the *felafel* stands of He-halutz is the Hadar entrance to the **Carmelit**, Israel's only subway. While most visitors are accustomed to subways, the Carmelit is one of a kind. Its tunnel, hacked through the interior rock of the mountain, operates on the same principle as San Francisco's cable cars: one train hurtling down from the Carmel Center at the top of the mountain hauls the other train up the steep incline from sea level. Even the cars are designed at an angle. From top to bottom, the trip takes seven minutes. ❏

BELOW:
a well-stocked
souvenir shop.

The Baha'i Gardens

The Baha'i Complex dominates the Mount Carmel hillside in Haifa. The complex includes the world's longest hillside gardens as well as the golden domed Baha'i Shrine and the palatial Seat of the Universal House of Justice (Baha'i World Headquarters).

The centerpiece of the hillside garden, midway down on terrace number 10 (of 19), is the gold-domed Shrine of the Bab. Completed in 1953, the building contains the tomb of Siyyad Ali Muhammed – the Bab – a Muslim in Persia who proclaimed the coming of a "Promised One" in 1844. He was executed for heresy in 1850, and his disciples brought his remains to Haifa in 1909.

Haifa became the center of Baha'i activity because the man that the Baha'is believe was the "Promised One" – Husayn-Ali, Baha'u'llah – was exiled from Persia and settled in what was then Palestine under the Ottoman Turkish empire. He is buried near Akko where he died in 1892. Baha'u'llah's son, Abbas Effendi, instructed believers to purchase large tracts of Mount Carmel overlooking Haifa Bay, which Baha'u'llah had foreseen as the world headquarters of the Baha'i faith.

The Baha'i religion emerged from Muslim society (though the Baha'is hate to be called a Muslim sect). The Baha'u'llah transformed the religion into a universal one; he taught that he himself and the Bab were the latest of nine manifestations of God after Abraham, Moses, Christ, Mohammed, Krishna, Buddha and Zoroaster. Some 2 million of the world's estimated 5 million Baha'is live in India; other concentrations are in Iran, where they are a persecuted group, and the US.

Few Baha'is live in Israel, but some 700 volunteers from abroad serve in the Baha'i World Center, the spiritual and administrative center of Baha'ism. The Baha'is do not engage in any missionary activity in Israel.

In addition to the Shrine of the Bab and the Seat of the Universal House of Justice – the faith's international governing body – two administrative buildings are being built.

Extending from the summit of Mount Carmel, this unique hillside terraced garden, completed in 2001, spreads out spectacularly along the northwestern slope of the mountain. The hillside garden has a classically European ambiance. The terraces are lined with stone balustrades, fountains and stone eagles. Black iron gates give access to the trees, bushes, flowerbeds and neatly manicured, very green lawns. But the garden's crowning glory is its breathtaking panoramic view of Haifa Bay and the Mediterranean Sea stretching serenely to the horizon.

Amram Mitzna, the former Labour party leader who was Mayor of Haifa when the gardens were first opened, said: "We have been incredibly lucky. Not many cities get a park like this for free."

Indeed, the Shrine of the Bab and the Baha'i Gardens are open to the public for free. However, guided tours must be booked at least 24 hours in advance (tel: 04-8313131). Dress modestly. Various tours start from three entrances – from the bottom in the German Colony opposite Bet Hagefen, mid-way from Zionism Avenue near the Golden Shrine, and from the top at 61 Yefe Nof. ❏

RIGHT: the Baha'i Gardens look over Haifa.

CENTRAL AND SOUTH COAST

*Crusader ruins, pioneer settlements and citrus groves line
the coast, but for most people the sand and the surf
are the major attractions*

Map
on page
226

F rom the environs of Caesarea in the north to Ashkelon in the south, Israel's central and south coast is citrus country – the fertile Sharon Plain. In Hebrew the word for citrus, *hadar*, is the same as the word for "splendor" and in the proper season both meanings are equally appropriate as much of the strip from seashore to foothills grows lush with groves and ripe, hanging fruit. However, Israel's growing population means that the orange groves are being transformed into housing estates, industrial zones and shopping centers. Yet the citrus crop was never indigenous to the area, and well into the 19th century the central coast was a miasma of malarial swamps. By the turn of the century, however, the development of pumps, which could raise the buried groundwater to the soil surface and the importing of eucalyptus trees from Australia, which soak up surplus moisture, harnessed the land to the needs of its pioneer settlers, who set about draining the marshes and cultivating new orchards.

Today, citrus is Israel's most valuable agricultural export. The varieties under cultivation run the spectrum, with the sweet "Jaffa" oranges and their kin dominating along the coast, grapefruit mainly thriving in the thicker, river-washed soil further inland, and lemons thriving on the hills. The citrus harvest is from November to April, and this is when the fruits are at their most intoxicating, swinging ripely off their evergreen branches, their scent wafting out over the road to the sea.

PRECEDING PAGES:
the beach at
Herzliya.
LEFT: Caesarea's
Roman aqueduct.
BELOW: planting a
seedling at a
coastal kibbutz.

The Carmel Range

The Carmel Range takes its name from the words Kerem-El, meaning "Vineyard of God." It runs for about 25 km (16 miles) along the coast, rising to some 500 meters (1,650 ft) and falling steeply to the Mediterranean. Today it contains **Mount Carmel National Park ❶**, (open daily round the clock; tel: 04-8231452; fee per car, extra fee for overnight camping), located south of Haifa University on Highway 672. This is Israel's largest national forest preserve, lush with hilly woodlands, well-marked hiking trails, picnic facilities and breathtaking vistas. Almost one-tenth of the 8,500-hectare (21,000-acre) park is a nature preserve where deer and gazelle roam freely.

An extra fee is charged for entering the **Khai Bar Nature Reserve** (daily 8am–4pm and until 5pm Mar–Sept; tel: 04-9841752; fee) where rare fallow deer from Iran, previously extinct in this region, have been re-introduced.

Just beyond the park, to the south on 672, tucked among the slopes and valleys of the Carmel Range, are the Druze villages of **Daliyat el-Karmel ❷** and **Isfiya**. Surrounded by tawny precipices plunging to verdant valleys carpeted with tangled foliage, the villages are easily accessible by car or bus. The market

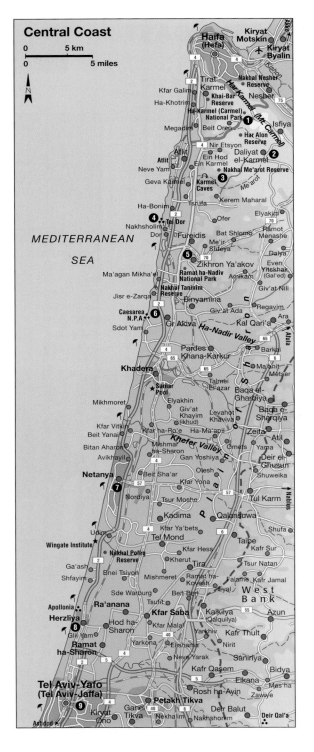

Central Coast

0   5 km

0   5 miles

N

MEDITERRANEAN

SEA

places offer traditional handicrafts and pleasant cafés where Turkish coffee and succulent pastries can be enjoyed under the trees. The **Carmelite Monastery** at **Muhraka**, nearby, stands over the site where Elijah defeated the Baalists.

Winding down through the mountainside on highway 721, the road arcs through the gorges of a severe, astonishingly attractive landscape: the region is known as **Little Switzerland**. Kibbutz Beit Oren tucked between the pines here operates a guesthouse. At the crest of the ridge lies the ultimate view of the Carmel coast.

Just to the south, on the right-hand side in the **Nahal Mearot Nature Reserve ❸** (daily 8am–4pm and until 5pm Mar–Sept; tel: 04-9841750; fee), you come to one of three caves inhabited by Neanderthal Man 50,000 years ago and discovered in 1929. The caves contained flint tools and dozens of skeletons that provided anthropologists with revelations about the lifestyle of these early hunters.

Turn left at highway 4 and left again onto 7111 to reach Ein Hod. Ensconced amid gnarled olive trees and Moorish arches, the artists' colony of **Ein Hod** was conceived in 1953 as a rugged oasis of creativity, and today provides living and working space for some 200 artisans. The gallery and restaurant in the town center warmly welcome company.

The Carmel Coast

Down on the coast you will come to the imposing Crusader fortress of **Atlit**, perched wearily on the rocks above the Mediterranean. At present the ruins are off-limits to the general public as this is a military zone.

Slightly further south, past Ha-Bonim beach and the moshav of the same name, you come to one of Israel's most active on-going archaeological sites: **Tel Dor ❹**. The excavations have as yet only unearthed a fraction of this sprawling ancient city, but the ruins on display, including Canaanite, Israelite and Hellenistic finds, indicate a vast metropolis of tens of thousands of inhabitants.

Map on page 226

Archaeology aside, this is a site of enormous natural beauty, the lagoons and water washing against the cliffs complementing the rolling hills of Mount Carmel inland.

Abutting the *tel* just to the south is the lovely beach of **Nakhsholim** (Breakers), and there is a kibbutz of the same name with a roomy guesthouse and a friendly atmosphere. In the grounds is an illuminating **Maritime Museum** (Sun–Thur 8.30am–2pm, Fri 8.30am–1pm, Sat 10.30am–3pm; tel: 04-6390950; book in advance), housed in a turn-of-the-century building which was once a glass factory. The museum holds a selection of treasures culled from underwater excavations, and their exhibits range from Phoenician catapult balls to relics dating from Napoleon's naval misadventures off this shore in 1799.

Along the length of this coast, rows of vegetables sheathed in white plastic dot the roadsides, often under the stately presence of towering cypress or eucalyptus trees. Towards evening, when the hues in the sky drift into violet, lilac and pale orange, the landscape looks as if it had been painted by Claude Monet.

Take a turning inland just after Nakhsholim on 7011, and after a short distance south on 4 (passing the tranquil Arab town of Fureidis (Paradise) you reach the town of **Zikhron Ya'akov** ❺, which was established in 1882 in memory of James (Jacob) Rothschild, the father of the great benefactor of Israel's first settlers, Baron Edmond (Benjamin) de Rothschild. The **Aaronson House and Museum** (Sun–Thur 8.30am–3pm, Fri 8.30am–1pm; tel: 04-6390120; fee), just off the main street (Hameyasdim St.), details the lives of Aaron and Sarah Aaronson. Aaron was a botanist who, in the early 1900s, isolated durable strains of wheat for cultivation in Palestine. He and his sister are enshrined in legend because of their role in organising the pro-British "Nili" spy ring during resistance to the oppressive Turkish regime. Caught by the Turks, and afraid she would give away information, Sarah shot herself in her home in 1917.

Beach apartments at Nakhsholim.

Rothschild's Tomb

A minute's drive to the south on 652 is **Rothschild's Tomb**, built in the 1950s to house the remains of the Parisian banker and his wife Adelaide. Situated amid a fragrant garden (Yad Hanadiv) of date trees, sage, roses and other flowers, this sensuously designed landscape opens up to a magnificent panorama of the Upper Sharon, while a concrete map indicates the locations of the settlements made possible by Rothschild (whose generosity lingers today in the bar-room phrase "put it on the Baron's account"). The tomb itself is contemporary and tasteful; the site, all told, is one of the most significant in Israel.

Two km (1 mile) further south is **Binyamina**, also named after the great benefactor. Many of the wineries in the Zichron Ya'akov and Binyamina region welcome visitors. Try Tishby at 33 Hameyasdim in the main street of Zichron (04-6288195) and Binyamina Wineries in Binyamina (04-6288042).

Heading south towards Caesarea on highway 4, one immediately enters the area of the excellent bird-watching country of the **Kabara Marshes**, where some of the early Zionist settlements were established in the early 20th century. The Crocodile River bears testimony to the once intimidating nature of the terrain, but the last crocodile here died in the late 19th

BELOW: the coast at Tel Dor.

century. You can view the birds and the river on the coast just south of Ma'agan Mikhael in the Nakhal Taninim Reserve.

Crusaders at their best

Although its greatest historical importance was as a Roman colony, it is to the Crusader ruins at **Caesarea** ❻ (daily 8am–4pm, Mar–Sept until 5pm; tel: 04-6361358; fee) that tourists flock by the busload today, and they are as impressive as any in Israel. It takes a good half-day just to take in the site, while the visual impact of Crusader arches, crumbling walls and smashed Roman pillars is constantly disarming, and attests to the layered history of habitation here. Despite being one of Israel's most lauded archaeological sites, Caesarea is difficult to reach via public transportation, which means that individual tourists must either rent a car, stay overnight nearby, or join a tour. Note that Caesarea cannot be reached from the coastal motorway (highway 2) but only highway 4 further inland.

While settlements in the region date back as far as Phoenician times, the history of the city only really began with the Romans in 22 BC when the royal master-builder Herod the Great founded it, naming it in honor of the emperor Augustus. Around the year 6 BC it was designated the official residence of the governors of Judea, and for 500 years Caesarea was the capital of Roman administration in Palestine. At the time of Jesus, Pontius Pilate lived here, and St Paul was imprisoned here for two years before being sent to Rome from this port.

The great Jewish Revolt in AD 66 began in Caesarea, and in the struggle that followed the city's prisons saw the torture and execution of many captive Jewish zealots. In AD70 the Roman general Vespasian was crowned emperor here. With the Bar-Kochba uprising, many notable Jews once again met their deaths

BELOW: the Roman Amphitheater at Caesarea.

here, among them the great sage and spiritual leader Rabbi Akiva, in 135. (The rabbi is commemorated in the nearby community of Or Akiva.)

During the period of Pax Romana, the city was a center of Hellenistic and, later, Christian culture. The Crusaders, under Baldwin I, captured the city in 1101, and during the next 200 years Caesarea changed hands with confusing frequency. King Baldwin believed it held the Holy Grail, which Jesus sipped from at the Last Supper, but the massive fortifications that so commend it today were only added after 1254, with the re-conquest of the city by Louis IX. Muslim forces captured the city in 1265 (and again in 1291), and Caesarea never regained its importance, being pillaged over the centuries by successive rulers.

The contemporary visitor to Caesarea enters the **Crusader City** through a vaulted gatehouse, after passing over a bridge across a wide moat. The walls around the city, which slope down precipitously from an imposing height, are perhaps the most awe-inspiring monument here; walking the breadth of this imposing redoubt, imaginative tourists can easily picture the spectacle of hand-to-hand combat that took place here time and again. Inside the city are numerous ruins of Crusaders' homes and streets. Along the waterfront, Roman pillars used as foundation stones by the Crusaders jut out among the waves.

Outside the entrance to the Crusader City, a Byzantine Street of Statues represents the city that preceded the Crusaders, its headless figures pondering the passing of their power. Some 500 meters (550 yards) south of the city walls is the restored **Roman Amphitheater** (hours as for the Crusader ruins). This arena witnessed mass executions in Roman times. More recently it has hosted popular summer concerts; past performers have included Isaac Stern and Eric Clapton.

The handsome aqueducts stretching north from the city once conducted fresh spring water; today they provide shade for lounging bathers on Caesarea's wonderful beaches. Inland from the ruins is one of the few golf courses in Israel, in the grounds of the elegant and pricey **Dan Caesarea Hotel**.

Cities of wealth and taste

The region just north of Netanya is the **Valley of Hefer** (Emek Hefer, in Hebrew), and although it isn't really a valley the area gets a mention in the Old Testament. This marshy plain is inextricably linked to the efforts of the pioneers of the 1930s, whose sweat and foresight revitalised the land, enabling it to be as productive as it is today. Kfar Vitkin was among the first of these new settlements and today it is among the country's largest moshavim (collective farming settlements).

The only remarkable thing about the city of **Khadera**, just south of Caesarea is its huge power station on the coast, you can't miss noticing the chimneys, which supplies 60 percent of the country's electricity. However, the electricity company can take credit for cleaning up the River Khadera and planting an attractive parkland along its banks, just south of the power station.

About 10 km (6 miles) south of Khadera is **Mikhmoret** beach, beautiful and seldom crowded. Here you can find sandy coves to nestle in and extraordinary sunsets from atop the cliffs.

Several kilometers further south lies **Netanya** ❼,

Map on page 226

Modern sculpture at Caesarea.

BELOW: archaeologists sift through rubble at Caesarea.

(www.netanya.muni.il), the capital city of the Sharon region. Founded as a citrus colony in 1929, Netanya has blossomed. It has an attractive beach and promenade, a population of nearly 200,000 and a galaxy of budget-priced hotels, often filled to capacity with both Europeans and Israelis. Most of the hotels are clustered along King David and Machnes streets, by the beachfront. The Tourist Information Office (Sun–Thur 9am–5pm; tel 09-8827286) is in Independence Square (Kikar Ha'atzmaut) at the end of Herzl Street just before the seafront.

Hub of the diamond trade

Netanya is also the center of Israel's formidable diamond industry, the country's second most important export after high-tech electronics. Inaugurated by immigrants from Belgium and the Netherlands in the early years of the state, the business has grown to the extent that, since 1974, Israel has held the title of world's number-one exporter of polished diamonds (the raw stones being imported from Asia and Africa). The dealing is all done in Ramat Gan near Tel Aviv, but much of the cutting and polishing is performed in Netanya.

Heading south from Netanya, we pass over the Nahal Poleg (Poleg River), at one time set in an unpleasant morass, now tamed as the **Nakhal Poleg Nature Reserve**, which is to the east. Close by stands the Wingate Institute, Israel's premier center for sports and physical training instruction. It is named after Charles Orde Wingate, a British officer who served in Palestine from 1936 to 1939, and who helped instruct the Jewish police force in defensive fighting techniques that would later prove invaluable in the War of Independence. Wingate reputedly carried a Bible with him, reinforcing the Jews' knowledge of their land through appropriately quoted passages.

TIP

Several companies offer opportunities to buy diamonds. Taub & Company, the largest, has an extensive showroom of precious stones. Guided tours include the chance to see the diamond craftsmen in action.

BELOW: graceful ruins by the sea.

High living

The city of **Herzliya** ❽ (pop. 95,000) is home to many of Israel's wealthiest citizens. It is a favorite with diplomats and ambassadors, and business executives, who are only too happy to take advantage of the stylish beaches and company, and whose villas stud the slopes above the shore amid such ritzy five-star hotels as the Sharon, Accadia and Daniel. To the west of highway 2 is the most expensive part of the city, Herzliya Pituach, between the high-tech park (which also has many of Israel's finest restaurants) and the coast.

On the seafront road a kilometer north of Herzliya is **Appolonia** (Tel Arshaf) in the Sidma Ali National Park (daily 8am–5pm; free). On this site are the ruins of an ancient Hellenistic city and a Crusader fortress. On the southern edge of Herzliya seafront is the city's marina, which has a large upscale shopping mall.

The coastal highway from Herzliya to Tel Aviv winds past modest memorials. On the shore side of the highway a faded ship's hull commemorates immigrants who died attempting to gain refuge in Palestine in the final years of the British Mandate. A short way on, a metallic rectangle standing atop a layered curve of a pedestal commemorates the 34 people killed in a 1978 sea-launched terrorist attack.

The South Coast

The Mediterranean coast means many things to Israelis. It is, first and foremost, the spine of the country, in terms of population as well as geography. The coastal plain is the site of the country's most luxurious hotels, and some of its most important ruins. It is a prime transportation corridor and the location of the fertile Sharon Plain, the source of Israel's citrus industry. Its harbors service industry, military and tourist needs alike.

Map on page 226

Herzliya beach lookout point.

BELOW: the beach at Herzliya.

For the average Israeli the Mediterranean coast means one thing: recreation. From April to October, from Yad Mordekhai in the south to Rosh ha-Nikra at the northern tip, thousands of bronzed sabras flock in droves to the sands, to bake in the sun, play paddle-ball along the water's edge, swim, wade, run, sail, tan, and then watch everyone else do the same. While many of the best-known beaches are a kaleidoscope of human activity in the summer, there are lesser known ones which offer fewer facilities but equally pleasant access to sun and sand. Because of the density of resources, it's not unusual to take a dip against a backdrop of an ancient aqueduct, or the looming silhouette of a power plant.

Israel's first communities

Israel's southern coast stretches from **Tel Aviv** ❾ (*see page 241*) to the tip of the Gaza Strip. The whole area from Tel Aviv to Ashdod is historically known as Darom (the South). In ancient times it was a seat of wisdom, thanks to Yavne (*see below*), and in the 20th century it became the location of some of the new country's first, and southernmost, communities.

The coastal road from Tel Aviv runs through the resort-suburb of Bat Yam and then, to reach two of these early communities, you must turn inland. The more important of the two is **Rishon Le-Tsiyon** ❿, meaning "First in Zion," which was founded in 1882 by Polish and Russian Zionists.

After struggling for five years, the community was given new life in 1887 by Baron Edmond de Rothschild who, in one of his first acts as Israel's benefactor, established vineyards here. He imported shoots of grape vines from Beaujolais, Burgundy and Bordeaux, and the vineyards flourished, producing mainly sweet wines for Jewish ceremonial occasions. After years of Rothschild ownership,

TIP

Only swim on beaches where life guards are on duty. The Eastern Mediterranean has a deceptively strong undercurrent and each year 120 people, many of them tourists, drown in Israel. Avoid the Mediterranean in late June and early July when the sea is full of jellyfish.

BELOW:
a rabbi enjoys those good vibrations.

Map below

the company became a cooperative in 1957, and today the Carmel Oriental Vineyards produce a wide variety of cheaper and expensive wines.

Also to Rishon Le-Tsiyon's credit are the first synagogue built in Israel in modern times (1885), the first kindergarten to teach in Hebrew, and the first Hebrew cultural center, where the national anthem *Ha-Tikva* (The Hope) was composed and sung for the first time. Rishon Le-Tsiyon has expanded enormously in the past 20 years, eating up the sand dunes between the west of Highway 4 and the coast. The city now has a population of 230,000, although it is considered a suburb of Tel Aviv rather than an independent entity. Turn west on 441 to reach Rishon's industrial zone, which has the country's largest shopping malls and amusement park (**Superland**).

Yavne Yam, the ancient port of Yavne, and the swimming beach of **Palmakhim**, said to offer Israel's finest surfing, as well as the site where Judas Maccabeus gained a victory over Greek forces in the 2nd century BC, are just south of Rishon, reached along highway 4311 off of Highway 4. This is where the Sorek River flows into the sea. The Palmakhim air base several kilometers inland is Israel's space launch site and every few years bathers are surprised by a rocket heading for the stars.

Over the years the Jewish National Fund has planted 250 million trees, partly to landscape, partly to slow soil erosion. Special attention is given to the seven trees mentioned in the Bible – fig, date, grape, pomegranate, olive, palm and carob.

Yavne

As you continue south along Highway 4, the next place of note is **Yavne ⑪**, a town which proffers a rich history. The legend goes that in AD 70, when the fall of Jerusalem seemed imminent in the war against Rome, the renowned Rabbi Yohanon Ben Zakkai appeared before the Roman general Vespasian to request permission to found an academy here, predicting that one day the general would

LEFT:
the Mameluke tower at Yavne.

South Coast

Tel Aviv-Yafo (Tel Aviv-Jaffa) ⑨

0   10 km
0   10 miles

N

Bat Yam
Tel Yona   Beit Dagan
Rishon Le-Tsiyon ⑩
Palmakhim   Nes Tsiyona
Kh. Yavne Yam   Ayabot

MEDITERRANEAN SEA

Yavne ⑪   Rekhovot
Nir Galim   Dnaya   Kiryat Ekron
  Kidron
Ashdod ⑫   Gedera
  Bitsaron
Kh. Ashdod Yam   Shtulim
  Talmei Yekhi'el   Ekron
Tel Ashdod
Giv'a 69   Kiryat Mal'akhi
Nitsanim   Masu'ot Yitskhak
The Open Museum
Ashkelon ⑬   Yo'av Fortress
Nir Yisrael   Menukha
  Gal'on
Mavki'im   Khamei Ya'av Hot Spring   Kiryat Gat
Zikim   Memorial Monuments   Uza
Yad Mordekhai ⑭   Gvar'am   Eitan   No'am
  Khelets   Lakhish
Beit Lahiya   Erez   Bror Khayil   Akhuzam
Jabaliya   Beit Hanun   Shikma
  Sderot   Shikma
⑮ Gaza   Metalsim   Dorot   Rukhama
  Nir Moshe
  Sa'ad   Nir Akiva
Alumim   Tkuma   Klakhim
Shuva   Be'er Sheva

become emperor. The prophecy came true shortly afterwards, and the request was granted. Whether or not the legend is true, Yavne did become the site of a great academy, and is known as the site where the Mishna, the great commentary on the Bible, which adapted Judaism to a modern framework, was started.

The *tel* of Yavne today consists of a lone Mameluke tower, built on Crusader ruins on top of a ridge. More recently, Yavne is notable as the site of a small atomic research reactor, Israel's first, built in 1960 by architect Philip Johnson.

Philistine cities

Flowers bloom on a coastal kibbutz.

Still on the coast, some 10 km (6 miles) south, is **Ashdod** ⑫ with its concrete skyline. Its Philistine history now long behind it, Ashdod is a burgeoning man-made harbor, Israel's most important deep-water port, and, if not much of a gift to tourism, a striking example of commercial success.

Re-founded only in 1957, Ashdod grew in five decades to a city of over 200,000 people, and is bursting at its seams with rugged vitality. Its populace includes Arabic-speaking Jews, Indian Jews, sabras and ex-Soviet Jews, among them a large community from Georgia, known as "Gruzinim." From Memorial Hill, just below the lighthouse, there is a clear view of the port, with great ships lined up to carry away exports such as potash and phosphates.

Outside the city, to the southeast, lies the grave of the ancient metropolis, **Tel Ashdod**. The site is quite literally a *tel* (mound), as little remains other than a hillock and the scattered shards of Philistine pottery. Returning towards the highway, keep an eye out for the sycamore trees which dot the environs, and which

BELOW: tetrapods in Ashdod's port.

bear a sometimes edible fruit.

Ashdod marked the northernmost advance of the Egyptian army in 1948, and

supposedly hosted Gamal Abdel Nasser himself. At the point where the road crosses the stream-bed, just east of the city, two relics of that period can be found. The first, the railroad bridge parallel to the road, is a reconstruction of the original, which was blown up by the commandos of the Israeli Givati Brigade, whose nickname was the Foxes of Samson. To the west of the bridges a small white pillbox, built by the British in World War II, stands in lonely vigil.

On the coastal highway 7 km (4 miles) south of Ashdod is the access road (3631) to **Nitsanim**, one of the country's finest strips of beach. Just inland from the beach are freshwater pools.

Ashkelon, an ancient trading post

One of the world's oldest cities, **Ashkelon** ⓭, some 40 km (25 miles) south, has retained far more of its Philistine heritage. Situated on a crest of dunes above the sea, Ashkelon is an amalgam of industrial plants, contemporary apartment towers and lovely beaches. But it is the archaeological park that makes it special, and thoughtful preservation has ensured that the area is rewarding for visitors.

The multi-layered ruins of this strategic harbor city attest to the diversity of the people who have lived here over the centuries. Lying along the famous Via Maris, the roadway linking Egypt and Syria, the city was a trading center from its earliest days, its exports including wine, grain, and a variety of local onion which is now known as a scallion, after its place of origin. In the early 12th century BC the town was conquered by the Philistines, in their sweep of the southern coast, and in the following years it grew to become one of the five great Philistine cities – the others being Ashdod, Gaza, Gath and Ekron.

The next two centuries witnessed bitter rivalry between the Philistines and the Israelites, and although the Jews never took the city it filtered into Jewish history through the story of Samson, whose exploits included his victory with the jawbone of an ass, the episode in which he set fire to the Philistine fields by tying torches to foxes' tails, and his famed ill-fated romance with Delilah.

When King Saul died at the hands of the Philistines, it prompted David's oft-quoted lament: "Tell it not in Gath, publish it not in the streets of Ashkelon, lest the daughters of the Philistines rejoice, lest the daughters of the uncircumcised triumph" (II Sam 1, 20). Three centuries later Ashkelon was still a Philistine stronghold, provoking the wrath of the prophet Zephaniah, who, in one of the final books of the Old Testament, proclaims, "For Gaza shall be forsaken, and Ashkelon a desolation: they shall drive out Ashdod at the noonday, and Ekron shall be rooted up" (Zeph 2, 4).

Eventually, of course, they all were. Taken in the ensuing centuries by Assyrians, Babylonians and others, Ashkelon once more experienced growth in the years of Greek and Roman rule. Herod the Great was supposedly born here, and contributed greatly to the city. Ashkelon fell to the Arabs in the 7th century, and briefly to the Crusaders in 1153, and, in the process, was pillaged of its monuments and stones. In 1270 the city was destroyed completely by the Sultan Baibars.

Today most of the city's antiquities are encompassed within the **National Park** (daily 8am–4pm Mar–Sept

Map on page 233

TIP

Yachtsman sailing into Israel can now berth at new marinas in Ashkelon, Ashdod and Herzliyah as well as at the well-established facilities in Tel Aviv and Yafo.

BELOW:
Roman pillars in the sea at Ashkelon.

Map on page 233

8am–5pm; fee). Here, near the seafront, one can ramble by the ruins of Herodian colonnades and ancient synagogues, along a Roman avenue presided over by the headless statue of Nike, goddess of victory, in and a long-abandoned Roman amphitheater. The site is surrounded by a grass-covered Crusader wall while, on the beach below, fallen pillars rest forlornly against the pressing of the tides.

The modern city consists of three distinct residential areas: **Midgal**, a former Arab town, to the east, and **Afridar**, a newer suburb, along the shore, founded in 1955 by Jews from South Africa. A third neighborhood linking the two was built in the 1990s to house new immigrants from the former Soviet Union. Afridar, distinguished by its tall, fenestrated clock-tower, is the pleasant downtown area where one can find the commercial center and two preserved Roman sarcophagi.

There are a number of hotels here, including Holiday Inn Crowne Plaza and Dan Gardens, as well as many bed-and-breakfast places near the seafront. The beaches are fine for bathing, and enjoy such biblical names as Samson Beach, Delilah Beach, Bar-Kochba Beach, and so on. Other notable sights include the Roman-era **Painted Tomb**, and, in Barnea to the north, the remains of a Byzantine church and 5th-century mosaic.

Dagon – the name of one of Ashkelon's hotels, is Hebrew for mermaid.

The end of the road

Ten km (6 miles) further south along Highway 4 lies the kibbutz of **Yad Mordekhai ⑭**. Named after Mordekhai Anilewitz, who died leading the Jews in their uprising against the Nazis in the Warsaw Ghetto in 1943, the kibbutz was founded that same year by Polish immigrants, and played a pivotal role during the Israeli War of Independence. Attacked by the Egyptian army as it made its advance north in May 1948, the settlement managed to hold out against vastly superior Egyptian forces for six days, thereby allowing Tel Aviv to muster adequate defense.

BELOW: a statue of Anilewitz guards Yad Mordekhai.

Several structures at the kibbutz commemorate the heroic episode; the morbid but effective battlefield reconstruction includes cut-out figures of the advancing Egyptian soldiers, and a taped narration describes the course of events.

Close by, the imposing **museum** (daily 8am–5pm; tel: 08-7720529; fee) houses displays about the fighting and the four kibbutzim that stood together here, and a memorial to the Polish-Jewish community which was annihilated during the Holocaust. On a ridge nearby are the graves of those who fell defending the young settlement.

Overlooking today's community, the statue of Anilewitz stands in defiant pose, grenade in hand, while behind him rests the fallen water tower, its rutted surface preserved in commemoration of all it withstood. The overall effect of Yad Mordekhai is unquestionably sobering rather than joyful, yet it does provide a potent insight into the mentality of this small nation, which has time and again been besieged by hostile forces.

Four km (2½ miles) further south is the **Erez Checkpoint**, the northern frontier crossing to the Gaza Strip and the scene of many bloody encounters between Palestinians and the Israeli army. ❏

Gaza

Gaza, ⑮, from which Israel removed all its settlements in 2005 despite passionate resistance from the settlers, is one of the world's most densely populated areas, with 1.4 million Palestinians living in a narrow strip only 6 km wide and 45 km long (4 by 28 miles). It begins at the Shikma River in the north and extends to the Egyptian border at Rafah. Gaza was once a part of the seafaring Philistine federation; it was here that the illustrious Samson met the beguiling Delilah, who turned out to be his nemesis.

According to Arab tradition, Samson is buried under the site of the Great Mosque, a structure built by the Crusaders in 1150 and transformed into a mosque by the Mamelukes. Gaza has hosted (not always willingly) Muslims, Crusaders, Ottoman Turks, the British, and even Napoleon's soldiers, since Samson's time. In 1948 Egyptian soldiers were perched on this gateway to Palestine, and Egypt retained control after Israel's independence.

About a fifth of the 800,000 Palestinian Arabs displaced by the 1948 fighting ended up in Gaza. Egypt's President Gamal Abdel Nasser organised the first fedayeen (underground fighters) and encouraged guerrilla warfare against Israel. Israel responded in 1956 with the Sinai Campaign, during which it briefly occupied the Sinai Peninsula and the Gaza Strip. In the Six Day War of 1967, Israel seized the territory from Egypt again.

In Palestinian circles, Gaza was always seen as being led by the more prosperous and better educated West Bank population. But surprisingly the Gazans took their place in the front line of Palestine's confrontation with Israel by initiating the 1987 Intifada and it was to Gaza that Yasser Arafat returned to triumphantly in 1994.

Before travelling to Gaza, it is important to keep abreast of current political events and to heed security measures. There is little to see in the way of tourist sights, but the street life is an attraction. Arab women in long black robes, plastic baskets balanced on their heads, walk through the streets and camps, passing children in crisp school uniforms, emblazoned with the Palestinian flag. The city centers are busy with merchants selling a variety of wares: cotton clothing (the word "gauze" comes from Gaza), terracotta pottery (a speciality), wicker furniture, and mounds of camel-hair carpets.

The coastline has some excellent beaches and, if peace and stability are ever achieved, these golden sands could well provide the basis for an important tourist industry. The sandy land here is very fertile and Gaza has thriving agriculture with much citrus.

But, since the armed takeover of the Gaza Strip by Hamas in early 2007, peace and stability seems further away than ever. Hamas's refusal to recognize Israel and its insistence on firing rockets into the adjacent Northern Negev does not bode well for the future coexistence of Arabs and Israelis in the region. ❑

RIGHT: bringing in the day's catch in Gaza.

TEL AVIV

This detailed tour of Israel's capital of style finds a biblical flavour in Old Yafo, and round-the-clock pulsating energy in the rest of the city

Maps:
Area 226
City 242

Tel Aviv (www.tel-aviv.gov.il) ❾ is the essence of modern Israel. If Jerusalem represents the past yearning down the centuries by Jews to return to their biblical roots and the promise of future redemption when the Messiah comes, then Tel Aviv is about the present. Tel Aviv is about the pursuit of material gain and pleasure. It is a city of high-rise office towers, shopping centers, golden beaches, upmarket restaurants, nightclubs and – most of all – boundless, bustling infectious energy. Tel Aviv is hedonistic while Jerusalem is holy. Tel Aviv is sexy while Jerusalem is sacred.

Tel Aviv is Israel's commercial capital, while Jerusalem is the country's political capital – even so, the international community does not recognize Jerusalem's primacy and places its embassies in Tel Aviv. And the two cities vie for the title of cultural capital. Tel Aviv's mayor, Ron Huldai, likes to tell visitors that his city spends far more on culture than Jerusalem and to be sure if culture is defined as music and dance, drama and art, then Tel Aviv takes the title of Israel's cultural capital.

Despite their differences, Tel Aviv and Jerusalem live side by side just a 50-minute drive apart, complementing each other rather than clashing. The dislike of each city's residents for the other never goes beyond taunts.

PRECEDING PAGES:
Tel Aviv's beach.
LEFT: the city seen from Shalom Tower.
BELOW: the city's busy road system.

Old and new

Tel Aviv may be a city of the present but it has a fascinating history. Some 100 years ago the sand dunes north of Yafo (Jaffa) were transformed into a middle-class garden suburb. The founders named the city Tel Aviv after something old and something new. *Tel* means an archaeological mound, while *Aviv* is Hebrew for spring.

Of course, Tel Aviv as we refer to it today is not truly 100 years old. In 1950 the modern Tel Aviv municipality was formed to include Jaffa just to the south. Jaffa, where Jonah set sail on his ill-fated voyage, is one of the world's oldest ports, with a history stretching back centuries before even before biblical times. The Neve Tsedek neighborhood which links Jaffa to Tel Aviv was established in 1887.

The original city of Tel Aviv around the impressive Rothschild Boulevard's western end had (and still has) large town houses and spacious thoroughfares. Tel Aviv quickly expanded as Jews left overcrowded Jaffa and immigrants from fashionable cities in Central and Eastern Europe fleeing anti-Semitic prejudice heard that there was now a modern Hebrew city with 20th-century utilities. Tel Aviv rapidly spread northwards and eastwards. The 1930s were good years for Tel Aviv as German immigrants fleeing Nazi persecution brought prosperity, culture and know-how. They intro-

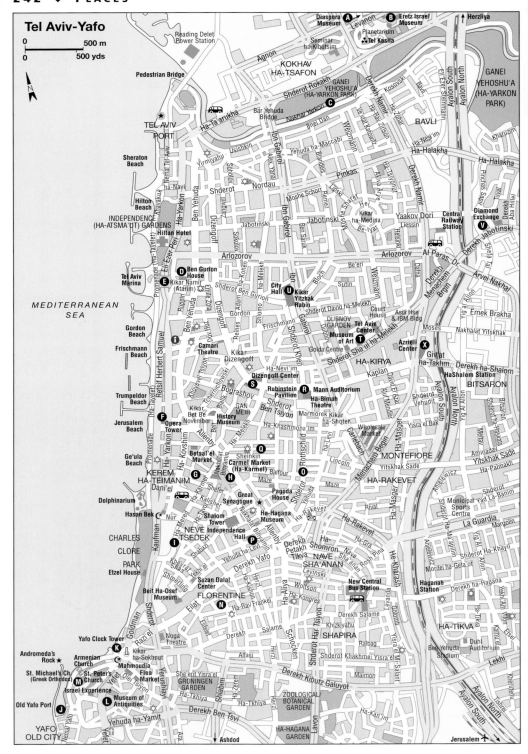

Tel Aviv-Yafo

0 _____ 500 m
0 _____ 500 yds

Map on page 242

duced the Bauhaus architecture, which characterizes early Tel Aviv and earned it the name of the White City.

Oddly enough the early 1940s were prosperous times too. And, with World War II keeping clear of Palestine, the global hostilities actually boosted the economy as the British used Palestine as a strategic military and economic base. However, the news seeping through from Nazi-occupied Europe, and the German advance on Egypt meant that few Tel Avivis could really enjoy their affluence.

It was in Tel Aviv that David Ben Gurion proclaimed independence in 1948 and the city soon fell on hard times. Austerity did not suit Tel Aviv's sense of style and panache and tens of thousands of immigrants from Arab countries were settled in hastily constructed suburbs to the south. To this day, Tel Avivis refer to *tzafonim* (northerners) and *daromim* (southerners). The former are middle-class, liberal Ashkenazim, the latter working-class Sephardim. In recent decades the differences have become blurred. Many Sephardim have made it to the affluent fleshpots of north Tel Aviv, while many of the residents of south Tel Aviv are new immigrant Ashkenazim from the former Soviet Union.

Tel Aviv was also the name given to the Hebrew translation of Theodor Herzl's book Altneuland *(Old-new Land), in which he conceived of the Jewish State.*

Even in the 1960s, '70s and '80s Tel Aviv never recovered the sense of style and international prominence that it felt it deserved. At best it had a shabby charm accentuated by those glorious beaches. It was often compared to Latin American cities – a comparison which irked its residents who aspired to European elegance and American dynamism.

But until the high-tech boom of the 1990s Tel Aviv was a city still searching for its true identity. Like manna from heaven, high-tech fitted in very nicely with the city's image of itself: young, dynamic, leading-edge, innovative and "cool." Most importantly, it brought in the billions of dollars any city needs if it wants to look and be attractive. Even today, cosmopolitan Tel Aviv is still a provincial city – more like Minneapolis or Manchester than London or New York. But don't say that to its residents – they might be offended.

BELOW: at play on Tel Aviv's Corniche.

Greater Tel Aviv

Tel Aviv's population today is a surprisingly small 360,000. But this figure is deceptive and here, once again, Jerusalem has stolen Tel Aviv's clothes as the country's largest city. The Israeli government has steadfastly refused to amalgamate Tel Aviv with its surrounding suburbs because it would then overtake Jerusalem in size. In fact, visitors are not aware that they have left Tel Aviv to enter Ramat Gan or Givatayim to the east, or Holon and Bat Yam to the south. When Israelis talk of Gush Dan (the Dan block – this region belonged to the tribe of Dan in biblical times) – or Greater Tel Aviv, they refer to a metropolitan area encompassing 2½ million citizens. And that doesn't include Netanya 30 km (19 miles) to the north and Ashdod 40 km (25 miles) to the south, each cities of 200,000. Jerusalem is only 60 km (37 miles) to the east and it is not uncommon for people to commute from the holy city to Tel Aviv and vice versa.

Orientation

The most important streets to get to know are the six major north–south axes running parallel to the coast-

*Celebrating on
Independence Day.*

BELOW: model
of a Florentine
synagogue at
Bet Hatefusoth.

line. Ha-Yarkon runs along the coast itself, with Allenby/Ben Yehuda and Dizengoff running close alongside slightly inland. Ibn Gabriol, a kilometer inland, is where City Hall is located. The next two north–south roads are more for transportation in and out of the city – Derekh Petakh Tikvah becomes Derekh Namir and the road to Haifa, while the Ayalon Highway is Tel Aviv's main urban freeway or motorway, transporting vehicles in an out of the city. The railway runs in between the carriageways of the Ayalong Highway.

There are no west–east roads in the center of the city which will take you directly through from the seafront to the Ayalon Highway. If traveling by car, try Kibutz Galuyot in the far south, Arlozorov in the north (one-way east to west), Pinkas/Nordau or Shderot Rokach.

Tel Aviv University

We will start our tour of Tel Aviv in the salubrious suburbs in the far north of the city surrounding Tel Aviv University campus (www.tau.ac.il). On the eastern side of the neatly manicured lawns of the campus, the country's largest university, is the **Museum of the Jewish Diaspora (Bet Hatefusoth)** Ⓐ (open Sun–Thur 10am-4pm, Fri 9am–1pm; fee; tel: 03-7457800; www.bh.org.il; fee) on the university campus. When it was founded in 1979, it was, in concept and methodology, a radical departure from the accepted notion of a museum, for, apart from a few sacramental objects, Bet Hatefusoth contains no preserved artefacts. Its principal aim is reconstruction.

The body of the main exhibit is handled thematically, focusing on general themes of Jewish Life in the Diaspora: family life, community, religion, culture, and the return to Zion. Its striking displays include a collection of beautifully

intricate models of synagogue buildings from across the globe. A memorial column in the central atrium commemorates Jewish martyrdom through the ages. An audio-visual depiction of the migrations of Jews is presented in the hall known as the **Chronosphere**. Four video study-areas enable visitors to view documentary films selected from a catalogue, while a computer system allows them to trace their own lineage. Special exhibitions highlight topics related to Jewish communities around the world.

Nearby in **Ramat Aviv**, cross to the western side of the campus and then go south and west along Levanon, is the sprawling **Eretz Israel Museum** ❸ (open Sun–Thur 10am–4pm, Sat 10am–2pm; tel: 03-6415244; www.eretzmuseum.org.il; fee). The museum is the region's most comprehensive storehouse of archaeological, anthropological and historical findings. Its spiritual backbone is **Tel Kasila**, an excavation site in which 12 distinct layers of civilization have been uncovered, its finds including an ancient Philistine temple and Hebrew inscriptions from 800 BC. The complex consists of 11 pavilions, including exhibits of glassware, ceramics, copper, coins, folklore and ethnography, and a planetarium.

Next door to the Eretz Israel Museum, immediately to the west, is the **Palmach History Museum** (book in advance, tel: 03-6436393) which also breaks new ground in museum presentation by telling the story of Israel's fight for independence using actors and theatrical sets.

River Yarkon and Tel Aviv port

Defining the northernmost limit of the city proper, rather than the municipal entity, is the River (**Nakhal**) **Yarkon** ❸, which once marked the border between the tribes of Dan and Ephraim. Today the river is lined with rambling **parkland**

Map on page 242

TIP

In front of the Carlton and Marina hotels is Tel Aviv's large seawater swimming pool. Aerobic exercise sessions are held on the beach in the summer, and a roller-skating rink operates in the evening near the pool.

BELOW: boating on the Yarkon.

TIP

Tel Aviv has two tourist
information offices.
● Lobby of City Hall: 69
Ibn Gbriol St. Open
Sun–Thur 9am–2pm
(tel: 03-5218500).
● 46 Herbert Samuel
St. corner Geula St.
(on the seafront) Open
Sun–Thur 9.30am–
5.30pm, Fri 9.30am–
1pm (tel: 03-5166188).
The tourist police are
also located in this
office (tel: 03-5165382).

and serves to accommodate scullers who row along it in the cooler hours of
the day. Near the river's western rim can be seen the dome and chimneys of the
Reading Power Station, while the greenery of the city's exhibition grounds
marks the river's eastern limit. Swimming in the river is strictly prohibited
however inviting the cool waters may seem and swallowing a mouthful is likely
to lead to a life threatening lung infection.

To the south of the Yarkon River is the trendy quarter known as **Little Old Tel
Aviv** where three of the city's major north-south roads begin: Ha-Yarkon, Ben
Yehuda and Dizengoff. There are a large number of cafés, restaurants and bars
in this quarter – and Tel Aviv's disused port has now been rejuvenated in a project often compared to London's Covent Garden or San Francisco's Fisherman's
Wharf. Tel Aviv Port itself as a working dock and harbor only had a relatively
brief existence. It was opened in 1936 as a Jewish-owned port to compete with
the British-run port in nearby Jaffa, which was frequently strikebound by Arab
stevedores protesting against the allegedly pro-Zionist policies of the Mandate
authorities. The Port was closed down in 1965 because its relatively shallow
waters could not harbor the large vessels shipping goods to and from Israel, and
custom was diverted either to Haifa in the north or Ashdod to the south.

There are currently 16 restaurants, cafés and bar in the Tel Aviv Port complex,
including half a dozen fish and seafood restaurants (not kosher) and a French
bistro. However, there is a kosher dairy restaurant and most of the cafés are
kosher too. The area also has a dozen fashion stores, a shop selling and renting
diving equipment, two nightclubs, and several wedding halls. You don't need to
be a paying customer to visit the Port. Even if you don't want to eat out or
party, Tel Aviv Port, linked by a seafront promenade to the city in the south,

BELOW:
Kikar Namir at dusk.

Map on page 242

makes an ideal destination for an evening stroll, with the sea breezes tempering the city's spring and summer humidity.

To the south stretches **Independence Gardens**, a strip of green offering a stirring view of the Mediterranean from its cliffs. Alternatively, there is a path on the promenade below. Independence Gardens hides among its shrubbery various archaeological finds, and in the evening it is the gathering spot of the city's gay community.

Just inland, in Ben Gurion Boulevard, after the Tel Aviv Hilton, is **Ben Gurion House** **D** (open: Sun, Mon 8am–5pm, Tues–Thur 8am–3pm, Sat 8am–1pm; tel: 03-5221010; www.ben-gurion.org.il; fee). This was formerly the home of Israel's first prime minister and today a public museum housing the personal mementos of David Ben Gurion and a 20,000-volume library.

Hotels and best beaches

The seaside promenade is dotted with cafés, restaurants, ice-cream parlors and the like, all offering free sea air and costly refreshments. On summer nights the promenade is clogged with people on foot and in cars, manoeuvring for some sea breeze after the day's oppressive heat.

The **marina**, for many years the largest in the Middle East until the Herzliya marina opened to the north, rents out sailing and motor-boats, and equipment for windsurfing, seasurfing, water-skiing, diving and other water sports.

You can't help notice – but should avoid – **Kikar Namir** (still known locally by its former name, **Kikar Atarim**) **E**, a concrete monstrosity squatting over the marina, at the end of Ben Gurion. This open-air mall offers concrete mushroom sunshades, tourist items and a chance to lose one's way. Its cafés, pizzerias and restaurants, tolerable in the sunlight, turn seedy at night.

The city's main hotel district lies along the coast here. From the north of the city to the south, the coastline is dominated by an imposing row of hotels lined up like dominoes, including (among others) the Hilton, north of Arlozorov, and the Carlton, Sheraton and Dan. The **Opera Tower** **F** to the south of the hotels is a distinctive building which houses apartments, restaurants, shops, jewellery stores and a cinema.

Each hotel has its own beach strip (the beaches are all public), most of them quite civilized, with showers, easy chairs and refreshment facilities. Marking the end of the hotel line to the south, across from the Dan Panorama and David Intercontinental, is the **Dolphinarium**, a white elephant, now unused, obscuring the magnificent view of Old Yafo from Tel Aviv's coast.

Where east meets west

Just inland, several blocks south of Opera Tower, is the **Kerem ha-Teimanim** (Yemenite Quarter) **G**, its exotic winding streets a jolt back in time, preserving the look and feel of the Yemenite community which settled here a century ago. Here, in Arab-style stone houses, is the best place to sample the spicy, pungent Yemenite cuisine. Pundak Shaul, Zion, Pninat Hakerem and Maganda are among the best Yemenite

When talking pictures arrived at the end of the 1920s, the cinema management, successfully pressured by the powerful Labor Federation, continued paying the unemployed orchestra members' wages for 18 months.

BELOW: a striking apartment building at Beach Promenade.

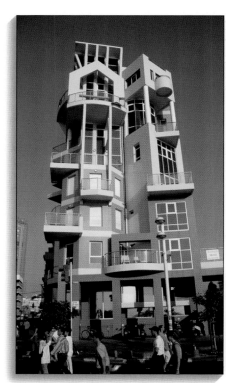

Architecture

Tel Aviv has been named a UNESCO World Heritage Site because of its unique collection of International Style (Bauhaus) buildings. The city has more than 1,500 such buildings, by far the largest number of any location worldwide, with most of them to be found in Rothschild Boulevard, and the roads to the north.

Beneath Tel Aviv's high-tech glass towers, it's hard for the visitor to pick out the Bauhaus buildings. The understated cubic style is often hidden behind trees, and in many instances urban grime. But many of the buildings have been restored to their former glory, and property developers are rehabilitating many more, usually adding on expensive penthouses, which are carefully designed (with close municipal supervision and encouragement) to enhance the entire structure.

The original architects would probably not have approved. Bauhaus appealed to the early Zionists because of its "no-nonsense" minimalist and socialistic style.

Until the emergence of Bauhaus in the 1920s, Tel Aviv buildings had an eclectic style with oriental and European designs alongside each other and sometimes incorporated in the same building. Bauhaus architecture itself, which had developed in Germany after World War I was simple. In the wake of new engineering developments, architects at the Bauhaus school were asked to forget everything they had been taught. For example, walls could now be built around steel frames and no longer had to support the building. There was also a social aspect to the architecture, which appealed to socialists as the new style was able to provide less expensive homes for the less affluent, while using less land.

Eventually Hitler threw the Bauhaus school out of his country because it was un-German. It became known as the International Style and the fact is that architects around the world like Le Corbusier in Paris had been developing similar ideas of architecture.

Many of the architects who left Germany were Jews who found their way to Tel Aviv and influenced the design of the city. Old post cards and pictures from the 1930s show Rothschild Boulevard in its full glory and also reveal why the first Hebrew city was once called the White City. Unfortunately, with urban grime taking a wicked toll on white walls the White City soon lost its luster.

Many of the buildings are being restored in their original white. Number 71 Rothschild is such an example. That building's strip passages between apartments on the upper floors are typical of the straight lines, rectangles and cubes that make up the International style design.

Engel Street, a delightful mews off Rothschild to the east, which is made up entirely of Bauhaus buildings, and Dizengoff Circle are both excellent places to appreciate the full cumulative effect of Bauhaus architecture. Property developers and homeowners wishing to comprehensively renovate a building are entitled to loans and grants from the municipality but they must restore all features, including re-opening enclosed balconies. Indeed, much work needs to be done, with dozens of the Bauhaus buildings looking like neglected slums. ❏

LEFT: the Bauhaus style suited early settlers.

restaurants in the country. Like the Yemenite Quarter, Tel Aviv's market-places are an inseparable part of the Levant. The biggest and best known of these is the **Carmel Market (Ha-Karmel)** , stretching along from Kerem ha-Teimanim to Allenby. Always crowded with shoppers and hagglers, the market is a medley of colors, smells and sounds. A large variety of exotic fruits, vegetables and herbs can be found here, as well as clothes, shoes, pickled foods and pitta bread at bargain prices.

To the left of the entrance to the Carmel Market on Allenby street is a pedestrianised street called **Nakhalat Binyamin**. Here, on Tuesdays and Fridays, arts and crafts traders bring their wares to parade and sell. A great place for present-shopping, as the artisans combine jewellery with juggling, cactus plants with camel bags, and wood carvings with wonderful art. On these days and throughout the week, the streetside cafés are crowded.

Between the Yemenite Quarter and Neve Tsedek, on the fast road to Yafo, is the **Hasan Bek Mosque**, contrasting sharply with the contemporary high-rise near it. Built in 1916 by Yafo's Turkish-Arab governor, the mosque was intended to block the development of Tel Aviv towards the sea. During the War of Independence the mosque served as an outpost for Arab snipers. In 1992 it was sold by its local Muslim owners to a Tel Aviv businessman who planned to open a nightclub there. After protests of outrage from the Arab world the mosque was bought by the Egyptian government, which has refurbished both the exterior and interior.

Neve Tsedek

Inland from the Dan Panorama Hotel is the city's oldest quarter, **Neve Tsedek** ❶ (not counting Yafo). It was founded in 1887 as a suburb of Yafo, and is a pic-

Map on page 242

TIP

Tel Aviv has 14 km (9 miles) of beaches. The Jerusalem Beach near the Hasan Bek Mosque is gender segregated for religious bathers. Some secular women prefer this beach, where they're not pestered by eager Romeos.

BELOW: vegetables for sale in Carmel Market.

Stone head in Yafo.

turesque maze of narrow streets flanked by low-built Arab-style houses. At the time the quarter was considered a luxury suburb, despite the crowded housing and less-than-sanitary conditions. In recent years the quarter's quaint old dwellings have taken the fancy of artists and well-to-do families, who have restored them and replanted the inner courtyards.

The **Neve Tsedek Theater**, otherwise known as the Suzan Dalal Center, which specializes in avant-garde drama, opened in the building of the city's first girls' school, which was also the first all-Hebrew school in Israel. This is also the home of the **Batsheva Dance Company** and the **Inbal Dance Company**. With the theater's opening in a magnificent plaza dotted with orange trees, several colorful galleries, restaurants and nightclubs popped up, lending a new vitality to the century-old streets.

Yafo, where it all began

Neve Tsedek stretches southwards to Yafo, the place where it all began. It is said that, when God got fed up with his creatures, he brought the Great Flood on the world to wipe the slate clean and start afresh. After the flood subsided and Noah's Ark landed on Mount Ararat, Noah's youngest son Japheth found a pleasant hill overlooking a bay and settled down, naming the site "Yafo" (Hebrew for beautiful). One of the world's oldest cities, Yafo has retained its biblical flavor, spiced by centuries of historical events and myths. The famous Cedars of Lebanon to be used by King Solomon in building the Temple in Jerusalem were shipped to Yafo – even then an important Mediterranean trading port. The miracle of raising Tabitha from the dead was performed by the Apostle Peter when he stayed at the Yafo house of Simon the Tanner (Acts 9, 36–42).

BELOW:
Yafo is a popular
center for boating.

Some 3,400 years ago Yafo was conquered by the Egyptians. Subsequently Alexander the Great, Herod, Richard the Lionheart, Napoleon, and the Turks (among others) all passed through, alternately destroying and building. The British took over from the Ottomans at the end of World War I, and Yafo returned to Israel during the War of Independence in 1948.

Jewish residence was resumed in Yafo long before that, in 1820, when a Jewish traveler from Constantinople settled here. Soon after came a larger community, mainly North African merchants and craftsmen, who merged with the local Arab community. By the time of Israel's independence the city had close to 100,000 residents, over 30,000 of them Jewish. Modern Yafo has retained its Eastern flavor, and today holds a colorful medley of immigrants from North African and Central European countries as well as a community of more than 20,000 Arabs.

Old Yafo today

Old Yafo was reconstructed and renovated in 1963, with cobbled paths and winding alleys twisting through the massive stone fortifications surrounding the city. Today it sports an artists' colony, art galleries, craft shops, tourist shops, seafood restaurants and nightclubs. The **Old Yafo Port ❿**, destined for demolition, is still the home port of the local fishermen, who haul in their catch every dawn. Their findings end up in the cauldrons of the town's many restaurants, three of which are located right in the old port, overlooking the pier and bobbing boats.

Looking seawards one can make out a cluster of rocks, the largest of which is said to be Andromeda's. But recent renovation of the pier, which included the bombing of some of the formation, nearly blew the rock out of existence. For the rest, time seems to have stood still. Primitive ovens still churn out an infinite variety of oriental-spiced pitta breads, and the ancient streets hum with aggressive shopkeepers, pastry vendors and meandering passers-by.

Old Yafo begins at the **Clock Tower** Ⓚ on Yefet, built in 1906 by the Turks and facing the local police station. The tower's stained-glass windows each portray a different chapter in Yafo's history. Opposite the tower, past an arched entranceway, is a large courtyard, once the Armenian Hostel which served as a central station for travelers going to Jewish settlements throughout the country. Walk past the police station and, on your right, an entrance leads to the **Mahmoudia Mosque**, built in 1812 and named after Yafo's Turkish governor.

Turning right from Yefet onto Mifrats Shlomo, towards the renovated section of Old Yafo, one passes the **Yafo Museum of Antiquities** Ⓛ (open Sun–Thur 9am–1pm, Tues also 4–7pm, Sat 10am–2pm; fee), where archaeological exhibits from many years of excavations trace the city's development. Erected in the 18th century, the building was the Turkish governor's headquarters and local prison. Later it won acclaim throughout the Middle East as the soap factory of the Greek Orthodox Damiani family. The sidewalk opposite the Museum offers one of the best views of Tel Aviv's beaches and coastline.

The Franciscan **St Peter's Church** Ⓜ is further along, on one side of Keddumim Square. The **St Louis Monastery** in the courtyard was named after the

Map on page 242

Romantic dining at Yafo.

BELOW:
Old Yafo Port.

French king who arrived at the head of a Crusade and stayed here in 1147. The monastery later served as a hostel for pilgrims to Jerusalem and was known in the 17th century as "The Europeans' House." Napoleon also relaxed here after conquering Yafo.

A little way north and towards the sea is the minaret of the **Jama El-Baher Mosque**, located next door to the first Jewish house in Yafo, built in 1820. The **Armenian Convent** and church here mark the site of a 17th-century pilgrims' inn. A magnificent renovated Turkish mansion behind the museum, once a Turkish bath house, has been converted into a nightclub and restaurant, **El-Hamam**.

At the top of the hill, past the Pisgah Park, **Horoscope Path** begins to wind its way through the Yafo wall. It goes all the way to the lighthouse at the wall's southern entrance, on the corner of Shimon Haburski. At the center of the renovated section is a square called **Kikar Kedumin**, in which the Yafo excavations present a reconstruction of the city's multi-faceted history; this is also one of Tel Aviv's most popular evening spots. Down an alleyway to the right is **Simon the Tanner's House** (daily 8am–7pm; fee) where, in addition to performing miracles, Peter is believed to have received divine instruction to preach to non-Jews.

On the southern side of the wall, along Pasteur, a modern structure rather spoils the beauty of the ancient walls. This is a shopping area including restaurants and cafés. Further along Pasteur Street is the **Horace Richter Gallery**. From here you can descend to the port and its delightful fish restaurants.

Back on Yefet, turn left and walk down the hill crossing the road. Just before the traffic lights on the right is **Abulafia**, Yafo's first pitta-bread establishment (dating back to the 1880s). It reputedly does its briskest business on Passover and Yom Kippur when droves of bread-craving Israelis queue outside. The area

For home thoughts.

BELOW:
St Peter's Church.
RIGHT:
Yafo Museum
of Antiquities.

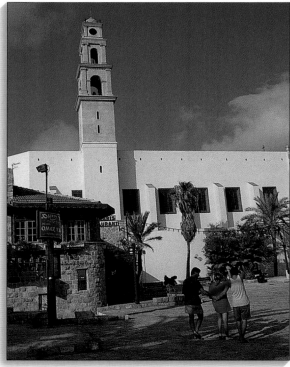

Map on page 242

is especially lively after dark, when Tel Aviv's night-owls descend on Yafo.

Yafo's famous **Flea Market** lies in the next complex of alleys just east of here. It specialises in antiques, copperware ("antique" specimens made while you watch), jewelry and second-hand junk. It isn't open on Saturdays.

To the northeast of Yafo lies **Florentine** , an ugly ramshackle neighborhood, which is nevertheless considered Tel Aviv's most trendy and bohemian quarter, with a flourishing nightlife, often compared to New York's Meatpacking District and London's Hoxton. East of Florentine is the new Central Bus Station, a vast complex of shops, offices and eateries. Other than stopping to grab a quick, great-value *felafel* with as much salad as you want, it is advisable to board your bus as quickly as possible. The area to the north, the old bus station, is even seedier, and is best avoided. The Central Bus Station now has an overhead walkway leading across the Ayalon Highway to the Haganah railway station.

Financial district

Immediately north and west of the Bus Station is the city's financial district. The streets are overlooked by the **Shalom Tower**, on Herzl, for many years the tallest building in Israel but superseded by the two high-rise towers of the Azrieli Center overlooking the Ayalon highway. The tower soars 35 floors – and 140 meters (460 ft) – above the city, an austere white rectangle. Its main significance lies in its location. Here stood one of the first buildings to be erected in Tel Aviv – the Herzliya Gymnasium (High School). Built in 1910 on the first thoroughfare, the school was a symbol of pioneering and became the cultural and economic nucleus of the town. It was torn down in 1959. All that remains of it is a huge fresco on the wall of the tower, created by artist Nahum Gutman.

Today **Rothschild Boulevard** 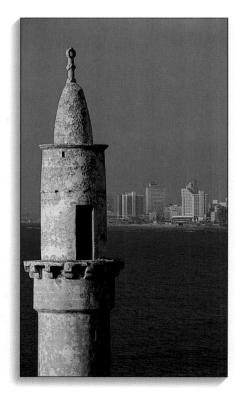, an appropriate name, at its western end, forms the heart of Israel's financial district. Built in 1910 over a dried river-bed, the boulevard was once Tel Aviv's most elegant address. It's again elegant, its central promenade dotted with trees, benches and refreshment kiosks as well as a cycle path, and its buildings embrace a jumble of styles. At number 13 the Betsal'el style (named after the Betsal'el Art School in Jerusalem) combines European and Oriental design.

The public museum, **Independence Hall** , is at number 16, the former residence of the city's first mayor, Meir Dizengoff. The Declaration of Independence was signed here on 15 May 1948, and it was also the first home of the Knesset (parliament) until it moved to the Opera Tower building on the beach, then to Jerusalem. The second and third floors comprise the **Bible Museum** (open Sun–Fri 9am–1pm, Sat 10am–2pm; fee).

Across the road is the **Israel Defense Forces** (Ha-Hagana) **Museum** (open Sun–Thur 9am–4pm; tel: 03-5608264; fee), located in the former residence of Haganah commander Eliahu Golumb. Here, and dotted around the city are square brown signs that refer to the original use of the buildings. Before Israel's independence the resistance forces fought underground from these positions, against both the British and the Arabs. The IDF (Israel Defense Forces) headquarters

TIP

Tourists staying in Tel Aviv are entitled to three free English-language guided walking tours. For details, phone the Tel Aviv Municipality's tourism department at 03-5218214 or ask at the Tourist Information offices.

BELOW:
Tel Aviv's coast, viewed from Yafo.

is still located in Tel Aviv at the Kirya, originally a German Templar settlement, turned into their headquarters by the British, before being taken over by the IDF. This explains where Saddam Hussein was aiming for when his forces fired Iraqi missiles at Tel Aviv in the 1991 Gulf War.

Breuer House at number 46 was built in 1922; it has tiny decorative balconies, a pagoda-like wooden roof, a minaret, and a large enclosed garden. On the verge of demolition in 1948, it was saved when the Soviet ambassador requested it for his headquarters. It served as the Soviet Embassy until 1953, when diplomatic relations with the USSR were severed. Renovated in the 1990s, it now houses Sotheby's Israel offices.

The large abstract sculpture in Ha-Bima Square is the work of Menashe Kadishman.

Typical Bauhaus-style buildings may be seen at numbers 89, 91 and 140, and on nearby Engel, recently converted into a pedestrian mall.

Sheinkin, ❶ which stretches eastwards off Rothschild further along, is the bastion of Israel's trendy, leftist and secular community, although the ultra-orthodox Lubavitchers (Habad) have their Tel Aviv headquarters in Sheinkin too. The local equivalent of New York's Greenwich Village or London's Notting Hill, Sheinkin is only just being discovered by tourists. Stretching from Allenby all the way east to Yehuda ha-Levi, it is a street that has it all. Don't bring a car on Friday when it is virtually closed to traffic to allow shoppers to buy wallpaper, furniture or home appliances, to discover a second-hand fake-fur coat, bind a book, buy eggs in a shop selling only farm-fresh produce, have their hair done, or simply sit sipping coffee or alcohol on one of the street's many cafés.

BELOW:
many office blocks are ultra-modern.

Sheinkin is renowned for its leading fashion designs, and hip Tel Avivians who can be seen flaunting their funky outfits and the latest chic hairstyles. At the

western end of Sheinkin is the Betsal'el Market, reputed to have the best *felafels* in Israel, as well as the usual discount quality fashion items and bric-a-brac.

A walk on Bialik

Further west along Allenby, **Bialik** is another pleasant street dating from the city's early days. At number 14 is the **Rubin Museum** (Mon, Wed, Thur 10am–3pm, Tues 10am–8pm, Sat 11am–2pm; tel: 03-5255961; www.rubin museum.org.il; fee), the former residence of Israeli artist Reuven Rubin. A short walk from here is **Bialik House** (same hours as Rubin House; tel; 03-5254350), once the home of Israel's national poet, Haim Nahman Bialik. Built in 1925, it has a little tower and dome, a prominent pink balcony and arched columns, like those of the Doge's Palace in Venice.

The Opera House.

The post-1948 city

To the east of this neighborhood, at the northern end of Rothschild and the eastern extremity of Dizengoff, is Tel Aviv's premier cultural complex including the **Ha-Bimah Theater**, the **Mann Auditorium** and the **Rubinstein Pavilion ®**. During the Russian Revolution a group of young Russian-Jewish actors formed a collective and dreamed of a Hebrew theater. The dream came true in Tel Aviv, dozens of years later. The Ha-Bimah Theater (ha-Bimah means "the stage" in Hebrew), built in the square of the same name, originally had creaking wooden chairs and lousy acoustics: today it has two theaters (one seating 1,000 and a smaller one with seats for 300), revolving stages, and simultaneous translation into several languages during the high season.

Just next to the theatre is the **Mann Auditorium**, the home of the Israel Phil-

BELOW: fast food, international style.

harmonic Orchestra. Tickets here are highly prized and hard to get. The third building in this complex is the **Rubinstein Pavilion** (Mon, Wed 10am–4pm, Tue, Thur 10am–10pm; Fri 10am–2pm Sat. 10am–4pm; tel: 03-5287196; fee), a branch of the Tel Aviv Museum which specializes in modern art exhibitions. The little park in the middle of the complex hides the chic brass-and-chrome **Apropos Café.**

Dizengoff's cafes

This arts complex is at the start of **Dizengoff ⑤**, once the city's most fashionable thoroughfare and although less grand today, still one of Tel Aviv's principal streets. Café-going is a major part of any self-respecting Tel Avivian's way of life. Some people go to cafés for their first coffee of the day; others conduct business meetings or entertain guests; retired people spend their mornings over cappuccinos and croissants. On a sunny day you may get the impression that the entire city is on holiday, sipping coffee at sidewalk cafés.

Much of Israeli café activity still takes place along Dizengoff, although Sheinkin is more trendy, and pedestrianized Nakhalat Binyamin a more convenient café location. Young, upbeat and action-packed, this street is a constant parade of beautiful people, window shoppers, tourists, actors, models and in-vogue popstars, vagabonds, soldiers and business people. A seat in a Dizengoff café is an excellent vantage point for observing the human panorama.

At no time is Dizengoff more glamorous or crowded than on Friday afternoons, when groups of Tel Avivians congregate to unwind from the long work week with friends, try to chat up girls, catch up on gossip, and learn of the night's best parties.

The fountain in the centre of Dizengoff Circle was designed by a leading Israeli artist, Yaakov Agam. The same Agam style adorns the side of the Dan Hotel on Ha-Yarkon.

BELOW: part of the Sheinkin scene.

A block north of the Ha-Bimah complex is the **Dizengoff Center**, a modern multi-level shopping complex offering everything from offbeat pets to oriental carpets, complete with cinemas, restaurants, sports shops and banks. Those who like to combine sightseeing with food can then eat their way along this end of Dizengoff which is crowded with snack bars and restaurants, offering everything from fruit juice, pizza and hamburgers to Hungarian *blintzes* and *shwarma*.

The raised piazza with the sculpture-fountain spouting in its center is **Kikar Dizengoff**. Originally a traffic roundabout, the pedestrian level has since been lifted above the street, creating a peculiar urban hub but allowing the free flow of people above and traffic below.

The next street to cut across Dizengoff is Gordon. Works of the great masters, such as Picasso and Chagall, are displayed here beside paintings by leading Israeli artists such as Agam, Gutman and Kadishman. Although these works are displayed in galleries, which are essentially stores, it is the Tel Aviv custom to walk in, around and out of these stores along Gordon and adjoining streets like Dov Hoz, as if you were in a museum.

Map on page 242

Outside the Museum of Art.

More arts off Ibn Gabirol

Ibn Gabirol also runs north through the city from the Ha-Bimah Theater. To the right of Ibn Gabirol on Sha'ul ha-Melekh Street, a rival cultural complex, the **Tel Aviv Museum of Art** ❶ (Mon, Wed 10am–4pm, Tues, Thur 10am–10pm, Fri 10–2pm, Sat 10–4pm; tel: 03-6961297; www.tamuseum.co.il; fee), has four central galleries, an auditorium which often features film retrospectives, numerous other halls, a sculpture garden, a cafeteria and a shop. There are exhibitions of 17th-century Dutch and Flemish masters, 18th-century Italian paintings, Impressionists, post-Impressionists, and a good selection of 20th-century art from the US and Europe, in addition to modern Israeli work.

Next to the museum, the **Tel Aviv Center for Performing Arts** was inaugurated in the 1990s. This attractive new building includes the New Israel Opera and a theater and auditorium.

At the corner of Sha'ul ha-Melekh and Weizmann are several of the more striking modern edifices in the city, the most unusual being **Asia House**, created by architect Mordechai Ben-Horin in gleaming white to resemble a horizontal series of giant rolling waves. Its entrance hall holds a permanent exhibit of sculpture under a pastel-colored mosaic ceiling. The **IBM Building** next door towers above, a three-sided cylinder supported on a mushroom-like shaft. Designed by Israeli architects Yasky, Gil & Silvan, it creates a handsome profile for the city skyline. Across the street, the red slated roofs of the **German Templar Colony** (1870–1939) provide one more architectural style in a city of contrasts.

On the other side of the Kirya, the IDF's headquarters, is the **Azrieli Center.** For several years these three towers – one round, one triangular, and one square – were the tallest buildings in Israel, although they have since been surpassed by Aviv Tower in Ramat Gan. Travel up to the 49th-floor observatory of the round tower for one of the best views in Israel, although it is marred by heat haze in the summer (Sun–Thur 10am–8pm, Fri 10am–6pm, Sat 10am–

BELOW: the fountain in Dizengoff Circle.

Map on page 242

Tel Aviv has been cited in an Economist Intelligence Unit report as the 10th most expensive city in the world.

BELOW: Asia House and the flowing IBM building.

8pm; tel: 03-6081179; fee). The Azrielli Center, with direct access to the Shalom railway station, is one of Israel's largest shopping malls.

Moving back westwards to Ibn Gabirol, the road leads northwards to the central square of the city, next to the headquarters of the municipality. It was here, when it was then known as Kikar Malchei Yisrael (the Square of the Kings of Israel), on 4 November 1995 that Prime Minister Yitzhak Rabin was assassinated after a huge demonstration in support of the peace process. The square was immediately renamed **Yitzhak Rabin Square** (**Kikar Yitzhak Rabin**) **U**, and there is an unusual memorial close to the spot where he fell, at the northern end of the square, just behind the steps to the City Hall. Portraits, paintings and graffiti cover the area as the people's memorial to a man respected by many of differing convictions.

East along Jabotinski is **Kikar Hamedina**, where the road makes a huge circle and contains many of the country's most expensive clothes stores. Further east, a dense forest of high-rise buildings suddenly looms on the horizon. Technically speaking, the Diamond Exchange district is in adjoining Ramat Gan rather than Tel Aviv. The gleaming office blocks contain not only the diamond traders, who handle some $7 billion-worth of diamonds each year, but also many of the country's most successful high-tech enterprises. The **Diamond Exchange** **V** has a museum (Sun–Thur 10am–4pm, Fri 8am–noon; tel: 03-5760219; www.diamond-il.co.il; fee), which tells the story of diamonds. The Diamond Exchange complex also contains Israel's tallest building, the 69-storey Aviv Tower *(see photograph, page 117)*.

Further to the east, **Ramat Gan**, with a population of 150,000, also contains Bar Ilan University, Sheba Medical Center, Israel's largest hospital, and a **safari park** where lions, elephants, hippopotami and other Asian and African animals entertain passing cars (Sat–Thur 9am–4pm Fri 9am–1pm; tel: 03-6313531; www.safari.co.il; fee).   ❑

Nightlife

In the late 1980s an advertising campaign for Tel Aviv's nightlife revolved around the slogan "The City That Never Stops". The label has stuck. Tel Avivans are proud of their energy and stamina, working hard by day and playing hard at night. Nightlife in Tel Aviv, as throughout Israel, starts late. The restaurants don't get busy until after 10pm, and the bars, cafés and nightclubs start filling up from midnight onwards. But if night birds start late in terms of time they start early age-wise. Parents will often take small children to bars and cafés at midnight, while unaccompanied 14-year-olds roam the streets well into the early hours. Israeli parents take the relaxed attitude that there is nothing youngsters can do at three in the morning that they couldn't do at three in the afternoon.

In any event, Tel Aviv's streets are jammed with pedestrians of all ages, as well as cars, well into the early hours of the morning, especially at the weekends (remember that the weekend days off are Friday and Saturday).

At night tourists might do well to stick to the seafront. Tel Aviv's Mediterranean coast stretches from the fashionable restaurants of Tel Aviv Port and Little Old Tel Aviv in the north, through the male gay pick-up venue in Independence Gardens (Gan Ha'atsma'ut), to the cafés popular with teenagers to the south of the hotel district, and the sleazy red-light district behind the Opera Tower.

Further south are the restaurants of the Yemenite quarter and then Yafo with its nightclubs and fish restaurants. Perhaps the latter are the most delightful night-time experiences. Taboun is the pick of these. Enjoying a meal with the sound of the sea lapping against the shore is not only romantic but can also be a delicious relief from the city's stifling humidity.

But, humidity aside, those who want to search inland for the core of Tel Aviv nightlife are also not starved of choice. Culture fiends tend to hang out in the vicinity of the Ha-Bimah Theatre/Mann Auditorium complex at the beginning of Dizengoff. Further north on Dizengoff, near the junction with Gordon, Israelis like to stroll around at night popping into art galleries and sipping coffee at nearby cafés. Gallery crawling is also the done thing in Old Yafo.

Dizengoff, however, is no longer the main after-dark attraction. The trendiest neighborhood is Sheinkin, a narrow street to the north of the financial district which runs eastwards from the Yemenite Quarter. Sheinkin offers an abundant choice of small restaurants, cafés and bars. Sheinkin is trendy for the middle-aged but Florentin to the south (northeast of Yafo) is the pulsating, hip place for the young, whether bohemian, artsy, affluent or just looking for a good time.

Remember that the essence of Tel Aviv nightlife is outdoors. As elsewhere in the Mediterranean there is a fine dividing line between a café and a bar and it is acceptable to just have a drink in a café, or go to a pub for a meal or a soft drink or coffee. Nothing is nicer than to find an outdoor table and watch the world go by. The night crowds can be noisy and lively but drunkenness is very rare. Indeed, Israelis are infamous for spending long hours in bars nursing one beer. ❑

RIGHT: keeping cool in a Tel Aviv club.

THE INLAND PLAINS

*Don't rush through the plains between Tel Aviv and Jerusalem
or you'll miss the monasteries, caves and splendid views
of the Judean foothills*

Map
on page
264

I t's not the most acclaimed tourist area in the Holy Land, nor is it the most famous for its ruins, and many visitors pass through this region, from Tel Aviv to Jerusalem and back, never venturing from the main roads. Yet the consistent flow of conquerors, immigrants, wayfarers and settlers has left its mark on the landscape, and the area – still the central crossroads of the nation – is rich in history.

Rising from the flat coastal plain into the gently rolling Judean foothills, this area has always been one of the most densely populated in the country. Some of the first modern Jewish settlements in the 1880s and 1890s were established here. Today several of these villages have grown into cities; while others, with their lush vegetation and smell of cow dung, convey an air of tranquility at odds with the hectic pace of so much of modern Israel.

Ground-breaking research

Start your journey at **Rekhovot ❶**, about 20 km (12 miles) south-east of Tel Aviv. This is the home of the **Weizmann Institute of Science** (www. weizmann.ac.il), the research and development center named after Chaim Weizmann, the country's first president, and situated near the northern entrance to the city on Highway 412. Weizmann was also an organic chemist of international renown, and for many years the leader of the Zionist movement. His scientific research assisted the British war effort during World War I, towards the end of which he was instrumental in securing the Balfour Declaration. Founded in 1934, the Weizmann Institute originally concentrated on local agriculture and medicine, but in 1949 it was transformed into a world-class research institute. Today it has a staff of 2,500 researchers and graduate students, with over 400 research projects in the pipeline in such fields as cancer cures, hormones, immunology, aging, cell structure, atomic particles and astrophysics. Children will enjoy the hands-on **Clore Science Park** (Mon–Thur 9pm–5pm, Fri 9pm–2pm; tel: 08-9344401).

The center's moving spirit in its early years was Meyer Weisgal, an American showbiz impresario who, in addition to raising millions of dollars for the institute, used to pace the grounds picking up discarded cartons, plastic bags and even matchsticks. The institute is still one of the tidiest places in Israel. There are daily guided tours of the grounds. The view from the top of the futuristic atomic particle accelerator is good, and Weizmann's house, designed by Erich Mendelsohn in 1936–37, is worth seeing.

Opposite the Weizmann Institute is another prestigious academic campus: the **Hebrew University's Faculty of Agriculture**, one of the world's leading

PRECEDING PAGES: Jewish and Arab children together in Neve Shalom. **LEFT:** the Tel Aviv–Jerusalem railway. **BELOW:** the greenhouse effect.

Thorny bloom in the Judean foothills.

research centers in this discipline, which has played an important role in the development of the country's leading-edge farming capability.

Slightly north of Rekhovot on Highway 40 from the southern entrance to the city lie Ramla and Lod (Lydda). They were originally Arab towns, but many of their inhabitants fled during the War of Independence in 1948. Today they are two of the few mixed Jewish-Arab communities in Israel.

Ramla ❷ has three important mosques: the 8th-century **White Mosque**; the **Mosque of the Forty**, built by the Mamelukes in 1318; and the **Great Mosque** (Sun–Thur 8am–11am; fee), situated west of the bus station near the market and built on the site of the Crusader Cathedral of St John. The **Vaulted Pool**, an underground cistern in the town's center, dates from the 9th century. The **British War Cemetery**, 2 km (1¼ miles) east of Ramla, has become a place of pilgrimage for Israeli children, who seek the grave of Private Harry Potter, a previously anonymous British soldier, who was killed in action in Hebron in 1939 aged 19.

North of **Lod** is **Ben Gurion International Airport**, named after Israel's first prime minister. Lying in the shadow of soaring jetliners, Lod was an important town during the biblical and Second Temple periods. Visit the ancient **Sheikh's Tomb**, in the center of the derelict old town, built over the ruins of a 12th-century Crusader church, in the basement of which is allegedly the **Tomb of St George**. The fact that the church is not open to visitors suggests that the patron saint of England and legendary slayer of dragons is not really buried here.

The Judean foothills

East of Ramla, in the Jerusalem foothills (take road 443), is the site of **Modi'im**, the birthplace of the Hasmonean family, leaders of the 2nd-century BC revolt

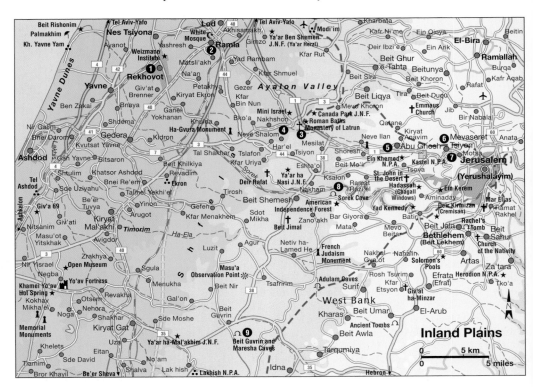

Map on page 264

against the Syrian-Greek empire which then controlled Judea. The revolt began in Modi'im when an official ordered the people to sacrifice a cockerel on a pagan altar, in accordance with the imperial policy of fostering Hellenisation and repressing Judaism. Mattitiahu, a local priest, and his five sons killed the official and his military escort, triggering the conflict. The revolt, led by Judas Maccabeus, the third son, expanded all over Judea, resulting in the recapture of the Temple and the restoration of Jewish worship in Jerusalem.

Not much remains of ancient **Modi'im**, but an attractive park has been laid out, with a model of a village of the period of the revolt. Visitors can bake pitta bread in the ancient-style ovens, handle replicas of ancient agricultural implements and spin yarn. At Hanukkah, the festival commemorating the revolt, a torch is lit at Modi'im and carried in relays to Jerusalem to light candles at the Western Wall. Next to Modi'im is **Neot Kedumim**, a biblical landscape reserve which presents the plants and agricultural lifestyle of biblical times (Sun–Thur 8.30am–sunset, Fri 8.30am–1pm; tel: 08-9770777; www.n-k.org.il; fee). Children will also enjoy the nearby **Kfar Daniel Monkey Park** (Sun–Thur 10am–5pm, Fri 9am–2pm, Sat 10am–3pm; tel: 08-9285888; fee).

Now return to the main road to Jerusalem, and travel the 15 km (9 miles) south on Highway 1 to the French Trappist **Monastery of Latrun** ❸ (just across the old border with Jordan). The monks make and sell wine, which complements the locally produced cheeses. The remains of a 12th-century Crusader fortress called **Le Toron des Chevaliers**, and an almost perfectly preserved Roman villa and bath house, are also located nearby.

Mini Israel

A kilometer back north on Highway 424 is **Mini Israel**, with miniature models of the country's principal sites (*see feature on pages 268–69*).

A little to the north on Highway 3 is **Canada Park**, a recreation center with vineyards, almond orchards, ancient fig trees and adventure playgrounds. In the park are the ruins of a village thought to be the Emmaus of the New Testament, where according to St Luke's Gospel the risen Jesus was seen. Emmaus was also the site of one of the Hasmoneans' greatest victories.

If you take Highway 3 southwest from Latrun you will shortly come to **Neve Shalom** ❹, a heartening experiment in Jewish-Arab coexistence. The only settlement founded specifically for people of the two groups to live together, it runs special courses where Jewish and Arab schoolchildren learn about each other's cultures and has a Jewish–Arab kindergarten and elementary school.

Back towards Jerusalem, Highway 1 enters the gorge of **Shaar Hagai**, west of Latrun, then climbs steeply through the wooded hills. They weren't always so green; when the first Jewish pioneers arrived, they saw a hilly desert stripped of trees by centuries of abuse. The early forests were made up almost entirely of indigenous Jerusalem pine, which still dominates, but foresters are diversifying for both ecological and aesthetic reasons, planting cypress, acacia, eucalyptus, pistachio, carob and varieties of the local scrub oak.

TIP

You can pick up the train at Bet Shemesh railway station for the scenic ride through the hillsides to Jerusalem.

BELOW: the Monastery of Latrun.

Back on the main road, you may be surprised to see dozens of ruined vehicles by the roadside, painted brown to prevent them from rusting. They are, in fact, relatively new vehicles but represent the remains of burnt-out armored vans and buses which carried supplies to besieged Jerusalem in the 1948 war, and which sit permanently at the spots where convoys were destroyed. Jutting out from a hilltop farther ahead is the more formal **Monument to the Road Builders**, its aluminium spars pointing compellingly to the capital beyond. The nearby settlements of Shoresh, Neve Ilan, Kiryat Anavim and Ma'ale ha-Khamisha offer guesthouses with stunning views of the Judean hills; all of them have attractive swimming pools and comfortable accommodation.

A little further along are three Arab villages, each of them with features of interest. The largest, **Abu Ghosh ❺**, is named after the Arab clan which still comprises the majority of its inhabitants. It has two fine churches and a French Benedictine monastery. A sacred spring, where Jesus is said to have drunk, is situated in a garden of towering pines and old palm trees. Some great local Arab restaurants offer tasty spiced pitta bread, *hummus* and *tahina*.

Nearby **Ein Naquba** is the only Arab village built by the State of Israel from scratch; it was constructed for villagers whose homes were taken over by new immigrants after they fled from their village of Beit Naquba in the 1948 war.

Although most of its fruit trees and vegetable plots are watered by modern methods, neighboring **Ein Rafa** has an irrigation system that dates back to biblical times. Some 4 hectares (10 acres) of land are watered by a natural spring, which flows into the individual plots according to a traditional eight-day rota system, stringently observed by the villagers.

Between the two villages and the main road right by the exit from Highway 1

The church at Abu Ghosh.

BELOW: stalactites in Sorek Cave.

at the Ein Khemed interchange is **Ein Khemed** (or Aqua Bella) (daily 8am–4pm Mar–Sept to 5pm; tel: 02-5342741; fee), a landscaped camping site and nature reserve with a stream flowing through it and a restored Crusader farm. Up the hill is the Jerusalem outer suburb of **Mevaseret Tsiyon ⑥**, built beneath **Kastel** (daily 8am–4pm Mar–Sept to 5pm; tel: 02-5330476; fee) an important Arab fortress (the name derives from Castle) and site of a key battle for Jerusalem in 1948. The fortress has been preserved as a memorial to those who died, and some bunkers and pillboxes have been restored. There are magnificent views of the surrounding Judean Hills and the gleaming expanse of Jerusalem.

Continuing in the direction of Jerusalem you will come to the village of **Motsa ⑦**, and the stump of **Herzl's Cypress**. Planted by the founder of modern Zionism on his visit to the Holy Land in 1898, the tree became a place of pilgrimage, and was later cut down as an anti-Zionist gesture. A glass case has been built around the stump, and it is traditional for presidents of Israel to plant a tree in the surrounding garden as a symbol of the continuing growth of Zionism. On the curve of Highway 1 at the bottom of the hill is a restored 19th-century synagogue with remains of a Byzantine synagogue in the basement.

The Jerusalem corridor

From Kastel, take Highway 3965 south to the junction of 395. Here is **Sataf**, where there are clearly visible remains of a 4,000 BCE Chalcolithic village with some of the oldest agricultural traces in the region as well as the remains of a pre-1948 Arab village. Two springs, Ein Sataf and Ein Bikura, flow into the Sorek riverbed below and the terraces have been converted to show how they would have been farmed in biblical times.

Take Highway 395 westwards. **Kibbutz Tsova** has the ruins of a Crusader castle called Belmont and a hotel of the same name. Travel down the road to Beit Shemesh and back eastwards along 3855 and 3866 to the spectacular **Sorek Cave ⑧** (Sun–Thur, Sat 8.30am–3.45, Fri 8.30am–12.45pm; tel: 02-9911117; fee), which extends across some 6 hectares (15 acres) of the **Avshalom Nature Reserve**. Discovered by chance during routine quarrying, it is by far the largest cave in Israel and contains stalactites and stalagmites of breathtaking beauty. After viewing a film about the formations, visitors walk down a path in the cave, which can take about 45 minutes.

Just to the south back along Highway 38 is the **Valley of Elah**, where David killed Goliath, the Philistine from Gath. The battle is described in I Samuel 17. The actual site of the encounter is not marked; today a kibbutz and a TV satellite receiving station stand in the valley.

South of here, further along 38 and turn right onto 35 on the road to Kiryat Gat, is the ancient site of **Beit Guvrin ⑨**, opposite a modern kibbutz of the same name. There are many Crusader ruins here, but it is the **Maresha Caves** that are of special note (daily 8am–4pm, Mar–Sept to 5pm; fee; 07-6811020). There are hundreds of these bell-shaped caves, caused by ancient Roman quarrying. Some of them are even earlier, dating to Greek and even Phoenician times. ❑

Many wineries in the Valley of Elah welcome visitors. Try the visitors' center at Kibbutz Tzora, just west of Bet Shemesh (Sun–Fri 10am–1pm; tel: 02-9908261).

BELOW: the remains of Roman engineering in the Maresha Caves.

THE WORLD'S BIGGEST MINIATURE MODEL

Mini Israel provides a polyurethane panorama of the entire country, from the traffic-clogged streets of Tel Aviv to the ski lifts of Mount Hermon

Israel may be a small country but it is still impossible to take in all the major sites in a single visit. One solution is a trip to Mini Israel where 350 model buildings, the snow on Mount Hermon, Red Sea fish and much more can all be seen on a 5-hectare (13-acre) site. The attraction, which has good disabled access, is an ideal introduction to Israel or a summing up at the end of a vacation.

Located mid-way between Tel Aviv and Jerusalem, Mini-Israel is just a 20-minute drive from Ben Gurion International Airport. The largest of the world's 45 miniature model parks, it was built by private investors with assistance from Madurodam in Holland. The attraction, which opened in 2001, is set out like a Star-of-David. This overcomes several problems. First, Israel's long, thin shape would make the park impossible to walk around without backtracking. Second, the country has no consensus borders anyway. Most models are on a 1:25 scale and are a delight of detail.

WHERE TO FIND IT

Mini Israel is located on Highway 424, 1 km north of Latrun – just off Highway 1. Buses leave for it from major hotels in Tel Aviv, Jerusalem, Netanya and Herzliya (check with your hotel). Open Sat–Thur 10am–6pm in April, until 8pm in Sept and Oct, until 9pm in May and June, and until 10pm in July and Aug; Fri 10am–2pm.
Food: self-service restaurant and snack bars.
Recommended tour time: 2–3 hours.
Tel: 08-9222444. Fax: 08-9214122
E-Mail: info@minisrael.co.il
Website: www.minisrael.co.il

△ **MINI MONASTERY**
It's easy to judge the authenticity of the model of Latrun Monastery since the original is close by and can be seen in the distance from Mini Israel.

▷ **BACK TO THE WALL**
The miniature figures at the Western Wall sway in prayer. Behind the wall is a scale model of Jerusalem's Dome of the Rock.

THE BIG EFFORT TO THINK SMALL

DIVERSE RESIDENTS
Mini Israel's 30,000 mini-residents include every type of Israeli imaginable as well as the distinct clothing of dozens of Christian sects. The miniature Jews by the Western Wall sway, while Muslims on the Temple Mount kneel down.

MINI PLANTS
This realism at Mini Israel extends to nature as well. The park has 50,000 plants including 20,000 miniature trees such as olives, palms, cypresses, and pomegranates. All this greenery is fed by 25 km (15 miles) of irrigation pipes.

IMMIGRANT ARTISTS
Most of the models were created by new immigrant artists from the former Soviet Union. Many have been asked to undertake the models for Turkey's new miniature park.

MINI-ISRAEL AT NIGHT
From March to September the best time to visit Mini Israel is in the early evening. Visitors not only avoid the oppressive daytime heat, but as twilight approaches more than 2,000 light bulbs are turned on to illuminate the models and enable them to be seen from an enchanting new angle.

◁ **FIELD OF DREAMS**
The players move in grooves and the crowd waves in Jerusalem's Teddy Stadium.

▽ **HEAVENLY CREATURES**
The animals enter two by two in this model of the Biblical Zoo, Jerusalem.

THE WEST BANK

*This remains a contentious area, but its holy sites, biblical
lands and ancient cities still draw pilgrims and tourists*

Hugging the Jordan River to the east and the amber-hued walls of
Jerusalem to the west, stretching out over the cities and valleys
of Samaria to the north and the tumbling Judean Hills to the
south, the West Bank is perhaps the geographical center of the Middle
East, and the epicenter of all the tensions that area has come to represent. It lies at the very heart of the Holy Land, holding such revered
sites as Bethlehem, Hebron, Shilo and Jericho within its domain.

For centuries, Jews, Christians and Muslims have paid homage here,
and today pilgrims still flock to its shrines. Scattered throughout the
region, these places are often claimed by more than one religion, and
such spots lend a physical immediacy to age-old conflicts. More than
a millennium has not erased the tension in this contested land.

After the end of the British mandate in 1948 the West Bank, including East Jerusalem, was occupied by Jordan. In 1967 it was captured
by Israel, making 300,000 Palestinians into first-time refugees while
another 150,000 picked up their belongings for the second time. Many
moved to Jordan proper. In the mid-1970s Yitzhak Rabin's Labor
government began setting up Jewish settlements in the West Bank,
exploiting the messianic spirit of right-wing extremists, for what they
saw would subsequently be a bargaining chip in future peace negotiations with the Arabs. But the bluff came back to haunt the Israeli
left. When the right-wing Likud came to power for the first time in
1977, the pace of Jewish settlement became rapid, the West Bank
was officially renamed Judea and Samaria, and the declared policy
was the eventual annexation of all of the Land of Israel.

Rabin was returned to power in 1992 and in 1994 he took the first tentative steps to restore the Occupied Territories to the Palestinian people,
with the all the major cities becoming part of the Palestinian Authority.
Ehud Barak proposed giving almost all the West Bank, including much
of East Jerusalem, to the Palestinians, but the offer was rejected. Many
of the cities were re-occupied by the IDF between 2000 and 2005 during fierce fighting in the Second Intifada. In 2005, for the first time,
Jewish settlements were abandoned in Northern Samaria within the
framework of Ariel Sharon's disengagement policy. Today most of the
West Bank is separated from Israel by a harsh concrete Security Wall.

Between the army outposts, Jewish settlements and refugee camps,
a trip to the West Bank necessarily provokes political awareness. But
much of the landscape appears unchanged since the days of Abraham,
David, or Jesus. With the political and spiritual both so firmly
entrenched here, your sense of wonder is sure to be heightened. However, in this period of ongoing negotiations, and despite optimism
about the peace process, the area is to be approached with caution. ❑

PRECEDING PAGES: a shepherd at work in the West Bank.
LEFT: a tour visits the Greek Orthodox Monastery of St George at Wadi Kelt.

Map on page 276

LANDS OF THE BIBLE

Bethlehem is the high spot for many visitors to the West Bank,
but the pastoral landscapes of the Bible also have
many other interesting sites to explore

Israelis call the northern part of the West Bank by its biblical name, Samaria (Shomron in Hebrew), while south of Jerusalem is known as Judea (Yehuda). The road running through the heart of the West Bank, along the ridge of the mountain chain 800–1,000 meters (2,625–3,280ft.) high, is known historically as the King's Highway and was an alternative trading route to the Via Maris (Mediterranean coastal road) linking Mesopotamia to Egypt 5,000 years ago. These mountain ridges, with a cooler, less humid climate, attracted much of the region's population, and the King's Highway passes through five of the eight West Bank towns under autonomous Palestinian rule, as well as Jerusalem.

Known today as Route 60, the highway is a worthwhile trip for the adventurous, passing through stunning countryside and pastoral biblical landscapes as well as the Palestinian urban enclaves. Clearly, when the security situation is tense it is impracticable to travel this route and it may be necessary to change taxis at Israeli/Palestininan roadblocks.

Highway 60, which comes down from the Galilee, enters the West Bank through the Jezreel Valley about 14 km (8 miles) south of Afula. The most northerly of the Palestinian autonomous zones is **Jenin**, the focus of the bitterest fighting in the second Intifada. To the south is the picturesque Dotan Valley, dropping dramatically to the west. It was here, so the story goes, that Joseph was sold to Egyptian traders by his jealous brothers. It is this region that Israel abandoned three Jewish settlements – the first ever in the West Bank – in 2005.

Omri's stately capital

A little over 10 km (6 miles) north-west of Nablus and 30 km (18 miles) south of Jenin is the site of one of the most impressive ruins in the Holy Land: **Sebastya ❶** (Shomron National Park: open daily 8am–4pm, fee). Once called Samaria, it was the capital of the northern Kingdom of Israel upon King Omri's accession to power in 887 BC. He and his son, the ill-tempered Ahab, built magnificent palaces and temples inside a circular protective wall. Ahab incurred the wrath of the Lord by adding temples to Baal and Astarte, cult figures favored by his wife, Jezebel.

The remains of **Ahab's Palace** adjoin the impressive steps which led to Herod's **Temple of Augustus**, constructed *circa* 30 BC. Herod's grandiose style is not lost in the rubble, and parts of many of his massive constructions still stand. In addition to Herod's work, Sebastya's ruins include an enormous hippodrome, the acropolis, a basilica, and many remains of Israelite and Hellenistic walls. The colonnade-lined street is a majestic reminder of Sebastya's opulence.

In the village of Sebastya, just outside the Roman

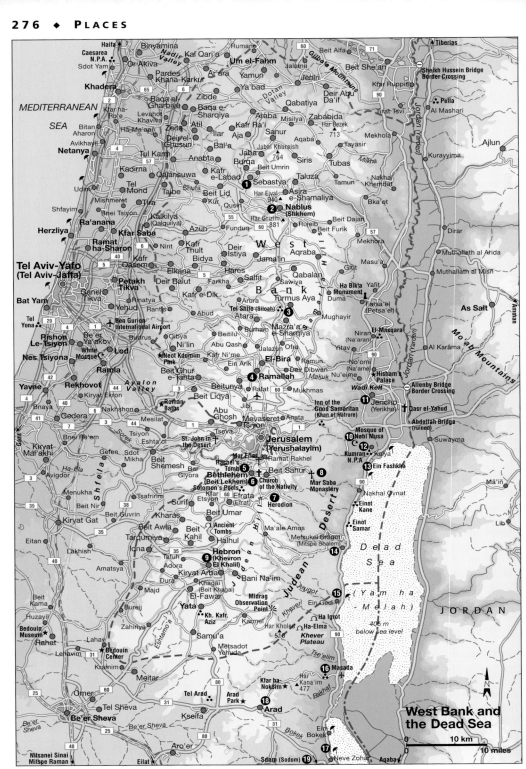

West Bank and the Dead Sea

0   10 km
0   10 miles

wall, lie the ruins of a Crusader cathedral. It is reputed to stand over the tombs of the prophets Elisha and Obadiah and of John the Baptist. This site is included in the **Mosque of Nabi Yaya**, in which a small chamber is believed to hold the head of John the Baptist.

Some 10 km (6 miles) further south is **Nablus** ❷ (Shkhem in Hebrew), which is many things to many people. The largest city in the West Bank, with an estimated population of over 100,000, it is chock-full of sites with biblical resonances. From a distance, Nablus looks like a *pointilliste* painting: innumerable blue doors dot houses neatly spread across a hillside. Within earshot there's a cacophony of sounds: honking car horns, the majestic *mu'ezzin* calling the Muslim faithful to prayer, and the ululations of Arab women.

Rich in history, the area just outside today's city center is mentioned in Genesis as the place where Jacob pitched his tents. **Jacob's Well**, located here, is still in use by Nablus residents. According to St John's Gospel (4, 25–26), Jesus stopped here for refreshment, weary from his travels. He spoke to a Samaritan woman who drew water from the well. "I know that the Messiah cometh, which is called Christ," she told him, whereupon Jesus responded, "I that speak unto thee am he." Adjoining this structure is a Greek Orthodox convent built on the remains of a Crusader church.

Nearby, the **Tomb of Joseph** is a shrine reputed to hold the great man's bones "in a parcel of ground which Jacob bought of the sons of Hamor the father of Shkhem" (Joshua 24, 32). (Defying scripture, there is another cenotaph for Joseph at the Tomb of the Patriarchs in Hebron.)

During the time of the Judges, Abimelech, the son of Gideon, had himself proclaimed king here; some 200 years later, in 928 BC, the 10 northern tribes

Map on page 276

TIP

Before venturing into the West Bank, check on the prevailing political climate. Modest dress (no shorts) is recommended. Several companies offer group tours, though these invariably have a Jewish nationalistic theme.

BELOW:
fruit stall, Nablus.

THE WEST BANK BARRIER

It was conceived in the tradition of the Great Wall of China – to keep out the barbarians – but it has attracted the opprobrium of the Berlin Wall. Its 670-km (420-mile) length varies from a 5-meter (16-ft) high wire-and-mesh fence-like structure set in a concrete base to an 8-meter (26-ft) high solid concrete wall incorporating watchtowers. With a deep ditch on one side, the barrier seems to many to symbolize the gulf between Israelis and Palestinians.

The Israeli government, announcing the plan in 2002, said the purpose was to exclude Palestinian suicide bombers. Some opponents within Israel feared it might be interpreted as the future border with a Palestinian state. But the wall, estimated to cost $2 million a kilometer, didn't simply follow Israel's pre-1967 boundaries. It embraced significant chunks of the West Bank containing Israeli settlements, thus enabling Palestinians to condemn it as a blatant land grab.

The effects on many Palestinians were more than symbolic. According to one United Nations report, the wall separated more than 200,000 Palestinians from their hospitals, schools and workplaces. Farmers claimed their livelihoods were threatened when the wall separated their homes from their land. The only consolation was that few expected it to have the longevity of the Great Wall of China.

called on Jeroboam to be king, and for several years Shkhem served as the capital of the new northern kingdom of Israel. Going farther back into biblical history, Abraham probably stopped in Shkhem just after he arrived in Canaan, and some believe that here he was given the covenant between God and man.

The Samaritans

Standing like gate-posts at the south-eastern entrance to Nablus are two historic peaks, **Har Eival** and **Har Grizim**, named by Moses as the mountains of cursing and blessing. After the conquest, Joshua built an altar on Har Eival. The Samaritan ceremony of the Paschal sacrifice on Har Grizim is a colorful tourist attraction – but not for the squeamish as lambs are slaughtered.

Har Grizim is the center of the Samaritan religion. The sect's origins date back to 720 BC when Assyria swept through the northern kingdom. Returning from exile in 538 BC, the Jews shunned the Samaritans for their intermarriage with the conquerors, although the Samaritans claimed strict adherence to the Mosaic Law. Today, about half the 500 remaining Samaritans (they were tens of thousands strong during the Middle Ages) celebrate the Passover holiday.

In Biblical times the city of **Shilo** (Siloah) ❸ stood equidistant between Nablus and Bethel. According to the Bible, it was at Siloah that the main division of the Promised Land among the 12 tribes was made and where the cities were allocated. In the 11th century BC it was the religious center for the Israelite tribes, and for over 200 years it was the sacred ground for the Ark of the Covenant. It was here that the great prophet Samuel's mother Hannah prayed for his birth. In time, the Philistines defeated the Israelites, captured the ark, and burned Siloah to the ground. Today the *tel* of Siloah spans less than 3 hectares (8 acres), although

Tenacious flora.

BELOW:
winter in Samaria.

Map on page 276

archaeologists have unearthed remnants of civilizations dating to the Bronze Age (1600 BC). There is also a large modern Jewish settlement nearby.

As you travel south of Nablus en route to Ramallah, limestone terraces climb up and down the hills, retaining all the mineral-rich soil they can. Knotty olive trees edged with flora grace the landscape. These olives are harvested by the local farmers, who transport them to the villages for pressing. Twelve km (7 miles) north-west of Ramallah, **Bir Zeit** is the largest of the West Bank's five major Palestinian universities. Built by the Israelis in 1972, it is an active center of hostility to the Israeli government; Israeli and self-imposed closures often occur.

Just north of Ramallah, two towns atop nearby hills serve as natural landmarks: **Bethel** and **Ai**. Bethel is prominent in early biblical narratives as the site where Jacob dreamed of a ladder ascending to Heaven. At this spot he made an altar and called it Beit El, or House of God. This is also where the Ark of the Law remained until the time of the Judges. Ai was one of the earliest cities captured by Joshua and the Israelites during their military conquest of Canaan.

The Palestinian town of **Ramallah** ❶ sees itself as the capital of the West Bank. Much smaller than Nablus, and without the historical significance of Jerusalem, Ramallah is most remarkable for its affluence. Streets and streets of large, luxurious villas testify to the town's wealth. While adjoining El Bira is predominantly Muslim, Ramallah itself is mainly Christian, and almost every Ramallah family has immediate relatives living in the USA. Ramallah provides much of the intellectual fervor and financial fuel for the Palestinian national movement. The town's status was further enhanced by the fact that Yasser Arafat's widow Suha is a Christian from Ramallah (she converted to Islam before marrying the Palestinian leader), and the Palestinian Authority frequently meets here as an alternative to Gaza. Ramallah's importance was consolidated when Arafat spent his last years virtually imprisoned by the IDF in the Mukatar government complex north of the city. His is also buried here, although in a "mobile" grave that the Palestinians plan moving to Jerusalem "when the time comes" *(photograph on page 78).*

Demographically speaking, Ramallah is in effect part of the Jerusalem conurbation, as the southern suburbs of Kalandia lead into the northern neighborhoods of Israel's capital – Atarot (which has Jerusalem's airport as well as a large industrial zone), the affluent suburb of Beit Ha'nina and the Shu'afat refugee camp.

Bethlehem is in the same manner also part of the Jerusalem metropolitan area. The southern Jerusalem neighborhood of Gilo almost touches the town of Christ's birth, while somewhere within Jerusalem's city limits, Samaria becomes Judea.

The Jewish settlements in this region such as Adam, Psagot and Bet El can be reached via a by-pass road to the east of the Ramallah road, going through the northern Jerusalem suburb of Pisgat Ze'ev.

Judea

There is no clear boundary marking the transition of the hills of Samaria to those of Judea, as both are part of the same central range of high ground, reaching from above Ramallah in the north through the Judean cities of Bethlehem and Hebron. Yet the **Judean Hills** have sustained

TIP

Hiring a car in Israel to travel in Palestinian-controlled territory creates insurance problems. To facilitate matters, try hiring from an East Jerusalem Arab company like Petra (tel: 02-5820716; fax: 02-5822668).

BELOW: St Catherine's Church in Bethlehem.

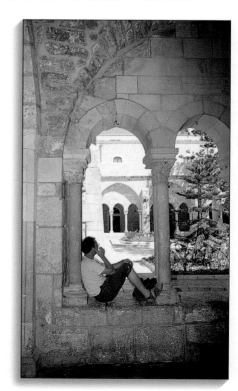

a body of legend as a wellspring of the Old and New Testaments. To the east, marking the descent of the range into the Jordan Rift Valley, lies the **Judean Desert**, which over the centuries served as a place of refuge for prophets, monks and kings. Judea is as elusive as it is revered; all around, the arid rolling hills remind you of biblical times and belie the tensions below the surface.

The approach to Bethlehem, just south of the border within the Palestinian autonomous zone, holds **Rachel's Tomb** ❺ (still inside Israeli-held territory), where the wife of the Patriarch Jacob and mother of Joseph and Benjamin is said to be buried. The shrine is one of the holiest in Israel, a place of worship for Jews and Muslims. The modest dome over the site was rebuilt by the British philanthropist Sir Moses Montefiore in 1841, at the place where, it is said, "Jacob set a pillar upon her grave."

A sign to the Grotto.

Shrines of Bethlehem

Centuries after Rachel, Boaz married Ruth after she gleaned his fields. (Their great-grandson David, became the poet-king of Israel.) On the eastern edge of **Bethlehem** ❻ lies the **Field of Ruth**. It is near the Arab village of **Beit Sahur** (House of the Shepherd), and is believed to be the field where the angel appeared to the shepherds to announce the birth of Jesus.

On **Manger Street**, which leads directly into the hub of the town, up a flight of stairs, you'll find three huge water cisterns hewn out of rock, said to be **David's Well**. When he was battling the Philistines in their garrison here, thirst prompted David to cry "Oh that one would give me water to drink of the well of Bethlehem, which is by the gate." But, offered the water drawn from the well of his enemies, he refused to drink it.

BELOW: the Milk Grotto Church.

Map on page 276

Today, music, bells and churches grace the town. The area teems with pilgrims during the holidays, and the festivities don't stop after Christmas and Easter. The pomp, ornate decor and beautiful displays continue year-round.

Christ was born in Bethlehem. The exact routes taken by the Nazarene in life remain unknown, and the Gospels do not even agree on chronology, but over the ages there has been a broadening consensus on the exact site of his birth. Following the road into Manger Square, you come to the **Church of the Nativity** (open daily dawn–dusk), entered by stooping through a small entrance, reduced to such a size by the Crusaders for defense purposes. The original basilica was built in 325 by Emperor Constantine the Great. The foundation for it is the cave revered in Christian tradition as the place where Jesus was born, which is mentioned in the writings of St Justin Martyr just 100 years after Christ.

Beyond the vestibule is the nave; much of this interior, including the towering wooden beams, dates from Emperor Justinian's rebuilding in the 6th century. At the front of the church, downstairs, is the **Grotto of the Nativity**, where the altar features a barely discernible 12th-century mosaic. But the eye is riveted to a gleaming star on the floor of this small space, inscribed in Latin *Hic de virgine Maria Jesus Christus natus est* (Here Jesus Christ was born of the Virgin Mary). Next to the ornate and gilded grotto is the **Chapel of the Manger**, where Mary placed the newborn child.

The Church of the Nativity adjoins several churches of varying Christian denominations. The most celebrated on Christmas Eve is **St Catherine's**, from which Bethlehem's annual midnight Mass is broadcast worldwide.

A few minutes' walk down Milk Grotto Street will take you to the **Milk Grotto Church**. Its milky white color gives it its name; the legend is that while Mary was feeding the newborn Jesus, some of her milk splashed to the stone floor and permanently whitened it. Today stone scrapings are sold to pilgrims to improve breastfeeding.

Outside the churches and shrines, countless self-appointed tour guides promise to show you all you wish to see. They often know some interesting tidbits about the history of the town, but you must pay for this "freely" offered information or be hounded around Manger Square and its environs. All over town, but particularly in the square, vendors offer a wide array of religious articles and artifacts. They are freshly minted but traditionally inspired, often of olive wood, ceramics or Jerusalem stone. If you are persistent but not too pushy, you can bargain and take care of all your Christmas shopping in one go.

As you look north, steeples rise from the hillside maze of houses, proclaiming the city's sanctity to the 15,000 Arab Christians who live here. Among the various religious institutions is an Arabic-language university directed by the Catholic Order of the Brothers of Christian Schools; known as **Bethlehem University**, it was established with Israeli assistance.

Castles in the wilderness

Some 8 km (5 miles) east of here is the desert citadel of **Herodion** ❼ (daily 8am–4pm, fee) – take Route 356 in southern Jerusalem past Har Homa and towards

The Crimean War in 1854 began as a result of an ownership dispute between the Catholic and Greek orthodox churches over a corner of the Church of Nativity. The Ottoman Turks sided with the Catholics while the Russian Orthodox church rushed to defend their Greek brothers.

BELOW: the citadel of Herodion.

Nokdim and Tekoa. This is one of the most outstanding of Herod the Great's architectural conceits. A monstrous circular protective wall struck with four watchposts guarded Herod's living space; included in the layout were hot baths, arcades, a synagogue, and numerous other luxuries. The banqueting hall of the palace is as immense as a football stadium. In 2007 a Hebrew University professor discovered the tomb of Herod, 100 meters from the site.

The Mar Saba area is inhabited by Bedouin, who claim to descend from the monastery's ancient caretakers, who came here from Byzantium.

Even more remote, dug into the canyon walls overlooking the Kidron River to the northeast, is the blue-domed **Mar Saba Monastery** ❽ – it is so out of the way that you should not attempt to reach this location without a guide. St Saba used this serene niche in the desert as a retreat for study and worship, and in AD 492 he established the monastery named after him. In the 7th century, Persians and Arabs ruined the monastery and murdered the monks; it was rebuilt, however, and early in the 8th century John of Damascus came to the site. The writing he completed here made an important contribution to Christianity and is representative of Christian/Islamic differences at the time. Today the most prominent feature of the hermitage is the huge protective wall surrounding the complex. Among the finds displayed inside are the robed remains of St Saba himself, returned here in 1965 from Venice, where they had been preserved for over 700 years. Also on view are the skulls of the hundreds of monks killed by the Persians in 614. Women are not allowed to enter the monastery.

Along the path to Mar Saba is the church of **St Theodosius**, where the three wise men are said to have rested after they worshiped the infant Jesus, and where St Theodosius died in 529 at the age of 105.

Roughly 8 km (5 miles) from Bethlehem, as you head south towards Hebron, lie the dark-green cisterns known as **Solomon's Pools**. Tradition attributes them to the

BELOW: Mar Saba Monastery.

Map on page 276

great Jewish king in the 10th century BC; archaeology suggests they date from Roman times. In either case, an aqueduct carried water from here to the population of Jerusalem, and today the cisterns still serve as a source of water for the city.

Passionate Hebron

Close to 25 km (15 miles) south of Bethlehem is the ancient city of **Hebron ❾**. The city represents layers of history, but its agricultural and urban community is progressive. Farmers, goat-keepers, shepherds and food packers have made great strides in production by mechanizing their tasks.

The town also has a major **Islamic University**, which enrols nearly 2,000 Arab students. In existence since 1971, this institution is noted for promoting Palestinian culture and nationalism, much to the chagrin of the Israeli authorities who close the facility every so often, citing anti-Israel activity.

Hebron is definitely not the place to sport your knowledge of Hebrew (unless you are in the small Jewish settlements in the city center), but any attempt to speak a few words of Arabic is appreciated by the local people. The chances are that you'll be beckoned into a web of merchants' stalls or to a private home for a cup of tea. Turning down such an invitation will offend, but steer clear of controversy. Debating the merits of Israel's presence on the West Bank, for example, is ill-advised, especially since this is the last Arab town, under the Oslo Agreements, from which Israel has not fully retreated. Hebron remains volatile, with a Jewish enclave in the south-eastern part of the city.

Meander through the criss-cross of alleyways in the Hebron *kasbah*. Here you will find a variety of artisans crafting pottery, compressing and sculpting olive wood, and blowing the colorful glass for which Hebron is widely known. Fresh fruits can be bought along the roadsides and in the souk. Hebron-grown peaches, pale and sweet, are in demand all over the Middle East, and Hebron's produce, including dried and fresh fruits as well as many types of vegetables, is transported (with Israeli agreement) to Arab countries by way of the Allenby Bridge.

The Jewish presence in Hebron dates back to when God gave Abraham his son Isaac as well as Ishmael. Abraham chose this airy hill as the burial ground for his family, and today the **Tomb of the Patriarchs** (open daily, dawn to dusk) dominates the city and is visited by both Jews and Muslims. According to Genesis, Abraham bought the Cave of Machpelah from Ephron the Hittite as the burial site for his wife Sarah.

Here all three Patriarchs and their wives are believed to be buried, and their cenotaphs compose the center of the edifice: Abraham and Sarah in the center, Jacob and Leah on the outer side of the enclosure, and on the other side, within the mosque area, Isaac and Rebecca. More expansive folklore further contends the site holds the graves of Adam, Eve, Esau, and all 12 sons of Jacob as well.

Just outside the structure is **Joseph's Tomb**, at least in name; according to the book of Joshua (24, 32), Joseph's bones were laid to rest instead at Shkhem (Nablus) after their transport from Egypt.

The entire rectangular building gives the impression of a massive fortress, and was built with typical

Abraham was the father of both the Jewish and Arab people through his two sons Isaac and Ishmael. When Ishmael and his mother Hagar were banished from his father's house, God told Hagar that her son's descendants would be a great nation in perpetual conflict with the offspring of Isaac.

BELOW:
the Tomb of the Patriarchs.

architectural confidence by Herod the Great. The Arabs later made a mosque of it, and the Crusaders made it a church during their stay, adding the roof-top crenellations. In 1188 it was taken by Saladin and again turned into a mosque.

Eight hundred years after Abraham, David was crowned King of Israel in Hebron, and later made it his capital. With David's capture of Jerusalem from the Jebusites in around 1000 BC, the capital was shifted, although Hebron remained one of the four holy cities of Israel, along with Jerusalem, Tiberias and Safed. The city's Jewish community survived the destruction of both Temples and remained until the year 1100, when it was expelled by the Crusaders. The population increased and dwindled alternately over the centuries. In 1929, and again in 1936, the community was wiped out in anti-Jewish riots, and after that it was not until 1967 that Jews re-entered Hebron. In 1968 a group of Jewish settlers gained *de facto* rights to settle in the area, although not in Hebron's Arab center. The result is a suburb called **Kiryat Arba** (Hebron's name in biblical times), over-looking the city from a nearby hill.

Today's tensions

Both Jews and Muslims claim descent from Abraham, and the Hebron area (particularly the Tomb of the Patriarchs) is a center of separate worship and mutual confrontation. Adding to the friction is the fact that a mosque covers part of the site, which had at one time been a synagogue.

The situation in Hebron has been tense ever since the 1967 War, and Israeli soldiers are on constant patrol in the area. Violent clashes between Jews and Arabs have riddled the town. Due to sporadic unrest here, it is best to consult the Israeli Government Tourist Office in Jerusalem before traveling to Hebron. Be sure

The roadsigns are to the West Bank Jewish settlement of Efrata. But the residents call it Efrat, claiming that the authorities got confused by the Hebrew suffix "a" which means "to" when the city is mentioned in the Bible as Efrata – meaning to Efrat

BELOW:
tilling the soil
in Samaria.

you plan your return trip in advance, however – Hebron is the one place in the West Bank where you should not spend the night.

Map on page 276

On the outskirts of Hebron stands the gnarled but living **Oak of Abraham**, believed to be 600 years old. It is reputed to be on the site where Abraham was visited by three angels who told him of Isaac's impending birth. It is owned by Russian monks, who have a small monastery here. This place's ancient name is Mamre; Abraham supposedly built an altar and a well here, and Herod's structure on the site was where Bar-Kochba's defeated troops were sold into slavery.

North of Hebron, along the road to Bethlehem, lies the **Etsyon Bloc**, where the agricultural-religious community of Kibbutz Ha-Dati was founded in 1926. It was abandoned in the Arab riots of 1929, and in 1948 its new settlers were wiped out in the War of Independence. The Etsyon Bloc and the surrounding Hebron Hills were retaken by the Israeli army in June 1967, and several months later **Kibbutz Kfar Etsyon** was resettled by children of the original kibbutznikim. The Jewish city of Efrat now dominates the hillside.

A Greek Orthodox monk.

From Kfar Etsyon the highway leads directly back to Jerusalem, some 14 km (8 miles) away, through a newly constructed series of tunnels and bridges that bypasses Bethlehem. Just off the highway is the kibbutz of Ramat Rakhel which offers an inspiring view of the desert, and nearby to the south is the 11th-century Crusader monastery **Mar Elias**. Elijah supposedly slept here when fleeing from Jezebel. Close by, Israeli archaeologists recently uncovered a Byzantine church. It has attractively preserved mosaics, and, more importantly, the Greek Orthodox Church recently proclaimed that the large flat stone in the 4th-century complex is to be called "The Mary Stone". The belief is that the pregnant Mary rested on this rock on her way south to Bethlehem.

BELOW: a detail at Hisham's Palace.

To reach Jericho, travel the highway down from French Hill to Ma'ale Adumim, or through the new tunnel under Mount Scopus past the Hebrew University. After **Ma'ale Adumim**, the largest Jewish city in the West Bank, follow the highway down through the inspiring and billowing stone hills of the Judean Desert to the lowest point on earth: the Dead Sea.

Hidden hermitage

On the road northeast of Jerusalem to Wadi Kelt, reached from Highway 1 down to the Dead Sea, turn right near Mitzpe Yericho. Here, the silence is so pure that it creates a ringing in your ears. For 1,600 years, since the age of the Patriarchs, monks have inhabited this surreal place, where the **Wadi Kelt River** meanders through a dramatic gorge in the canyon between Jericho and Jerusalem. This 35-km (22-mile) stretch includes ruins on top of ruins, monasteries, eerie hermits' caves and surprising watering holes. Honeycombing the rock face are hollowed-out niches which serve as cells for monks, who live off the fruit of the land. The **Greek Orthodox Monastery of St George** (open Mon–Sat 8am–5pm) is just over a century old, but its community long precedes it. Hasmonean, Herodian and Roman remains line this circuitous course.

South of Jericho, off the Jerusalem-Jericho highway, is the astounding **Mosque of Nabi Musa** ❿. It appears out of nowhere in the middle of nowhere. Here Muslims worship at the Tomb of Moses. The Mamelukes constructed the mosque in the 13th century, providing a high cenotaph for Moses. It is open during the times of Muslim prayer, and all day Friday. Only Muslims are admitted in April, when thousands make their pilgrimage. The Muslim route to Nabi Musa intersects the procession of Christians making their Easter pilgrimages to al-Maghtes on the Jordan River, and clashes have resulted.

BELOW:
the Monastery of St George.

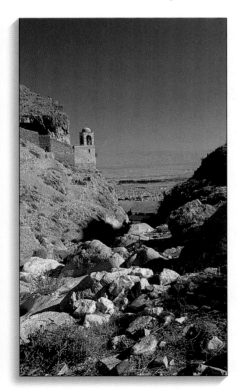

The walls of Jericho

The northern border between Israeli-held land and the Palestinian autonomous zone of Jericho is marked not by an international frontier but the **Oasis Casino**. The casino, a huge investment by an Austrian leisure chain, opened in 1998 just inside Palestinian territory but was closed in 2000 following the start of hostilities. However, it is slated to re-open soon. Such gambling is illegal in Israel, and the casino is aimed at those who otherwise would have to travel to Egypt or Turkey to gamble. Even though it holds 2,000 people, long entrance queues can form at weekends and holidays.

Jericho must have been a prime spot for the earliest city-dwellers on earth some 10,000 years ago. Widely considered to have sprouted the first agricultural community, the town today is once more centered on agriculture. It is ensconced in an oasis in the midst of barren land; its greenery is nurtured by underground springs, the secret of the town's endurance. It was the first Arab town in the West Bank to be handed over to the Palestinian Authority (both in 1994 and 2005).

In times past, rulers used this spot as a warm-weather retreat. One such was Hisham, the 10th Umayyid caliph, who built the fabulous **Hisham's Palace**, about 3 km (2 miles) from the city, in the 8th century. An enormous aqueduct supplied water from the nearby Ein Dug Springs to a cistern, which then doled it out to the palace as needed. The carvings and monumental pillars are awesome, and the palace floors contain examples of the finest Islamic mosaics.

A few kilometers south of the palace is **Elisha's Spring**, a fountain which the Jews believe was purified by the prophet after the populace claimed it was harmful to crops: it is referred to by Arabs today as Ein-es-Sultan. Nearby is the preserved floor of a 6th-century synagogue, featuring a mosaic menorah in its center, within the walls of a Jericho home.

Ancient **Jericho** ⓫, which lies under Tel es-Sultan, is where the walls came tumbling down on the seventh day after they were encircled by Joshua and the Children of Israel. Archaeological excavations confirm that settlements here date to 8,000 BC, when hunters and gatherers completed the transition to sedentary life, becoming the earliest practitioners of agriculture and animal husbandry.

Jericho today is a sleepy town of 7,000 people, with most of the activity confined to its center. Here, men and women gather to sit on rattan stools, talk, sip coffee, or play backgammon. The markets are ablaze with fruit and vegetables, and huge bunches of dates and bananas swing from their beams. The cafés offer authentic Middle Eastern foods and refreshment.

In the stark wilderness outside this small town, Jesus tempted by the devil on a peak the Bible calls the **Mount of Temptation** (also called Qarantal). Hinged to the rock face here is a **Greek Orthodox Monastery of the Temptation**, constructed in front of the grotto where Jesus was said to have fasted for 40 days and nights. A cable-car takes visitors up to the monastery.

Along the River Jordan

Some 10 km (6 miles) east of Jericho, at a ford north of the Dead Sea known as **al-Maghtes**, Jesus is said to have been baptized "and it came to pass in those days, that Jesus came from Nazareth of Galilee, and was baptised by John in Jordan" (Mark 1, 6–9). Not surprisingly, this **Site of the Baptism** is one of the places favored today by Christians as an authentic location.

Mark Twain described the Jordan River as "so crooked that a man does not know which side of it he is on half the time. In going 90 miles it does not get over more than 50 miles of ground. It is not any wider than Broadway in New York." It is true that the symbolism attached to this stream – its muddy waters barely flowing in winter – far exceeds its actual size.

The **Allenby Bridge** (open Sun–Thur 9am–2pm, Fri and Sat 7am–noon) is the river crossing from the West Bank to Jordan. During the 1967 war it was reduced to scaffolding and jammed with Palestinians fleeing to Jordan. It has been rebuilt, and its traffic is strictly monitored by Israeli security. It is the gateway for West Bank produce into the market places of the Arab world. Visits are exchanged by families and friends on both sides of the Jordan, and many West Bank residents go to Amman for banking and commercial links. Although Israel and Jordan are officially at peace, the Palestinian community living between the two still constitutes a security threat. The strict security surrounding the bridge is a potent reminder that peace is tentative. ❑

Map on page 276

BELOW: the cable car from Jericho to the Mount of Temptation.

"We are trying to show that these are wondrous animals."

THE DEAD SEA

*You can float in the salt water and bathe in the therapeutic mud
at the lowest spot on earth, then visit Masada, Israel's
most spectacular archaeological site*

Map
on page
276

Christian pilgrims traveling here over the centuries were aghast at the lifelessness they encountered and gave the **Dead Sea** its name. It's an apt one, for the most saline body of water on the face of the earth contains no life of any sort, and for most of its history there has been little life around it either. Yet today it is a source of both life and health: the potash contained in its bitter waters is an invaluable fertilizer, exported all over the world, while the lake and the springs that feed it are said to have cured everything from arthritis to psoriasis since ancient times. Sun-worshippers from Scandinavia and health fanatics from Germany fill its spas and hotels, seeking remedies and relaxation. Tourists and Israelis come here to breathe in the abundant oxygen, float on the water's salty surface, and marvel at the rugged panoramas.

Situated some 400 meters (1,300 ft) below sea level in a geological fault that extends all the way to East Africa, the Dead Sea is the lowest point on the face of the globe, and is surrounded by the starkest scenery the world has to offer. Steep cliffs of reddish flint rise sharply to the west, contrasting with beige limestone bluffs and the blinding white salt flats of the plain. Across the shimmering gold surface of the water to the east, the mauve and purple mountains of the biblical Moab and Edom are almost indistinguishable in the morning, gaining visibility throughout the day. In late afternoon their wadis and canyons are heavily shadowed, forming a spectacular backdrop of ragged earth.

Mild and pleasant in winter, the Dead Sea basin is an oven in summer. The hot air has an almost solid presence, and the glare from the sun is ferocious.

The Dead Sea is drying up as a result of the use of the waters of the River Jordan by both Israel and Jordan and the mining of minerals. Indeed, the sea has already separated into two lakes, although it will be many thousands of years still until the Dead Sea completely disappears. On the Israeli side, dykes built for the potash plant form a network of artificial lakes designed for the extraction of chemicals; they are also used by bathers.

LEFT:
it's hard to sink in
the salty Dead Sea.
BELOW: the mud is
said to keep skin
young and fresh.

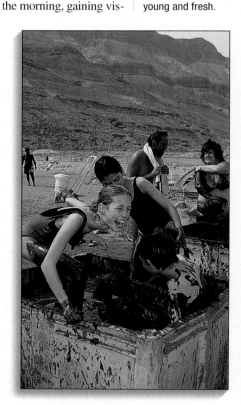

The Judean Desert

The **Judean Desert**, the area between the hills of Judea and the Dead Sea, was a region of hermits, prophets and rebels. David hid here from Saul. The Hasmoneans, who raised the banner of Jewish independence from the Syrian-Greek empire in the 2nd century BC, regrouped here after their initial defeat. Jesus retired to the desert to meditate, and the Essenes established a community in its desolate wastes. The Jewish War against Rome of AD 66–73 started with the capture of the Judean desert fortress of Masada.

Israel's pre-1967 border with Jordan ran just north of

Fun in the mud.

Ein Gedi, about halfway up the western shore of the Dead Sea, so only the southern half of the Judean desert was in Israel. Some of the sites described here became accessible to Israelis only after the Six Day War, and may revert back to Arab administration. However, the highway down from Jerusalem and along the western shore of the Dead Sea runs through desert and is under the complete control of the Israeli authorities, making it safe to travel at all times.

On descending from Jerusalem, the first available opportunity to "float" in the Dead Sea is at **Kalya Beach** (open daily 8am–sunset; tel: 02-9942391; fee) on the north west shore. It is clearly signposted. Kalya offers several beaches – one is a nudist beach for members only – as well as a swimming pool and water park. Bathing here is a unique experience: the swimmer bobs around like a cork, and it's possible to read a newspaper while sitting on the surface. The salinity of the water – ten times that of the oceans – can make it painful if you have a cut or scratch. Emperor Vespasian threw manacled slaves into the sea to test its buoyancy. Most modern bathers go in voluntarily. Non-swimmers can float easily, but must be careful to maintain their balance. The bitter taste of even a drop can linger all day, and a mouthful of Dead Sea water should be avoided.

The scrolls of Kumran

On the northwest shore of the Dead Sea is the Essene settlement of **Kumran** ⑫ (open daily 8am–4pm, until 5pm Mar–Sept; tel: 02-9942235; fee), where the Dead Sea Scrolls were found. The Essenes, an ascetic Jewish sect of the Second Temple period, deliberately built their community in this inaccessible spot. It was destroyed by the Romans in AD 68.

BELOW:
a cave at Kumran.

In the early summer of 1947 a Bedouin shepherd stumbled across the most exciting archaeological discovery of the century: scrolls, dating from the first centuries before and after Christ, preserved in earthenware jars. Some of these documents were acquired by Israel in rather dramatic circumstances. Eliezar Sukenik, Professor of Archaeology at the Hebrew University, was offered by an Armenian dealer the chance of buying a collection of ancient scrolls. He was shown a fragment briefly and was impressed by its antiquity – but, to see the collection, he had to travel to Bethlehem. It was the period just prior to the establishment of the State of Israel, and Jerusalem was a war zone; Bethlehem was in the Arab-controlled area, and dangerous for Jews. Sukenik approached his son Yigael Yadin for advice. Yadin, an archaeologist himself, and at that time chief of operations of the new Israel Defense Forces, replied, "as an archaeologist, I urge you to go; as your son, I beg that you do not go; as chief of operations of the army, I forbid you to go." Sukenik did go to Bethlehem, at considerable personal risk, and managed to buy three scrolls. He could not complete the purchase of the other four, which were eventually taken to the United States and later re-purchased for Israel by Yadin.

Subsequent searches of the caves unearthed other scrolls and thousands of fragments, most of which are now on display in Israel, either in the Shrine of the Book at the Israel Museum in Jerusalem or in the Rockefeller Museum. They have revolutionized scholarship of the Second Temple period and thrown new light on the origins of Christianity, indicating that Jesus may have been an Essene, or at least was strongly influenced by the sect. The scrolls have revealed the mood of messianic fatalism among the Jews of that time, explaining both the emergence of Christianity and the fervor of the Jewish rebels in their hopeless war against Rome. The scrolls have also disclosed much about the nature of the Essene way of life and their beliefs, ritual and worship.

The partly reconstructed buildings of Kumran are on a plateau some 100 meters (330 ft) above the shore and are well worth a visit. Numerous caves, including those where the scrolls were found, are visible in the nearby cliffs, but are not accessible to the tourist. Near the caves is a tourist center, run by the neighboring **Kibbutz Kalya**, which also offers accommodation and runs the aforementioned beach and water park.

Salt baths

The oasis of **Ein Fashkha** ⑬ (open daily 8am–4pm, until 5pm Mar–Sept; fee;), where the Essenes grew their food, is 3 km (2 miles) to the south. Today it is a popular bathing site, although only in the fresh water pools. The Dead Sea's alarming evaporation means that there is no longer access to the sea itself, which is surrounded by mud and quicksand.

Some 14 km (9 miles) south of Kumran is the kibbutz of **Mitspe Shalem** ⑭. The original site, on a cliff overlooking the sea, has been converted into a field school, **Metsukei Dragot**, which offers desert safaris in jeeps, rock climbing and rappeling. Past the school there is access to the steep-sided **Murabbat Canyon**, which contains caves where other 1st- and 2nd-century scrolls were dis-

Map on page 276

TIP

Take care: people do drown in the buoyant Dead Sea each year. They are usually elderly people who, after lying on their backs in the water, don't have stomach muscles strong enough to help them stand up. They panic, flip over, and drown floating face down.

BELOW: the ruins of an Essene village.

covered. The canyon descends to the Dead Sea, but at that point it is sheer and unscalable. A walk down the canyon from the field school is a memorable experience, but not to be undertaken alone. Would-be hikers are advised to go in a group from the school, with expert guides.

Also found in the Murabbat caves were fragments relating to a later revolt against Rome in AD 32–35 led by Simon Bar Kochba, including a letter written by Bar Kochba himself to one of his commanders.

Ein Gedi

Less than 15 km (8 miles) further south is the lush oasis of **Ein Gedi** , site of a kibbutz, a nature reserve and another field school. A particularly beautiful spot, with the greenery creeping up the steep cliffs beside the springs, Ein Gedi is the home of a large variety of birds and animals, including gazelles, ibex, oryx, foxes, jackals and even a few leopards.

Birdwatching in the desert.

The most popular site for hiking and bathing is **David's Spring**, which leads up to a beautiful waterfall, fringed in ferns, where tradition says David hid from King Saul, when he was the victim of one of the king's rages. "Then Saul took three thousand chosen men out of all Israel, and went to seek David and his men upon the rocks of the wild goats," (I Sam 24, 2). According to the biblical account, David crept up on Saul as he slept and cut off a piece of the king's robe, proving he could have killed him but desisted. A tearful reconciliation followed.

BELOW: cooling off at Ein Gedi.
RIGHT: the free-roaming ibex.

On most days, summer and winter, the area around David's Spring is thronged with visitors, so the more energetic may prefer to hike along the course of **Nakhal Arugot**, a kilometer south. This canyon is full of wildlife and has deep pools for bathing. Both Nakhal David and Nakhal Arugot are nature reserves.

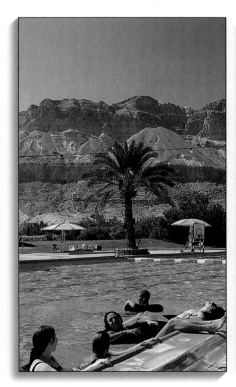

Map
on page
276

Kibbutz Ein Gedi runs a guesthouse, a youth hostel and a spa for bathing in the Dead Sea water and nearby sulphur springs and mud baths. A camping site, and an additional youth hostel and restaurant are situated on the shore below the kibbutz near the Ein Gedi spa.

A little further south is the canyon of **Nakhal Khever**. Of particular interest here are two caves: the **Cave of Horror**, where 40 skeletons dating from the time of the Bar Kochba revolt were discovered, and the nearby **Cave of Letters**, in which 15 letters written by Bar Kochba to his commanders were found. As with Murabbat, visitors are not advised to climb to the caves alone.

Masada

About 20 km (12 miles) south of Ein Gedi, towering almost 300 meters (1,000 ft) above the Dead Sea shore, is the rock of **Masada** ⓰ (daily 8am–4pm, until 5pm Mar–Sept; tel: 08-6584117/8 (entrance fee and cable car fee), the most spectacular archaeological site in Israel. Part of the line of cliffs which rise up to the Judean desert plateau, Masada is cut off from the surrounding area by steep wadis to the north, south and west.

It was on this desolate mesa, in 43BC, that Herod the Great seized an existing fortress and used it as a retreat from his potentially rebellious subjects. Visitors to the site can wander through the magnificent three-tiered palace which extends down the northern cliff; the Roman bath house, with its ingenious heating system; the vast storehouses; the western palace with its fine mosaics, and the huge water cisterns hewn in the rock. They can appreciate the view of the remarkable desert landscape from the summit, which can be climbed easily from the west via the Roman ramp, ascended by cable-car from the east or, more energetically,

In Hebrew the Dead Sea is called the Salt Sea and in Arabic the Stinking Sea. Both names are apt.

BELOW: the fortress of Masada.

climbed via the **Snake Path**, also from the east. These features alone make the fortress worth a visit, but it is the story of the epic siege of the fortress in the Jewish War against Rome which has made Masada a place of pilgrimage second only to the Western Wall.

In AD 66 a group of Jewish rebels known as Zealots, and also called the Sicarii – named after the *sica* (dagger), their favorite weapon – seized Masada from its Roman garrison, triggering the Jewish War against Rome. Securing their base there, the Sicarii proceeded to Jerusalem, where they took over the leadership of the revolt. In bitter in-fighting between the rebel groups their leader was killed, and they returned to Masada to regroup.

The new Sicarii leader, Elazar Ben-Yair, waited out the war at Masada, joined from time to time by other groups. He was still in possession after the fall of Jerusalem in AD 70. Three years later the Roman Tenth Legion arrived to put an end to this last Jewish stronghold. With its auxiliaries and camp followers, the legion numbered over 15,000. Defending Masada were fewer than 1,000 Jewish men, women and children. Herod's store-rooms were still well supplied. The Romans destroyed the aqueduct feeding the cisterns from dams in the wadi, but the cisterns had enough water for a prolonged period and were accessible from the summit.

The legion constructed a wall around the rock, which blocked the main possible escape routes, reinforced by camps, and then built an earth ramp, reinforced by wooden beams and shielded by stone, which pointed like a dagger at the perimeter wall of the fortress.

The final defenses were set on fire, and when the blaze died down the Romans entered Masada to discover the bodies of the defenders laid out in rows. Repudiating defeat and refusing slavery, the men had first killed their own families and then themselves, drawing lots for a final 10 to carry out the act, one last electee killing the other nine and finally committing suicide.

The account in *The Jewish War* by Flavius Josephus has become one of the legends of modern Israel. In recognition of the symbolic importance of the site, young soldiers being inducted into the armed forces today swear their oath of allegiance atop the fortress and vow: "Masada shall not fall again."

The excavations by Yigael Yadin in the 1960s uncovered the magnificence of Herod's fortress and palaces, but the most moving finds were of the Zealots' living quarters in the casement wall, their synagogue and ritual baths, the remains of the fire, and fragments of their final meal. The skeletons of a man, woman and child were uncovered in the northern palace; more were found in a nearby cave, where they had apparently been thrown by the Romans.

The country caught its collective breath when the discovery was announced of a set of inscribed pottery shards, which may have been the lots cast by the defenders to decide who would kill the others. One of them was inscribed "Ben Yair."

Sodom's soothing spas

Ensconced along the shore just north of biblical Sodom, the resorts of **Ein Bokek** and **Neve Zohar** ⓱

Times change. Two generations ago the Sicarii who held out against the Romans at Masada were viewed by all Israelis as heroes. Today, they are generally seen as fanatics who gave up their lives for a hopeless cause.

BELOW: the cistern at Masada.

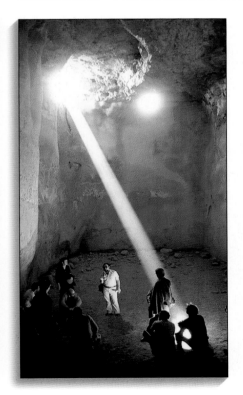

attract health-seekers from across the globe, with a wide range of accommodation based around the mineral springs. Famous since the 1st century AD, the healing waters are believed to cure a spectrum of ailments, from skin disease to lumbago, arthritis and rheumatism *(see page 299)*. The clinics, run by medical staff, offer sulphur baths, mineral baths, salt baths, mud baths, massage and exercise programs. The prices range from reasonable to expensive, the latter in five-star hotels where the spas are actually on the premises.

Don't miss the mud if you do stay; Cleopatra is said to have sent slaves here to fetch it for her, and today Dead Sea Mud has once more become a sought-after export as a natural moisturizer.

Arad, old and new

Between the spas and the chemical plant a road (Highway 31) wends its way westwards into the mountains, climbing over 1,000 meters (3,300 ft) in less than 25 km (15 miles), to **Arad ⑱** Israel's first planned town.

Arad has a history of human habitation going back 5,000 years, but while the modern town is constructed on an elevation near the Dead Sea to ensure a mild climate, the historic settlement is set in farming land 8 km (5 miles) further west along Highway 31 and turn north onto 2808. The ancient mound of **Tel Arad** (daily 8am–4pm, until 5pm Mar–Sept; tel: 08-7762170; fee) has been excavated and partly reconstructed. Sections of a Canaanite town of the 3rd millennium BC have been found, with pottery from the First Dynasty in Egypt, indicating trade between the two nations at that time.

A 10th-century BC fortress from the time of King Solomon was the next settlement. Far smaller than the original Canaanite city, the enclosure contained a

Map on page 276

Spa hotel at Ein Bokek.

BELOW: covered in Dead Sea mud.

Map on page 276

TIP

The **Flour Cave** (called after its chalk walls) is located in Nahal Pratzim and is a narrow fissure in the rock enclosed from the top. Turn inland along desert tracks opposite the Dead Sea works towards the Amiaz Plain. Bring a flashlight.

BELOW: cult basin at Tel Arad.
RIGHT: visiting the caves at Ein Bokek.

sanctuary modelled on the Temple in Jerusalem, with a courtyard, an outer chamber and a Holy of Holies, the only one of its kind ever discovered.

Archaeologists found the remains of a burnt substance on two smaller altars inside the Holy of Holies. Analysis showed it to be traces of animal fat, indicating sacrifices. This is consistent with the denunciations of the prophets, recorded in the Bible, of continuing sacrifices on the "high places". King Hezekiah, who ruled Judah from 720 to 692 BC, heeded the advice and "removed the high places and broke the images".

Modern Arad, founded in 1961, was the most ambitious new town project of its time. It was meant to provide housing, health services and tourism facilities plus regional industries. It was well placed to utilize the natural resources, and mineral spas at the Dead Sea, and offered dry desert air, suitable for asthma treatment. Architecturally, it was conceived as a fortress against the desert: the buildings were grouped around squares; the paved walkways were shaded by houses; greenery was planted in small concentrations which did not require too much water. The six basic neighborhoods and the town center were compact: less than a mile across. Arad is an interesting example of theory being changed by practice. It was initially assumed that the inhabitants would wish to cluster together in the desert environment, but this did not prove to be the case, and the planners were forced to modify their designs to meet demand for more space.

Arad is the epitome of planned pioneering: the rational creation of a town, adapted to the desert and utilizing its resources. King Uzziah, the Bible records, "built towers in the wilderness". Constructed only a few miles from where the king's buildings stood, Arad's apartment blocks are Israel's new towers in the desert, a symbol of today's Israel: a modern community arising where an ancient one used to exist.

Sodom, "city of sin"

From Arad, take the road back to Neve Zohar, then south to **Sodom** (Sdom) ⑲. There is a peaceful atmosphere about modern Sodom which, despite its oppressive heat, makes it an unexpectedly calm place to swim, stroll or sunbathe. This is in stark contrast with the "cities of sin," Sodom and Gomorrah, which were destroyed with fire and brimstone for the decadence and sexual perversion of their inhabitants. The Bible is rather coy regarding the exact nature of these sins, but homosexuality and buggery are implied (originating the term "sodomite").

According to the story, God allowed Lot, Abraham's nephew, to escape with his family, but his wife, disobeying instructions, looked back, and was turned into a pillar of salt. On the Dead Sea shore there is a cave with a hollow tower. Called **Lot's Wife**, the pillar is said to be the remains of that unhappy lady. Take a walk inside, lick your finger, and taste the salt.

Further south, the conveyor belts, funnels and ovens of the **Dead Sea Mineral Works** grind and roar day and night. Articulated trucks move ponderously out of the yard, hauling the potash, magnesium and salt down the Arava to Eilat, or up the ridge to the railway and Ashdod ports. ❑

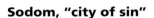

FOUR SEAS KEEP VISITORS IN THE SWIM

The Med, the Red and the Dead – and, of course, the Sea of Galilee: Israel's four seas offer a wide variety of pleasures and experiences

According to the map, Israel has four seas, but in reality there are only two. The Sea of Galilee and the Dead Sea are actually lakes, relatively small bodies of water linked by the River Jordan.

Also known as Lake Tiberias, the Sea of Galilee is a mere 230 sq. km (88 sq. miles) in size. Surrounded by the picturesque hills of the Galilee and the Golan, the lake is edged by artificial beaches. Although only some 100 km (60 miles) further south, the Dead Sea lies amid a barren, majestic sweep of mountainous rocky desert. Set at the lowest point on earth, 400 meters (1,300 ft) below sea level, it has a unique mineral composition, including a 30 percent salt content which makes bathers float. The sea has now split in two as a result of evaporation and excessive mining of potassium and bromides.

The Red Sea, another 200 km (125 miles) to the south, a northern finger of the Indian Ocean, is the closest that tropical waters come to Europe. Beneath the surface, fish of all shapes, sizes and colors, and exquisite coral formations, can be seen. At Coral World Underwater Observatory, a submarine – yellow, of course – takes those who can afford it on underwater sightseeing trips.

Sandy beaches dominate the 200-km (125-mile) Mediterranean coastline from Rosh ha-Nikra to Ashkelon. The beaches are beautiful but can get very crowded at weekends with Israelis escaping the city heat.

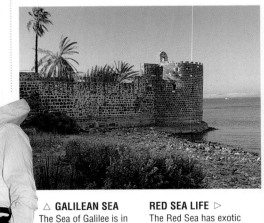

THE VEST OF LIFE ▷
There is absolutely no divine protection against drowning in the Holy Land. Taking precautions is wise: many don't, and there are more than 100 deaths by drowning every year.

△ GALILEAN SEA
The Sea of Galilee is in fact a vast reservoir providing Israel with more than one third of its drinking water.

RED SEA LIFE ▷
The Red Sea has exotic tropical marine life, guaranteed winter sunshine and opportunities for a wide range of water sports.

◁ **FLIPPING OUT AT THE BEACH**
Israel's glorious Mediterranean beaches turn some people head over heels with enthusiasm.

▽ **EIN BOKEK**
Bathers at Ein Bokek on the Dead Sea enjoy an oxygen-rich atmosphere and sunbathing that is free of ultra-violet rays.

MUD, MUD, GLORIOUS MUD

Despite its slimy, salty nature, the Dead Sea is extremely therapeutic. The fashionable and fun way to let the sea's minerals work wonders on your body is by covering yourself in Dead Sea mud. Among the minerals found in the water are bromine, which soothes the nerves, and iodine and magnesium which ease arthritis, rheumatism, psoriasis and skin problems as well as respiratory complaints. The mud can be applied professionally by medical staff in the region's hotels within the framework of comprehensive treatment, or simply slapped on by the sea.

There are also sulphur baths available at Ein Gedi and Ein Bokek. Other health advantages to the Dead Sea region include the high level of oxygen in the low-altitude air, and evaporating gases which rise from the sea and create a filter which takes out the sun's harmful ultra-violet rays. Thus the cancerous risks of sun-bathing are reduced, despite searing summer temperatures of 40°C (104°F). The winter average is a delightful 21°C (70°F).

△△ **HISTORIC PORT**
At Yafo Port, Jonah set sail on his ill-fated voyage, and Solomon imported cedars from Lebanon to build the Temple.

△ **DIVERS' PARADISE**
Israel has the highest number of qualified divers per capita in the world, with over 50,000 registered.

Map
on page
302

THE NEGEV

*King Solomon's Mines and the market at Be'er Sheva are not the
only sights in the Negev – there are magnificent craters,
nature reserves, and a high-tech university*

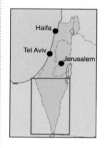

The very name "Negev" conjures up an image of the rugged outdoors, jeeps,
camels, frontiersmen – an unforgiving expanse of bleak wastes, sunlight
and sharp, dry air. It is every bit as vast and intimidating as it sounds, containing 60 percent of Israel's land area but less than 10 percent of its population.
Yet the Negev is far from barren: it supports successful agricultural communities,
a sprawling "capital", a complex desert ecosystem, and – since Israel relinquished the Sinai in 1982 – a variety of defense activities.

The Hebrew word means "parched", and the Negev is indeed parched, with
rainfall varying from an annual average of 30 cm (12 inches) in the north to
almost zero in Eilat. But don't expect white sand and palm trees. The northern
and western Negev is a dusty plain slashed with wadis: dried-up river-beds
which froth with occasional winter flash floods. To the south are the bleak flint,
limestone, chalk, dolomite and granite mountains, with the Arava Valley to the
east dividing them from biblical Edom, today part of Jordan.

History

The Negev is saturated with history. In Abraham's time, around 2,000 BC, the
area was inhabited by nomadic tribes. When the Children of Israel left Egypt
(around 1280 BC) the warlike Amalekites blocked
their path to the Promised Land. Joshua eventually
conquered Canaan and awarded the Negev to the tribe
of Simeon, but only the northern part was settled.
King David extended Israelite rule over the Negev in
the 10th century BC, and his son Solomon built a
string of forts. Solomon also developed the copper
mines at Timna, and the port of Etzion Geber (Eilat).
After the division of the kingdom into Israel and
Judah, the area was occupied by the Edomites, who
were expelled by the Nabateans in the 1st century BC.

In the Middle Ages the Negev was an important
Byzantine center. In subsequent centuries it remained
the domain of nomadic Bedouins until the start of
Zionist immigration in the 1880s. But it was not until
1939 that the first successful kibbutz, **Negba**, northwest of Be'er Sheva, was established. Three other outposts in the western Negev were created in 1943, and
a further 11 were thrown up on a single day in 1946.

The Jews fought hard for the inclusion of the Negev
in the new State of Israel, and the UN partition plan
awarded most of it to the Jewish state. The rest was
won in the War of Independence of 1948, when the
Egyptian and Transjordanian armies were expelled.

David Ben Gurion, Israel's first prime minister,
believed passionately in the development of the Negev,
and went to live in what was then a tiny isolated kibbutz, Sde Boker, when he retired.

LEFT:
the visitor center
at Mitspe Ramon.
BELOW: rare blooms.

Gaza
Rafeh (Rafi'akh)
Ein-ha-Bsor
Kholit
Gyulot
Tse'elim
Urim
Ofakim
Eshkol Park N.P.A. (Ha-Bsor)
Khativat ha-Negev Monument
Omer
Tel Aviv-Yafo
Tel Arad
Arad Park
Ein Bokek
Neve Zohar
Atubotayim Cave

Be'er Sheva
Tel Sheva
Nevatim
Aro'er
Kseifa
Arad

Khalutsa Sands
Retamim
Revivim
Revivim Observation Point
Har Keren 334
Nitsanei Shait (Kadesh Barne'a)
Kmehin

Agur Sands
Ashalim
Tlalim
Boker Plateau
Irus Yerukham Reserve
Metsad Yerukham
Yerukham

Yerukham Ridge
Dimona Mountains
Efe Mountains
Ben Gurion Park J.N.F.
Dimona
Mamshit National Park
Ami'az Plain
Ash alim
Ami'az Plain
Peres
 Har Sdom
Sdom (Sodom)
Safi
Ne'ot ha-Kikar Reserve
Ein Tamar
Ne'ot ha-Kikar

Nitsana Border Crossing
Ezuz
Kisji'a Hills
Korkha Valley
Ancient Farm
Shivta
Midreshet Ben Gurion
Sde Boker
Ben Gurion House
Ben Gurion Burial Place
Ha-Makhtesh (The Large Crater)
Khatira Mountains
Memorial Monument
Yamin Plain
Memorial Monument
Tsin
Har Hahar 278

Negev (Ha-Negev)
Ein Ovdat N.P.A.
Ovdat N.P.A.
Nafkha Plateau
Har Tsin Reserve
Khatseva
Metsad Khatseva
Ein Khatseva
Khatseva
Idan

Barne'a Plateau
Har Arikha 895
Alpaca Ranch
Suka ba-Midbar
Planetarium
"Tsel Midbar" Visitor Center
Desert Sculpture Park
Mitspe Ramon
Makhtesh Ramon (Ramon Crater)
Har Ardon 722
Kamal
Marzeva
Metsok ha-Tsinim Reserve
Sheizaf
Ein Yahav
Makhteshim Reserve
Nakhal Sheizaf Reserve
Ein-Yahav

S i n a i
E G Y P T
Ramon Reserve Geological Park
Nekarot
Khadav Plateau
Keinan Ridge
Omer Hights
Sapir
Tsofar
Omet Ridge
J O R D A N

Har Khtsun
Har Sagi 996
Arod
Barak Plateau
Paran
Tsofar Plateau

Har ha-Negev Reserve
Cave Paintings
Karkom Ridge
Paran Desert
Paran
Menukha Ridge 13
Tsekhikha Hills
Menukha Plain
Petra 15

Ha-Nekhalim ha-Gdolim Reserve
Paran Plain
Nakhal Shitim
Notsa Ridge
Yafruk Plain
Al Quwayra

Khiyon Plain
Ne'ot Smadar (Shizafon)
Ya'alon
Yahel
Gharandal
Räs an-Naqab

Uvda Cliffs
Neve Kharif
Uvda Valley
Uvda
Ktura Reserve
Lotan
Grofit
Al Kuntillah
Shakharut
Samar
Ktura
Yotvata
Khai Bar Reserve
Yotvata 10

Timna Cliffs
Rock Paintings
Ancient Mines
Red Canyon
Har Uziyahu 844
Pillars of Amram
Rakham
Timna Valley
Elifaz
Timna 11
King Solomon's Pillars
Dom Palm Tree

Netafim Border Crossing
Harei Eilat Reserve
Dolphin Reef
Marine Museum
Eilot
Eilat 14
Arava Border Crossing
Al 'Aqaba

Eilat
0   1 km
0   1 mile
Timna
Eilot
Aqaba 1
Ha-Melekha (Salt Evaporation pools)
Eilat
North Beach
Harbor
Taba
Reef Ha-Dolfinim
Ha-Almogim (Coral) Nature Reserve
Coral World Underwater Observatory
Gulf of Eilat (Gulf of Aqaba)

Negev
0   10 km
0   10 miles

Map on page 302

Capital of the Negev

Although it has become comparatively civilized, **Be'er Sheva ❶** still has something of its old frontier atmosphere: brash, bustling, and bursting with energy. You don't see too many suits or ties here.

Despite planners' efforts to create a new center further east near the shopping mall, the old city remains the real center of the town. The municipality acknowledged this through an urban renewal program which included the refurbishment of the **Negev Museum** in Ha'atzmaut St. (open Sun–Thur 8.30am–3.30pm Tues 8.30am–2pm 4pm–6pm Fri & Sat 10am–1pm; tel: 08-6206570).The unusual rectangular formation of its streets was the work of a German engineer who served with the Turkish army in the years before World War I. The rest of Be'er Sheva, a monument to the great improvisation phase of Israel's development, is laid out like an English garden city, without consideration for climatic and topographical conditions.

But the town, thrown up hastily while Israel was doubling its population with an influx of immigrants, couldn't have been built in any other way. There was no time for proper planning. Today, with a population of 200,000, a flourishing industrial base, a university, hospital, medical school, music conservatory, dance school, an orchestra and arts center, Be'er Sheva is Israel's fourth city. If it's a mess, it's a triumphant mess. Be'er Sheva is the capital of the Negev, providing services for the surrounding population. The regional offices of the companies extracting potash, phosphates, magnesium, salt and lime are all here, alongside new factories for everything from ceramics to pesticides. Be'er Sheva has got in on the high-tech act, too, with an advanced technology park in **Omer**, 10 km (6 miles) north of the city, near the affluent suburb of the same name.

The town accommodates people from over 70 countries, the earlier immigrants from Romania and Morocco rubbing shoulders with more recent arrivals from Argentina and the former Soviet Union. An Arab town until 1948, it is now a predominantly Jewish community, but several hundred Bedouin have moved here from the surrounding area and form an important part of the population.

City sights

Every Thursday morning there is a **Bedouin market** on the southern edge of town, for which a special structure has been built. The Bedouin still trade their camels, sheep and goats here, but in recent years the market has become a tourist attraction, providing opportunities to buy all kinds of arts and crafts.

The name Be'er Sheva means "well of the swearing", in memory of the pact sworn between the patriarch Abraham and a local ruler, Abimelech, in which Abraham secured the use of a well to water his flocks. There is a dispute as to the location of the actual **Well of the Swearing**. The traditional site is at the bottom of the main street in the old town, but more recently archaeologists have suggested that it is the 40-meter (130-ft) well excavated at the site of Tel Be'er Sheva, some 6 km (4 miles) east of the modern city.

The **Ben Gurion University of the Negev** (www. bgu.ac.il), founded here in 1969, is one of Israel's largest universities, with a student population of 17,000 studying courses in, among others, humanities,

TIP

A new rail link to Be'er Sheva was opened in 2001, with stations at the university and city center. There is a direct link to Tel Aviv. Change at Lod for Jerusalem.

BELOW: a Bedouin trader at the weekly market.

TIP

To learn more about
Bedouin culture, travel
to the Joe Alon
Museum of Bedouin
Culture – 24 km (15
miles) north on High-
way 40 and east along
325 to Lahav (Sat–
Thur 8am–4pm, Fri
8am–1pm; tel: 08-
9913322; www.
joealon.org.il; fee).

BELOW:
the futuristic library
at Be'er Sheva's
Ben Gurion
University.

sciences, engineering and medicine. In this respect the university has transformed the town from a desert backwater into a modern community, with its
own sinfonietta orchestra and light opera group. Its contribution to the surrounding environment should not be overlooked. Impressively, the university is
researching projects on water resource management and carrying out magnesium research and arid zones studies.

About a mile to the northeast, overlooking the city, (near Omer on Highway
60) is the **Khativat ha-Negev** Monument to the Palmach, which captured Be'er
Sheva in the War of Independence. Designed by sculptor Dani Karavan, who
spent five years on the project, its trenches, bunkers, pillboxes and tower (through
which visitors are encouraged to climb and crawl) create a claustrophobic atmosphere evocative of a siege. The sinuous concrete edifice is a worthy commemoration of the bitter battle for the Negev between the Egyptian army and the
fledgling Israeli forces backing the kibbutz outposts during the 1948 war.

South of the monument is an animal hospital, attached to the life sciences
department of Ben Gurion University. It includes a camel clinic.

The Negev Bedouin

Southeast of the hospital, next to ancient Tel Be'er Sheva, is **Tel Sheva ②**, a
modern village built for the local Bedouin. It is the first of five Bedouin villages
in the Negev gradually replacing the traditional tented camps of the nomads,
which, as a rule, are spread out over a large area. High-walled courtyards separate the houses, in an attempt to preserve as much privacy as possible.

The concept was developed by an Arab architect, and its logic seemed unas-
sailable, but in fact the Bedouin were not keen on Tel Sheva, and subsequent
developments have encouraged the former nomads to
build their own homes. Israel's Bedouin claim large
tracts of the desert over which they formerly grazed
their herds, but the lands were never registered, and
this has led to disputes with the government. In most
cases the Bedouin have been given title to the land
around their camps.

Where the land has been appropriated by the government, as in the case of the **Nevatim Airforce Base**
east of Be'er Sheva, monetary compensation has been
awarded. But at present 75,000 Bedouin, about half
the Negev Bedouin, are fighting for government recognition of some 45 "unrecognized" villages. They are
steadfastly refusing to move into six new towns such
as Tel Sheva, proposed by the government. However,
although the campaign is bearing fruit, with the government recognizing Bedouin ownership of the land
in five villages, the Negev tribesmen must then continue fighting to be connected up to basic utilities like
water, sanitation and electricity.

Ancient Tel

Several kilometers before Tel Sheva is **Tel Be'ersheva
National Park** (daily 8am–4pm, until 5pm Apr–Sept;
tel: 08-6467286; fee). Tel Be'er Sheva was recognized
in 2005 as a UNESCO Heritage site, along with Tel
Megiddo and Tel Hatzor in the north. This tel sits near
the confluence of the Be'er sheva and Hebron Rivers,

Map on page 302

where settled land meets the desert. Archaeologists working at Tel Be'er Sheva have uncovered two-thirds of a settlement from the early Israelite period (10th century BCE), when a fortified administrative city was built on the tel. The site has unparalleled importance for the study of biblical-period urban planning.

The meticulously planned waterworks are evidence of tremendous engineering expertise. The centerpiece of the water system is a huge rectangular shaft dug 15 meters (50 ft) into the ground. The walls of the shaft are tiled with pieces of stone. The shaft descends into a large reservoir, fed by the floodwater that flowed through the Hebron River. A 70-meter (230-ft) well, Israel's deepest, was also discovered on the site. Large parts of the ancient buildings have been reconstructed using mud blocks. Visitors will want to see the well, the city streets, the storehouses, the public buildings and private homes, the city wall and gates, and the reservoir. Especially interesting is the reconstructed horned altar, parts of which were found on the site. There is also an observation tower.

The western Negev

Immediately west of Be'er Sheva along Highway 2357 is **Kibbutz Hatserim,** where modern drip irrigation was invented. Just past the kibbutz is the **Khatserim Air Force Museum** (Sun–Thur 8am–5pm, Fri 8am–1pm; tel:08-990 6853; fee) which records the history of the Israel Air Force and exhibits the aircraft which enabled the country to consolidate its presence in the region.

West from Be'er Sheva along Highway 25, the Negev is flat and dull, more suitable for settlement than for tourism. It is an area of cotton and potatoes as well as extensive wheat fields, irrigated by the run-off from the National Water Carrier, which ends in this area.

The soil in the Eshkol region is called loess – a type of very fertile sand which is great for growing winter crops like tomatoes and cucumbers as well as melons and peppers.

BELOW: alternative mode of transport if fuel runs low.

The first Negev kibbutzim were built in this region in the 1940s, and, after the peace treaty with Egypt, some of Israel's northern Sinai settlements were moved to Pithat Shalom (the Peace Region) next to the international border in 1982. East of these communities along Route 241 lies the **Eshkol National Park** (Ha-Bsor) (daily 8am–6pm) 3,300 hectares (750 acres) of trees, lawns and playing fields with an amphitheater, a swimming pool and a natural pond, surrounded by cat-tails and cane and stocked with fish.

Known locally as Kemahin by the Bedouin, the desert around Nitsana yields truffles each March when local people can be seen scouring the land for the highly prized food.

The Western Negev road, which goes south from this region, is designated as a military area, as it is right on the Egyptian border, and travelers using it have to fill in forms provided by the military. Since the peace treaty with Egypt in 1978 it is not regarded as dangerous, but the army wants to know who is using it so that travelers are not stranded there after dark. The southern sector of the road winds attractively through the **Negev mountains**, providing some spectacular views of Sinai to the west and the Negev to the east.

Shivta

There is a road (number 222) from Eshkol to the junction at Mashabei Sade, just past the Revivim Observation Point. This road passes the former Nabatean set-tlement of **Khalutsa**. From Mashabei Sade, follow the road towards the Egypt-ian border and you will come to **Shivta** ❸, to the south in the Korkha Valley, a Nabatean city later rebuilt by the Byzantines in the 5th century. An Arab tribe, the Nabateans dominated the Negev and Edom in the first centuries BC and AD. Although less accessible than Ovdat (*see page 319*), Shivta is still relatively well-preserved, with three churches, a wine press and several public areas still intact. There is also a direct route from Be'er Sheva to Shivta. Shivta, together with the

BELOW: the ancient site of Mamshit.

region's other three Nabatean settlements – Ovdat, Mamshit and Khalutsa – were named a UNESCO Heritage Site in 2005, called the incense or spice route.

Nitsana ❹, 25 km (16 miles) further west at the intersection of the western highway, is one of three active border crossings to Egypt (open daily 8am–4pm). The village also located at Nitsana – a desert outpost which now has a thriving school for young new immigrants and a seminar center for desert science – was founded in 1987 and lies just next to the border.

To reach Eilat from Nitsana, you can continue down the road, which hugs the Sinai border, but there are two other main routes to the pleasure resort on the Red Sea. From Be'er Sheva the main highway leads down the eastern side of the Negev, through the **Ha-Arava**, and that is the one to take if your aim is simply reaching the sunny beaches. Alternatively, a narrow, beautiful, scenic road goes right through the middle of the desert. The traveler may well feel that the Negev between Be'er Sheva and Eilat is a mythical badland dividing Israel from the Red Sea paradise to the south, but there is plenty to see on both routes.

The Arava

The eastern route takes you past the moshav of **Nevatim**, settled in the early 1950s by Jews from Cochin in southern India. Even within the kaleidoscope of the Israeli population these beautiful, dark-skinned people stand out as "more different"than others. In the past few years they have become famous for growing winter flowers, exported by air to Europe. This industry, which takes advantage of the mild desert climate, has been taken up by others and become a major Israeli export.

Further east, the development towns of **Yerukham** and **Dimona**, built in the mid-1950s, were settled primarily by immigrants from North Africa. Yerukham has a park, 10 km (6 miles) south of the road, which is a rare green patch in the arid grey-brown wasteland, but so far the dust tends to dominate the man-high trees. Nearby is an artificial lake, created by a dammed wadi, fed by the winter rains. A huge variety of birds migrate across the Mediterranean coast from Africa to Europe in the spring and return in the autumn; Israel is one of their favorite way-stations.

Dimona is home to the fierce harsh desert climate which many thought would prove too much for people to live and work in. The few original settlers have now blossomed into a town of 35,000. Although it's called the "Flower of the Desert" Dimona is known more for its nuclear plant and Black Hebrew community than for its flora. A small Indian Jewish community also resides here, and their delicatessens supply great Indian spices and poppadums.

Southeast of Dimona, on Highway 25, the dome of Israel's infamous **Nuclear Research Station** looms in the plain behind its numerous protective barbed-wire fences.

Nearby is the site of **Mamshit** ❺ (daily 8am–4pm, until 5pm Apr–Sept; tel: 08-6556478; fee), called Kurnab by the Arabs. A fine example of a Nabataean site of the 1st century AD, it contains the remains of two beautiful Byzantine churches and a network of ancient dams. The settlement was also famous for breeding Arabian horses. Nearby is the **Camel Farm** of Mamshit,

Map on page 302

There is an alpaca farm near Mitspe Ramon. Although imported from Latin America and not indigenous to this region, the alpaca is actually the closest cousin to the camel.

BELOW:
an immigrant from Cochin works with winter flowers.

home to the original ships of the desert. It is still worth a visit even if this alternative mode of travel is not to your taste. Safaris, 4-wheel-drive tours, rappeling and hiking are among the other options.

South of the road is **Ha-Makhtesh Ha-Gadol** (**The Large Crater**) ❻, a spectacular geological fault (take 206 to the south and then 225). Further east, **Ha-Makhtesh Ha-Katan** (**The Small Crater**) is less extensive but more beautiful, with geological layers in some locations exposed like a rainbow cake. Their origin is unknown. One theory ascribes the Negev craters to volcanic activity; another suggests the fall of large meteors in the distant past.

A spectacular road

The old road south – today a dirt-track – cuts through the desert south of the small crater, connecting with the Arava Valley via **Scorpions' Pass**. The most spectacular road in the southern desert, it plunges down a series of dizzying loops that follow each other with frightening suddenness. To the right are the heights of the Negev, great slabs of primeval rock, slammed together. Below are the purple-grey lunar formations of the **Tsin Valley**, with the square-shaped hillock of **Ha-har** rising up from the valley floor. Be warned: the rusty metal drums that line the road have been unable to prevent accidents.

The main road from Mamshit (Highway 25) reaches the Arava Valley south of the Dead Sea, at the Arava Junction, near the moshav farming village of **Neot ha-Kikar**. Situated in the salt marshes and utilizing brackish water, it has become one of the most successful settlements in Israel, exporting a variety of winter vegetables to Europe. In the 1960s Neot ha-Kikar was settled by an eccentric group of desert lovers, who established a private company. As initial attempts at farming the area proved less than successful, they set up a desert touring company for trips by camel and jeep to the less accessible locations of the Negev. Those initial settlers eventually abandoned the village, but their company (still called Neot ha-Kikar) continues to thrive, with offices in Tel Aviv and Eilat.

Similar tours are run by the Society for the Protection of Nature in Israel, which, among its noteworthy spectrum of activities, offers a four-day camel tour starting at **Ein-Yahav**, a moshav some 80 km (50 miles) south.

The road through the Arava is bordered by the flint and limestone ridges of the Negev to the west; 19 km (12 miles) to the east tower the magnificent mountains of **Edom** in Jordan, which are capped with snow in winter. These mountains change color during the day from pale mauve in the morning, to pink, red and deep purple in the evening, their canyons and gulleys etched in grey.

To the south lies the **Paran Plain**, the most spectacular of the Negev wadis, which runs into the Arava. The road twists through the timeless desert scenery before joining the southern stretch of the Arava road on its way to Eilat. You can continue on this route, taking in the Khai Bar Nature Reserve and Timna (*see page 311*), but we will return to Be'er Sheva and take the central desert road through the Negev Plateau.

TIP

If you are going into the Tsin Valley as an independent traveler, remember that it should be negoiated very slowly in a 4-wheel drive vehicle, or else on foot.

BELOW:
an observatory at Mitspe Ramon.

The Negev Plateau

The most interesting route south is also the oldest and least convenient, but it passes a number of interesting sites, the first of which is **Sde Boker ❼**, some 50 km (30 miles) south of Be'er Sheva. Either take Highway 40 south directly from Be'er Sheva or Highway 204 from Dimona and Yerukham. The kibbutz was the final home of David Ben Gurion, Israel's first prime minister, and his wife, Paula. Their simple, cream-colored tombstones, which overlook the Wilderness of Tsin, form a place of pilgrimage for Israeli youth movements and foreign admirers. The old man is said to have selected his burial place, with its view of beige and mustard limestone hills, the flint rocks beyond, and the delicate mauve of Edom in the hazy distance.

The **Sde Boker College**, south of the kibbutz and overlooking Ben Gurion's grave, is divided into three sections: Ben Gurion University's Institute for Arid Zone Research coordinates desert biology, agriculture and architecture; the Ben Gurion Institute houses the prime minister's papers and records, and the Center of the Environment runs a field school and a high school with an emphasis on environmental studies.

South of the college is **Ein Ovdat**, (daily 8am–4pm, until 5pm Apr–Sept; tel: 08-6555684; fee) a steep-sided canyon with freshwater pools fringed with lush vegetation. Rock badgers, gazelles and a wide variety of birds inhabit this oasis, where the water is remarkably cold even in the heat of summer. A swim can be refreshing, but the water is deep and sometimes it is difficult to climb out onto the slippery rocks. Lone hikers should not take the risk, and parties of visitors should take it in turns, leaving some out of the water to haul out their companions. There are paths up the sides of the cliffs, with iron rungs and railings in the difficult parts.

Map on page 302

Sculpture at Ovdat.

BELOW: ruined villa at Ovdat.

Reconstruction at Ovdat

A few kilometers further south is **Ovdat** , (daily 8am–4pm, until 5pm Apr–Sept; tel: 08-6586391; fee) the site of the Negev's main Nabatean city, built in the 2nd century BC. Situated on a limestone hill above the surrounding desert, Ovdat was not only excavated but also partly reconstructed in the early 1950s. With its impressive buildings, burial caves, a kiln, workshop and two Byzantine churches, it is one of the most rewarding sites in the country; but what makes it fascinating is the reconstruction of Nabatean and Byzantine agriculture.

With their capital at Petra (today in the Kingdom of Jordan), the Nabateans' achievements in farming the desert are unsurpassed. Their technique was based on the run-off systems of irrigation. Little rain falls in this part of the desert, but when it does, it is not absorbed by the local loess soil; it cuts gulleys and wadis, running in torrents to the Mediterranean in the west and the Dead Sea and the Arava in the east. The run-off system collects this water in a network of fields and terraces, fed by dams, channels and slopes. Variations include gently sloped fields in which each tree has its own catchment area.

A botanist, Michael Evenari, working with archaeologists and engineers, has reconstructed Ovdat and two other farms, growing a variety of crops without the help of piped water: fodder, wheat, onions, carrots, asparagus, artichokes, apricots, grapes, peaches, almonds, peanuts and pistachios are among them.

What started as research into ancient agriculture has proved to be relevant to the modern era, as the system could provide valuable food crops in arid countries of the third world using only existing desert resources, thus preserving the delicate ecological balances. Indeed, although the ancient Nabateans managed to grow grapevines here 2,000 years ago, they didn't irrigate them with salt water.

TIP

Kibbutz Yotvata produces some of the best dairy products in Israel. Try some at the cafeteria beside the gas station.

BELOW:
King Solomon's
Mines at Timna.

Map on page 302

New scientific research using saline water has begun to reap rewards in the form of cabernet sauvignon and sauvignon blanc.

Mitspe Ramon

A half hour south of Ovdat is the development town of **Mitspe Ramon** ❾, perched at an elevation of 1,000 meters (3,300 ft) along the northern edge of the **Makhtesh Ramon**, the largest of the three craters in the Negev (40 km/ 25 miles long and 12 km/7 miles wide). Despite its vast size, the crater comes into view quite suddenly: an awesome sight. Among the finds have been fossilized plants and preserved dinosaur footprints dating back 200 million years to the Triassic and Jurassic periods. Mitspe Ramon has an observatory, connected with Tel Aviv University, which takes full advantage of the dry desert air. In the Makhtesh Ramon a geological trail displays the melting-pot of minerals present in the area, evident from the patches of yellow, ocher, purple and green that tint the landscape.

Start off at the **Mitspe Ramon Visitors Center** at the edge of town (open Sun–Thur 8am–3.30pm, Fri 8am–1pm; fee), which not only explains about the crater's unique geological formations but also offers a splendid view.

From here the road snakes south, joining with the eastern route near the Jordanian border just before Ktura. The next stop is at **Kibbutz Yotvata**, 50 km (30 miles) north of Eilat, with the fascinating **Khai Bar Nature Reserve** ❿ (daily 8am–5pm; tel: 08-6373057; buy tickets at the Visitors Center). At this unusual game park, conservationists have imported and bred a variety of animals mentioned in the Bible, which had become extinct locally: wild asses, ostriches and numerous varieties of gazelle. A holiday village, with modest but comfortable accommodation, swimming pools and a mini-market, is on-site, as is the **Arava Visitors' Center** with a museum and audio-visual display of the desert. **Ktura**, a kibbutz 16 km (l0 miles) to the north, offers horse-riding.

Timna

Timna ⓫, 24 km (15 miles) further south, (daily 8am–4pm except Fri 1pm, in Jul–Aug 8am–8.30pm except Sun & Fri 1pm; tel: 08-6316756; www.timna-park.co.il; fee) is the site of **King Solomon's Mines**, a little to the south of the modern copper mine. The ancient circular stone ovens for roasting the copper ore look simple enough, with stone channels to the collection vessels for the metal, but the air channels were skilfully angled to catch the prevailing north wind which comes down the Arava. The late archaeologist Nelson Glueck, who excavated the mines, called the ventilation system "an ancient example of automation."

The area surrounding the mines has been developed as privately owned park, with an artificial lake and a network of roads, including a fine scenic route in the northeast of the park to facilitate touring. Highlights include **King Solomon's Pillars**, a natural formation of Nubian sandstone, and the redoubtable **Mushroom Rock**, a granite rock shaped like a mushroom. The time-worn remains of a settlement, a fortress and two Egyptian sanctuaries used by the ancient mine-workers can also be seen. From here, it's just 30 km (18 miles) to Eilat and the Red Sea. ❑

Nitsanei Sinai (Kadesh Barne'a), on the Sinai border, was the only one of Solomon's fortresses to be rebuilt.

BELOW: the giant Mushroom Rock.

EILAT

Map on page 302

Eilat is a hedonistic playground, a birdwatcher's delight, and a jumping-off point for visits to Jordan to see the great Nabataean city of Petra, and to the Sinai in Egypt

Remote from the rest of Israel, **Eilat** ⑫ is searing hot and parched dry. But, with guaranteed year-round sunshine – average January temperatures of 21°C (70°F) – the closest tropical waters to Europe with remarkable marine life and coral formations, and the unique flora and fauna of the only land link between Africa and Europe/Asia, Eilat has a lot to offer.

Consequently Eilat is one of Israel's most popular tourist resorts. Holiday-makers migrate instinctively, like the billion birds who fly overhead twice each year journeying back forth between Africa and Europe. Most of the visitors to Eilat are Israelis who feel that they are vacationing *hutz la'aretz* (abroad). Others simply say they're off to *sof olam* – the end of the world. And anyone who drives from the populated central part of Israel across that "Great Bald Spot," known as the Negev Desert might be inclined to agree with them.

Eilat is Israel's southernmost community. It is the state's flipper-hold on the Red Sea. It is also a mecca (if such a word can be used in Israel) for snorkelers, scuba-divers, windsurfers, water-skiers, swimmers, sailors, sandcastle builders, sun-worshippers, tropical-fish fanatics and birdwatchers.

Eilat's single significant industry lies in assisting visitors to do nothing productive. It is a sensual city, which caters for people who like magnificent natural beauty, lazy afternoons, spicy food and cold beer. To help keep down prices, the Israeli government has made Eilat a zone free of sales tax (VAT), although overseas visitors are anyway exempt from this tax.

PRECEDING PAGES: Eilat's Dolphinarium. **LEFT:** fishing by the Underwater Observatory Marine Park. **BELOW:** the North Beach.

First city

Eilatis whimsically call their town Israel's "First City," because it was the first piece of land in what is now Israel to be occupied by the Children of Israel after the Exodus from Egypt (Deuteronomy 2, 8). But Moses was only a tourist; he moved north to find milk and honey soon afterwards.

A few centuries later King Solomon built a port here and called it Etzion Geber. With the help of his friend King Hiram of Phoenicia, he sent a fleet of ships east to the land of Ophir, "and fetched from thence gold, four hundred and twenty talents, and brought it to King Solomon," (I Kings 9, 26). Since there were about 3,000 shekels to the talent, and about a half-ounce to the shekel, the sailors must have lugged some 20 tonnes of gold back to Jerusalem.

Eilat changed hands many times during the following centuries. The Edomites grabbed it for a while, and then King Uzziah took it back for the Israelites. The Syrians later wrested it away from him. A succession of conquerors marched through – Nabateans, Greeks, Romans, Mamelukes, Crusaders, Ottoman Turks and others. The Crusaders left behind their 12th-

The restaurant at the Underwater Observatory.

century fortress at Coral Island, just south of Taba. The celebrated Colonel T.E. Lawrence, popularly known as Lawrence of Arabia, trekked through here after his conquest of Aqaba across the bay.

The most recent army to conquer Eilat was the Israel Defense Forces, which swooped down on this exotic pearl during Operation Uvda in March 1949 and scared the daylights out of several sleepy lizards and a tortoise living in the ruins of Umm Rashrash, an otherwise uninhabited mudbrick "police station," which stood all alone in what is now the center of the town. Although the United Nations had allocated Eilat to Israel in its partition plan, the capture of this corner of the Promised Land in the War of Independence was so hastily organized that Israeli troops arrived without a flag to proclaim it as part of their new state. So, a soldier with artistic talent was issued a bed sheet and a bottle of blue ink with which to produce an Israeli flag of appropriate dimension and design.

Development town

BELOW:
Eilat has seen a building boom in recent years.

The new flag didn't fly over very much, but the Israeli authorities knew that Eilat was located in a highly strategic position, and rapid steps were taken to create a town. It was strategic because it provided Israel's only access to the Indian Ocean, and trade with Asia, East Africa, Australia and the islands, including vital oil supplies from pre-revolutionary Iran and subsequently the manufactured goods on offer from Japan, Korea and China. Holding on to Eilat also meant a break in land continuity between Egypt and Jordan, thus offering a military advantage to the defense forces.

In the rush to create a city on the Red Sea, Eilat's builders, as throughout Israel, didn't invest much in fine architecture. Instead, they went for fast, sim-

Map on page 302

ple, sturdy construction of apartments to house immigrants trickling in from the horrors of Nazi-occupied Europe, and the expulsions by Arab states such as Iraq and Yemen. Visitors to Eilat can see some of the older 1950s apartment buildings still standing like concrete bastions on the hillside. They're still quite serviceable and are occupied by Eilati families who have affectionate nicknames for them, such "Sing Sing," and "La Bastille."

As the city expanded, other neighborhoods grew further up the slopes of the Eilat Mountains. Improved architecture didn't spare them from satirical nicknames. One neighborhood built about a kilometer up a steep hill west of the center of town is locally know as the "Onesh" district. In Hebrew, *onesh* means "punishment" and anybody who walks this distance from the center of town on a hot day will appreciate the appropriateness of this sobriquet. In recent years, prosperity has produced colonies of villas around the town, unleashing a new generation of nicknames, which are still to stand the test of time.

Attractions in Eilat include the Kings City Biblical Theme Park near the North Beach and the IMAX Theater, a 3D cinema located in a blue pyramid opposite the airport with a screen eight stories high.

Crisis and boom

Egypt's President Gamal Abdel Nasser also realised the strategic value of Eilat and its potential as a multi-million-dollar tourist playground. In May 1967 he imposed a blockade on Eilat and shut down its shipping by closing off the Straight of Tiran off of the Sinai peninsula, including the vital oil supplies from Iran. Next, he ordered the UN peace-keeping forces out of Sinai and moved his own army into the mountains north-west of Eilat, within clear view of Jordan. With one quick push, the fear was, he could have cut off Eilat, linked up with the Jordanian Arab Legion and created a solid, integrated southern front against Israel. Eilat was in an extremely vulnerable position until the Israeli pre-emptive

LEFT: a beachside café. **BELOW:** security check at an Eilat shopping mall.

strike against Egyptian air fields deprived Nasser of the vital air cover his troops would need. The following six days witnessed Israel's lightning conquest of Sinai, and the removal of military threats against Eilat.

Even after 1967, Eilat didn't really take off as a tourist destination. For most Israelis it was a stop-off point en route to Sinai, where the desert was more dramatic and the diving and marine life even more remarkable. The return of Sinai to Egypt and growing affluence in Israel enabled Eilat to begin to grow. And grow it has. Today the city has about 40 hotels, including many of the major international chains.

Most of the tourists are Israelis, who drive the four-hour trans-desert trek from Jerusalem and Tel Aviv for their holidays and can withstand average summer temperatures of 40°C (104°F). But many others, especially in winter, are foreigners who take charter flights from Europe directly to Eilat. Arkia, Israel's domestic airline, also operates several flights a day from here to other cities in Israel, and the Sinai.

Plenty of rocks

An adage grew up among Eilatis, "If we could export rocks, we'd all be millionaires." The key to Eilat's tourism has been to twist the adage to bring the foreigners to the rocks. Nearly all of these rocks are pre-Cambrian, formed by the forces of the Earth in the epochs before the beginning of life on the planet. Aeons ago they covered the land facing the north, where the ancient Tethys Sea flowed over what is now the state of Israel.

To the south extended the primordial megacontinent of Gondwanaland. Gondwanaland eventually drifted apart to form India, Africa, South America, Aus-

TIP

Eilat is a free-trade zone, which means it has no sales tax. As a result, many items are cheaper than elsewhere in the country.

BELOW: windsurfing at dusk.
RIGHT: camping out at Taba.

Map on page 302

tralia and Antarctica, and the bed of the Tethys Sea was pushed up to form the bedrock of Israel. Geologists are forever pottering about the Eilat Mountains, picking at chunks of granite, gneiss, quartz-porphyry and diabase. In some places they are after an attractive bluish-green malachite which merchants in town call Eilat Stone, a type of copper ore which can be shaped and given a high polish. In fact, this stone has been used in jewelry-making in the region for thousands of years, and is still very evident in many Eilat tourist shops.

For those who like to see their rocks in the rough, there are the Eilat Mountains, spectacular ascents of colorful stone. In some areas it appears as if their volcanic genesis was fast-frozen, and their flowing magmas interrupted in full flood. Erosion here has taken some bizarre and incredibly beautiful courses. In places it is possible to walk through narrow canyons with walls towering hundreds of meters vertically, but just a meter or two apart. The harsh desert wind has carved monumental pillars among the mountains, particularly in the sandstone regions, such as the **Pillars of Amram** (named after the father of Moses), some 9 km (5 miles) north of Eilat and 3 km (2 miles) west of the main highway. The site is laced with lovely ravines and clusters of imposing natural columns.

About 4 km (2¼ miles) south of Eilat, along the coastal highway leading to Sinai, is the entry to **Solomon's Canyon**, a popular hiking area. A dusty granite quarry at the mouth of the canyon tends to obscure the formations lying beyond, but those following the path markers in the **Harei Eilat Nature Reserve ⓭** will be treated to an exotic geological adventure. As you enter the canyon, **Ha-Metsuda** (The Stronghold) rises to the left. This great rock was vital to Eilat's defences against invasion from the Sinai coast. The path then leads another 16 km (10 miles) up into the mountains, twisting and turning along the route of the

The dolphins at Dolphin Reef enjoy human company. In the 1990s a group of very pregnant British women came out to give birth in the sea with the dolphins. But the Israeli Ministry of Health refused to allow the women to do so.

LEFT: geological field trip.
BELOW: camels wait by the marina.

canyon. Hikers pass first beneath **Har Yehoshafat**, then **Har Shlomo**, and then **Har Uziya**, each of which towers more than 700 meters (2,300 ft) overhead.

Eventually the trail crosses the paved **Moon Valley Highway** which leads into central Sinai. Across the highway, the trail continues on to the spectacular cliffs and oasis at **Ein Netafim** (the Spring of the Drops), which trickles across a barren rock into a picturesque pool at the foot of an imposing cliff. Further along is **Red Canyon**, another impressive natural wonder of erosion-sculpted sandstone.

Seaside sojourning

Welcome to the Dolphinarium.

Beaches are a year-round attraction in Eilat. Even in the summer, when temperatures can range well above baking at 40°C (l05° F), the waters of the Red Sea are cool and soothing. Midwinter swimming, however, is usually left to the Europeans and Americans, while native Eilatis stare from the shore, bundled up in parkas to dispel the wintry gusts, which usually hover at around 15°C (roughly 60°F).

Eilat has a number of distinct and attractive beaches, spanning 11 km (7 miles), ranging from fine sand to gravel. **North Beach**, close to the center of the town and to the west of the marina and lagoon, is the local hangout for sun-worshippers. The bay is protected, the swimming is easy, and dozens of hotels line the shore. The eastern end of North Beach also has inexpensive bungalows and even camping facilities for those on a tight budget.

BELOW:
water sports are
a main attraction.

Further south is the **Dolphin Reef** (open 9am–5pm, Fri–Sat until 4.30pm; tel: 08-6300111; www.dolphinreef.co.il; fee), a private beach where you can swim with the dolphins. If you have a license you can hire diving equipment and dive with them too. There are qualified guides to accompany divers. The dolphins are very friendly – so much so that they are sometimes used in therapeutic programmes for children with disabilities.

A little further down the coast, past the navy station and port facilities, is **Coral Beach Nature Reserve** (daily 8am–5pm; tel: 08-6376829; fee). This reserve includes a fine sandy beach and a truly spectacular coral reef. Here visitors can rent diving masks, snorkels and flippers from the reserve's office and swim along any of three marked routes which lead over different parts of the coral reef. Special markers set into the reef itself identify different types of coral and plants growing there, as well as some of the more common fish.

The reserve also has changing rooms, showers, snack and souvenir stands and other tourist amenities. But tourist-friendly though it may be, this is a monitored nature reserve. Swimmers must be very careful not to bruise any of the coral. Removal of any pieces of coral is taken very seriously indeed and will result in the culprit paying a visit to the local judge.

Observing fish

Further south is the **Underwater Observatory Marine Park** (open Sat–Thur 8.30am–5pm, Fri 8.30am–4pm; tel: 08-6364200; www.coralworld.com; fee), an unusual commercial aquarium and undersea observatory. Here the visitor walks out on a long pier to the observatory building, which is set into the reef

Map on page 302

itself. Descending the spiral staircase within the observatory, one emerges into a circular room with windows facing out into the coral reef at a depth of 5 meters (16 ft). All sorts of fish swim freely about outside the window, and the many colors and shapes of the living reef are astonishing sights which should not be missed.

There is also a museum which exhibits the marine life and coral on a comprehensive A–Z basis, a shark tank and, for an extra fee, a yellow submarine, the *Jacqueline*, which will take you on one-hour underwater trips. Nothing quite as lovely has been seen since Jules Verne's Captain Nemo retired the *Nautilus*. Also, for an additional charge, the Oceanarium offers a 3-D cinema show with a screen surrounding the viewer, while even the seats move.

Those who abjure actually going into the water might be more inclined to ride on it instead. A large marina and lagoon at North Beach is the mooring for many boats and yachts, from expensive charter schooners to more affordable windsurfing craft. There are also several glass-bottomed boats for reef-viewing, and a number of water-skiing speedboats available for charter. Licensed diving clubs which will rent diving equipment and offer diving courses include Lucky Divers, Red Sea Divers, and Eilat Aqua Sport.

Observing birds

Birdwatching too, is a year-round attraction in Eilat, and several dozen species of resident bird can be found in the mountains and deserts, by the seashore and among the fields of neighboring **Kibbutz Eilot**. The spring migration season, however, is particularly dazzling and is the best time to be here. Millions upon millions of migratory birds fly across the Eilat region on their northward journeys

TIP

You can learn to dive while in Eilat: several schools advertise prominently in the town.

BELOW: the submarine offers one-hour underwater trips

from warm wintering havens in Africa to their breeding grounds scattered across Eurasia. Great waves of eagles and falcons fill the sky and highly respected ornithologists keep producing reports giving strangely precise figures such as 19,288 steppe eagles, 26,770 black kites and 225,952 honey buzzards in the course of a single migration season.

Sharp-eyed birdwatchers will also pick out booted eagles, snake eagles, lesser spotted eagles, imperial eagles, marsh harriers, sparrowhawks and osprey. And then come the pelicans and storks in their tens of thousands. There is a ringing and birdwatching center north of the north beach near the salt flats where many of the migrating birds stop off for a nibble after traveling across the sea and or desert.

The King Solomon Hotel.

For those looking for a leisurely holiday there are scores of restaurants ranging from inexpensive pizza parlors and *felafel* stands, through reasonably-priced places selling very good seafood, to high-priced haute cuisine in the Eilat Center, the New Tourist Center and the Hotel District. Most of the larger hotels also have nightclubs, discos and other entertainments. The **Red Sea Jazz Festival** each August has become an annual summer fixture, drawing thousands of jazz fans to several nights of live entertainment by local acts and international stars.

Aqaba and Petra

In the wake of the Middle East peace process Eilat has become a popular base for visits to Sinai in Egypt and Petra in Jordan. The region is marketed as a Middle Eastern French Riviera and its region's tourist industry is flourishing.

BELOW: the rosy facades at Petra.

The **Arava Crossing** to Jordan, northeast of Eilat, has offered access to the Hashemite Kingdom since the peace accord was signed with Israel in 1994. The frontier can be reached along a road running eastwards off the main Arava

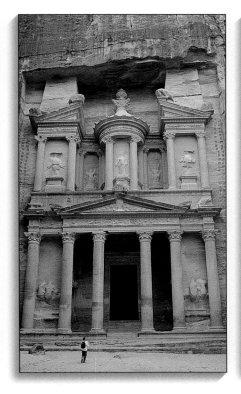

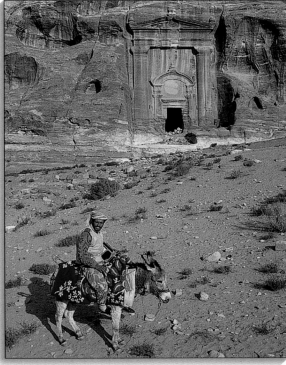

highway several kilometers north of Eilat, not far from Kibbutz Eilot. The Arava Checkpoint is open Sun–Thur 6.30am–8pm and Fri–Sat 6.30am–6pm. It is closed on Yom Kippur and Id el Fitr. Passport holders can enter Jordan without a visa if they pay a $10 charge. It is not yet possible to take vehicles from Israel into Jordan. Bus 16 leaves Eilat Central Bus Station once an hour for the border crossing.

The town of **Aqaba** ⓮ is unexceptional. Sitting alongside Eilat on the northern shore of the Red Sea, Aqaba is Jordan's only outlet to the sea and therefore a busy port. The tourist infrastructure here is much less significant than in Eilat, making the beaches quieter. The name Aqaba was given to the town in the 14th century by the Mamelukes, and it was the first town captured from the Turks in 1917 by the Arab forces led by T. E. Lawrence (Lawrence of Arabia).

By far the most popular excursion into Jordan involves traveling northwards some 120 km (75 miles) to the fabulous Nabatean city of **Petra** ⓯. Reached through a narrow canyon, Petra is best known for the dramatic tomb and temple facades carved into the Nubian sandstone mountains. The pink, red and purple-hued mountain walls would be exquisite enough, but in addition there are the romance and history of the location, which lay forgotten for nearly 2,000 years until "rediscovered" by the Swiss explorer Ludwig Burckhardt in 1812.

Visiting the Sinai

The Sinai was captured by Israeli forces in 1967 and returned to Egypt in 1982 under the Camp David peace treaty. It remains a popular playground for Israelis who built up a tourist infrastructure along the Red Sea coast during the years when they held the territory. Since then the Egyptians have greatly expanded

Maps:
pp 302
and 323

In 1845 Petra was immortalized in a poem by the English cleric John W. Burgon, in which he described it as "a rose-red city, half as old as time".

BELOW:
rugs for sale
in the Sinai.

Map on page 323

TIP

In the Sinai and Negev take heed when Bedouin warn of flash floods in the winter. The skies may be clear but heavy rains can sweep down through dry canyons and river beds. The Bedouin, smelling the rainwater in the air, know what's coming.

BELOW:
St Catherine's Monastery, in the Sinai.

the region's tourist facilities, but vast stretches of the Sinai remain gloriously isolated. It is more rugged and spectacular than the Negev, and everything here is on a grander scale.

The Sinai can be reached from the **Taba Border Crossing**, 10 km (6 miles) south of Eilat. The Taba enclave itself, which has a Hilton Hotel with a casino, is technically in Egyptian territory, but is open to all who can produce valid passports. The crossing into the Sinai is open 24 hours a day, seven days a week, closing only for the Jewish festival of Yom Kippur and the Muslim festival of Id el Fitr. Visas for a two-week stay in the Sinai peninsula only are given at the frontier itself for a small fee, but people wishing to visit the rest of Egypt must obtain a visa from an Egyptian consulate in Eilat or elsewhere. Bus number 15 will take you to the border, and there are buses and taxis on the Egyptian side running through Sinai and on to Cairo. Passenger cars can be taken into the Sinai for a modest fee.

Sharm al-Shaykh

There are three major resorts along the Sinai's Red Sea coast: **Nuwayba** ❶, 60 km (38 miles) south of Eilat, **Dahab** ❷, 135 km (85 miles) south of Eilat, and **Sharm al-Shaykh** ❸, 225 km (140 miles) south of Eilat. You can stop en route to eat fresh fish in one of the coastal villages. Desert safaris to nearby wadis and oases are offered from all these locations, but an even bigger attraction than the stunning desert landscapes is the marine life, and especially the coral reefs.

The Sinai is considered one of the world's premier locations for divers. Generally speaking, the coral formations are more remarkable to the south, with Sharm al-Shaykh being the favorite choice of seasoned divers. Conservationists are inceasingly concerned about the harm caused to coral at Ras Mohammed National Park; this is mainly due to over-harvesting and damage from ships' anchors, but also to illicit souvenir-hunting.

St Catherine's and the burning bush

The other major attraction of Sinai is **St Catherine's Monastery** ❹ (open daily 9.30am–noon; closed public holidays). reached from a road running southwest for 35 km (21 miles) from a point midway between Nuwayba and Dahab. Built by funding from the Byzantine ruler Justinian in the 6th century on a site where some believe the burning bush spoke to Moses, the monastery is today home to Greek Orthodox monks. It has a magnificent basilica and a splendid fresco depicting the transfiguration of Christ. The tiny Chapel of the Burning Bush stands on the spot where the biblical event is said to have taken place.

The nearby summit at an altitude of 2,640 meters (8,660 ft) offers a breathtaking view of the desert.

All-inclusive tours to both Sinai and Petra involving overnight stays are available from the many travel agents in Eilat. As the price and content of these tours vary quite a lot, it is worth shopping around for the best value. ❏

Diving in Eilat

Eilat is one of the world's top destinations for warm water diving. What makes its marine environment especially magical are the exquisite coral reefs, the colorful and remarkable array of tropical fish and the clearness of the water with average underwater visibility of 30 meters (100 ft). An extra incentive to visit Eilat is the 350 days of sunshine a year.

Black-belt divers consider diving in the Sinai in Egypt to the south of Eilat to be much better, but the tourist infrastructure there is less well developed. Moreover, Eilat's lack of currents due to its location in a sheltered bay at the northern end of the Red Sea combined with the shallowness of the reefs greatly reduces the dangers associated with diving. It also means that Eilat is nicknamed the "underwater classroom" because of the large numbers of budding divers who flock to the resort to learn the skills of scuba diving.

The safety factor is also enhanced by the fact that diving in Israel is strictly regulated by Knesset legislation. It is a criminal offense for any of the several dozen diving equipment businesses in the city to rent out equipment to a person who can't present a valid diving license issued by an internationally recognized organization such as PADI (Professional Association of Diving Instructors).

Most of the diving clubs are located near Coral Beach, several miles south of the city center, and if you do not have a license, then a typical diving course for beginners takes five full days of instruction from classroom theory through to pool training and ultimately the real thing.

The less adventurous need not be denied the fantastic spectacle of Eilat's underwater world. Snorkeling is simple to do. Simply buy or rent a snorkel, wade in and stick your head under water. Alternatively, many of the diving clubs have snorkeling tours – a bit like a nature hike with a professional guide.

There are dozens of other ways to enjoy the Red Sea from above the water. The bay's strong breezes are ideal for windsurfing and for those who prefer to travel faster there is no lack of water skiing (including jet skis, tube skis and bob skis for the initiated). If you don't want to get your feet wet, then you can hire a kayak, canoe, rowing boat or speed boat, while a glass-bottom boat is ideal for appreciating the marine life.

There is also the yellow submarine, located inside the Underwater Observatory Marine Park (see page 321). The Marine Park itself is probably the best place for non-divers to enjoy Eilat's incredible underwater seascapes. ❏

Practical information

For renting diving equipment or taking courses it is best to head for Coral Beach:
● Aqua-Sport: P.O.B. 300, Eilat; Tel: 08-6334404. Fax: 08-6333771. email: info@aqua-sport.com. Website: www.aqua-sport.com
● Red Sea Lucky Divers: P.O. Box. 4191, Eilat; Tel: 08-6323466. Fax: 08-6370993. email: luckysue@luckydivers.com. Website: www.luckydivers.com

RIGHT: the lack of currents and the shallowness of the coral reef make diving relatively safe.

TRAVEL TIPS

TRANSPORT

GETTING THERE AND GETTING AROUND

GETTING THERE

The website of the Israel Airports Authority has information in English about all Israel's airports and land border crossings: www.iaa.gov.il

Travel Security
For decades before 2001's terrorist attacks on America – in fact, since aircraft hijacking began in the late 1960s – Israel's border and aviation security has been rigorous. Since 9/11, international travel and aviation authorities have adopted the security norms tried and tested by Israel over the decades (often in consultation with Israeli experts). For example, as a matter of procedure since the 1970s, the door to the pilots' cockpit has been locked at all times, and Israeli fighter aircraft are scrambled to escort any plane that doesn't respond to air traffic control routine calls as it approaches Israeli airspace. Passengers taking flights to and from Israel should get to the airport two to three hours before take-off and expect a thorough search of their baggage with detailed personal questioning as to the purpose of their visit.

By Air

Ben Gurion International Airport
The main hub for international air traffic is Ben Gurion International Airport, which is located in Lod (Lydda), near the Mediterranean coast, 15 km (9 miles) southeast of Tel Aviv, 50 km (30 miles) west of Jerusalem and 110 km (68 miles) southeast of Haifa.
Terminal 3: International passengers

arrive and depart from Terminal 3, a new, spacious facility.
Terminal 2: this is a relatively small terminal near the eastern entrance to the airport used for domestic flights.
Terminal 1: this old terminal is being refurbished and will be used at a future date when the new terminal's traffic reaches capacity level.
About 40 percent of international flights in and out of Ben Gurion International Airport are operated by El Al Israel Airlines, the country's national carrier, which was privatized in 2005. El Al carries nearly 2 million passengers a year. Most major airlines from North America and Europe have regular flights to Israel as well as many charter companies.
The airport has ATMs, banks and a post office which is open 24 hours a day (except Friday night/Saturday).

Useful Numbers

Ben Gurion International Airport: 03-9755555.
Flight arrival and departure information at Ben Gurion International Airport: (03) 9723344
Transport and parking information at BG airport: (03) 9723339
Government Tourist Office: (03) 9715555
Lost Property & Tourist Police: (03) 9715444 or (03) 9755555 the press 2
24 Hour Left Baggage Service: (03) 9712130
Jet Set Club Lounge: (03) 9731659 – executive facilities including Internet and fax access for a small fee.
King David Suite: (03) 9716892 Executive facilities for El Al business-class passengers.

To and From Ben Gurion International Airport

Train: A new rail link to the airport was inaugurated with the opening of Terminal 3. Details about times of trains and fares are available on the internet: www.israrail.org.il. There is no train service on the Jewish Sabbath from Friday sunset to Saturday evening or on public holidays. There are no trains after midnight and before 3am. There is a regular service to Tel Aviv and from there to most major cities in Israel. For Tel Aviv's hotel district, take the train to Tel Aviv Merkaz (Central) and catch a taxi from there.
Taxis: Taxis to Jerusalem cost about NIS 160 ($40) and to Tel Aviv about $28.
Shared Taxis: This service to Jerusalem costs about $12 per person. For booking a shared tax from your hotel or any other address in Jerusalem back to the airport, telephone Nesher (02) 6257227, 6231231, 6253233. This service to Haifa costs about $20 – for booking back to the airport phone Amal: (04) 8662324.
Buses: Timetables available on www.egged.co.il or tel: (03) 6948888. The 475 goes to Tel Aviv every 20 minutes; the 947 to Jerusalem or Haifa (via Netanya) every 30 minutes. There are no buses on the Jewish Sabbath from Friday sunset to Saturday evening.
Car Hire:
All the major car hire companies operating in Israel have offices at the airport:
Avis: tel: 03-9773200. www.avis.co.il
Best: tel: 1-800-22-015.
www.best-car.co.il
Eldan: tel: 03-9773400/1 9773407.
www.eldan.co.il

Hertz: tel: 03-9772444. www.hertz.co.il
Budget: tel (03)-9711504.
www.budget.co.il
Shlomo SIXT: tel: 1-700-501-502.
www.sixt.co.il

Hotels:

There are no hotels next to the airport. The Avia Hotel is a 10-minute drive away and operates a free shuttle. Tel: 03-5393333.
www.inisrael.com/avia/

Check-In at home or at a hotel

El Al provide a check-in service for its customers at the passenger's home or hotel, which can be ordered from 48 hours before the flight. Phone *2678. Service is available Sun–Thurs 7am–10pm and Friday 7am–12noon. The service eliminates waiting on line for a security check, thus significantly reducing the time spent at the airport and enabling you to arrive comfortably without your luggage, with only your carry-on bag. With this service you receive your boarding card at home or hotel and can proceed directly to Passport control. Security regulations require every person using the service to be present when receiving the service.

OTHER AIRPORTS

With the exception of Eilat Airport and Uvda Airport in the Negev, which take in a limited number of international flights bound for Eilat, all Israel's other airports are for domestic traffic only, although in certain circumstances arrangements can be made for private planes to land.
Sde Dov (Tel Aviv) Airport: (03) 6984500
Haifa Airport: (04) 8476111
Eilat: (08) 6363838
Rosh Pina (North): (06) 6936478.
Uvda: (08) 6375880

Private planes

Pilots interested in flying their own planes to Israel should provide the Israel Airports Authority with all mandatory information at least 48 hours in advance of the estimated time of arrival and await clearance before commencing the flight. For further information contact: Israel Airport Authority, POB 7, Ben Gurion International Airport, 70100 Israel, Tel. 03-9774500.

By Sea

The main ports are Haifa and Ashdod. Several shipping lines offer a regular service from Greece and Cyprus to Haifa port, and many Mediterranean cruises include Israel in their itineraries. Official ports of entry for foreign yachts and boats, in addition to these, include the marinas at:
Ashdod: Tel: (08) 8557246 Fax: (08) 8556810. Email: bmarina@netvision.net.il
Ashkelon: Tel.(08)-6733780. Fax (08)-6733823. Email:
marine_nm@netvision.net.il. Website www.ashkelon-marina.co.il
Eilat: Tel: (08)-6376761.
Fax (07)-6375454.
Herzliya: Tel: (09)-9565591.
Fax (09) –9565593.
Email: info@herzliya-marina.co.il.
Website www.herzliya-marina.co.il
Tel Aviv: Tel. (03)-5272596. Fax (03)-5272466. E-Mail: marinata@zahav.net.il.
Website: www.telaviv-marina.co.il.
Contact the marina of your choice and reserve berthing several weeks in advance, providing full particulars concerning your vessel. When 80 km (50 miles) off the Israeli coast, report (IMOT) to Haifa Radio 4xo and to the Israeli Navy. Stand by VHF channel 16.

Landing-for-the-Day

If you visit Israel on a cruise ship or yacht, you will be given a Landing-for-the-Day card, which permits you to remain in the country for as long as your ship is in port, and you need not apply for a visitor's visa. This applies only to people wishing to enter Israel for tourism purposes.

By Road

FROM JORDAN:

Following the signing of a peace agreement between Israel and Jordan in 1994, communications between the two countries have improved considerably (Israel now recognizes Jordanian stamps in passports and visas, and vice versa). Visitors now have several border crossings to choose from: the Allenby Bridge (easiest for travel between Amman and Jerusalem/Tel Aviv), the Jordan River Crossing (near Beit She'an) and the Arava Checkpoint (between Eilat and Aqaba).
Allenby Bridge, near Jericho, some 40 km (25 miles) from Jerusalem, is the main crossing-point. For information tel: (02) 9941038
The visa requirements are the same as those at any other point of entry into Israel (it is not possible to get an Israeli visa upon arrival at the bridge and, as yet, it is still not possible to get one in Jordan). The bridge is open Sun–Thurs 8am–4pm and on Friday and the eves of holidays 8–11am. It is closed on Saturday and on Jewish holidays. At Allenby Bridge, a Tourist Information Office is open at the same time as the bridge. Other facilities are: currency exchange, post office, public telephones, cafeteria, toilets, porters and *sherut* (service) taxis to Jerusalem, Jericho, Bethlehem, Hebron, Ramallah and Gaza.
For opening hours and restrictions at points of entry between Jordan and Israel, check details with Israel's Ministry of Tourism, or contact the border:
Jordan River (near Beit She'an): (06) 6586448. Sun–Thurs 6.30am–10pm Fri–Sat 8am–8pm, closed Yom Kippur and Id el Fitr.
Arava (Yitzhak Rabin) Checkpoint (near Eilat): (07) 6336812 Sun–Thur 6.30am–8pm and Fri–Sat 6.30am–6pm. Hourly bus service – route 16 – from Eilat. Checkpoint closed on Yom Kippur and Id el Fitr.

FROM EGYPT:

Points of entry open between Israel and Egypt are Nitsana, Rafah and Taba, open 363 days a year (the exceptions are Yom Kippur and the first day of Id el Fitr).
Nitsana, the main point of entry, is about 60 km (37 miles) southwest of

BELOW: Israel's transport facilities are mostly ultra-modern.

TRANSPORT
ACCOMMODATION
EATING OUT
ACTIVITIES
A – Z
LANGUAGE

Be'er Sheva, and is open between 8am and 4pm, tel: (08) 6564666. It is served by Egged bus 44 from Be'er Sheva.

Rafah, 50 km (30 miles) southwest of Ashkelon, is open between 8.30am and 5pm, tel: (08) 6734205. This border crossing is not recommended as those crossing must reach the border in an armoured behicle due to tensions between Israelis and Palestinians.
Taba, just south of Eilat, is open 24 hours a day, tel: (08) 6372104. Take bus 15 from Eilat.

Entry Requirements

Visas and Passports
Tourists are required to hold passports valid for Israel, which are valid for at least six months from the date of arrival. Stateless persons require a valid travel document with a return visa to the country of issue. Citizens of the USA, Canada, the European Union, Australia and New Zealand do not need a visa to enter Israel, only a valid passport. For citizens of these countries, there are no special health requirements.

Financial Restrictions
When entering Israel, unlimited amounts of money can be brought into and out of the country and freely converted to and from New Israeli Shekels (NIS). But sums of more than NIS80,000 (about US$20,000), which are converted or deposited in a bank must be reported to the Bank of Israel within the framework of international regulations to prevent money laundering. Banks will provide appropriate forms.

Visa Extensions
Those entering Israel on vacation can only stay for three months and are not allowed to work for money. Anyone wishing to enter the country for work, study or permanent settlement must apply for the appropriate visa at an Israeli Diplomatic or Consular Mission before leaving their own country. Due to a rise in illegal workers in Israel, even visitors from North America and Western Europe may be refused entry if they do not have return tickets, sufficient funds for their stay, or an Israeli citizen prepared to vouch for them.

Entry and Exit Formalities
All visitors to Israel, including diplomats, are required to fill in an entry form, AL-17, upon arrival. This form should be supplied on the flight to Israel.

Visitors who intend continuing to Arab or Muslim countries (except Egypt and Jordan) after their visit to Israel should ask the frontier control officer to put the entry stamp on this form instead of in their passports, as they may subsequently be refused entry into countries hostile towards Israel if an Israeli stamp appears on the passport itself.

Extensions of Stay
Tourists who wish to stay in the country for longer than three months must obtain an extension of stay. This applies also to citizens of those countries which are exempt from entry visas, and generally requires the stamping of your passport. The extension may be obtained through any district office of the Ministry of Interior – an appointment for this purpose must be made ahead of time.
The main offices are located at:
Jerusalem: General Building, 1 Shlomtsion ha-Malka. Tel: (02) 6290239 (call 10am–2pm Sun–Thur).
Tel Aviv: Shalom Meyer Tower, Visa Department, 9 Akhad Ha'am. Tel: (03) 7632534 (call 8am–3pm Sun–Thur).
Haifa: Government Building (opposite Municipality), 11 Hassan Shukri. Tel: (04) 8633349 or 8633353 (call 1.30pm–3.30pm Sun–Thur).

GETTING AROUND

Public Transport

Buses
Buses are by far the most common means of public transportation for both urban and inter-urban services (although the railways are making a rapid resurgence). Services are regular and the fares are reasonable, though the prices have risen substantially in recent years due to the withdrawal of government subsidies.

Historically the Egged Bus Cooperative, one of the world's largest bus companies, had the franchise to operate almost all buses in Israel outside of the Greater Tel Aviv region, while the Dan Bus cooperative had the franchise in Tel Aviv. But for the past five years all new bus lines are subject to a public tender, and many new companies have won these tenders. However, Egged and Dan remain the dominant bus companies.

Egged has a fleet of more than 3,300 modern air-conditioned buses

operating routes throughout the country. Services are punctual and, if anything, impatient drivers tend to leave half a minute before time. If traveling to Eilat, it is advisable to reserve seats several days in advance.
Egged information Tel: 03-6948888. Route details and timetables are available in English at www.egged.co.il The site offers updated information about discounted and multi-ride tickets for various periods and in various cities, discounts for children and students, bus maps etc.
Egged runs the urban routes in Jerusalem, Haifa and Eilat.
Lost Property: Tel Aviv (03) 6383924 Jerusalem: (02) 5685670
Bus 99 – $10 per adult and $8 per child – allows you to travel around 25 major tourist points in Jerusalem on a double-decker, London-style bus – alighting and getting back on again when you feel like it.
Dan Bus: Information on city buses in the Greater Tel Aviv region www.dan.co.il/english/
Times: Buses do not run from Friday before sundown until Saturday after sundown. Inter-urban bus services start around 6am and finish in the early evening except for the Tel Aviv–Jerusalem and Tel Aviv–Haifa lines which continue until midnight. Urban services run from 5am to just after midnight.
Locations: The Jerusalem Central Bus Station is in Yafo, at the western entrance to the city. The Tel Aviv Central Bus Station is a vast shopping mall complex on Levinski in the south of the city (connected to Haganah Railway Station). Haifa has two bus stations: Hof Hacarmel (connected to the railway station of the same name) at the city's southern entrance and Checkpost at the northern entrance to the city.
There are no bus services on the Sabbath, or on Jewish holidays except within Haifa, Eilat and Arab cities.

Trains
Israel Railways has undergone major expansion and upgrading in recent years. The railway now reaches most major cities (except Eilat and Tiberias) and tickets are slightly more expensive than for comparable rides on buses. Since 2001, stations were opened, among others, at Tel Aviv University, Tel Aviv Hahganah (to link with the Central Bus Station), Be'er Sheva and Rishon Lezion. New stations were opened in 2004 at Ben Gurion International Airport, in 2005 at Jerusalem (Malkha), Jerusalem Biblical Zoo and Ashkelon, and in 2007 at Modlin.

For information on schedules and fares Tel (03) 5774000
www.israrail.org.il
There is no train service on the Sabbath, or on Jewish holidays.

Metro

Israel's only subway operates in Haifa and is called the Carmelit. This recently renovated system is in fact an underground cable car. It is also the quickest way of getting about Haifa. The train runs from Central Mount Carmel to downtown Haifa every 10 minutes and makes six stops. The trip takes 9 minutes. It operates Sun–Thur 6am–10pm, Fri 6am to 1 hour before the Sabbath, and Sat from sunset to midnight. See map at: www.urbanrail.net/as/hai/haifa.htm

Shared Taxis (Sherut)

The sherut is Israel's own indigenous mode of transportation, operating in and between main cities every day but Shabbat; some private companies or owners operate on Shabbat as well. Individuals share a mini-bus or cab, which can take up to 10 people at a fixed price, usually equivalent to the bus fare for the same route.
In Jerusalem sheruts between cities leave from near the central bus station, and, in from near Kikar Tsiyon (Zion Square) in the city centre. In Tel Aviv the sheruts leave from near the Central Bus Station for Jerusalem, Haifa and most other cities. Local sheruts follow the main bus routes, making similar stops in quicker time and charging the same fare. In all Israeli cities, taxi drivers will often follow bus routes charging a similar fare; but beware – they can become opportunistic about the price when faced with a tourist.

Taxis

Taxis offer a quick and convenient mode of travel in Israel. You can phone for a taxi in any major city, or hail one in the street.
All urban taxis have meters, whose operation is compulsory. If the driver wants to turn off the meter he may be trying to take you for a ride in more ways than one. Tipping is not compulsory, but is appreciated.
Prices are fixed between cities, and the driver will tell you your fare in advance, or show you the official price list if you ask for it.

Driving

Israelis drive on the right and with Mediterranean creativity. There is a lot of horn honking, overtaking on the inside and general improvisation, but life on the road is not as chaotic as in many other Mediterranean countries. With well over 2 million vehicles on the roads, Israel has one of the world's most densely populated road systems.
There are around 450 fatalities each year from road accidents, which is comparable with death rates on Western European roads. Drinking and driving offenses are relatively rare and weather conditions are good. All cars are legally bound to have air-conditioning.
Bringing your car into Israel is virtually impossible and is not recommended. It can be brought in by land from Jordan or Egypt but this is fraught with bureaucratic problems – not least from Israeli customs and excise officials.

Strict Law Enforcement

Laws are strictly enforced, and it is necessary to wear seat belts at all times (both front and back) and strap children under four into appropriate seats. Speed limits are 90–100 kph (55–60 mph) on highways and 50–70 kph (30–40 mph) in urban areas. Keep your passport, driver's license and other papers with you at all times. Police tend to be lenient with tourists but can take you straight in front of a judge if they wish. There are many speed traps on major highways with fines of up to $170 for exceeding the speed limit by more than 15 percent.
Talking on a cellular/mobile phone that is not in a hands-free installation is also an offense which police strictly enforce with a fine of $170. There are speed cameras on many highways and there are also cameras at many traffic light intersections prime to photograph cars crossing the lights one second after the lights have turned red.
Note: Israelis tend to move off very quickly at traffic lights the moment they turn green, making it especially dangerous to shoot a red light even before the one-second grace that the police give drivers before issuing a ticket.
Fuel: Most cars manufactured in the past decade (all vehicles are imported) take unleaded gasoline or diesel called benzine and solar in Hebrew respectively. Fuel is cheaper in Israel than in Western Europe but more expensive than in America. In Eilat, a VAT-free zone, you do not pay the usual 15.5 percent VAT charge (sales tax) on fuel.

Parking

Parking is very difficult in the major city centres and it is best to look for a parking lot. These can cost $2 an hour in Jerusalem, and up to $4 per hour in parts of Tel Aviv. If a curbside is marked in blue and white, you need a ticket, which you can purchase in batches of five from kiosks, lottery kiosks and stores. Each ticket costs about $1 and allows you to park for an hour. You must tear out the right time, month and day and display the ticket on the curbside window.
These tickets must be displayed from 7am to 6pm. Outside these hours, parking is usually free, though it is prohibited in some residential areas of Tel Aviv. In Jerusalem most blue and white curbsides have parking metres or nearby machines to dispense tickets.
If you fail to display a ticket, or the ticket has expired, you are liable for a $20 fine, though this need not be paid for several months.
Do not ignore red-and-white marked curbsides or No Parking signs. Here you may be clamped with a "Denver boot" or towed away. In either instance it will cost you $20 (or more) and a lot of wasted time in redeeming your car.

BELOW: tipping taxi drivers isn't compulsory but is appreciated.

Highway Six

Highway Six is Israel's first toll highway, running a length of 86 km (54 miles) from north to south parallel to the Mediterranean about 15–25 km (9–15 miles) inland. Extensions stretching further north and south are under construction. The highway is especially useful when traveling from Jerusalem to Haifa and the north because it misses out the heavily congested Tel Aviv region and during morning and evening rush hours can reduce what would otherwise be a three-hour trip between Jerusalem and points north by one hour.

The toll is collected electronically. The highway is being built on a BOT basis by a private consortium. The speed limit on the highway is 110 kph (70mph). Cameras photograph vehicles' number plates and send the bill by mail to the owners several months later. A one-way journey of about 70 km (44 miles) costs $5 and subscriptions are available.

Note: car-hire firms take an additional one-off handling fee of $11 for using Highway Six.

For more information: www.kvish6.co.il; Tel: 03-9081111. To report accidents or emergencies when actually on the highway, tel: 1-800-28-6666

Hiring a Car

Car-hire companies require drivers to be over 21 and to have held a full license for at least one year. Drivers must present an international driving license, or national license if written in English or French, plus a passport and international credit card.

Many of the world's principal car-hire companies have outlets here. Israel's largest car-hire company, Eldan, also has offices overseas. These companies can supply you with a car at the airport and allow you to leave it there on departure. They have a network of offices around the country.

Car hire is expensive (at least $300 a week for a small 1600cc saloon). Traffic is usually heavy, and parking is difficult in Israel's big cities. Hiring a car, though convenient, is not necessarily vital for the centre of the country, which has good bus, rail and taxi services.

However, hiring a car can be the best way of touring the Galilee or the Negev, and it can be cheaper off-season (Oct–Apr) or if you do a deal with one of the many local, smaller companies. But in general it is much cheaper to book a car as part of a package deal (flight, hotel, car) with a travel agent overseas.

As everywhere in the world,

carefully check that there is no damage to the car, that the spare wheel, jack and other equipment are in place, and that oil and water are sufficient before accepting a car.

Note that car hire companies will deduct parking and police fines from your credit card. They will also take the toll charge from Highway Six – about $5 for a one-way journey and an $11 handling fee. This latter charge is a one-off fee and will be deducted only once, however many times you use Highway 6.

Payments in foreign currency are exempt from VAT (16.5 percent) and rates usually include just theft insurance. Commercial vehicles cannot be hired with VAT exemption.

CAR-HIRE COMPANIES

(See Ben Gurion Airport section for details about car hire offices there.)

Hertz (www.hertz.co.il): 18 David ha-Melekh, Jerusalem.
Tel: (02) 6231351. Fax: (02) 6247248. E-Mail: hertzjerusalem@hertz.co.il
144 Ha-Yarkon, Tel Aviv.
Tel: (03) 5223332. Fax: 03-5230937.
Avis: (www.avis.co.il) 22 David ha-Melekh, Jerusalem.
Tel: (02) 6249001/2.
E-Mail celine@avis.co.il
113 Ha-Yarkon, Tel Aviv.
Tel: (03) 6884242.
Budget: (www.budget.co.il) 22 David ha-Melekh, Jerusalem
Tel: (02) 6248991. Fax: (02) 6259456. E-Mail: info@budget.co.il
Also at: 99 Ha-Yarkon, Tel Aviv
Tel: (03) 5245233. Fax: (03) 5245234
SIXT: (www.sixt.co.il) 14 David ha-Melekh, Jerusalem.

BELOW: car hire is costly in Israel.

Tel: (02) 6248204/5.
112 Ha-Yarkon, Tel Aviv.
Tel: (03) 5249764.
Central Reservatiuons 1-700-501-502
Best-Car: (www.best-car.co.il)
159 Yaffo, Jerusalem. Tel: (02) 5389226
3 Arlozorov Tel Aviv. Tel-(3) 5244122.
Eldan: (www.eldan.co.il) 24 David ha-Melekh, Jerusalem.
Tel: (02) 6252151. Fax: (02) 6252154.
114 Ha-Yarkon Tel Aviv. Tel: (03) 5271166. Fax: (03) 5271174.
Eldan USA: 1114 Quentin Road 2nd Floor, Brooklyn, New York 11229 USA. Toll Free: 1-800-938-5000.
Local: 1-718-998-5500.
Fax: 1-718-336-2216.
Eldan UK:
136B Burnt Oak Broadway, Edgware, Middlesex HA8 0BB.
Tel - 020 8 951 5727.
Fax - 020 8 951 5786.

Specialist Tours

So much history gets missed without an expert guide to explain the significance of each site, so it is well worth joining an organized tour. Major tour bus companies include:
Egged Tours.
Tel: 1700-70-75-77. www.egged.co.il
United Tours.
Tel: (02) 6252187 (03) 6162656.
www.inisrael.com
Diesenhaus Unitours/Galilee Tours.
Tel: (03) 5651313. Fax: (02) 6240579. www.diesenhaus.com

Pedestrians

Drivers cannot be relied upon to stop at pedestrian crossings. And pedestrians can't always be relied on not to wander casually into the road. The safest place to cross is at traffic lights. Beware at right-turn filters where the pedestrian light is green but traffic may still pass. In Jerusalem and other cities, police hand out fines to pedestrians who cross at red pedestrian lights.

Hitchhiking

This is a highly acceptable form of getting around, within and between cities. Hitchhiking stations, looking rather like bus stops complete with shelters, are provided at major junctions. But the competition can be fierce, with preference given to hiking soldiers. Women should beware of predatory males.

ACCOMMODATIONS

HOTELS, YOUTH HOSTELS, BED & BREAKFAST

CHOOSING A HOTEL

There is a wide choice of accommodations in Israel, from deluxe suites in high-class hotels through to budget hotels, bed and breakfasts and youth hostels. But there is a lack of charm about Israeli hotels, many of which were built in recent decades, offering modern comfort and convenience without much character. Unique Israeli forms of accommodations include kibbutz guesthouses (relatively expensive rural retreats) and Christian hospices (more luxurious than they sound, usually with a 19th-century European ambience, and not to be confused with hospitals for the terminally ill). Both these accommodations offer an unusual taste of Israel.

In the past decade bed and breakfasting has become increasingly popular in Israel, while the *zimmerim* (taken from the German) are widely popular in northern Israel. Ideally this is some sort of country lodge, chalet or log cabin, in a rural retreat, though often it is a less romantic prefabricated structure. Youth hostels range from hole in the wall downtown joints through to the facilities of the Israel Youth Hostel Association, which are usually well appointed, and of three-star hotel quality (with prices to match).

PRICE BANDS FOR ALL ACCOMMODATION CATEGORIES:

$	under $100
$$	$100–$160
$$$	above $160

These prices are for double rooms per night and usually include breakfast.

Kibbutz Guest Houses

Visitors wanting a truly Israeli experience should try a kibbutz guesthouse. They usually offer all the facilities of a luxury hotel plus the chance to get acquainted with kibbutz life at first hand. Though many of these guesthouses are in isolated rural areas, especially in the northern Galilee, others are located in the countryside but just 20 minutes or so by bus or car from Jerusalem or Tel Aviv. Many kibbutzim have opened country lodges (*zimmerim*). These are fairly inexpensive and guest can benefit from kibbutz facilities like swimming pools, sport and fitness amenities and good value meals in the dining hall.

For further information, contact
Kibbutz Hotels Chain
90 Ben Yehuda,
Tel Aviv 61031.
Tel: (03) 5608118.
www.kibbutz.co.il.
For kibbutz reservations in the US:
Israel Tourism Center
Tel.: 888-669-5700, 201-556-9669.
Fax: 201-556-9668.

Following is a list of recommended kibbutz guesthouses.
Ramat Rachel Hotel & Spa
Kibbutz Ramat Rachel, M.P. North Judea, Jerusalem 90900.
Tel: (02) 6702555.
Fax (02) 6733155. E-Mail:
info@ramatrachel.co.il
www.ramatrachel.co.il
Although within the city limits, the kibbutz grounds offer a stirring view of the Judean Desert. The kibbutz is adjacent to an unusual olive garden
$$$
Maaleh Hachamisha Kibbutz Hotel
Kibbutz Maaleh Hachamisha, Judean Hills (near Jerusalem).
Tel: (02)-5331331. (02) 5342144.
E-Mail: maale5@kibbutz.co.il
Hilltop retreat with excellent facilities on the airport and Tel Aviv side of Jerusalem.**$$$**
Kibbutz Tsuba Belmont Hotel
Kibbutz Tsuba (near Jerusalem).
Tel: (02) 5347090. Fax: (02) 5347091.

BELOW: springtime is an attractive time of year on a kibbutz.

Inexpensive apartments near Crusader fortress on a hilltop. **$$**

Shfayim Guesthouse,
Kibbutz Shfayim (near Tel Aviv/Herzliya).
Tel: (09) 9595595.
Fax: (09) 9595555.
E-Mail: shefayim@netvision.net.il
www.h-shefayim.co.il.
Close to the Mediterranean coast and a short bus ride away from Tel Aviv. **$$**

Nahsholim Kibbutz Hotel
Kibbutz Nahsholim, M.P. Hof Carmel 30815 (Haifa).
Tel: (04) 6399533. Fax: (04) 6397614.
E-Mail: nahsholim@kibbutz.co.il
www.nahsholim.co.il
Great location on the coast south of Haifa. **$$**

Nof Ginosar Hotel
Kibbutz Ginosar (near Tiberias).
Tel: (04) 6700300. Fax: (04) 6792170. E-Mail: ginosar@netvision.net.il
www.ginosar.co.il
On the shores of the Sea of Galilee close to the sacred Christian sites of Ein Tabgha and Capernaum. **$$**

Kfar Blum Guesthouse,
Kibbutz Kfar Blum (Upper Galilee).
Tel: (04) 6836611.
Fax: (04) 6836600.
E-Mail: pastoral@kbm.org.il
www.kfarblum-hotel.co.il
Idyllic location along the banks of the River Jordan in the Upper Galilee. The kibbutz hosts a classical music festival each August.**$$**

Moshav Keshet
Ramat Hagolan 12140
Tel: (04) 6962505 Fax: (04) 6961702 E-Mail:
keshetyo@netvision.net.il
Ideal base on the Golan Heights for Mount Hermon. **$**

Ein Gedi Guest House
Kibbutz Ein Gedi (Dead Sea)
M.P. Dead Sea 85525.
Tel: (08) 6594222. Fax: (08) 6584328. www.eingedi.co.il
Overlooking the remarkable Dead Sea and Judean desert, close to the spa and the kibbutz has a rare tropical garden. **$$**

Eilot Hotel
M.P. Eilot 88805.
Tel: (08) 6358816.
Fax: (08) 6358846.
Closest kibbutz to Eilat, several km north of the Red Sea resort. **$$**

Christian Hospices

Another fascinating Holy Land experience is the broad array of Christian hospices. Originally designed principally for pilgrims, and owned by churches, these hospices cater for all comers, including many Israeli Jews on vacation, who enjoy the old-world European charm of these establishments. Because these locations are often subsidized by the church that owns them, they offer excellent value.

The term hospice is misleading. Some, like Notre Dame in Jerusalem, owned by the Vatican, resemble luxury hotels. Others reflect the ethnic origins of their founders. The Sisters of Zion convent in the Jerusalem suburb of Ein Kerem is like a pension in Provence, while St Andrew's Church in Jerusalem could be a guest house in Scotland and even serves mince pies and mulled wine at Christmas. For a full list of hospices in Israel, contact the Ministry of Tourism, Pilgrimage Promotion Dept., POB 1018, Jerusalem.

IN JERUSALEM

Notre Dame
P.O.B. 20531, Jerusalem, opposite the New Gate.
Tel: (02) 6279111.
Fax: (02) 6271995.
Luxurious accommodations, splendid 19th-century architecture and one of Jerusalem's best (non-kosher) restaurants. Superbly appointed opposite the Old City walls. Owned by the Vatican which has extensively renovated the building. $$

YMCA,
26 David ha-Melekh, P.O.B. 294, Jerusalem 91002.
Tel: (02) 5692652.
Fax: (02) 6253438.
Stylish 1930s building opposite the King David Hotel. Recently refurbished and made more upscale. **$$**.

St Andrew's Scots Memorial Hospice
1 David Remez St. P.O.B. 8619, Jerusalem 91086 (opposite the old railway station).
Tel: (02) 6732401.
Fax: (02) 6731711.
Intimate guesthouse atmosphere in central location. No kippers, but there is sometimes haggis. $

Austrian Hospice
37 Via Dolorosa, P.O.B. 19600, Jerusalem 91194.
Tel: (02) 6274636.
Fax: (02) 6271472
Grand and ornate 19th-century building on the Via Dolorosa that served as a hospital for many years but was renovated in the late 1980s. $$

Our Sisters of Zion,
Ein Kerem.
Tel: (02) 6415738.
Fax: (02) 6437739.
Delightful Provençal-style pension in Ein Kerem. Spacious gardens filled with olive trees and grape vines and comfortable accommodations. $$

IN NAZARETH

Casa Nova Franciscan Hospice
Casa Nova St. P.O.B. 198, Nazareth
Tel: (04) 6456660
Fax: (04) 6579630
Opposite the Basilica of the Anunciation the Franciscan brothers lend the hospice an Italian atmosphere with Italian cuisine to go with it. $

St. Margaret's Anglican Hospice
Ofraneg St. P.O.B. 7, Nazareth 16100.
Tel: (04) 6573507.
Fax: (04) 6567166.
Up the hill from the Basilica with excellent views of the city and a less religious atmosphere than the Catholic hospices. $

In Tiberias

Sea of Galilee Hospice
P.O.B. 104, Safed Road, Tiberias 14101.
Tel: (04) 6723769.
Excellent base for the Christian sites around the Sea of Galilee. $

IN HAIFA

Carmelite Pilgrim Center "Stella Maris"
P.O.B 9047, Haifa 31090.
Tel: (04) 8332084.
Fax: (04) 8331593.
Located on the slopes of Mount Carmel with good views of the bay. $

BELOW: Nazareth (population 70,000) is the country's largest Israeli-Arab city.

HOTELS

Until the late 1990s, the Ministry of Tourism graded hotels from one to five stars according to size, service and facilities. This system has now been discontinued, making it more tricky to monitor the quality of a hotel.

Hotels require guests to check out by midday, but on Saturday and holidays guests can retain their rooms until the Sabbath or holiday finishes in the evening. Check-in is usually after 3pm.

Prices can be more expensive during the high season, which is Easter/Passover, July to August, Jewish New Year and Christmas. But there is a wide range of hotels catering for every pocket down to the cheapest youth hostels, which charge about $10–$15 a night. Hotel rates are generally quoted in dollars and include a 15 percent service charge. If you pay in foreign currency you are exempt from 16.5 percent VAT. Eilat is VAT-free.

Akko

Palm Beach,
Sea Shore, P.O.B. 2192 Akko 24101.
Tel: (04) 9877777.
Fax: (04)9910434.
E-Mail: palmbeach@netvision.net.il
The hotel has its own private beach and is a 20-minute walk from Akko's Old City. **$$**

Arad

Nof Arad
Rehov Moav, Arad.
Tel: (08) 9957056.
Fax (08) 9954053.
Great views of the desert and Masada from the western approach. **$$**

Ashkelon

Dan Gardens
56 Rehov Hatayasim, Ashkelon Beach Front.
Tel: (08) 6711261.
Fax: (08) 6710066.
www.danhotels.com
Excellent value in probably Israel's quietest Mediterranean resort. **$$**
Holiday Inn Crowne Plaza
9 Yekotiel Adam Street,
P.O. Box 944,
Ashkelon 78100.
Tel: (08) 6748888.
Fax: (08) 6718822.
www.afi-hotels.co.il
More luxurious but still off the beaten track. **$$$**
Samson's Gardens Hotel
38 Hatamar Street, Ashkelon,
78450.
Tel: (08) 6734666.
Fax: (08) 6739615.
E-Mail: shimsho@zahav.net.il
Good value near the beachfront. **$**

Be'er Sheva

Paradise Negev
4 Henrietta Szold, Be'er Sheva 84102.
Tel: (07) 6405444.
Fax: (07) 6405445.
www.fattal-hotels-israel.com
Unexceptional accommodations, but a convenient stop-over if you want to get to the Bedouin market early. **$$**

The Dead Sea

All hotels in the Dead Sea region offer medically supervised facilities. The sea's unique mineral content is beneficial for a range of ailments, including psoriasis, rheumatism and respiratory problems. Many European health services send patients to the Dead Sea for treatment.
Le Meridien Dead Sea Resort and Spa Hotel
Resort & Spa, Ein Bokek, Dead Sea.
Tel: (08) 6591234.
Fax: (08) 6591235.
www.fattal-hotels-israel.com
This large hotel, formerly the Hyatt Regency, offers therapeutic treatment based on the Dead Sea's minerals and has a range of recreational facilities. **$$$**
Hod Hotel
Ein Bokek, Dead Sea.
Tel: (08) 6688222.
Fax: (08) 6584606.
www.hodhotel.co.il

Cheap and comfortable and near the Dead Sea in the main hotel district. **S**
Magic Nirvana Hotel
Ein Bokek, Dead Sea.
Tel: (08) 6689444.
Fax: (08) 6689400.
www.nirvana.co.il
Set away from the main hotel district for those who prefer isolation in this most isolated of locations. **$$**
Tsell Harim
Ein Bokek, Dead Sea.
Tel: (08) 6688111.
Fax: (08) 6688100.
E-Mail: tsellhar@netvision.net.il
www.tsell-harim.co.il
Also cheap and comfortable, this hotel is located by the sea. **$**
Tulip Inn Dead Sea Fattal
Ein Bokek Dead Sea.
Tel: (08) 6684666.
www.fattal-hotels-israel.com
Very popular with English-speaking tourists and has its own Dead Sea spa alongside the regular swimming pool. **$$$**

Eilat

Isrotel King Solomon's Palace,
North Beach.
Tel: (08) 6363444.
Fax: (08) 6334189.
www.isrotel.co.il
Elegantly designed hotel overlooking the marina with an excellent choice of restaurants and consistently rated by guests as the city's best value hotel, though far from the most expensive. **$$**
Princess Hotel,
nr Taba border crossing, P.O.B. 2323 Eilat.
Tel: (08) 6365555.
Fax: (08) 6373590.
E-Mail: princess@isdn.net.il
Well away from the town and near the Egyptian border, this hotel is a self-contained complex of swimming pools and restaurants. **$$$**
Dan Eilat
North Beach, Eilat.
Tel: (08) 6362222.
Fax: (08) 6362333.
www.danhotels.com
The flagship hotel in the city of Israel's leading chain. Good service and

good value. **$$$**
Isrotel Lagoona
North Beach, Eilat.
Tel: (08) 6366666.
Fax: (08) 6366699.
www.isrotel.co.il
Tranquil location north of the city, on the lagoon, with a good view of the Red Sea. **$$**
Magic Sunrise Club Hotel
Tel: (08) 6305333.
Fax: (08) 6305350.
www.fattal-hotels-israel.com
Located slightly inland with a shuttle to the beach, the hotel has excellent sports club facilities. **$$**
Magic Palace
North Beach, Eilat.
Tel: (08) 6369999.
Fax: (08) 6369998.
www.fattal-hotels-israel.com
Built for a family holiday with small children; grown-ups without offspring should steer clear. **$$**
Red Rock,
POB 306, Eilat.
Tel: (08) 6373171.
Fax: (08) 6371705.
Great location by the beach and near the center of town. Comfortable but unexceptional. **$$**
Orchid Hotel
Coral Beach, Eilat.
Tel: (08) 6360360.
Fax: (08) 6375323.
E-Mail: orchid@netvision.net.il
Set on the hillside above Coral Beach south of the city, the hotel is comprised of separate cabins built like a Thai village. **$$**
Etzion
1 Sderot Hatamarim, Eilat.
Tel: (08) 6370003.
Fax: (08) 6370002.
www.hoteletzion.co.il
Far from the beach, but in the town and near the central bus station. **$**
Moon Valley
POB 1135, Eilat.
Tel: (08) 6366888.
Fax: (08) 6334110.
E-Mail: sarahmic@internet-zahav.net
Cheap, clean and comfortable. It's as well the hotel has its own swimming pool because it is a 10-minute walk from the beach. **$**
Red Sea Sports Club
Coral Beach.

Tel: (08) 6382222.
Fax: (08) 6382200.
www.redseasports.co.il
Compact and comfortable: this is the place to be if you enjoy diving. The hotel also offers courses for beginners. **$**

Haifa

Dan Carmel
85–87 Hanasi Boulevard, Haifa.
Tel: (04) 8306306.
Fax: (04) 8387504.
www.danhotels.com.
The city's most stylish hotel, located on Mount Carmel, with a breathtaking panorama of Haifa Bay and the azure-coloured Mediterranean. **$$$**

Le Meridien
10 David Elazar St., Haifa.
Tel: (04) 8508888.
Fax: (04) 8501160.
www.fattal-hotels-israel.co.il
Very large hotel located right on the beach at the southern entrance to the city near the railway station and bus station. **$$$**

Dan Panorama
107 Hanasi Boulevard, Haifa.
Tel: (04) 8352222.
Fax: (04) 8352235.
www.danhotels.com
Right on the summit of Central Carmel. The rooms looking west offer a breathtaking view of the bay. **$$**

Eden
8 Shmariyahu Levin St.
Tel: (04) 8664816.
Compact and convenient in the center of town. **$**

Carmel Forest
Carmel Forest, Haifa.
Tel: (04) 8307888.
Fax: (04) 8323988.
www.isrotel.co.il
Located out of the city in the Carmel forest. Ideal for nature lovers with a splendid view of the Mediterranean.

Herzliya

Dan Accadia
Derekh Hayam, Herzliya.
Tel: (09) 9597070.
Fax: (09) 9597090.
One of Israel's oldest and most elegant luxury hotels, this is the pick of the accommodations in this upscale resort to the north of Tel Aviv. **$$$**

The Daniel
Ramot Hayam St.
Tel: (09) 9528282.
Fax: (09) 9528280.
E-Mail: danirl-hotel@inisrael.com
On the seafront with no expense spared on the palatial decor. **$$$**

Sharon
5 Ramot Yam St., Herzliya 46748.
Tel: (09) 9525777.
Fax: (09) 9572448.
E-Mail: Sharon@sharon.co.il
www.sharon.co.il
Good location on the seafront and good value. **$$**

Eshel
3 Ramot Yam St., Herzliya 46748.
Tel: (09) 9568208.
Fax: (09) 9568797.
Small 36-room hotel on the seafront. **$**

Jerusalem

Addar
53 Nablus Road.
Tel: (02) 6263111.
Fax: (02) 6260791.
www.addar-hotel.com
A relatively new and comfortable Arab hotel in an old building opposite St.George's Cathedral. **$$**

American Colony
Nablus Road, Jerusalem.
Tel: (02) 6279777.
Fax: (02) 6279779.
www.americancolony.com
Jerusalem's oldest hotel has much character and charm and is favoured by the foreign press corps on account of its location between West and East Jerusalem. **$$$**

Caesar Hotel
208 Yafo, Jerusalem
Tel: (02) 5005656
Fax: (02) 5382802.
Modern and nondescript, but by the Central Bus Station, this hotel is ideal for itinerant tourists. **$**

Christmas
Ali Ibn Abi Taleb Street, East Jerusalem.
Tel: (02) 6282588.
Fax: (02) 6264417.
E-Mail: garo@netvision.net.il
Attractive small Arab hotel in the heart of East Jerusalem with a delightful garden. **$**

David's Citadel
7 David ha-Melekh.
Tel: (02) 6211111.
Fax: (02) 6211000.
www.tdchotel.com
Formerly the Hilton, this

attractively designed and well appointed hotel is near the Jaffa Gate and downtown Jerusalem. **$$$**

Holiday Inn Crowne Plaza
Givat Ram, Jerusalem.
Tel: (02) 6588888.
Fax: (02) 6514555.
www.afi-hotels.co.il
Landmark high-rise building at the entrance to the city, opposite the Central Bus Station, this hotel offers luxury accommodations for modest prices. **$$**

Holyland Hotel
Bayit va-Gan, Jerusalem.
Tel: (02) 6437777.
Fax: (02) 6437744.
E-Mail: holyland@isracom.co.il
Away from town near the Second Temple model, with a laid-back ambience and great view of West Jerusalem. **$$**

King David Hotel
23 David ha-Melekh, Jerusalem.
Tel: (02) 6208888.
Fax: (02) 6208882.
www.danhotels.com
Israel's premier hotel, where political leaders and the rich and famous stay. It has style and an old-world ambience, but in terms of quality of service its newer rivals try harder. Has beautiful gardens overlooking the Old City. **$$$**

Inbal
3 Jabotinski, Jerusalem.
Tel: (02) 6756666.
Fax: (02) 6756777.
www.inbal-hotel.co.il
Formerly the Laromme, overlooking the Liberty Bell Garden, this delightfully designed hotel has attracted some world leaders away from the King David. **$$$**

Itzik Hotel
141 Yafo.
Tel: (02) 6243879.
Fax: (02) 6243879.
E-Mail: hotel_iz@netvision.net.il
Comfortable and clean, 20 rooms with B&B atmosphere, with interesting location in the heart of the Makhane Yehuda fruit and vegetable market. **$**

Jerusalem Pearl
POB 793, Jerusalem.
Tel: (02) 6226666.
Fax: (02) 6226649.

www.danhotels.com
Superbly located opposite the Old City walls near the Jaffa Gate. **$$$**

Mount Zion
17 Hebron Road, Jerusalem.
Tel: (02) 5689555.
Fax: (02) 6731425.
www.mountzion.co.il
Originally an ophthalmology hospital, built over a century ago, this building was converted into a luxury hotel overlooking the Old City walls in the 1980s. **$$**

Olive Tree Hotel
23 St. George St., Jerusalem.
Tel: (02) 5410410.
Fax: (02) 5410411.
www.royal-plaza.co.il
One of the city's newest hotels is between the Damascus Gate and Mea Shearim. **$$**

Palatin Hotel
4 Agrippas St., Jerusalem.
Tel: (02) 6231141.
Fax: (02) 6259323.
E-Mail: palatinj@netvision.net.il
A clean and comfortable hotel, with a central location in West Jerusalem. **$**

Prima Palace
6 Pines St.
Tel: (02) 53841111.
Fax: (02) 5381480.
www.prima.co.il
Colourful ultra-orthodox in the heart of West Jerusalem. **$$**

Prima Royale
3 Mendele St., Jerusalem.
Tel: (02) 5663111.
Fax: (02) 5610964.
Comfortable and convenient, opposite the Dan Panorama but smaller and less expensive, and well located for walks into both the New and Old Cities. **$$**

Regency
32 Lekhi, Mount Scopus, Jerusalem.
Tel: (02) 5331234.
Fax: (02) 5815947.
Stylish interior, Commands

a splendid view of the Old City. **$$**

Reich Hotel
1 Hagai St. Beit ha-Kerem, Jerusalem.
Tel: (02) 6523121.
Fax: (02) 6523120.
E-Mail: reichhtl@zahav.net.il
Located in the leafy suburbs of Beit ha-Kerem, the hotel is not far from the city and the Bus Station. **$$**

Renaissance
6 Wolfson Street, Jerusalem.
Tel (02) 6599999.
Fax: (02) 6511824.
E-Mail: renjhot@netvision.net.il
Large and luxurious near the western entrance to the city, this is Jerusalem's largest hotel with the biggest banqueting facilities. **$$$**

Seven Arches
Mount of Olives.
Tel: (02) 6267777.
Fax: (02) 6271319.
E-Mail: svnarch@trendline.co.il
Built on a desecrated Jewish graveyard, making it unkosher for religious Jews, but offers classic view of the Old City. **$$**

Metula
Arazim
Tel: (04) 6997143.
Fax: (04) 6997666.
Charming Swiss-style village high in the mountains on the Lebanese border. **$**

Nazareth
Mary's Well
Paulus IV Road, Mary's Well Square.
Tel: (04) 6500000.
Fax: (04) 65000055.
www.rimonim.com
Large hotel in the city. **$$**

Renaissance
P.O.B. 44011 Nazareth 1600.
Tel: (04) 6028600.
Fax: (04) 6028666.
www.renaissancehotel.co.il
Large hotel on the edge of the city. **$$**

Nahariya
Sol Marine
Ha'alyah St., Nahariya.
Tel: (04) 9950555.
Fax: (04) 9950556.
Pleasing hotel near the seafront in Israel's northernmost Mediterranean beach resort. **$$**

Netanya
The Seasons
Nice Boulevard.
Tel: (09) 8601555.
Fax: (09) 8623022.
www.seasons.co.il
On the cliffs overlooking the sea the city's smartest hotel. **$$$**

King Solomon
18 Hma'apilim, Netanya.
Tel: (09) 8338444.
Fax: (09) 8611397.
Pick of the budget-price hotels in Netanya. Near the beach and center of town. **$$**

Grand Yahalom Hotel
15 Gad Machness, Netanya.
Tel: (09) 8624888.
Fax: (09) 8624890.
Located in Netanya's hotel district opposite the sea; makes a pleasant base for touring the country. **$**

Safed
Ruth Rimon Inn
Artists' Quarter, Safed.
Tel: (04) 69994666.
Fax: (04) 6920456.
www.rimonim.com
The best hotel in the city, with relaxing hillside views. **$$$**

Ron
Hativat Yiftah St., Safed.
Tel: (04) 6972590.
Fax: (04) 6972363.
Small hotel in the heart of the old town. **$**

Tel Aviv
Carlton
10 Eli'Ezer Peri Street.
Tel Aviv 63573.
Tel: (03) 5201818.
Fax: (03) 5271043.
www.carlton.co.il
Overlooking the marina, the hotel offers excellent views of the Mediterranean. **$$$**

Dan Tel Aviv
99 Ha-Yarkon, Tel Aviv 63432.
Tel: 03-5202525.
Fax: 03-5480111.
www.danhotels.com
The city's veteran luxury hotel offers excellent sea views and is renowned for comfort, style and convenience. **$$$**

Dan Panorama
10 Kaufmann, Charles Clore Park, Tel Aviv.
Tel: 03-5190190.
Fax: 03-5171777.
www.danhotels.com
Away from the main hotel

district, the Dan Panorama is conveniently close to Yafo and offers good value for a luxury hotel. **$$$**

David Intercontinental
12 Kaufman Street, Tel Aviv.
Tel: (03) 7951111.
Fax: (03) 7951112.
www.interconti.com
Adjacent to the Dan Panorama near Old Jaffa, this is the city's largest hotel and is often favored by the business community due to its proximity to the financial district. **$$$**

Sheraton City Tower
14 Zisman Street, Ramat Gan.
Tel: (03) 7544444.
Fax: (03) 7544445.
www.sheraton.co.il
Technically this hotel is in Ramat Gan and not Tel Aviv and is ideal for the Diamond Exchange and central railway station, though far from the beach. **$$$**

Tel Aviv Hilton
Independence Gardens, Tel Aviv.
Tel: (03) 5202222.
Fax: (03) 5224111.
www.travelweb.com
Generally accepted as the city's most luxurious hotel. Very fashionable with Tel Aviv high society, with prices to match. **$$$**

Tel Aviv Sheraton
115 Ha-Yarkon, Tel Aviv 63573.
Tel: (03) 5211111.
Fax: (03) 5233322.
www.sheraton-telaviv.com
Challenges the Hilton's claim to be the city's paramount hotel. **$$$**

Adiv Hotel
5 Mendele, Tel Aviv.
Tel: (03) 5229141.
Fax: (03) 5229144.
www.adivhotel.com
Friendly, comfortable and convenient with self-service restaurant. Situated just over the road from the seafront and beach. **$$**

Howard Johnson Express Shalom
216 Ha-Yarkon, Tel Aviv 62405.
Tel: (03) 5243277.
Fax: (03) 5235895.
www.hojo.com
Well located for Tel Aviv Port and the beach. **$$**

Imperial Hotel
66 Ha-Yarkon, Tel Aviv.
Tel: (03) 5177002.
Fax: (03) 5178314.

www.imperial.co.il
In the heart of the city's hotel district, this comfortable hotel is well located for the beach and walks to the Dizengoff shopping and nightlife district. **$$**

Metropolitan
11/15 Trumpeldor St. Tel Aviv.
Tel: (03) 5192727.
Fax: (03) 5172626.
www.hotelmetropolitan.co.il
Well located for the beach and center of town, this hotel is comfortable and convenient but otherwise ordinary. **$$**

City
9 Mapu St., Tel Aviv.
Tel: (03) 5246253.
Fax: (03) 5425555.
www.atlashotels.co.il
Near the beach and center of town, this clean and comfortable hotel puts a roof over your head. **$**

Deborah Hotel
87 Ben Yehuda, Tel Aviv.
Tel: (03) 5278282 (03) 5278304.
www.atlashotels.co.il.
Pleasant hotel and location in the northern part of the city though it's a 5-minute walk from the beach. **$**

Tiberias
Holiday Inn Tiberias
Habanim St. Tiberias.
Tel: (04) 6728555.
Fax: (04) 6724443.
www.afi-hotels.co.il
Great view of the Sea of Galilee. **$$$**

Sheraton Moriah
1 Eliezer Kaplan, Tiberias.
Tel: (04)6792233.
Fax: (04) 6792320.
E-Mail: avr0004@ibm.net
On the lakeside in Tiberias, this is one of the city's oldest and most stylish hotels. **$$**

Aviv
66 Hagalil, Tiberias.
Tel: (04) 6712272.
Fax: (04) 6712275.
Conveniently located next to the old city of Tiberias. **$**

Bed & Breakfast
With the exception of the Galilee, there is a very limited amount of B&B accommodation in Israel, partly because Israelis live in relatively small

apartments, so rarely have rooms to offer.

Good Morning Jerusalem.
9 Coresh Street, Jerusalem 94144
Tel: (02) 6233459
Fax: (02) 6259330
E-mail: gmjer@netvision.net.il
Located in downtown West Jerusalem opposite the bus station, gives information on many available B&Bs in the city and throughout Israel. Overnight prices are no more than $60 per couple.

Country Lodges (Zimmerim)

Located mainly in the rural north, Galilee and Golan, these include:
Noga Country Lodging
Maale Gamla, Golan Heights.
Tel: (04) 6732430.
Fax: (04) 6732430.
Great view of the Sea of Galilee. $
Beit Alfa
MP Gilboa.
Tel: (04) 6533026.
Fax: (04) 6533882.
E-mail: bb-ba@betalfa.org.il
In the Lower Galilee opposite the Gilboa Mountains. $

Vacation Apartments

For a longer stay in one place, it can be very economical to rent an apartment, with its own kitchen etc. For families it can mean a cheap way of accommodating the children; for couples, individuals or groups, it can be a more natural experience of the country, living as the locals do. As with vacation accommodations, options range from the economical to the luxurious. A few recommended places are:
Rivka's Holiday Apartments
52 Azza St, Jerusalem.
Tel & Fax: (02) 6436211.
Sea Tower Apartment Hotel
1 Trumpledor St., Tel Aviv 63433.
Tel: (03) 7953434.
Fax: (03) 5172613.
The Home Apartment Hotel
106 Ha-Yarkon, Tel Aviv.
Tel: (03) 5222695.

Fax: (03) 5240815.
E-Mail: thehome@internet-zahav.net

Campgrounds

Israel is a good place for camping, with campsites providing excellent touring bases for each region. They offer full sanitary facilities, electric current, a restaurant and/or store, telephone, first-aid facilities, shaded picnic and campfire areas, and day and night watchmen. They can be reached by bus, but all are open to cars and caravans. Most have tents and cabins, as well as a wide range of equipment for hire. All sites have swimming facilities on the site or within easy reach.

There is a reception and departure service for campers at Ben Gurion International Airport. If you telephone (03) 9604524 on arrival, a camping car will come within a very short time to take participants to the reception camping site at **Mishmar Hashiva**, about 10 km (6 miles) from the airport. A similar service is available from Mishmar Hashiva to the airport upon departure, if you stay the last night there.

On arrival in Israel, campers can obtain assistance from the Tourist Information Office in the Arrivals Hall of the airport. At the reception camp at Mishmar Hashiva, campers are given maps and folders and are individually advised on touring the country.
Reception Site: Mishmar Hashiva, tel: (03) 9604524. Fax (03) 9604712
E-mail: israelcc@hotmail.com

Camping Sites

Beit Zait (near Jerusalem).
Tel: (02) 5346217.
Ein Gedi (by Dead Sea).
Tel: (08) 6584342.
Eilot (near Eilat).
Tel (08) 6374362.
Neve Yam (near Haifa).
Tel: (04) 8844827.
Kibbutz Ma'ayan Baruch (Upper Galilee).
Tel: (04) 6954601.

Youth Hostels

There are 25 youth hostels throughout the country, operated by the Israel Youth Hostel Association (IYHA), which is affiliated to the international YHA. They offer dormitory accommodations or private double rooms, and most of them provide meals and self-service kitchen facilities. There is no age limit. Some hostels also provide family accommodations. Individual reservations should be made directly with the hostel.
SOME USEFUL ADDRESSES:
Head Office–IYHA
P.O.B. 6001, Jerusalem 91060.
Tel: (02) 6558400.
Fax: (02) 6558432.
E-Mail: iyha@iyha.org.il
Website: www.youth-hostels.org.il
Agron, Jerusalem
2 Agron, 94266 Jerusalem.
Tel: (02) 6258286.
Fax: (02) 6221124.
E-Mail: agron@iyha.org.il
Bayit Va Gan, Jerusalem
8 Hapisga St. Bayit VeGan, Jerusalem.
Tel: (02) 6423366.
Fax: (02) 6423362.
E-Mail: betbg@zahav.net.il
Jewish Quarter, Jerusalem
2 Ararat St. P.O.B. 7880 Jewish Quarter, Jerusalem.
Tel: (02) 6288611.
Fax: (02) 6262036.
E-Mail: iyhtb@iyha.org.il
Ein Kerem, Jerusalem
P.O.B. 16091, Jerusalem 91170.
Tel: (02) 6416282.
E-Mail: iyhbt@iyha.org.il
Yitzhak Rabin, Jerusalem
1 Nachman Avigad St. (near Israel Museum) P.O.B. 39100, Jerusalem 91390.
Tel: (02) 6490141.
Fax: (02) 6796566.
E-Mail: rabin@iyha.org.il
Ein Gedi, Dead Sea
D.N. Dead Sea 86980.
Tel: (08) 6584165.
Fax: (08) 6584445.
E-Mail: eingedi@iyha.og.il
Beit Yatziv, Be'er Sheva
79 Hatzmaut St., POB 7, Be'er Sheva.
Tel: (08) 6227444.
Fax: (08) 6275735.
E-Mail: beit_yatziv@silverbyte.com
Carmel, Haifa
18 Rehov Tzvia Veitzhak, Haifa.
Tel: (04) 8531944.

Fax: (04) 8532516.
E-Mail: haifa@iyha.org.il
Eilat
P.O.B. 152, Eilat 88101.
Tel: (08) 6370088.
Fax: (08) 6375835.
E-Mail: eilat@iyha.org.il
Meyouchas, Tiberias
2 Jordan St., P.O.B. 81, Tiberias 14100.
Tel: (04) 6721775.
Fax: (04) 6723072.
E-Mail: tiberias@iyha.org.il
Poriah, nr. Tiberias
P.O.B. 232, Tiberias 14101.
Tel: (04) 6750050.
Fax: 6751628.
E-Mail: poria@iyha.org.il
Tel Aviv
36 Bnei Dan, P.O.B. 22078 Tel Aviv 62260.
Tel: (03) 5441748.
Fax: (03) 5441030.
E-Mail: telaviv@iyha.org.il
Tel Hai
P.O. Box 9001 MP Upper Galilee 12100, Tel Hai.
Tel: (04) 6940043.
Fax: (04) 6941743.
E-Mail: telhai@iyha.org.il
Masada
MP Dead Sea, Masada 86901.
Tel: (08) 9953222.
Fax: (08) 6584650.
E-Mail: masada2@iyha.org.il
Karei Deshe, Sea of Galilee
MP Korazim 12365, Kare Deshe.
Tel: (04) 6720601.
Fax: (08) 6724818.
E-Mail: kdeshe@iyha.org.il

Other private youth hostels:
Gesher
10 Hamelekh David, Jerusalem.
Tel: (02) 6241015.
Fax: (02) 6255226.
www.gesher.co.il
St. George
Nablus Road, Jerusalem.
Tel: (02) 6282573.
The No. 1 Hostel,
84 Ben Yehuda St. 4th Floor, Tel Aviv.
Tel: (03) 5237807.
Fax: (03) 5237419.
Gordon Hostel
2 Gordon St cnr. Ha Yarkon, Tel Aviv.
Tel: (03) 5238239.
Fax (03) 5237419.

PRICE CATEGORIES

These prices are for double rooms per night and usually include breakfast.

$	under $100
$$	$100–160
$$$	above $160

E ATING OUT

RECOMMENDED RESTAURANTS, CAFES & BARS

WHAT TO EAT

Eating is a national pastime in Israel, one engaged in as much and as often as possible. On the street, at the beach, in every public place and in every home, day and night – you'll find Israelis tucking in to food.

The biblical residents of the Land of Canaan were nourished by the fertility and abundance of a land "flowing with milk and honey." But the milk was mainly from sheep and goats, and the honey from dates, figs and carobs. Much depended on the sun, the rains and the seasons. Food was simple; feast predictably followed famine. Times have changed – at least in the culinary sense.

Just as Israel is a blend of cultures from all over the world, so its cuisine is a weave of flavors and textures, contrasts and similarities. There is no definitive Israeli fare, just as there is no definitive Israeli. Rather, there is a rare merging of East and West, and the results are a profusion of culinary delights.

The predominant food style reflects the country's geographical location – somewhere between the Middle East and the Mediterranean.

When dining out, don't be led astray by signs telling you that the establishment serves "oriental" food. "Oriental" refers to the Middle East, rather than the Far East. "Oriental" Jews are those of Sephardic (Spanish, Italian or Arab) heritage. Each Jewish ethnic group, whether Moroccan, Libyan, Tunisian, Yemenite, Iraqi or native born (sabra) Israeli, has its own special dish and its own holiday fare.

Their foods are similar yet quite distinct from each other. Basic herbs and spices include cumin, fresh and dried coriander, mint, garlic, onion, turmeric, black pepper, and sometimes cardamom and fresh green chilli. Dark, fruity olive oil adds further fragrance.

Arabic food is considered "oriental", and both Arabic and Jewish meals begin the same way – with a variety of savory salads. *Hummus* – ground chickpea seasoned with *tahina* (sesame paste), lemon juice, garlic and cumin – is probably the most popular dip, spread and salad rolled into one. You'll also find the most astounding variety of aubergine salads you've ever seen; aubergine in *tahina*, fried sliced aubergine, chopped aubergine with vegetables, chopped liver-flavoured aubergine, and more. Assorted pickled vegetables are considered salads as well.

While the waiters may show some signs of disappointment, you can order a selection of these salads as a meal in themselves. Or you can follow them with kebab (grilled ground spiced meat), *shishlik* (grilled sliced lamb or beef with lamb fat), *seniya* (beef or lamb in *tahina* sauce), stuffed chicken or pigeon, chops or fish.

Don't expect pork in either a kosher or a traditional Muslim restaurant; both religions prohibit its consumption. Seafood, while forbidden by Jewish law and permissible by Muslim, is widely available. Shrimps and calamari are the predominant varieties.

Do try the fish, particularly in the seaside areas of Tiberias, Tel Aviv, Yafo and Eilat (there are no fish in the Dead Sea). Trout, gray and red mullet, sea bass and the famous St Peter's fish are generally served fried or grilled, sometimes accompanied by a piquant sauce. Authentic North African restaurants will also feature *harimeh* – hot and spicy cooked fish fragrant with an appetizing blend of tomatoes, cumin and hot pepper. And if you still have room, there's dessert. In Arabic restaurants this may mean *baklawa* (filo pastry sprinkled with nuts and sweet syrup) or other rich sweets, or fruit. In typical Jewish oriental restaurants it could mean caramel crème custard, chocolate mousse or an egg-white confection laced with chocolate syrup and called (for some unknown reason) Bavarian cream. Turkish coffee or tea with fresh mint ends the meal. If you do not want sugar in your coffee, tell the waiter in advance or your coffee will be liberally sweetened.

Snacks

Since Israelis are major-league eaters, snacks play a starring role in the day. Favorites include bagel-shaped sesame-sprinkled breads (served with *za'atar* – an oregano-based spice mixture available only in "ethnic" settings like the Old City of Jerusalem), nuts and sunflower seeds. Pizza, blintzes, waffles and burgers all come in and out of vogue.

But the ultimate sabra snack has to be *felafel* (fried chickpea balls served in pita bread with a variety of vegetables). Along the pavements of major streets you can usually find several adjoining *felafel* stands where you're free to stuff your pita with salads for as long as the bread holds out.

Tel Aviv's Betsal'el Souk is probably the most famous of the *felafel* centres. Located near the Carmel market, it features an entire street of *felafel* vendors, with the largest salad selection this side of the Mediterranean.

Fruit and Vegetables

A trip to the open-air Makhane Yehuda in Jerusalem or the Carmel market in Tel Aviv will reveal a sumptuous array of fruit and vegetables: everything from apples to artichokes, kohlrabi to celeriac. Sub-tropical fruits include kiwi, mango, persimmon, loquat, passion fruit, chirimoya and papaya. Fresh dates, figs, pomegranates and the world's largest strawberries are among the seasonal treats. In fact, near the Carmel Market in Tel Aviv, in Kerem Hatamanim and Jerusalem's Agrippas Street by the Makhane Yehuda market can be found the best selection of restaurants.

Meat & Poultry

If you like fowl and game, you will find chicken and turkey and, in more upscale restaurants, goose and mullard duck (an Israeli hybrid) excellent choices. While much beef is imported, all fowl is domestically raised.

Dairy Products

In biblical times water was scarce and unpalatable, so milk became a major component of the diet. Goat's milk was the richest and most nourishing; next came that of sheep, then cows and finally camels. Today's Israel continues the "land of milk and honey" tradition with a wealth of familiar cheeses (Camembert, Brie and Gouda), cottage cheese, and a wide variety of goat and sheep yogurt.

Breads

Pita bread with its pocket for tucking in meat, chips, *falafel* and anything edible would have brought a smile to the face of Lord Sandwich. Many restaurants will also offer *lafa,* a flat

bread from Iraq made into a sandwich by wrapping around whatever contents come to hand. In Yemeni restaurants several types of bread are served: *mallawah* (crispy fried, fattening and delicious), *lahuh* (light and like a pancake) and *jahnoon* (slow-baked strudel-like dough).

Eating Kosher

The laws of *kashrut* are extremely complex, but in practical terms they mean that many animals, most notably the pig, cannot be eaten at all. Furthermore, kosher animals such as the cow and chicken must be killed in a specific way (by having their throats cut), otherwise the meat is not considered kosher.

The blood must also be drained out of kosher meat, often making a steak, for example, somewhat desiccated and lacking in flavor. In addition, while most fish are permissible, all seafood (prawns, lobsters, octopus, etc.) is considered unclean. Finally, meat and milk cannot be consumed together at the same meal.

This said, many secular Jews disregard dietary laws, and most restaurants in Israel, especially those outside Jerusalem, are not kosher.

Outside of hotels, all kosher restaurants are closed on the Jewish Festivals and the Sabbath from sunset on Friday through to sunset on Saturday.

Drinking Notes

Soft Drinks

All the usual carbonated drinks such as colas are available. As in Britain, "soda" refers to soda water and not a flavored carbonated drink as it does in the United States. Diet and regular soft drinks are available. The most delicious and healthiest drinks to try are the wide range of fruit

juices. For a few dollars, street vendors will squeeze you an orange, carrot, grapefruit, kiwi or a dozen other fruits.

Tea & Coffee

Tea connoisseurs will be out of luck. Most Israeli establishments dip a feeble tea-bag into hot water. But they take their coffee seriously. Most popular are Middle Eastern coffee (*botz*), Bedouin coffee (*botz* with *hell* – a spice known as cardamom in English), Turkish coffee, Viennese coffee (*café hafuch*) and filter coffee. Instant coffee Western-style is known as *Nes*. Cafés and *espresso* bars, like their counterparts in Europe, have increasingly become the center of both social and business life.

Short and Strong

Turkish and Middle Eastern coffee can be very small and very strong. If you are thirsty, and not just in need of a caffeine-shot, order a glass of iced water with it. Remember to tell the waiter when you order if you don't want your coffee sugared.

Alcohol

Israel has a wide selection of wines. Over the past decade there has been a proliferation of quality wines from dozens of wineries big and small, many of them reasonably priced. There are several local beers, both bottled and draught, and a range of imported beers – but real-ale specialists will probably turn up their noses. There are both home-distilled and imported spirits and liquors. The local speciality is *arak*, very similar to Greece's *ouzo*.

Although Israel has none of the alcoholic inhibitions of its Islamic neighbors, most Israelis consume relatively small amounts of alcohol compared with Europeans and Americans. Excessive drinking, or even smelling of alcohol, is viewed with suspicion by society at large. A person who drinks, say, three pints of beer a day is quite likely to be branded an alcoholic.

There are plenty of bars and pubs, and all restaurants and cafés serve alcohol. Israelis will often go to a pub and spend the entire night nursing just one or two drinks. By the same token it is acceptable to sit at streetside cafés chatting for hours over just a coffee and cake.

Prices for Eating Out

Prices in restaurants are given in shekels:

$	under NIS 80 a person.
$$	NIS 80–250
$$$	more than NIS 250

BELOW: Israel's climate encourages outdoor eating during much of the year.

EILAT

RESTAURANTS

La Brasserie,
King Solomon's Palace Hotel.
Tel: (08) 6366444.
French-style brasserie, which offers excellent kosher French cuisine. Kosher. Open daily noon–midnight. **$$$**

Tandoori
King's Wharf (by the Laguna Hotel)
Tel: (08) 6333666
Excellent Indian restaurant, part of an Israeli chain set up by an Indian Jewish family, though don't expect curry and chips. Open daily noon–midnight **$$$**

The Last Refuge,
Coral Beach.
Tel: (08) 6373627.
South of the city by Coral Beach this restaurant has an excellent choice of fish and seafood. Open daily noon to midnight. **$$**

Denise Kingdom
Fish Hatchery, Laguna

Tel: (08)6379898
This kosher restaurant specializes in the denise fish and sea bass raised by kibbutz Eilot mainly for export to France. Adjacent to the restaurant is a fish farm and visitors center, which explains about the fish. Diners know that they are getting fresh fish straight from the farm and the salads are excellent too. The restaurant is open Sun–Thur noon–11pm–Fri, closes before sunset and reopens Saturday night **$$**

Eddie's Hideaway
68 Almogim St.:
Tel: (08) 6371137.
Perhaps the best restaurant in the city. Because of its out of the way location the restaurant will take your taxi fare from the hotel off your bill on presentation of a receipt. Eddie specializes in a range of creative meat and fish dishes Open daily

6pm–midnight **$$**

La Barracuda
Commercial Centre, Eilat.
Tel: (07) 6376222.
The place to come if you want to know what those peculiar-looking Red Sea fish really taste like. Open daily 11am–11pm. **$$**

Lotus Restaurant
by the Caesar Hotel, Eilat.
Tel: (07) 6376389.
The city's oldest Chinese restaurant, which combines Szechwan spicy cuisine with Cantonese sweet food. Open daily noon–midnight. **$$**

Shipudei Eilat
10 Ha'Oman St. Industrial Zone
Tel: (08) 6332343
The industrial zone, albeit with a different ambience to the rest of the Red Sea resort offers a choice of good-value kosher meat eateries including Shipudei Eilat. This is one of the few non-hotel kosher restaurants. Open Sun–Thur noon–11am Fri. **$**

CAFES

Milan Café
Red Shopping Mall, Eilat.
Tel: (08) 6374487.
Serves light dairy meals in a pleasant atmosphere.

Siesta
Dan Eilat
Tel: (08) 6362222
This café in a hotel offers a delightful selection of cakes and sandwiches – open daily 11am–midnight.

BARS & PUBS

The Three Monkeys
Promenade by the Royal Beach Hotel
Tel: (08) 6368888
The city's most popular English style pub – open daily 9pm–3am. Most of the large hotels in the resort also have pubs and bars.

HAIFA

RESTAURANTS

Douzan
35 Ben Gurion Street
Tel: (04) 8525444.
An unusual fusion of oriental and western food in an estern ambience. The restaurant's diverse cuisine echoes the relative ethnic tolerance of the city. Open daily 11pm–midnight. **$$**

Nof Chinese Restaurant
Nof Hotel, 101 Hanassi Boulevard, Haifa.
Tel: (04) 8354311.
The taste buds are stimulated by an amazing view of Haifa Bay. Open daily noon–12pm. **$$**

La Terrazza
46 Moriah Boulevard.
Tel: (04) 8101100.
Good value Italian and Mediterranean cusine with

a great view from the terrace. Open Sun–Thurs noon–midnight, Fri–Sat 8pm–1am. **$$**

Shawarma Ahim Sabah
37 Allenby
Tel: (04) 8552188.
Located in midtown Hadar, specialises in meat cut from the spit and eaten in pitta with a wide range of salads and relishes. Open daily 11am–12pm. **$**

BELOW: freshly made bagels.

CAFES

Yonk Ice Cream Café
23 Kibbutz Gluyot
Tel: (04) 8667929.
A long-established Haifa establishment that has managed to maintain its popularity. It offers excellent ice cream and coffee and also serves full

meals. Open Sun–Thur 11.30am–10pm, Fri 11.30am–5pm.

Eva's
51 Ha'atzmaut
Tel (04) 8663113
Located near the port Eva reputedly serves the best coffee in Haifa. Open Sun–Thur 7am–5pm, Fri 7am–1.30pm.

BARS AND PUBS

Bear Pub
135 Ha-Nassi Blvd.
Tel: (04) 8386563.
Located on the Central Carmel in one of the centers of the city's night life. Open Sun–Fri 11am–4am, Sat 6pm–4am.

TRANSPORT · ACCOMMODATION · EATING OUT · ACTIVITIES · A–Z · LANGUAGE

JERUSALEM

RESTAURANTS

Arabesque/American Colony Hotel
Nablus Road, Jerusalem.
Tel: (02) 6279777.
A la carte menu and a beautiful courtyard in which to dine. Open daily 6.30am–12pm. **$$$**

Arcadia
10 Agripas (in the alleyway).
French cuisine with Middle Eastern improvisations. Open daily 12.30pm–3pm 7pm–10.30pm. Best to make reservations. **$$$**

Darna
3 Horkenos Street.
Tel: (02) 6245406.
North African food and Moroccan atmosphere including authentic implements and ceremonial service. Kosher. Open Sun–Thur 7pm–11pm, Sat after sunset. **$$$**

La Regence
23 Ha Melekh David, King David Hotel.
Tel: (02) 6208888.
Considered the city's finest kosher restaurant. Nouvelle cuisine and traditional French cooking. Open Sun–Thur 7pm–10pm and Saturday after sunset. **$$$**

Kohinor
Holiday Inn Crowne Plaza, Givat Ram, Jerusalem.
Tel: (02) 6588888.
The only kosher restaurant in this chain of Indian restaurants serving delicious foods, including a choice of meat and vegetarian dishes. Open Sun–Thur noon–12pm Fri lunch and Sat night. **$$$**

Cardo Culinarium
The Cardo, Jewish Quarter, Old City.
Tel: (02) 6264155.
You've got to be in the mood for a laugh. Diners are compelled to wear togas and laurel wreaths. The restaurant was actually built in Roman times. Open Sun–Thur noon–3.30pm, 6.30pm–11pm. **$$**

Eucalyptus
4 Safra Square.
Tel: (02) 6244331.
Offers an unusual choice of local foods. Try the sorrel soup. Open Sun–Thur noon–10.30pm. **$$**

Notre Dame
8 Shivtei Yisra'el Street.
Tel: (02) 6288018.
Situated in the magnificent Notre Dame hospice complex, this is one of the city's finest restaurants but offers good value fare. Open daily 7pm–11pm. **$$**

Al Dente
50 Ussishkin St, Jerusalem.
Tel: (02) 6251479.
Small neighborhood restaurant in Rehavia offers its own unique Italian cuisine at modest prices. Kosher non-meat menu. Sun–Thur noon–11pm, Fri 11am–4pm, Sat 8–12pm. **$**

Taverna
2 Naomi St. Abu Tor.
Tel: (02) 6719796.
Located by the Abu Tor promenade, the Taverna commands great views of Jerusalem and the Judean desert. Interesting selection of cheeses and salads. Open Sun–Thur noon–11pm, Sat after sunset.

Philadelphia
9 E-Zahra, East Jerusalem.
Tel: (02) 6289770.
The city's most famous restaurant for Middle East cuisine. Excellent choice of *hors d'oeuvres* salads. **$$**

Shipudei Hagefen
74 Agripas, Jerusalem.
Tel: (02) 6253267.
The pick of the Middle East restaurants; near Makhane Yehuda market. Open Sat–Thur noon–11pm, Fri noon–4pm, Sat night. **$$**

Anna Ticho House
off Ha-Rav Kook, Jerusalem.
Tel: (02) 6244186.
Dairy food in a garden restaurant which forms part of a museum. Open Sun–Thur 11am–12pm, Fri 11am–3pm, Sat night. **$**

Simas
78 Agripas, Jerusalem.
Tel: (02) 4233002.
Speedy service and good value food in the cheapest steak house in town. Open Sun–Thur noon–11pm, Fri noon–4pm, Sat night. **$**

CAFES

Aroma
Mamilla Pedestrian Mall..
Tel: (02) 6241304.
This new branch of a national chain of quality coffee houses provides stirring views of the Old City walls. Open Sun–Thur 8am–12pm, Fri 8am–4pm, Sat 8pm–12pm.

Kaffit
35 Emek Refaim.
Tel: (02) 5635284.
Best known café in the fashionable German Colony. Open Sun–Thur 7.30am–1am, Fri 7.30am– to Shabbat, Sat night.

Moment
30 Azza.
Tel: (02) 5666756.
Attracts an intellectual crowd. Open Sun–Thur 7.30am–1am, Fri 7.30am– to Shabbat, Sat night.

Rimon Cafe
4 Lunz, Jerusalem.
Tel: (02) 6252772.
A popular hang-out by the Ben Yehuda Street Mall with a choice of light meals and cakes. Open Sun–Thur 8am–12pm, Fri 8am–3pm, Sat night.

BARS AND PUBS

Mike's Place
37 Yafo St., near Zion Square.
Tel: (02) 2670965.
English-style pub with live music and live TV soccer and a wide choice of draft beers and pub grub. Open daily 11am–3am.

Glasnost
15 Haleni ha-Malkah.
Tel: (02) 6256954.
One of many bars in the Russian Compound, such as Sergei's, Arthur's, Cannabis and Alexander. Along this street and its arteries is where the city's nightlife begins.
Open daily 6pm–2am.

BELOW: a *mezze* selection of salads makes a typical start to a meal.

TEL AVIV

RESTAURANTS

Boya
Old Tel Aviv Port.
Tel: (03) 5446166.
One of Israel's leading seafood restaurants where you can also savor the atmosphere of Tel Aviv's recent re-invention of its Old Port as a leisure complex. Open Sun–Thur 9am–1am, Fri–Sat 8pm–1am. **$$$**

Chinese Wall
26 Mikve Israel.
Tel: (03) 5603974.
This Chinese restaurant is one of the city's few top quality kosher restaurants outside of the hotels. Open Sun–Thur 11am–11pm, Fri 11am–4pm, Sat night. **$$$**

Raphael
87 Ha-Yarkon.
Tel: (03) 5226464.
Owner and chef Rafi Cohen, still only in his early 30s, is considered the country's leading chef. Cohen built his reputation in Jerusalem's King David Hotel where he adapted the cooking of his Moroccan mother. Open daily 6pm–12pm. **$$$**

Yin Yang
64 Rothschild Boulevard.
Tel: (03)-5606833.
A Chinese restaurant run by Israeli Aharoni, the country's best known celebrity chef. Open daily noon–12pm. **$$$**

Takamaru
4 Ha'Arba's, Tel Aviv.
Tel: (03) 5621629.
This is one of Israel's very few Japanese restaurants. Will not disappoint. Open Sun–Thur noon–11pm, Fri & Sat 8pm–12pm. **$$$**

Ba-Li
8 Ibn Gabirol, Tel Aviv.

PRICE CATEGORIES

Prices in restaurants are given in shekels
$ under NIS 80 per person.
$$ NIS 80–250
$$$ more than NIS 250

Tel: (03) 6955661.
Modest Yemenite restaurant with home-cooked food and authentic Yemenite soups and breads. **$$**

Elimelech
35 Wolfson.
Tel: (03) 5182478.
Excellent place for those who like traditional Eastern European kosher food. Located south of the business district. Lunches only Open Sun–Fri 9am–3pm. **$$**

Lillith
42 Mazeh.
Tel: (03) 6298772.
Fish-vegetarian restaurant in the heart of the financial district that focuses on healthy but tasty eating. Open Sun–Thur noon–12pm, Fri 10am–4pm, Sat night. **$$**

Taboon
Old Yafo Port.
Tel: (03) 6816011.
In a pleasant spot in Yafo's old port; specializes in oven-cooked Mediterranean fish. Open daily 12.30pm–midnight. **$$**

Zion
4 Peduim, Tel Aviv.
Tel: (03) 5178714.
The pick of the meat restaurants in the city's famous Yemenite Quarter (Kerem ha-Teimanim) by the Carmel Market. Open Sun–Thur noon–12pm, Fri noon–4pm, Sat night. **$$**

David's Ful
22 Peduim.
Tel: (03) 5160693.
An Egyptian restaurant in the Yemenite quarter specializing in inexpensive savory dishes based on *ful* (beans). Open Sun–Fri noon–6pm. **$**

Lev Harachav ("Wide Heart")
Rabbi Akiva, Carmel Market, Tel Aviv.
A no-nonsense, tasty and cheap authentic Israeli restaurant with excellent *hummus*. Open Sun–Fri noon–6pm **$**

Marsala
15 Yosef ha-Nasi Street, Tel Aviv.
Tel: (03) 5256515.
Delicatessen and eatery serving fresh sandwiches and salads. Open Sun–Fri 11am–5pm **$**

Rachmo Hagadol
98 Petakch Tikvah.
Tel: (03) 5621022.
The pick of the *felafel* eateries near the old Central Bus Station. Excellent, clean and astonishingly cheap. Open Sun–Fri 11am–6pm. **$**

CAFES

Ilan's Coffee Shop
90 Ibn Gvirol St.
Tel: (03) 5235334.

Excellent espresso. Open Sun–Fri 7.30am–7pm.

Orna and Ella
33 Sheinkin St.,
Tel: (03) 6204753.
One of the best-known cafes in the trendy Sheinkin area. Open daily 9am–1am.

Café Nordau
145 Ben Yehuda St.,
Tel: (03) 5240134.
One of the city's best known gay spots. Open daily 11am–1am.

BARS

Bugsy's
26 Florentine, crn of Washington St.
Tel: (03) 6813138.
One of the trendiest bars in the heart of the city's trendiest Florentine district with an interesting menu for vegetarians. Open daily 11am–3am.

Hashoftim
39 Ibn Gvirol St., corner of Hashoftim St.
Tel: (03) 6951153.
One of the city's oldest and best-known pubs. Open 6pm–2am.

Molly Bloom's Traditional Irish Pub
2 Mendele Street.
Tel: (052) 2330202.
The name says it all. One of many Irish pubs near the seafront. Daily 6pm–2am.

BELOW: the availability of fresh ingredients ensures that the quality of cuisine is high.

ACTIVITIES

FESTIVALS, THE ARTS, NIGHTLIFE, SHOPPING AND SPECTATOR SPORTS

FESTIVALS

The Israel Festival of Music and Drama takes place in May of each year, with the participation of the country's leading talent and world-famous visiting companies and artists. The festival centers on Jerusalem.

The Abu Ghosh Vocal Music Festival – June

Israel Festival – the country's premier international theater festival, every May.

The Jerusalem International Film Festival – July.

The Haifa International Film Festival – September/October.

The Karmiel Dance Festival – July.

Jerusalem International Arts & Crafts Fair – Sultan's Pool Jerusalem, every August.

Jerusalem International Puppet Festival – August, Jerusalem's Liberty Bell Park.

Klezmer Hasidic Jewish Music Festival – August, Safed.

The Red Sea Jazz Festival (Eilat) – August.

The Akko Fringe Theatre Festival – September/October during Sukkot (Tabernacles).

In addition, the **Jerusalem International Book Fair** is held every two years in March. An international **Harp Contest** takes place every three years, drawing young musicians from all over the world. The **Zimriya**, an international choir festival, is another well-established triennial event.

Spring in Jerusalem and **Spring in Tel Aviv**, annual festivals, include music, drama and dance, and the **Rubinstein Piano Competition** brings talented young artists from around the world to Israel.

Events in Haifa include the **International Flower Show** (Floris), when hundreds of thousands of flowers from all over the world, typical of their countries of origin, adorn the city.

Religious Festivals

Jews: Public holidays fall on the Jewish festivals listed below. On Rosh Hashana (New Year), Yom Kippur (Day of Atonement), the first and last day of Succot (Tabernacles), the first and last day of Pesach (Passover) and Shavuot, all shops and offices are closed and there is no public transport. On Holocaust Day, Memorial Day and Tisha B'Av, all places of entertainment and restaurants are closed.

Israel observes a solar–lunar year in accordance with Jewish religious tradition, with the New Year occurring in September/October, with the festival of Rosh Hashana. But the standard Gregorian system is also in daily use everywhere.

The working week runs from Sunday to Thursday, and most businesses are also open on Friday mornings. From sunset on Friday to sunset on Saturday, however, everything shuts down in observance of the Jewish Sabbath, or *Shabbat*. This includes all banks and public services, including buses and other forms of transportation. In Tel Aviv and Haifa, however, small mini-buses run along the main bus routes and inter-city *sheruts* (communal taxis) also run some services. On Saturday evening, most of the transport and other public services are resumed.

The Hebrew calendar is a lunar calendar, with a leap month added every two to three years to ensure that the year is also a solar one.

Jewish holy days, therefore, fall on different dates in the general calendar each year, so exact dates cannot be given. Therefore, the months only are indicated in the following list.

Christians: While the Catholic churches use the Gregorian calendar the Orthodox churches still use the Julian calendar, therefore Christmas and sometimes Easter are celebrated on different dates to the Western Churches.

Muslims: The Muslim calendar is completely lunar with festivals falling throughout the year in relation to the solar calendar – so, for example, Ramadan rotates backwards through the seasons – and generally Muslim festivals cannot be attributed to any single Gregorian month.

January/February

Christmas – January 6 for most orthodox Churches (Greek, Russian etc.) January 13 for Armenian Orthodox Christmas

Tu B'Shvat – (15th of the Hebrew month of Shvat) Jewish New Year for trees – mid-January to mid-February. Tree planting ceremonies around the country and activities by "greens."

March/April

Purim – (15th of the Hebrew month of Adar, or Adar Shani during a leap year) This one day festival recalls the biblical story of Esther. Set in Persia the Jews are saved from exter-mination after Queen Esther appeals to her husband King Ahasuerus. The festival is celebrated in walled cities like Jerusalem a day later than the rest of the country. Traditionally Jews go around in fancy dress, there are many carnival style dresses, and religious Jews are urged to get drunk (unless they're driving).

Pesach (Passover) – (15th–21th of Nisan). Celebrating the Jewish Exodus from Egypt, the festival lasts seven days, of which the first and last are public holidays. During this period, Jews abstain from bread and eat *matzot* – unleavened bread, similar to crackers.
Easter – The crucifixion and resurrection of Christ are celebrated (usually) the weekend after Passover. One of the central events is the Good Friday procession along the Via Dolorosa in Jerusalem.

May/June
Holocaust Day – (24th Nisan) memorial day for the 6 million Jews killed in the Holocaust. All places of entertainment are closed.
Memorial Day – (4th Iyar) memorial day for members of the security forces killed in action and victims of terror. All places of entertainment are closed.
Independence Day – (5th Iyar) Marks Israel's Declaration of Independence in 1948. A public holiday but public transport operates and shops are open. Sometimes falls in the last days of April.
Lag B'Omer – (18th Iyar) A Jewish bonfire night marks various favorable Jewish historical events down the centuries.
Shavuot (Pentecost) – (6th Sivan) 50 days after Passover this festival, which is a public holidays marks the giving of the Torah to Moses on Mount Sinai. It is also a harvest festival.

July/August
Tisha B'Av – (9th Av) a fast day to commemorate the destruction of both Temples. All places of entertainment are closed.

September/October
Rosh Hashana – (1–2nd Tishrei) – Jewish New Year.
Yom Kippur – (10th Tishrei) the most solemn day in the Jewish calendar as an individual's fate is sealed for the year to come. Fast day. Public holiday and no vehicles travel on the roads.
Sukkot (Tabernacles) (15–22 Tishrei) – Jews build tabernacles to remind themselves of their 40 years in the desert after leaving Egypt. The first and last days are a public holiday. The last day – Simchat Torah – marks the beginning and end of the annual Torah reading cycle.

November/December
Hanukkah (25th Kislev to 3rd Tevet) – The festival of lights recalls the Jewish victory over the Greeks.

Christmas – The Catholic, Protestant and other western churches celebrate the birth of Christ.

Muslim Festivals
Friday is a holy day for Muslims, and places of worship are closed to visitors during prayers on that day, as they are on all holy days. The most important Muslim holidays are:
Id el Adha, Sacrificial Festival (four days).
New Year.
Mohammed's Birthday.
Feast of Ramadan (one month of fasting from sunrise to sunset).
Id el Fitr, Conclusion of Ramadan (three days).

Religious Etiquette
Of obvious sensitivity is religious etiquette. When visiting holy sites, women should dress conservatively (no bare legs or shoulders), and men should wear shirts and long trousers. When visiting Jewish shrines or memorials, it's also standard for men to cover their heads; if you don't have a *kepah* or hat, a cardboard substitute is often provided. In some religious neighborhoods, especially in Jerusalem, these conservative rules of dress apply as general practise. While not all Israelis are observant, you should be aware that religious Jews see the Sabbath as a holy day and smoking or other informal behavior can be considered offensive. When visiting mosques and the Dome of the Rock, it is customary to remove shoes before entering.

Religious Services
Jews and Muslims will have no problems finding synagogues and mosques, which are virtually on every street corner in some neighborhoods.

Jewish
Jerusalem Great Synagogue
56 Ha-Melekh George.
Tel: (02) 6247112.
Chabad Synagogue
16 Yirmiyahu, Jerusalem.
Tel: (02) 5814755.
Centre for Conservative Judaism
4 Agron, Jerusalem.
Tel: (02) 6223539.
Union for Progressive Judaism
13 David ha-Melekh, Jerusalem.
Tel: (02) 6232444.
Tel Aviv Great Synagogue
110 Allenby.
Tel: (03) 5604905.
Beit Yisrael
Independence Square, Netanya.

Tel: (09) 8624345.
Haifa Central Synagogue
Rabbi Herzog.
Tel: (04) 8660599.

Muslim
The best-known mosques in Israel are the El-Aqsa Mosque (Tel: (02) 6281248) on Jerusalem's Temple Mount, the El-Jazzar Mosque in Akko and the White Mosque in Ramla. There are also many mosques in Arab towns and villages throughout Israel. Mohammed is said to have prayed in the El-Aqsa Mosque during his lifetime. and the Dome of the Rock is a shrine built on the rock where the Prophet is said to have risen to heaven after his death in Medina.

Christian
While Israel has much to offer every tourist, for the Christian pilgrim a trip to Israel is more than just a journey because here the pilgrim has the unique opportunity of tracing the footsteps of Jesus and the early Christians and visiting sites significant to the life and teaching of Jesus: Bethlehem, his birthplace; Nazareth, the town of his boyhood; the Sea of Galilee, scene of miracles and his ministerial teaching; Mount Tabor, site of the Transfiguration; the Garden of Gethsemane and Jerusalem, where he spent his last hours of prayer and agony; and Latrun, the site of a Trappist monastery, near the biblical Emmaus, where Jesus is said to have appeared after the resurrection.

Jerusalem
Armenian Cathedral of St James
Tel: (02) 6284549.
Mon–Fri 3am–3.30pm; Sat and Sun 2.30am–3.15pm.
Baptist House Center
Tel: (02) 6255942.
Prayer meetings Sunday 10.45am and 5.30pm, Wed. 1.30pm.
Coenaculum Franciscan Chapel
Tel: (02) 6272692.
7am–noon, 3pm–sundown. Ring bell.
Christ Church (Anglican)
Tel: (02) 6277727, Sun services 9.30am, 4.30pm, 6.30pm, Tues 6.15pm.
Church of the Dormition
Tel: (02) 5655300. 7am–12.30pm, 2–7pm.
Church of God Pentecostal (Mount of Olives near Coomodore Hotel)
Tel: (02) 6273899. Services Sun 10.30am.
Church of God (Seventh Day Adventists)
Tel: (02) 6731347. Services Sat 7pm.

Church of the Holy Sepulchre
Old City. Tel: (02) 6272692. For more
details about services for various
denominations, contact the Christian
Information Centre. (02) 6272692.
Danish Lutheran Church
Tel: (02) 5324254.
Dominus Flevit
Tel: (02) 6285837.
6.45am–11.30am, 3–5pm.
Ein Kerem: St John's
Tel: (02) 6413639. 5.30am–noon,
2.30–6pm (winter 2.30–5.30pm).
Ein Kerem: Visitation
Tel: (02) 6417291. 9am–noon,
3–6pm.
Flagellation
Tel: (02) 6282936. 6am–noon,
2–6pm (winter 2–5.30pm).
Garden Tomb
Tel: (02) 6283402. 8am–1pm,
3–5pm (winter 8am–12.30pm and
2.30–4.30pm). Sunday closed.
**Gethsemane, Church of Agony
and Grotto**
Tel: (02) 6283264. 8.30am–noon,
3pm–sundown (winter 2pm–
sundown).
Lithostrotos-Ecce Homo
Tel: (02) 6282445. 8.30am–4.30pm,
Sunday closed (winter 8.30am–4pm).
Lutheran Church of the Redeemer
Tel: (02) 6276111. 9am–1pm, 2–5
pm, Friday 9am–1pm; Sunday for
services only.
Monastery of the Holy Cross
Tel: (02) 5634442. Irregular hours –
phone in advance.
Russian Cathedral
Tel: (02) 6284580, by appointment.
St. Andrew's Scottish Church
1 David Remez St.
Tel: (02) 6732401.
Services in English Sun 10am; in
Dutch, Sun 4.30pm.
St Mary Magdalene
Tel: (02) 6282897. Irregular hours –
phone in advance.
St Anne's, Bethesda
Tel: (02) 6283258. 8am–noon,
2.30–6pm (winter 2–5pm).
St George's Cathedral
20 Nablus Road. Sun 8am, 11am,
6pm.
Tel: (02) 6282253 or 282167.
Open 6.45am–6.30pm.

Outside Jerusalem
Abu Ghosh Crusader Church
Tel: (02) 5342798. 8.30–11am,
2.30–5pm.
Bethlehem, Nativity Church
6am–6pm.
Bethlehem, St Catherine
Tel: (02) 6742425. 8am–noon,
2.30–6pm.
Bethlehem Shepherds' Field
Tel: (02) 2742242. 8am–11.30am,
2–6pm (winter 2–5pm).

Capernaum: "City of Jesus"
Tel: (06) 6721059. 8.30am–4.30pm.
Church of the Multiplication (Tabgha)
Tel: (04) 6700180. 8.30am-5pm daily
Church of Scotland, Tiberias
Tel (04) 6723769.
Emmaus: Qubeibeh
Tel: (04) 9952495 ext: 4.
6.30–11.30am, 2–6pm.
Latrun Monastery
Tel: (08) 9220065. 7.30–11.30am,
2.30–5pm.
Mount of Beatitudes
tel: (04) 6790978. 8am–noon,
2–4pm.
Mount Carmel: Stella Maris
tel: (04) 8337758. 6am–noon,
3–6pm (winter 3–5pm).
**Nazareth: Basilica of the
Annunciation & St Joseph's**
tel: (04) 6572501. 8.30–11.45am,
2–6pm, Sunday 2–6pm (winter
2–5pm).
Tabor Transfiguration
tel: (06) 6567489. 8am–noon,
3–5pm.
Tabgha: Multiplication of the Bread
tel: (06) 6721061. 8am–4pm.
The Christian Information Center,
inside the Old City's Jaffa Gate,
opposite the Citadel (Tel: 02-
6272692) (open daily 8.30am–1pm),
offers information on all churches,
monasteries and other Christian
shrines. The office also issues
certificates of Christian pilgrimage.

Baptismal Sites

An organized baptismal site has been
erected at Yardenit at the mouth of
the River Jordan, 8 km (5 miles)
south of Tiberias. Descent is by
steps or wheelchair-accessible ramp.
There is ample space for groups. The
site is open during daylight hours. Al-
Maghtes, near Jericho, also claims to
be the site of Christ's baptism, and
is accessible to pilgrims.

Direct Line

Jerusalem has a fax number direct to
heaven: c/o The Western Wall, (02)
5612222. The telephone company
places your fax in the cracks of the
wall. The Aish Hatorah Yeshiva in
Jerusalem offers a free service
enabling people to e-mail the wall.
E-mails are printed out and placed in
the wall – www.thewall.org

THE ARTS

Israel has a wealth of cultural and
artistic entertainments. Ticket
agencies in each city or town sell
tickets for concerts, plays and other
events. Annual festivals of all art,
cultural and musical events are

booked up well in advance.
Calendars of Events are available at
the tourist information offices.

Music

There are several orchestras, of
which the most famous is the Israel
Philharmonic, playing under the
baton of the great conductors of the
world (Zubin Mehta since 1991) and
featuring distinguished guest artists.
The Jerusalem Symphony Orchestra
gives a weekly concert in Jerusalem
in the winter season.
    There are frequent performances
by the Haifa Symphony Orchestra,
the Rishon Le-Tsiyon Symphony
Orchestra and the New Israel Opera.
Mann Auditorium (for Israel
Symphony Orchestra), 1 Huberman,
Tel Aviv. Tel: (03) 6211777.
www.hatarbut.co.il
Israel Opera Israel Opera House,
Sha'ul ha-Melekh Boulevard. Tel: (03)
6927777. www.israel-opera.co.il
Henry Crown Hall (for Jerusalem
Symphony Orchestra), Marcus,
Jerusalem. Tel: 1-700-70-4000.
www.jso.co.il
Israel Northern Symphony Haifa Tel:
(04) 8363131.
Israel Kibbutz Orchestra Tel: (09)
9604757.
Israel Andalusian Orchestra Tel: 1-
800-693-693.

Dance

Professional dance companies
include the Israel Classical Ballet,
the Batsheva Dance Company, the
Bat-Dor Dance Company, Kol
Hademana and the Kibbutz Dance
Company. Batsheva and Bat-Dor are
both modern dance groups. All
perform regularly in the three main
cities, as well as in other towns and
kibbutzim.
Suzan Dalal Centre, 6 Yekhi'el, Neve
Tsedek, Tel Aviv. Tel: (03) 5171471.
For Batsheva and Inbal Dance
Troupes,
Batsheva Tel: (03) 5160231.
Inbal Tel: (03) 5173711.
Israel Ballet Tel: (03) 6966610.
Kibbutz Contemporary Dance Co.
Tel: (03) 6925278.
Jerusalem Dance Theater Tel: (02)
6795626.

Theater

The theater is very popular in Israel,
and there are many companies
performing a wide range of classical
and contemporary plays in Hebrew,
including original works by Israelis.
The best known are the Ha-Bima and
Camari Theaters in Tel Aviv and the

Haifa Municipal Theater, which take their productions all over the country. In Jerusalem, the Centre for Performing Arts includes the Jerusalem Theater, the Henry Crown Auditorium and the Rebecca Crown Theater. Also Sultan's Pool Ampitheater, located beneath the walls of the Old City, is a must for a concert. Smaller companies offer stage productions in English, Yiddish and other languages. One such theater, Gesher (meaning bridge), founded in Tel Aviv in 1991, is the first Russian-speaking theater in Israel.

Jerusalem Theater, Marcus, Jerusalem.
Tel: (02) 5610011/5610293.
Khan Theater, David Remez, Jerusalem, tel: (02) 6718281.
Ha-Bima Theater, Tarsith Boulevard, Tel Aviv, tel: (03) 5266666.
Camari Theater, 101 Dizengoff, Tel Aviv, tel: (03) 5233335.
Beit Liessin Theater, 34 Weizmann, Tel Aviv, tel: (03) 6956222.

Movies

There are cinemas in all the big towns; most have three showings a day, one at about 4pm and two in the evening.

For about $7 you can see the latest Hollywood offerings. You'll also find the latest movies from France, Germany, Italy, Hungary and elsewhere. These films usually have English subtitles, but ask at the box office first if unsure.

Israel itself produces a dozen or so films a year, and these offer an insight into the local culture. These, too, have English subtitles. The local cinemathèques show golden oldies as well the more recent movies.
Jerusalem Cinemathèque, Derekh Hevron. Tel: (02) 5654333.
www.jer-cin.org.il
Tel Aviv Cinemathèque, 2 Sprintzach.
Tel: (03) 6938111.
Haifa Cinemathèque, Hanassi 142.
Tel: (04) 8383424.

Museums

Israel has more than 100 museums. The most important are:

Jerusalem

Israel Museum, reached from the Knesset along Kaplan to Derekh Ruppin (open Mon, Wed, Sat, Sun 10am–4pm, Tues 4–9pm, Thur 10am–9pm, closed Sun; fee; tel: 02-6708811, www.imj.org.il) is Israel's national museum and a leading showcase for the country's art, archaeology and Judaica. The

Museum's most famous exhibit is the **Shrine of the Book** which displays the Dead Sea Scrolls. These scraps of tattered parchment represent the oldest known copy of the Old Testament. The **Second Temple Model of Jerusalem** in AD66 is now in the Museum compound.
Bible Lands Museum (opposite the Israel Museum) (open Sun–Thur 9.30am–5.30pm, Wed. 9.30am–9.30pm, Fri 9.30am–2pm; fee; tel: 02-5611066; www.blmj.org) in Avraham Granot displays artefacts dating from biblical times. Along Ruppin north–east is the hands-on
Bloomfield Science Museum – near Israel Museum – (open Mon–Thur 10am–6pm, Fri 10am–2 pm, Sat 10am–3pm; fee; tel: 02-6544888; www.mada.org.il) is imaginative and popular with children.
Yad Vashem Holocaust History Museum (Sun–Thur 9am–5pm, Fri 9am–2pm; free; www.yadvashem.org) is a striking memorial to the 6 million Jews massacred by Nazi Germany. Daring in its design, the museum is housed in a linear, triangular structure (in the shape of a Toblerone container, if you'll pardon the trivial image), which stretches for 160 meters beneath the Jerusalem hillside. Only the apex of the structure is above ground forming a skylight. The gray concrete walls intensify the harshness of the structure, which gashes brutally through the Jerusalem hillside. The new Yad Vashem uses the latest multimedia means to recount the dreadful history from 1933 to 1945. It typifies Israeli daring and in this alone it is an eloquent and optimistic postscript to Europe's darkest hour.
Tower of David Museum of the

BELOW: the Ha-Bima Theatre, Tel Aviv.

History of Jerusalem (Tel: 02-6265310; Sun–Thurs 10pm–4pm in summer until 5pm and 10pm on Sun, Tues & Thurs. Closed Fri. Sat 10am–2pm; fee; www.towerofdavid.org.il) inside the body of the Citadel, which contains displays describing the tumultuous history of the city, figurines of Jerusalem characters, a 19th-century model of the Old City, and the multi-layered ruins of the structure itself. A multi-media show with a separate entrance describes the various moods of Jerusalem via numerous slide projectors.

Tel Aviv

Museum of the Jewish Diaspora (Bet Hatefusoth) (open Sun–Thur 10am–4pm, Fri 9am–1pm; fee; tel: 03-7457800; www.bh.org.il) on the university campus. Founded in 1979, it was when set up, in concept and methodology, a radical departure from the accepted notion of a museum, for, apart from a few sacramental objects, Bet Hatefusoth contains no preserved artefacts. Its principal aim is reconstruction. The body of the main exhibit is handled thematically, focusing on general themes of Jewish Life in the Diaspora: family life, community, religion, culture, and the return to Zion. Its striking displays include a collection of beautifully intricate models of synagogue buildings from across the globe.
Eretz Israel Museum (open Sun–Thur 9am–3pm, Sat 10am–2pm; fee; tel: 03-6415244; www.eretzmuseum.org.il). The museum comprises the most comprehensive storehouse of archaeological, anthropological and historical findings in the region. Its spiritual backbone is **Tel Kasila**, an excavation site in which 12 distinct layers of civilization were uncovered, its finds including an ancient Philistine temple and Hebrew inscriptions from 800 BC. The complex consists of 11 pavilions, including exhibits of glassware, ceramics, copper, coins, folklore and ethnography, and a planetarium.
Tel Aviv Museum of Art (Mon, Wed 10am–4pm, Tue Thur 10am–10pm, Fri 10–2pm, Sat 10–4pm; fee; tel: 03-6961297; www.tamuseum.co.il), has four central galleries, an auditorium which often features film retrospectives, numerous other halls, a sculpture garden, a cafeteria and a shop. There are exhibitions of 17th-century Dutch and Flemish masters, 18th-century Italian paintings, Impressionists, post-Impressionists, and a good selection of 20th-century art from the United States and Europe, in addition to modern Israeli work.

Art Galleries

The area around Gordon Street in Tel Aviv between Ben Yehuda and Dizengoff Streets is full of art galleries. Trendy Tel Aviv culture vultures will walk around the galleries at night as if they are public museums. This is acceptable behavior and casual visitors will not be approached by eager sales staff.

NIGHTLIFE

Nightlife starts late in Israel and is very vibrant. From 11pm onwards, Israelis are out on the streets of Tel Aviv, and also in Jerusalem and virtually every Israeli city. Street-side cafés and restaurants are busy until well after midnight, and bars and discos have a brisk trade right through the night. Because Friday and Saturday constitute the weekend, Thursday night is a big night out.

Tel Aviv seafront and other hotspots are crowded right through the night and it is remarkable to see the traffic jams along the seafront promenade at 3am. Nightclubs abound in the main cities and resort towns. Many have regular floor shows, while others offer more informal entertainment. Rock, jazz, folk and pop music are the usual fare. Jerusalem and Tel Aviv are the hot spots. Bohemian Florentin is another popular nightspot in Tel Aviv as well as the newly renovated Tel Aviv Port and Old Yafo Port.

Tel Aviv

Abraxas
40 Lilienblum St
Tel: 03-5104435
Betty Ford
48 Nahlat Binyamin
Tel: 03-5100650
Saloona
17 Tirza St Jaffa
Tel: 03-5181719
Shoshana Johnson
97 Allenby St
Tel:03-5607443

Jerusalem

Although lower-profile than that of Tel Aviv's, Jerusalem's nightlife is certainly vibrant. This is especially true between April and October when it is warm enough to stroll through the streets and sit outside at cafés and restaurants. The city's nightlife, as elsewhere in Israel, gets going after 10pm and the streets remain packed until well after midnight. The Ben Yehuda Street Mall and

adjacent pedestrian precincts at the bottom end of the street are especially busy. After 1am the focus moves over to the pubs and bars in the Russian compound, on the north side of Yafo. The Talpiyot Industrial Zone is where most nightclubs and discos are located, but if you're over 30, you may feel out of place. More mature revelers should stick to the clubs and bars in the large hotels.

Glasnost
15 Heleni ha-Malka Street.
Tel: (02) 6234523.
Bar in the heart of Jerusalem's Russian Compound.
Underground
1 Yoel Salomon St.
Tel: 02-6251918.
Dance club in downtown Jerusalem.
The Lab
28 Hebron Road
Tel 02-6292000
Trendy disco on the renovated compound of the old railway station also doubles as a small theater.

SHOPPING

Shops tend to open long hours usually 9am-9pm and even later on Saturday night. Shops are closed Friday afternoons and Saturday during the day.

A strange thing has happened in Israel in recent years. If once consumer goods were far more expensive than in the US and Western Europe, this is no longer necessarily the case. Imported branded household items do still tend to be considerably more expensive than overseas but many items, especially clothing, are less expensive than comparable goods in Western Europe (though not usually North America). In any event, it is worth looking through major clothes stores when in shopping malls including Castro, Golf and Fox.

Otherwise, shoppers will be hunting for items that were always good value in Israel such as exclusive jewelry and diamonds; oriental carpets and antiques; fashionable ladies' wear and elegant furs; leather goods; paintings and sculptures; ceramics; silverware and copperware; embroidery and *batiks*, and of course religious requisites, particularly Judaica. Several hundred shops are approved by the Ministry of Tourism. These shops display a sign stating "Listed by the Ministry of Tourism" and the Ministry's emblem (two scouts carrying a bunch of

grapes on a pole between them), which is the symbol of quality merchandise. Try the G.R.A.S. chain for good value arts and crafts gifts.

In addition, colorful oriental markets and bazaars are found in the narrow alleyways of the old cities of Jerusalem, Bethlehem, Akko, Nazareth and Hebron, and in Druze villages like Daliyat el-Karmel near Haifa. These sell handmade arts and crafts – including olive wood, mother-of-pearl, leather and bamboo items, hand-blown glass – and clothing, vegetables and fruit.

Duty-free shops are located at Ben Gurion and Eilat airports and at most of the leading hotels. Foreign-made articles such as watches, cameras, perfumes, tobaccos and liquors as well as many fine Israeli products may be purchased with foreign currency for delivery to the plane or ship prior to departure.

Judaica

Besides these items, Israel has a unique variety of traditional crafts and Judaica for sale, ranging from religious articles like *Menorahs*, *mezuzot* and spice boxes to wall hangings and statuary. They range from loving reproductions to stark minimalism.

Centers for buying fine crafts include several locations in Jerusalem, among them the House of Quality, Khutsot ha-Yoster (Arts & Crafts Lane), Yochanan Migush Halav, and the Me'a She'arim area. The latter for the best bargains while King David Street has the exclusive, upscale antique and Judaica stores.

Shopping Areas

In the Old City of Jerusalem and other Arab market places, bargaining is standard practise. Usually you can buy an item at 25 percent off by starting to haggle at half the quoted price. Avoid haggling if you are not really interested in buying or if an item is cheap. Brassware, carvings and fabrics are among the more popular buys. The center of Downtown Jerusalem is also full of souvenir and Judaica stores.

Other popular shopping places include the weekly Bedouin market in Be'er Sheva on Thursday mornings, the Druze markets in the north, such as Daliyat el-Karmel and Nakhalat Binyamin in Tel Aviv, where artisans trade their wares on Tuesday and Friday.

Shopping Malls

Malka Shopping Mall, Malkha, Jerusalem. Tel: (02) 6793261.

Azrieli Shopping Center, 132 Petach Tivah Road, Tel Aviv (by Hashalom Railway Station). Tel: (03) 6081199. **Dizengoff Center**, cnr. Dizengoff St. & King George St. Tel Aviv. Tel: 5251249.

Export of Antiquities

It is forbidden to export antiquities from Israel unless a written export permit has been obtained from the Department of Antiquities and Museums of the Ministry of Education and Culture, Jerusalem. This applies also to antiquities which accompany tourists who are leaving the country. Antiquities proved to have been imported to Israel after 1900 are exempted. Antiquities are defined as objects fashioned by man before the year 1700. A 10 percent export fee is payable on the purchase price of every item approved for export.

The articles must be dispatched by post, with an accompanying cheque for the appropriate amount, or taken in person, to: **The Department of Antiquities and Museums**, Rockefeller Museum, opposite Herod's Gate, POB 586, Jerusalem. It is advisable to telephone (02) 6278627 for an appointment first.

VAT (sales tax)

After your passport has been stamped by customs, apply to Bank Leumi in the exit hall. A refund of VAT (value-added tax) of 15.5 percent is made at the point of your departure. However, you must make sure that:
● The total net sum (after the 15.5 percent reduction) on one invoice is not less than $50. The following items are not included in this scheme: tobacco products, electrical appliances and accessories, cameras, film and photographic equipment.

● The purchased items are packed in a plastic bag with at least one transparent side; the original invoice (white) is placed inside the bag in such a manner that the entries on it can be read; the bag is sealed or glued shut; the bag remains sealed during your entire stay in Israel.

When arriving at the departure hall on leaving the country, you must present the sealed bag with the purchased goods to customs for approval of refund.

After checking and placing the stamp of approval on the invoice, the customs official will direct you to the bank counter where the refund will be made in US dollars.

Note that Eilat is a VAT-free zone, and these regulations do not apply to goods purchased there.

Also, many hotels and stores will exempt you from VAT if you pay in foreign currency.

How to Complain

Be persistent in arguing with shopkeepers if you have a complaint. You cannot expect a shopkeeper to respond to your problem if you do not articulate your grievance, and they are not accustomed to people accepting inferior goods or services without complaint. Be polite, but vocal. If all else fails, contact: **the Ministry of Industry, Trade and Labour's Consumer Protection Service**, 76 Maze, Tel Aviv, tel: (03) 5604611.

SPORTS

Participant Sports

Israel is an ideal place for sports enthusiasts. Here they will find

excellent facilities and an opportunity to combine interests such as skin and scuba diving, riding, tennis, golf, swimming and skiing with a general tour of the country. The Mediterranean climate guarantees most outdoor sports year round (the exception being snow skiing, which is available only in winter).

The Mediterranean shoreline, the Sea of Galilee and the Red Sea are ideal for **water sports**: swimming, surfing, sailing and water skiing. The marinas in Tel Aviv, Herzliya, Eilat, Ashkelon and Ashdod offer yachting as well as sailing. All the large hotels have swimming pools, and there are municipal or private pools all over the country. Skin and aqualung diving are especially popular along the Gulf of Eilat; centres at Eilat will rent equipment (to those with a valid international license and provide instruction for those without.

Fishing equipment, both for angling and underwater, can be hired along the Mediterranean and the Red Sea, though the latter is now a protected area, with fishing permitted only in certain places.

Tennis and squash courts are available at a number of hotels.

There is a fine 18-hole **golf** course at Caesarea and a 9-hole course north of Herzliya at Gaash. You can find **horseriding** clubs throughout the country. **Bicycles** can be rented in most cities, and cycling tours of the country can be arranged. During the winter, there is skiing on the slopes of Mount Hermon. Marches, races, and swimming competitions are organised by the Ha-Po'el and Maccabi sports organisations. The highlight of the year is the annual Jerusalem March, a highly organised event in which thousands of Israelis from all over the country, as well as overseas visitors, both individually and in groups, make a colorful and high-spirited pilgrimage to the capital. This event is usually held in April.

As the following list shows just about every sport is played in Israel.

SOME USEFUL PHONE NUMBERS:
Academic Sports Association
Tel: (03) 6486626.
Israel Archery Federation
Tel: (03) 6423799.
Israel Badminton Association
Tel: (03) 6494546.
Israel Baseball Association
Tel: (09) 9910945.
Israel Basketball Association
Tel: (03) 5622290.
Israel Boxing Association
Tel: (04) 9965933.
Israel Cricket Association
Tel: (03) 6425529.

BELOW: souvenirs on sale in a Jerusalem market.

Israel Cyclists Association
Tel: (03) 6490436.
Israel Equestrian Federation
Tel: (09) 8850938.
Israel Fencing Association
Tel: (03) 5671919.
Israel Football Association
Tel: (03) 5709239.
Israel Gymnastics Association
Tel: (03) 6491477.
Israel Handball Association
Tel: (03) 6497444.
Israel Hang Gliding Association
Tel: (052) 4601862.
Israel Ice Hockey Association
Tel: (03) 6059318.
Israel Judo Association
Tel: (03) 6478025.
Israel Olympic Committee
Tel: (03) 6498385.
Israel Paragliding Association
Tel: (03) 5338002.
Israel Rowing Association
Tel: (04) 6263801.
Israel Sailing Association
Tel: (03) 6482860.
Israel Shooting Federation
Tel: (09) 9570816.
Israel Swimming Association
Tel: (09) 8851970.
Israel Taekwando Association
Tel: (02) 6780175.
Israel Table Tennis Association
Tel: (03) 6486736.
Israel Tennis Center
Tel: (03) 6456655.
Israel Trampoline Association
Tel: (09) 7419497.
Israel Triathlon Association
Tel: (03) 6764008.
Israel Volleyball Association
Tel: (03) 6497444.
Israel Water Polo Association
Tel: (09) 8854325.
Israel Weightlifting Association
Tel: (03) 6408440.
Israel Wrestling Association
Tel: (03) 6472417.
Topsea Israel Surfing Center
Tel: (03) 5270125.
Raanana Squash Center
Tel: (09) 7448115.

Golf
Caesarea Golf Club
Tel: (04) 6109600.
Gaash Golf Club
Tel: (09) 9515111.

Skiing
Mount Hermon Ski Site
Tel: 04 6981337.

Sport for the Disabled
Etgarim – Israel Outdoor Sports and
Recreation Association for the
Disabled. Tel: (03) 5613585.
Israel Sports Centre for the Disabled
Tel: (03) 5754444

Water Sports

Israel is truly a diver's paradise. Its
mild climate ensures year-round
diving in the crystal-clear waters of
both the Mediterranean and Red
Seas, where hundreds of miles of
easily accessible coral reefs and
spectacular seascapes await the
diving enthusiast. A variety of diving
experiences includes underwater
photography, archaeological diving,
grotto and cave diving. It should be
noted that, unless divers have a two-
star license, they must take a special
diving course, though diving without a
license can be done if you are
accompanied by instructors.

Skin & Scuba Diving Courses

The courses for beginners last about
five days and cover the theory of
diving, lifesaving, physiology, physics
and underwater safety. The only
qualifications necessary are the
ability to swim, a certificate from a
doctor confirming fitness to learn
diving, and a chest X-ray. Beginners
can also go out on individual
introductory dives, lasting from one
to 1½ hours, accompanied
throughout by an instructor.
    It is possible to rent all the
necessary skin and scuba diving
equipment at the following centres:

Eilat

For renting diving equipment or taking
courses it is best to head for Coral
Beach:
Aqua-Sport: P.O.B. 300, Eilat.
Tel: 08-6334404 Fax: 08-6333771
E-Mail: info@aqua-sport.com
Website: www.aqua-sport.com
Red Sea Lucky Divers: P.O.B. 4191,
Eilat; Tel: 08-6323466.
Fax: 08-6370993.
E-Mail: info@luckydivers.com
Website: www.luckydivers.com

Tel Aviv
Octopus Diving Center, Tel Aviv
Marina.
Tel: (03) 5271440.
Email: info@octopuus.co.il
Web site: www.octopus.co.il

Spectator Sports

Soccer is the number one spectator
sport, with several matches every
week. Israeli teams participate in the
major European competitions.
Basketball is also very popular, and
Israelis are especially proud of the
Maccabi Tel Aviv basketball team,
which has won the European
championship twice. There are many
international matches during the
winter season at stadiums in the Tel
Aviv area.

Stadiums
**The Ramat Gan National Soccer
Stadium**, P.O.B. 3591 Ramat Gan
Tel: (03) 5709239. Fax: (03)
5702044.
Yad Eliahu Basketball Stadium,
Tel Aviv. Tel: (03) 5272112.

BELOW: the waters around Eilat are a big draw for diving enthusiasts.

A – Z

A HANDY SUMMARY OF PRACTICAL INFORMATION, ARRANGED ALPHABETICALLY

A ccidents

In case of a serious accident or emergency, telephone for an ambulance **101** and or police **100**. In such situations people are very helpful. Hotel receptionists or taxi drivers are obvious people to help but don't be afraid to stop passers by in the street.

B udgeting for a Visit

Israel can be very expensive or quite cheap, depending on how you live. Modest accommodations start at $50 a night and a luxury hotel might charge $150 or even more. But you can find a youth hostel for just $20 a night. Good negotiating skills can bring down prices considerably in all situations. A cheap meal in a restaurant is likely to cost $7 or $8 and a good meal with wine no more than $25 or $30. Best value is a falafel in pita bread and eat as much salad and chips as you want for just $3 or $4. A flat-fare bus ticket in a city costs $1 and the bus or train between Tel Aviv and Jerusalem is about $4. The taxi between the two cities would cost $30. A cinema tickets is $8.

C hild Care

Israelis love children and some people feel threatened by the forward behavior of strangers in the street or on the next restaurant table. They are likely to engage in conversation with your child and offer all types of sweets and candies. Israelis love children, who are expected to be seen and heard.

Eating: Restaurants, hotels and cafés are very flexible in meeting children's fussy food needs, but tend not to have a formal child's menu. Then of course McDonald's, Burger King, Kentucky Fried Chicken and Pizza Hut are always near at hand for kids who like familiar junk food.

Accommodation: Many hotels operate baby-sitting services and are very flexible in adding beds into the parents' room for a minimal additional child. Here, too, good negotiating skills and persistence can help.

Transport: Children under 5 travel free on buses but thereafter pay full fare unless a multi-ride ticket is acquired. On the trains children under 5 go free and get a 20 percent discount between 5 and 10. Children under 4 must be harnessed into special seats when traveling in cars (except taxis).

Places of Special Interest: The Israel Museum in Jerusalem has a children's wing (see museums) and the nearby Bloomfield Science Museum is designed with children in mind. Also in Jerusalem the Biblical Zoo is a must. Other attractions include the Ramat Gan Safari Park, the Monkey park at Kfar Daniel (near the airport) and Tzapari, bird park in Tel Aviv's Yarkon Park. There are major fun fairs in Tel Aviv and Risho Lezion called Luna Park and Superland respectively.

Dangers to avoid: The Mediterranean Sea is deceptively calm. There is a strong undercurrent and more than 120 people are drowned each year, many of them tourists. Be sure to bathe when lifeguards are on duty and keep a close eye on children even when paddling. Children are especially susceptible to the sun, particularly if they are fair-skinned. A high-factor sunscreen can help, but it's prudent to to keep children out of the sun and that, while in the sun, clothes cover as much of the skin as possible. Dehydration is a major problem and children should be encouraged to drink substantial amounts of liquid, preferably water.

Climate

For a small country Israel has very diverse climate zones. Israeli summers are long (lasting from April to October), hot and virtually rainless. During these months Tel Aviv and the coast are humid (average 70%), while the atmosphere in hill towns such as Jerusalem is drier and cooler (average 30%). Because Jerusalem is in the hills, summer evenings can be pleasantly cool. The winter season (from November to March) is generally mild, but quite cold in hilly areas (close to freezing at nights). Spells of rain are interspersed with brilliant sunshine. During the winter the Tiberias area on the Sea of Galilee, the Dead Sea and Eilat (all searingly hot in summer) have ideal warm, sunny weather.

The weather allows for year-round bathing: from April to October along the Mediterranean coast and around the Sea of Galilee; and throughout the year, though especially enjoyable in winter, along the Dead Sea shore and the Gulf of Eilat.

The best time to visit is early spring, when the hillsides are ablaze with flowers and the weather is still mild. Late autumn (November) is also very pleasant, while Eilat and the Dead Sea are best appreciated in the winter. The hot summers are strictly for those who enjoy high temperatures and know how to handle the heat (i.e. drink lots of liquid, use sunscreen, move slowly and stay in the shade).

Mean Temperatures
(minimum–maximum)

	Jan	April	July	Oct
Jerusalem				
°C	6–11	12–21	19–29	16–26
°F	43–53	53–69	66–84	60–78
Tel Aviv				
°C	9–18	12–22	21–30	15–29
°F	49–65	54–72	70–86	59–84
Haifa				
°C	8–17	13–26	20–30	16–27
°F	46–63	55–78	68–86	60–81
Tiberias				
°C	9–18	13–27	23–37	19–32
°F	48–65	56–80	73–98	65–89
Eilat				
°C	10–21	17–31	25–40	20–33
°F	49–70	63–87	78–103	69–92

Annual Rainfall

Jerusalem and Tel Aviv: 550mm (22 inches).

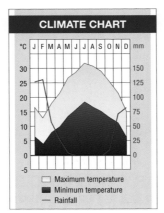

CLIMATE CHART

Galilee: 650mm (26 inches).
Eilat: 20mm (0.79 inches).
All rain falls between October and April, with most of it concentrated in December, January and February.

Clothing

Dress in Israel is informal by Western standards. Few people wear jackets and ties in the summer except for business occasions. However, even in the summer, Jerusalem can get quite cool in the evenings, and be sure to bring some conservative clothes for visiting religious sites. It is anyway recommended to keep arms, legs and shoulders covered to prevent sunburn. Also, wear a hat for sun protection.

Suggested packing lists might include the following:
Summer (April to October): slacks, shorts and open-necked shirts for men; plenty of light cotton daytime dresses and a slightly smarter dress for more formal occasions for women; light shoes, sandals and more solid shoes for touring; sunglasses, hat, swimsuit and beachwear; a light coat, jacket or sweater for cool evenings in the hills.
Winter (November to March): warm coat, sweaters, raincoat and hat, walking shoes, overshoes; shirts, slacks, sports jacket; woolen or heavy suit, blouses, skirts and slacks, long dress or evening skirt for women; lighter clothing and swimsuit for Eilat and the Dead Sea coast.

If you forget anything, you will find that the shops in Israel have high-quality clothes for all occasions at very reasonable prices.

Note: the sun's rays are extremely powerful in Israel even in the winter so bring a broad-brimmed hat, lots of sunscreen and a water bottle.

Crime

Israel has a high rate of non-violent crimes (theft of homes, cars, property, pickpocketing, etc.) but little violent crime (mugging, murder and rape). Do not leave valuables in hotel rooms, or cars, or leave wallets sticking out of pockets. Take all the usual precautions.

In terms of violent crime the security situation is the most pressing problem, but incidents are few and far between. Under no circumstances leave unattended baggage lying around in a public place – police sappers will blow it up within a few minutes. You should report all suspicious packages. Before taking trips to the West Bank or Gaza you should ask about the prevailing security situation there. To contact the police, tel: 100.
Drug Offenses: Hashish/marijuana is illegal, but prosecutions are rarely brought. Because neighboring Lebanon supplies much of the world's hashish, the drug is widely available in Israel, with peddlers frequenting bars. The use of heroin, also grown in Lebanon, is regarded much more seriously by the Israeli authorities, as are chemical drugs such as ecstasy.

Customs Regulations

The red–green customs clearance system is in operation at Ben Gurion Airport. Tourists with nothing to declare or bringing in the goods mentioned below may choose the Green Channel and leave the airport. Tourists bringing in other goods, even if they are exempt from duty, must use the Red Channel.

Green Channel

Every adult tourist may bring into the country, without payment of duty, the following articles, provided that they are for personal use: eau de Cologne or perfume not exceeding 0.2 litres (0.44 pint), wine up to 2 litres and other alcoholic drinks not exceeding 1 litre; tobacco or cigars not exceeding 250 grams or 250 cigarettes; gifts up to US$200 in value, including assorted foodstuffs not exceeding 3 kg (6½ lb), on condition that no single type of food exceeds 1 kg (2¼ lb).

Red Channel

Gift parcels sent unaccompanied – by post or by any other means – are liable to full import duties and Value Added Tax. Portable, expensive electronic items such as cameras, video cameras and lap-top computers may be taken into the country duty-free on condition that they are taken out on departure. These are meant to be for your use in Israel. You may have trouble explaining why you need to use a fax machine or VCR, and there are stiff fines (usually equal to the value of the item) for those attempting to smuggle such goods into Israel.

The following articles are also subject to declaration and deposits of duties and taxes, and the Red Channel must be taken: professional instruments (which can be held in the hand during operation) up to a value of $1,650; boat (rowing, sailing or motor) and a caravan trailer; scuba-diving equipment, portable and appreciably used; records in reasonable quantities.

Customs Deposits

The customs authorities are entitled to demand deposits or guarantees on any article brought in by a tourist or sent separately. This is usually enforced only for very expensive professional equipment or other costly items. The guarantees or deposits are returned to tourists when they leave the country and take the articles out with them. Since the formalities take some time, it is advisable to make all arrangements a day or two before departure, and preferably at the port of entry of the goods, so that the return of the guarantee can be carried out more conveniently.

For further information, contact:
The Department of Customs and Excise, 32 Agron, POB 320, 91000 Jerusalem, Tel: (02) 6703333

D isabled Access

For a list of tourist services for the disabled contact Yad Sarah: Yad Sarah House – Kiryat Weinberg, 124 Herzl Boulevard, Jerusalem 96187. Tel: (02) 6444444. Fax: (02) 6444508. info@yadsarah.org.il www.yadsarah.org
This internet site lists those museums and other places that are accessible for those in wheelchairs.

There have been major efforts in Israel to make the country accessible for the disabled but, while intentions are good, they are not always put into practise. The country has very progressive legislation on the disabled and by law all municipalities must make all junction crossings (ramps on sidewalks) and public buildings accessible for the disabled. To help the blind, pedestrian crossings at traffic lights make a loud flicking noise when the light is

green and pedestrians may cross. For information about disabled rights in Israel, see www.bizchut.org.il
Public Transport: For the most part inter-urban buses do not have access for the disabled, but urban buses do. In the past decade Israel Railways has bought rolling stock with low entry platforms for the disabled and then built several new stations that have no access for the disabled.
Public Buildings: Most museums and many public buildings in Jerusalem and Tel Aviv have wheelchair access but often spoil matters by having the odd stair requiring the disabled to request assistance.

E lectricity

Standard voltage in Israel is 220 volts AC (single phase 50 cycles). Most plugs are three-pin but in some instances can be two-pin. Adaptors and transformers can be purchased throughout Israel.

Embassies & Consulates
Jerusalem
UK Consulate General
19 Nashabibi, Sheikh Jarah.
Tel: (02) 5414100.
5 David Remez Square (West Jerusalem).
Tel: (02) 6717724.
US Consulate
16 Agron.
Tel: (02) 6227200. Fax: (02) 6285455 (West Jerusalem).
27 Derekh Shkem.
Tel: (02) 6282452 (East Jerusalem).

Tel Aviv
Australian Embassy
37 Shderoths Sha'ul ha-Melekh.
Tel: (03) 6950451.
www.australianembassy.org.il
Canadian Embassy
220 Rehov Hayarkon, 63405.
Tel: (03) 6363300. Fax: (03) 6363380.
Visa section, 7 Khavakuk ha-Navi.
Tel: (03) 5442878.
www.dfait.-maeic.gc.ca/telaviv
Embassy of The Republic of South Africa
Dizengoff 50 (Dizengoff Tower).
Tel: (03) 5252566.
Fax: (03) 5256481. www.safis.co.il
Ireland
Tel: (03) 6964166.
UK Embassy
192 Ha-Yarkon, Tel Aviv 63405.
Tel: (03) 7251222.
Fax: (03) 5271572.
Consular Section, 1 Ben Yehuda.
Tel: (03) 5100166.
Fax: (03) 5101167.
www.britemb.org.il

US Embassy
71 Ha-Yarkon, Tel Aviv 63903.
Tel: (03) 5103822.
Fax: (03) 51038328.
usembassy-israel.org.il

G ays & Lesbians

Homosexuality between consenting adults (aged 18 and over) became legal in Israel in 1988, when the Law of Equal Rights in the Workplace was also amended to ban discrimination against gay people. Tel Aviv has a Community Center housing support and study groups, a library and art gallery. Gay clubs abound in the city. Jerusalem also has a gay scene, albeit smaller.
Useful Address:
Jerusalem Open House, 7 Ben Yehuda Street, Jerusalem
www.gay.org.il/joh

Government

Israel is a democracy with a 120-member single chamber Knesset (parliament) elected every four years by all citizens aged 18 and over. Seats are allocated by proportional representation. The president, elected every five years by a secret ballot of Knesset members, is a titular head of state, rather like the British monarch. After elections he the President asks the leader of the largest party to become Prime Minister and form a government. Israel has no formal constitution, but the Supreme Court has the power to interpret Knesset legislation.

H ealth & Medical Care

There are no vaccination require-ments for tourists entering Israel except if they are arriving from infected areas.

Israel has advanced healthcare services with all Israeli citizens guaranteed medical attention by law. Visitors are advised to have medical insurance as even the shortest stay in hospital and elementary surgery is likely to cost thousands of dollars.

With more than 30,000 physicians for a population of 7 million, the country easily has the highest per capital number of doctors in the world. Lists of doctors, dentists and duty pharmacies are available from hotel receptions. A private consultation with a doctor is likely to cost $25. If in pain, Israelis tend to be expressive. So if you are sitting in the emergency room of a hospital with an appendix that is about to burst, go ahead and yell. If you stoically play the strong silent type, then staff will tend to assume you are not really in pain and others will be treated before you.

By far the biggest health problem affecting visitors stems from a lack of respect for the sun. Sunburn and sunstroke afflict bathers, while dehydration plagues those who over-exert themselves sightseeing.

Tourists should acclimatise gradually, apply suntan lotions liberally, keep indoors or in the shade between 10am and 4pm in the late spring, summer and early autumn, and wear light, comfortable clothes that cover legs and arms, and a hat and sunglasses.

Most importantly of all, it is vital to drink continually, even if you do not feel thirsty. Research has shown that the average person who is exerting him or herself in the heat of the day during an Israeli summer needs to drink 1 litre (over 2 pints) every hour to replace the body liquids lost through sweat.

The first symptoms of dehydration are tiredness, headache and lack of appetite. Advanced dehydration can express itself in unpleasant symptoms, from migraines and fever to diarrhoea and vomiting. Medication will not help. Recovery will come about through rest and sipping water, possibly with some salt added, though it is probably best to consult a doctor to ensure that the problem really is dehydration.

Upset stomachs are also common. Here, too, rest and a diet of water are the best medicine. Tap water is as drinkable as anywhere in the developed world, though mineral waters are available everywhere.

AIDS: The number of cases of Aids in Israel is considerably lower than in the countries of Western Europe, but is nevertheless on the increase. The usual precautions should be taken. The Ministry of the Interior requires all visitors seeking to extend their stay beyond three months to take an Aids test.

Useful Details:
Phone 101 – Ambulance
Hadassah (Hospital) Medical Organization, Jerusalem.
Tel: (02) 6777111.
Fax. (02) 6434434.
www.hadassah.org.il

Sheba Medical Center, Tel Hashomer near Tel Aviv.
Tel: (03) 5302534.
Fax: (03) 5303171.
www.sheba.co.il

To hire medical equipment contact:
Yad Sarah: Yad Sarah House – Kiryat Weinberg, 124 Herzl Boulevard, Jerusalem 96187. Tel: (02) 6444444. Fax: (02) 6444508.
info@yadsarah.org.il www.yadsarah.org

L eft Baggage

There are few left baggage facilities in Israel because of the security situation. One such 24-hour service is at Ben Gurion International Airport.
Tel: (03) 9712130.

Lost Property

Ben Gurion Airport: Tel: (03) 9715444.
Egged Buses: Tel: (03) 6388924 or (02) 5685670.
Otherwise phone the police: 100.

M aps

Insight FlexiMaps, which are laminated for durability and easy folding, are available to **Israel** and to **Jerusalem**. Few locally-produced maps are available in English. Some, published by Carta, are stocked by bookstore chains like Steimatsky.

Media

Television Stations

The Israel Broadcasting Authority (IBA) has a 10-minute news bulletin in English (currently at 4.50pm). Channel 2 and 10 are commercial stations, and then there is cable and digital television offered by two companies, Yes and Hot. These companies offer subscribers packages of up to 60 channels including Sky, BBC and CNN.

In addition, Israel can receive broadcasts from all its neighbors, including two English-language stations, Middle East Television, broadcast from Lebanon, and Jordan's Channel 6.

Radio Stations

The Government-run Israel Broadcasting Authority (IBA) modeled on the BBC has a comprehensive radio service broadcasting on six networks. On the foreign-language service there are English-language news bulletins several times a day. Listen to the news on the REKA network at 6.30am, 12.30pm and 8.30pm (local time) in the AM band on 954 kHz in the center and south of the country, and 1575 in the north and on the FM band: Jerusalem 101.3 and 88.2; Tel Aviv 101.2; Be'er Sheva 107.3; Haifa 93.7; Upper Galilee 94.4. At 10pm, English news may additionally be heard on 88.2 FM in Jerusalem and parts of Central Israel. A recording of the latest news can be heard on the internet at www.israelradio.org.

Other Israeli stations include the BBC World Service (1323 KHz), Voice of America (1262 KHz) and Jordan's English-language radio station

Print

Israelis are prolific newspaper readers. With several dozen daily newspapers and countless weekly and monthly magazines, they read more newspapers per head of the population than almost any other country in the world. Most of these newspapers are in Hebrew, the two largest being the afternoon journals *Yediot Ahronot* and *Ma'ariv*, which each sell over 600,000 copies of their Friday (weekend) edition. This is a very high number when you consider that there are only 7 million Israelis.

The *International Herald Tribune* is published daily in Tel Aviv, together with an English translation of the Hebrew daily *Ha'Aretz* (www.haaretz.com) which has a left-of-center editorial line. This is Israel's best-quality newspaper.

The *Jerusalem Post* (www.jpost.com) is published in English six days a week (except Saturday). Founded in 1932, the paper was originally owned by the Histadrut Trade Union Movement and supported the Labor Party. But in 1990 it was sold to the right-wing Conrad Black's Canadian-based Hollinger Corporation which ran into major difficulties in 2004. Under new management, the *Jerusalem Post* now takes a non-partisan line. The Friday paper has an English listing of what's going on in the arts, music, theater, television and radio. The paper also carries useful information about medical services, religious services, etc.

The *Jerusalem Report* (www.jrep.com) is an English-language magazine appearing every two weeks. It gives comprehensive news and features insights into Israeli life. It offers a more colorful alternative to the *Jerusalem Post*.

There is also a dynamic Arab press with over 20 publications, including six dailies and six weeklies. The Israeli Arab press is based in Haifa, while journals printed in East Jerusalem are aimed at a readership in the West Bank and Gaza.

The size and impact of the recent waves of immigration from Russia can be measured by the press. There are a dozen national papers printed in Russian, most of which are dailies. In addition there are several weeklies in

French, Spanish, Amharic, Hungarian, Romanian and many other languages.

Many of the leading newspapers and magazines from Western Europe and North America are available at newsagents the day after publication. In addition to the aforementioned newspaper internet sites in English, it is also possible to read *Globes*, Israel's daily financial paper in English on the web at: www.globes.co.il

Money

Israel has no currency controls and tourists can bring in and take out as much money as they want.

Israel's currency is the New Israeli shekel (NIS), which officially succeeded the old Israeli shekel in 1985. The shekel is divided into 100 agorot. Bills are issued in four denominations: 20 NIS (green with a portrait of former Prime Minister Moshe Sharett), 50 NIS (purple with a portrait of Nobel Prize-winner Shmuel Agnon), 100 NIS (grey with a portrait of former President Yitzhak Ben Zvi) and 200 NIS (reddish-brown with a portrait of former President Zalman Shazar). Change comes in the bronze coins of 5 agorot, 10 agorot, 0.5 shekel, and silver coins 1 shekel, 5 shekels and 10 shekels (silver and gold).

Exchange rates are the same in all banks and *bureaux de change*. The NIS is stable and floats freely against the world's major currencies, with a revised exchange rate each day according to supply and demand. Vendors are prepared to accept the world's better-known currencies but offer inferior exchange rates.

Banks are everywhere and generally open Sun–Thur 8.30am–1pm. Some branches are open until 3pm and some are open in the late afternoon 4pm–6pm. Some branches open Friday morning and all banks are closed on Saturday.

Bureaux de Change are everywhere too and it is usually more convenient in terms of queues and bureaucracy to change money here.

ATMs are everywhere. In the event of losing your card:
VISA: Tel (03) 6178800.
Mastercard/Eurocard & Diners Club: (03) 5723666.
American Express: 1-800-877-877.
VAT on purchases of more than $50 can be claimed back at Ben Gurion International Airport on presentation of a tax receipt.

P opulation & Size

With an annual growth rate of about 1.8% Israel's population reached 7.27 million in 2008. This number includes 1.5 million Arabs (about 1.3 million Muslims and 200,000 Christians and Druze). The largest cities are Jerusalem 800,000; Greater Tel Aviv, 2.5 million; and Greater Haifa 600,000.
Area: 21,000 sq. km (8,110 sq. miles) including administered territories and Palestinian autonomous zones.
Capital: Jerusalem.
Highest mountain: Mount Hermon (2,766 metres/3,962 ft).
Longest river: River Jordan (264 km/ 165 miles).

Postal Services

Post offices have many branches and can be identified by a logo of a white stag leaping across a red background. Post boxes are red. Letters take 5–9 days to reach Europe and America. Express service takes half the time, and Super Express (which is very expensive) about one-third of the time.

Post office hours are 8am–12.30pm and 3.30–6pm. Major post offices are open all day. On Friday afternoon, Saturday and holidays post offices are closed all day.

Postcodes

Israeli addresses include a zip code of five numbers after the city and before Israel (if sent from abroad). Use of the zip code is not compulsory, but mail will arrive more swiftly if it is used.

Public Holidays

The following Jewish festivals are also public holidays:
March/April: first and last days of Passover (Pesach).
May/June: Independence Day, Shavuot.
Sept/Oct: Jewish New Year (Rosh Hashanah); Yom Kippur, first and last days of Succot.
Note: The eve of a festival is like Friday with most businesses, banks, post offices etc. closing at lunch time.

T elephones

Israel's country code is **972** when phoning Israel from abroad.
There are still many public phones in Israel, many of which accept pre-paid cards bought in post offices or in some instances credit cards.
Within Israel:
02- Jerusalem
03- Tel Aviv
04- Northern Israel
08- Southern Israel
09- Herzliya and Netanya
These are the dial codes for the landlines of Bezeq the Israel Telecom Corporation, which is in the process of losing its monopoly on domestic calls. It should be stressed that national flat-rates are charged between area codes and it is no more expensive to phone within Jerusalem than to phone the north or south from Jerusalem.

Peak rates are about 2 cents a minute Sun–Thur 7am–7pm. After 7pm the price drop to less than 1 cent per minute. Friday after 1pm and all Saturday is also a cheap rate.
Four companies provide VOIP domestic calls:
072 – Golden Lines
073 – Globcall
074 – Bezeq International
077 – Hot

Overseas Calls:
Some country codes:
11 USA & Canada
44 UK
61 Australia
64 New Zealand
353 Ireland
27 South Africa
When phoning abroad phone use the following codes of international call providers then the country code.
012 – Golden Lines
013 – Barak
014 – Bezeq International
015 – Internet Gold
017 – Netvision
018 – Xfone
For details of tariffs which should be no more than six or seven cents a minute to Western Europe and North America.
Phone 1-800-012-012 for Golden Lines; 1-800-013-013 Barak etc.
For collect calls, phone 1828 (Golden Lines), 1838 (Barak) and so on.

Phone books are available only in Hebrew, but call 144 for directory enquiries.

Other useful numbers:
100   Police
101   Ambulance
102   Fire Brigade
166   Telephone repairs
199   Telephone company information

Israel's four mobile/cellular phone providers claim to have 7.1 million subscribers in a country of 7 million.
050 – Pelephone
052 – Cellcom
054 – Orange
057 – MIRS
059 – Paltel (Palestinian)

TRANSPORT

ACCOMMODATION

EATING OUT

ACTIVITIES

A – Z

LANGUAGE

Overseas cellular phones work in Israel provide you have made appropriate arrangements with your provider and phones can be hired in Israel for about $5 a day.

Tipping

In restaurants, if a service charge is not included, then 10–15 percent is expected. Israelis do not tip taxi drivers, but drivers will expect a small tip from tourists. Hotel staff such as porters (bell hops) will be happy with a few shekels for each item of baggage. Hairdressers also expect a small tip.

Tourist Offices

OUTSIDE OF ISRAEL:
United States
Tourism Commissioner for North America.
Tel: 001-212-499-5650.
Fax: 001-212-499-5645.
Information center (general public):
Tel: 001-800-596-1199.
Travel industry: 001-800-514-1188.
Website: http://www.goisrael.com/
Los Angeles
Israel Government Tourist Office, 6380 Wilshire Blvd. #1718.
Los Angeles, CA 90048.
Tel: (323) 658-7463.
Fax: (323) 658-6543.
New York
Israel Government Tourist Office, 800 Second Avenue, New York, 10017
Tel: (212) 499-5660
Fax: (212) 499-5645
Canada
Israel Government Tourist Office, 180 Bloor St. West, Suite #700, Toronto, Ontario M5S 2V6.
Tel: (416) 964-3784;
800 669-2369.
Fax: (416) 964-2420.
United Kingdom
180 Oxford Street,
London WID 1NN.
Tel: (20) 7434 3651.
Fax: (20) 7437 0527.

IN ISRAEL:
Arad, Paz Gas Station.
Tel: (08) 9954160.
Ben Gurion Airport.
Tel: (03) 9754260.

Eilat, 8 Beit Hagesher Street.
Tel: (08) 6309111.
Haifa, 48 Ben Gurion Street.
Tel: 1-800-305090.
Jerusalem Jaffa Gate.
Tel: (02) 6280403.
Nazareth, Casa Nova Street.
Tel: (04) 6750555.
Netanya, 12 Ha'atzmaut Square.
Tel: (09) 8827286.
Tel Aviv, Municipal Building, Ibn Gbriol.
Tel: (03) 5218500.
46 Herbert Samuel St.
Tel: (03) 5166188.
Tiberias, 23 Habanim Street.
Tel: (04) 6725666.
All these offices are open Sunday–Thursday 8.30am–5pm, Friday 8.30am–12am.

What to Read and View
Books

Altneuland – Theodor Herzl. The Zionist visionary's dream of what a Jewish homeland might be like.
Encyclopaedia Judaica – offers the most comprehensive information about Judaism and Israel.
Fathers and Sons – Amos Eilon. Entertaining account of the Zionist founding fathers.
My Michael – Amos Oz, Israel's leading contemporary novelist. Oz's other novels include *To Know a Woman* and *Elsewhere Perhaps*.
The Bible – This is where it all happened.
Exodus – Leon Uris's novel that became an epic movie.
The Diary of Anne Frank – Helps the reader understand what makes Israelis tick.
The Source – James Michener, basing his story on an archaeological site, Khatsor ha-Glilit in, creates fictional accounts of what might have happened in a Cannanite/Israelite/Palestinian village down the centuries.
The Little Drummer Girl – John Le Carré's Middle East novel.
The Wedding Canopy – Shai Agnon, the only Israeli winner of the Nobel Prize for literature.
The Reluctant Bride – A.B. Yehoshua, Israel's leading contemporary writer.
The Yellow Wind – David Grossman, about Israel's occupation of the

Palestinians.
To Jerusalem & Back – Saul Bellow, about the late Nobel prize winner's visit to Israel
From Beirut to Jerusalem – Thomas L. Friedman's account of his time as a *New York Times* correspondent in Lebanon and then Israel.
The New Middle East – Shimon Peres, the former Israeli Prime Minister's vision (often derided by the right) of a peaceful Middle East.
Durable Peace – Benjamin Netanyahu, a different vision of the future of the Middle East.

Videos

Exodus. Paul Newman wins independence for Israel – Otto Preminger's 1960 filming of the Leon Uris novel.
Cast a Giant Shadow. Kirk Douglas wins independence for Israel – Melville Shavelson's 1966 movie.
Raid on Entebbe. Yet more Israeli heroics in 1977 TV movie, with Peter Finch as Yitzhak Rabin.
The Little Drummer Girl. George Roy Hill's 1984 version of John le Carré's novel had Diane Keaton being recruited by Mosad.
Jesus Christ Superstar. Norman Jewison's poor 1973 version of the Tim Rice and Andrew Lloyd Webber musical was filmed by the Dead Sea and in the Judean Desert.

Websites

www.goisrael.com – official Israel Ministry of Tourism website.
www.goisrael.co.il – private company giving information about Israel.
www.parks.org.il – Israel's national parks website.
www.jerusalem.muni.il – Jerusalem municipality website.
www.jpost.co.il – *Jerusalem Post* newspaper site.
www.haaretz.com – *Haaretz* newspaper site.
www.tel-aviv.gov.il – Tel Aviv municipality site.
www.maven.co.il – Jewish web directory with comprehensive Israel section.
www.mfa.gov.il – Israel's Foreign Ministry.
www.cbs.gov.il – Israel's Central Bureau of Statistics.

L ANGUAGE

UNDERSTANDING HEBREW

History

Hebrew is the ancient language of the Old Testament, and is now spoken by the overwhelming majority of Israelis. Hebrew script is descended from Phoenician, which also gave rise to the Greek and ultimately the Roman and Cyrillic alphabets. With a lot of patience and persistence, it is just possible to make out the similarities with English letters. Even the names of Hebrew letters derive from their original pictorial meanings: *alef* and *bet* (which gave us the word "alphabet," via Greek) are, respectively, a bull's head and a house. The Hebrew language developed throughout Biblical and early times but remained fixed thereafter until the late 19th century.

During the intervening period, Hebrew was used solely for ritual and scholarly purposes, and played no part in ordinary daily life. Hebrew is thus the only language of antiquity to have been truly resurrected after lying dormant for many centuries.

Modern Hebrew

The modern language has uniform rules of grammar and pronunciation, though its vocabulary is eclectic and draws on the Bible, on the medieval languages of the Mediterranean, and on modern international scientific terminology. There is relatively little in the way of regional dialect, but Hebrew speakers or their ancestors may have brought with them other countries special words for cultural specialties, such as food, dress, and social customs.

Speakers of Hebrew from a Middle Eastern background tend to stress the guttural sound of some letters

more than those of European descent. The Middle Eastern pronunciation is supposed to be the authentic ancient pronunciation.

Hebrew has a masculine and feminine form of "you" – which means that the sentence changes slightly depending on whether you are talking to a man or a woman. These differences are indicated as *m/f* in the vocabulary section below.

Spelling

As of yet, there is no standardised spelling of Israeli place names. Thus one has: *"Acre"*, *"Akko"* and *"Acco"*; *"Nathanya"* *"Natanya"* and *"Netanya"*; *"Elat"*, *"Elath"* and *"Eilat"*; *"Ashqelon"* and *"Ashkelon"*; *"S'fat"*, *"Zefat"*, *"Tzfat"* and *"Safed"*, etc. As if to confuse the visitor deliberately, all such variations are used freely. This guide has attempted to standardise spellings, but do not be surprised if you come across many different versions of place names on maps and road signs.

Useful words and phrases

It is a good idea to know some basic Hebrew words and phrases before coming to the country. Deciphering the written language requires serious study, so we have provided simplified phoenetic transcriptions, with emphases indicated in bold type.

Essential Expressions

Yes	*ken*
No	*lo*
Okay	*be**seder***
Please	*bevaka**sha***
Thank you	*to**da***
good	*tov*
bad	*ra*
and/or	*ve/o-*

Greetings and Apologies

(all-purpose)	*shal**om***
Good morning	*bo**ker** tov*
Good evening	*erev tov*
Good night	*loyla tov*
Goodbye	*lehitra-**ot***
Sorry!	*sli**kha***
Don't mention it	*eyn be-ad ma*
Happy birthday	
	*yom hu**ledet** sa**me**-akh*
Congratulations!	*ma**zal** tov*
Best wishes!	*mey**tav** ha-ikhu**lim***

Communication difficulties

Do you speak English?	
	*[m]: ata meda**ber** ang**lit***
	*[f:] at meda**beret** ang**lit***
I don't speak much Hebrew	
	*[m]: ani lo meda**ber** har**be** iv**rit***
	*[f]: ani lo meda**beret** har**be** iv**rit***
Could you speak more slowly?	
	*[m]: tuk**hal** leda**ber** yo**ter** le-**at***
	*[f]: tuk**hli** leda**ber** yo**ter** le-**at***
Please write it down	
	*[m]: bevaka**sha** ktov et ze*
	*[f]: bevaka**sha** kit**vi** et ze*
Can you translate this for me?	
	*[m]: tuk**hal** letar**gem** et ze bish**li***
	*[f]: tuk**hli** letar**gem** et ze bish**li***
What does this mean?	
	*ma zot o**meret***
I understand	*ani me**vin** [f]: me**vina***
I don't understand	
	*ani lo me**vin** [f]: me**vina***
Do you understand?	*[m]: ata me**vin***
	*[f:] at me**vina***

Emergencies

Help!	*ha**tzilu***
Go away	*lekh mi**po***
Leave me alone!	*a**zov** oti*
Stop thief!	*ga**nav***
Call the police!	*haz-**ek**-mish**tara***
Get a doctor!	*kra lero**fe***
Fire!	*sre**fa***
I'm ill	*ani kho**le***
I'm lost	*ta-iti ba**derekh***
Can you help me?	*tuk**hal** la-a**zor** li*

Exclamations

At last!	*sof sof*
Go on . . [m]: *tamshikh* [f]: *tamshikhi*	
Nonsense!	*shtuyot*
That's true	*ze nakhon*
No way!	*beshum ofen lo*
How are things?	*eykh ha-inyanim*
Fine	*tov*
Not bad	*lo ra*
Not good	*lo tov*
Terrible	*nora*
You look great!	*ata nir-e nifla*
Why's that?	*madu-a ze*
Why not?	*madu-a lo*

Everyday purchases

stamps	*bulim*
envelopes	*ma-atafot*
writing paper	*neyar ktiva*
map	*mapa*
book	*sefer*
newspaper	*iton*
magazine	*magazin*
chocolate bar	*tavlat shokolad*
matches	*gafrurim*
pen	*et*
how much?	*kama?*

Sights

old town	*ha-ir ha-atika*
ruins	*ha-khoravot*
museum	*ha-muze-on*
art gallery	*galeriyat ha-omanut*
theater	*ha-te-atron*
historic sight	*ha-atar ha-histori*
park	*ha-park*

Eating Out

Can you recommend a good restaurant?	*tukhal lehamlitz al mis-ada tova*
inexpensive	*zola*
café	*beyt kafe*
restaurant	*mis-ada*
Middle Eastern	*mizrakhit*
Italian	*italkit*
Chinese	*sinit*
vegetarian	*tzimkhonit*
pizzeria	*pitzeriya*
steakhouse	*mis-adat stekim*
soup	*marak*
St Peter's fish	*amnun*
cod	*bakala*
trout	*shemekh*
salmon	*iltit*
shrimp/prawns	*khasilonim*
omelet	*khavita*
eggs	*beytzim*
beef	*bakar*
chicken	*of*
duck	*barvaz*
lamb	*tale*
liver	*kaved*
kidneys	*klayot*
carrots	*gezer*
cabbage	*kruv*
green beans	*she-u-it yeruka*
peas	*afuna*
mushrooms	*pitriyot*
rice/pasta	*orez/itriyot*

potatoes/fries	*tapudim/chips*
fruit juice	*mitz perot*
milk	*khalav*
bread	*lekhem*
butter	*khem-a*
rolls	*lakhmaniyot*
toast	*tost*
honey	*dvash*
jam	*riba*
marmalade	*ribat tapuzim*
lemon	*limom*
mustard	*khardal*
salt/pepper	*melakh/pilpel*
sugar	*sukar*
ketchup	*ketchup*
mayonnaise	*mayonez*
knife/fork	*sakin/mazleg*
spoon	*kaf*
plate	*tzalakhat*
cup/glass	*sefel/kos*
napkin	*mapit*
Where are the restrooms?	*eyfo hasherutim*
The bill, please	*kheshbon bevakasha*

Drinks

beer	*bira*
wine	*yayin*
red/white	*adom/lavan*
dry/sweet	*yavesh/matok*
mineral water	*mayim mineraliyim*
sparkling/still	*toses/lo toses*

Travel

airport	*nemal hate-ufa*
taxi	*monit*
train	*rakevet*
bus	*otobus*
station/bus stop	*takhanat*
one-way ticket	*bekivun ekhad*
round trip	*halokh vashov*
where is?	*eyfo?*
right	*yemin*
left	*smol*
straight	*yashar*

Colors

white	*lavan*
black	*shakhor*
red	*adom*
pink	*varod*
blue	*kakhol*
purple	*argaman*

Problems with Accommodations

I have a reservation	*yesh li hazmana*
May I see the room?	*efshar lir-ot et hakheder*
The air conditioning doesn't work	*ha mizug avir lo po-el*
There is no hot water/toilet paper	*eyn mayim khamim/neyar to-alet*
My room has not been made up	*lo sidru et hakheder sheli*
There are insects in our room	*yesh kharakim bakheder shelanu*
I've locked myself out of my room	*sagarti et atzmi mikhutz lakheder*
I'd like to move to another room	*ani rotze la-avor lekheder akher*
I'd like to speak to the manager	*ani rotze ledaber im hamenahel*
Are there any messages for me?	*yesh hoda-ot bishvili*

Payments

May I have my bill, please?	*efshar lekabel et hakheshbon bevakasha*
I think there's a mistake in this bill	*ani kkoshev sheyesh ta-ut bakheshbon*
Could I have a receipt, please?	*efshar latet li kabala bevakasha*

Yellow/Green

yellow	*tzahov*
green	*yarok*

Numbers

zero	*efes*
one	*ekhad*
two	*shnayim*
three	*shlosha*
four	*arba-a*
five	*khamisha*
six	*shisha*
seven	*shiv-a*
eight	*shmona*
nine	*tish-a*
ten	*asara*
hundred	*me-a*
thousand	*elef*
million	*milyon*

Days

Sunday	*yom rishon*
Monday	*yom sheni*
Tuesday	*yom shlishi*
Wednesday	*yom revi-i*
Thursday	*yom khamishi*
Friday	*yom shishi*
Saturday	*shabat*

Dates

yesterday	*etmol*
today	*hayom*
tomorrow	*makhar*
next week	*hashavu-a haba*

Months

January	*yanu-ar*
February	*februar*
March	*mertz, mars*
April	*april*
May	*may*
June	*yuni*
July	*yuli*
August	*ogust*
September	*september*
October	*oktober*
November	*november*
December	*detzember*

Seasons

spring	*aviv*
summer	*kayitz*
fall/autumn	*stav*
winter	*khoref*

ART & PHOTO CREDITS

AFP/Getty Images 78
ASAP Images/Mendrea 237
Sammy Avnisan 67, 69, 72, 182, 195, 215, 220T, 220,249, 263
Baubau/Mendrea 49
Lev Borodulin/Israelimages 213
Werner Braun 27, 87, 84, 105, 140, 168, 179, 194, 206, 209, 234, 283, 296, 310, 325
Central Zionist Archives 33, 36, 39, 41, 42
Bill Clark 77, 114, 266
Corbis 52
Mickael David/Authors Image/ Alamy 181
Christian Fischer/Bongarts/Getty Images 119
Neil Folberg 262, 270/271
4Corners Images 12/13
Elyssa Frank/Israelimages 63, 259
Eddie Gerrald 210, 254, 256, 306, 322L&R, 323
Getty Images 21, 51, 55
Eddie Gerard/Alamy 117
Shai Ginott/Israelimages 126
David Harris 23, 66, 101, 155L, 172L, 176/177, 202, 290, 294, 308
Beth Hatefutsoth 244
Hebrew University at Mt Scopus 164
Naftali Hilger/Israelimages 4/5, 9, 122/123, 317R
Hulton Getty 88
Hanan Isachar/Israelimages 108, 120/121, 176, 238/239, 240, 247, 250, 274, 287, 314, 316
Israel Hirshberg 227
Israel Government Press Office 45, 46, 79, 236, 318L
Israel Philharmonic 98
Yorman and Jane Korman 104
Axel Krause 324
Lyle Lawson 285322R
Library of the Jewish Theological Seminary of America 25
Yasha Mazur/Israelimages 75
Ram Meir/Israelimages 62

George Melrod 43, 211L, 234T, 235
Dinu Mendrea 57. 60, 68, 71, 118, 173, 243, 248, 260/261, 277, 293, 305
Radu Mendrea 89, 182
Sandru Mendrea 115, 160, 188, 191, 267
Garo Nalbandian/Israelimages 124/124
National Library, Givat Ram 18/19
Doron Nisim/Israelimages 278, 284
Gary-John Norman 17, 30/31, 64, 90, 110, 134, 135,136, 137, 143, 144L, 144R, 156T, 165, 169T, 170, 188T, 187, 192, 197, 197T, 199T, 200, 201, 202T, 207, 208, 209T, 211T, 211R, 216T, 219, 222/223, 227T, 229T, 229, 231, 250T, 251, 252T, 252R, 253, 257, 279, 280T, 280, 291, 292L, 295T, 295, 297, 300, 309T, 309, 312/313, 315, 316T, 320T, 322T
Richard Nowitz 1, 2/3, 4/5, 10/11, 14, 20, 28, 44, 54, 81, 61, 65, 70, 73, 74, 76, 82, 83, 85, 91, 95, 96, 99, 107, 109, 112/113, 116, 132T, 132/133, 141, 142T, 142, 145T, 147, 149T, 149, 150, 151, 152, 153, 154, 155R, 156, 157L&R, 163, 166, 167, 169, 173T, 174T, 182T, 186, 188/189, 191T, 191, 196, 198/199, 203, 212, 217, 225, 230, 245, 246, 251T, 255T, 257T, 258, 264T, 265, 266T, 275, 278T, 281, 282, 285T, 286, 288, 289, 290T, 292T, 292R, 301, 303, 304, 306, 307, 318R, 320, 333, all small cover pictures
P. Lavon Institute for Labor Research 37
Tusur (Tsuf) Pelly/Israelimages 53
Photri 130, 148L
Reinhard Schmid/Fototeca 9 x 12 317L
David Silverman/Getty Images 172

Silverprint Archives 35
Eitan Simanor/Alamy 53
Paul D. Slaughter/Image Bank/ Getty Images 221
Amantini Stefani/4 Corners Images 214, 224
Duby Tal/Albatross/Israelimages 241
Israel Talby/Israelimages 255
The Travel Image 139
Topham Picturepoint 40, 47, 48, 49, 56, 131
Tony Stone Worldwide 58/59, 173, 319

PHOTO FEATURES

Pages 92/93
all Eddie Gerald except: bottom left and bottom centre left Andrea Pistolesi
Pages 158/159
all Eddie Gerald except: main picture Richard Nowitz, top right Andrea Pistolesi
Pages 204/205
Top row left to right: Andrea Pistolesi, Andrea Pistolesi, Andrea Pistolesi, Richard Nowitz; Centre row: both Andrea Pistolesi; bottom row: Eddie Gerald, Andrea Pistolesi, Richard Nowitz, Andrea Pistolesi, Richard Nowitz
Pages 268/269
All pictures: Mini Israel
Pages 298/299
Top row lefto to right: Richard Nowitz, Eddie Gerald, Richard Nowitz, Richard Nowitz; Centre row: Eddie Gerald; Bottom row: Eddie Gerald

Cartographic Editor: Zoë Goodwin
Map Production: Colourmap Scanning Ltd, James Macdonald
©2008 Apa Publications GmbH & Co. Verlag KG, Singapore Branch

INDEX

Numbers in italics refer to photographs

TRULY ADVENTUROUS

TRULY ASIA

In the heart of Asia lies a land of many cultures, wonders and attractions. Especially for the adventure seeker to whom fear is not a factor. There are hundreds of thrills to experience. Mount Kinabalu. Mulu Caves. Taman Negara. These are just a few places where you'll always find that rewarding adrenaline rush. Where is this land, so challenging and exhilarating? It can only be Malaysia, Truly Asia.

Malaysia
Truly Asia

KUALA LUMPUR (Head Office): 17th Floor, Menara Dato' Onn, Putra World Trade Centre, 45 Jalan Tun Ismail, 50480 Kuala Lumpur, Malaysia.
Tel: +603-2615 8188 Fax: +603-2693 5884 Website: www.tourismmalaysia.gov.my